上海市人民政府 | 国际智库咨询
发展研究中心系列报告 | 系 列 报 告

INVESTMENT AND TRADE FACILITATION

提升投资贸易便利化水平
构建开放型经济新体制

2016上海国际智库咨询研究报告

Consultation Report of
Shanghai International Think Tank, 2016

上海市人民政府发展研究中心 编

EDITOR
The Development Research Center
of Shanghai Municipal People's Government

格致出版社 上海人民出版社

论坛现场
Conference Site

论坛现场
Conference Site

BitSE 公司联合创始人兼首席运营官陆扬作主旨发言
Keynote Speech by Sunny Lu, BitSE, Co-founder, COO

上海美国商会会长季瑞达作主旨发言
Keynote speech by Kenneth Jarrett, President of the American Chamber of Commerce in Shanghai

IBM 大中华区副总裁及华东华中区总经理郑军作主旨发言
Keynote speech by Jun Zheng, Vice President, Enterprise Business Unit, East & Central China

中国欧盟商会上海分会总经理琼安娜作主旨发言
Keynote speech by Ioana Kraft, General Manager of Shanghai Chapter, European Union Chamber of Commerce in China

中国（上海）自由贸易试验区管委会政策研究局副局长郑海鳌作主旨发言

Keynote speech by Haiao Zheng, Deputy Director-General at the Policy Research Bureau of China (Shanghai) Pilot Free Trade Zone Administration

麦肯锡咨询公司全球资深董事合伙人、全球基础设施与政府业务联席负责人李广宇作主旨发言

Keynote speech by Guangyu Li, Senior Partner from McKinsey & Company

波士顿咨询公司全球合伙人兼董事总经理周园作主旨发言
Keynote speech by Yvonne Zhou, Global Partner and Managing Director, Beijing, BCG

凯捷咨询（中国）有限公司首席运营官钱敏毓作主旨发言
Keynote speech by Alva Qian, COO, Capgemini China

德勤华东区主管合伙人刘明华作主旨发言

Keynote speech by Minghua Liu, Managing Partner of Eastern China, Audit Partner of Shanghai, China, Deloitte

埃森哲全球副总裁、大中华区副主席吴琪作主旨发言

Keynote speech by Qi Wu, Senior Managing Director and Vice Chairman of Accenture Greater China

上海 WTO 事务咨询中心经济学研究员姚为群作主旨发言
Keynote speech by Weiqun Yao, Research Professor of Economics, Shanghai WTO Affairs Consultation Center

北京大学全球治理研究中心副主任兼秘书长范德尚作主旨发言
Keynote speech by Fan Deshang, Deputy Director & Secretary General of Global Governance Studies Center at Peking University

高风咨询高级顾问黄昱作主旨发言

Keynote speech by Yu Huang, Senior Executive Advisor at GaoFeng Advisory

美中贸易全国委员会上海首席代表欧文作主旨发言

Keynote speech by Owen Haacke, Chief Representative, Shanghai Office, US-China Business Council

日本贸易振兴机构上海所所长小栗道明作主旨发言
Keynote speech by Michiaki Oguri, President of Japan External Trade Organization in Shanghai

普华永道中国中区市场主管合伙人、上海首席合伙人黄佳作总结发言
Summary statement by Elton Huang, PwC Central China Markets Leader, Shanghai Senior Partner

上海市商务委员会副主任申卫华作互动讨论

Roundtable discussion by Shen Weihua, Deputy Director General of Shanghai Municipal Commission of Commerce

上海市国有资产监督管理委员会副巡视员李咏今作互动讨论

Roundtable discussion by Li Yongjin, Deputy Inspector of the State-owned Assets Supervision and Administration Commission of Shanghai Municipal Government

上海市口岸服务办公室副巡视员武伟作互动讨论
Roundtable discussion by Wu Wei, Deputy Inspector of the Shanghai Municipal Office for Port Services

上海出入境检验检疫局党组成员、浦江局局长谢秋慧作互动讨论
Roundtable discussion by Xie Qiuhui, Member of the Party Committee of Shanghai Entry-Exit Inspection and Quarantine Bureau，Director of Shanghai Pujiang Entry-Exit Inspection and Quarantine Bureau

上海对外经济贸易大学教授陈子雷作互动讨论

Roundtable discussion by Chen Zilei, Professor at Shanghai University of International Business and Economics

上海发展研究基金会副会长兼秘书长乔依德作互动讨论

Roundtable discussion by Qiao Yide, Vice Chairman and Secretary General of Shanghai Development Research Foundation

上海电气集团副总裁张科作互动讨论
Roundtable discussion by Zhang Ke, Vice President of Shanghai Electric Group Co., Ltd.

上海国际港务（集团）股份有限公司战略研究部总经理丁嵩冰作互动讨论
Roundtable discussion by Ding Songbing, General Manager of Strategic Research Department, Shanghai International Port (Group) Co., Ltd.

上海新工联集团总经理范杰作互动讨论
Roundtable dscussion by Fan Jie, General Manager of Shanghai NIU (Group) Co., Ltd.

德意志银行董事总经理、首席运营官、董事会执行董事赵熙作互动讨论
Roundtable discussion by Zhao Xi, Managing Director, COO, Executive Director of Deutsche Bank, China

毕马威中国区高级合伙人、环球客户部负责人、中国及亚太区生命科学部负责人诺伯特·梅尔林作互动讨论
Roundtable discussion by Norbert Meyring, Senior Partner, Head of Global Accounts, Head of Life Sciences Division in China and Asia Pacific, KPMG China

雅培中国政府关系总监邵枫作互动讨论
Roundtable discussion by Shao Feng, Director of Government Relations, Abbott, China

中伦律师事务所合伙人李俊杰作互动讨论

Roundtable discussion by Li Junjie, Partner of Zhong Lun Law Firm

泰科电子政府关系经理邓凌玲作互动讨论

Roundtable discussion by Deng Lingling, Manager of Government Relations, TE Connectivity, China

嘉宾合影
Group photo of guests

PREFACE

序

　　建设中国（上海）自由贸易试验区，是以习近平同志为核心的党中央在新形势下全面深化改革和扩大开放的重大战略决策。自贸区建设的重要使命是，通过制度创新，与国际高标准投资贸易规则相衔接，构建开放型经济新体制，构筑法治化、国际化、便利化的营商环境，探索形成可复制可推广的改革成果。

　　为更好地服务上海自贸区和开放型经济建设，2016 年 12 月 9 日，由上海市人民政府发展研究中心主办，普华永道中国、上海发展研究基金会和上海国际智库交流中心联合承办，举行了"2016 年上海国际智库峰会"。本次峰会以"提升上海投资贸易便利化水平"为主题，吸引了来自普华永道、麦肯锡、埃森哲、波士顿咨询公司、德勤、IBM、凯捷、高风咨询、美中贸易全国委员会、上海美国商会、欧盟上海商会、日本贸易振兴机构、印度工业联合会等 20 余家国际智库专家参与。与会嘉宾探讨了国际投资贸易规则发展趋势，交流了各类企业在投资贸易实践中面临的问题，共同探索并提出了实际可行的解决思路和方案，形成了有价值的决策参考，达到了会议的预期效果。

　　这本国际智库研究报告生动再现了论坛现场的交流盛况，详实记录了专家学者的精彩观点。希望本书能够对关注和研究上海投资、贸易发展的人们有所裨益，助力更多国内外专家学者以前瞻性和战略性眼光，从更广阔的视野共同探索研究上海未来经济发展和现代化建设，更好地服务市委、市政府的科学决策和民主决策。

上海市人民政府发展研究中心主任

The construction of China (Shanghai) Pilot Free Trade Zone is an important strategic decision made under the leadership of the Central Committee of the Communist Party of China (CPC) headed by General Secretary Xi Jinping on the new situation of comprehensively deepening reform and expanding opening up. The ultimate missions of the establishment of the China (Shanghai) Pilot Free Trade Zone construction are to meet with the high standards of international investment and trade rules, establish a new system of open economy, build a legal, international and convenient business environment, and explore institutional reform achievements that can be replicated and promoted through systematic innovation.

To better serve the China (Shanghai) Pilot Free Trade Zone and open economy construction, the "2016 Shanghai International Think Tank Summit" was held on December 9th, 2016. It was sponsored by Development Research Centre of Shanghai Municipal People's Government, and jointly organized by PwC China, Shanghai Development Research Foundation and Shanghai International Think Tank Exchanges Center. The "2016 Shanghai International Think Tank Summit" was themed "Promote the Investment and Trade Facilitation in Shanghai", and attracted experts from more than 20 international think tanks, including PwC, McKinsey & Company, Accenture, Boston Consulting Group, Deloitte, IBM, Capgemini, Gao Feng Advisory, the US-China Business Council, the American Chamber of Commerce Shanghai, European Chamber Shanghai Chapter, the Japan External Trade organization (JETRO), Confederation of Indian Industry and etc. Experts and scholars exchanged views on the megatrend development of the formation of the international investment and trade rules and regulations, discussed the specific issues that various enterprises have been facing in the practice of investment and trade facilitation, and together explored and proposed feasible plans and solutions, formed valuable decision-making references, to meet the expectations of the summit.

The consultation report of 2016 Shanghai International Think Tank Summit recreates the grand scene of the exchange and it has a detailed record on the brilliant views of the guests. We hope that it can not only benefit those who concerns about and has been studying on the investment and trade development in Shanghai, but also help

提升投资贸易便利化水平，构建开放型经济新体制

more experts and scholars from home and abroad to explore and study the economic construction and modernization development for future Shanghai with a foreseeing, strategic and broader view, so as to better serve the scientific and democratic decision-making process for the CPC Shanghai Committee and Shanghai Government.

Wang Dezhong

Director General of the SDRC

CONTENTS

目 录

KEYNOTE SPEECHES

主旨演讲

区块链：新技术、新思路、新模式

陆　扬

BitSE 公司联合创始人兼首席运营官

最近我刚刚学到的非常有趣的理论，叫"技术阻碍理论"。说的是，任何一个新技术的发展，都诞生于对目前社会发展形成最大障碍的一些情况。比如：人类交通工具的诞生，来自人类想要自由旅行在空间上遇到的阻碍；互联网的诞生，来自大家交流、沟通，共同协作中遇到的阻碍。随着社会分工和协同的极大发展，现在我们又遇到了一些新的阻碍。就是信息不对称，流通不自由，信任不透明。这也就是区块链为什么诞生于今天这个世界的主要原因。

区块链从诞生之初，一直被认为是金融科技非常有力的一个组成部分。虽然区块链技术诞生于金融，很多人认为它是互联网金融下一代或者科技金融最核心的技术结构，但是我们认为，它在各方面，在社会各个行业，都有很大的作用。

随着计算机跟互联网技术的极大发展，并且伴随着越来越多的多方协同要求，整个人类社会都在加速数字化进程。比如，我国提出"一带一路"倡议，更是需要打破地域、国家、文化的界限，进行更加紧密的发展合作。在这个过程中，就会发现信息孤岛、信息不流通、互动不信任，变成了现在最大的障碍。区块链正是帮助我们跨越这个障碍最好的新技术。这种新技术给我们带来一种新的思维模式，将会对现有的模式带来很大的改变。传统的思维方式会考虑"我能做什么"，或者作为一个企业和监管方，我这一方能带来什么样的创新；但是区块链可以让我们从更大的层面思考整个行业，甚至整个社会一起能带来什么样的创新。

我们可以思考一个典型的应用场景：什么样的数据、操作模式，可以运行在区块链上？首先，它是非常有价值的数据；其次，它是公开、透明，并且允许多方共同参与的数据；同时，数据不希望被别人篡改，具有很强的信任性、安全性。符合这些条件的数据或者操作就可以放在区块链上，或者成为区块链的一个典型的应用场景。

举个例子。一个通用并唯一的产品 ID。唯一的 ID 目前已经应用了很长时间。比如设备都有一个序列号，这个序列号就是一个唯一的 ID。但是要把这个唯一的 ID 做到通用，就面临很多的挑战，因为不同的企业之间，ID 互相不被识别。区块链技术就可以使这种通用并且唯一的 ID 的实现成为可能。

我们的主要区块链即服务的平台产品——唯链，就是基于区块链技术，围绕唯一通用型 ID 建立的打通整个供应链体系的商品管理体系。

供应链领域是区块链一个非常好的应用场景。供应链最核心的三个基本要素是物流、信息流和资金流。目前，随着技术的成熟、各方面服务的优化，物流已经比较连贯，物流要素已经得到了非常大的完善。但通常情况下，信息流都是割裂并且不及时的。这就造成了供应链协同方面效率和成本的挑战。

在商品的整个生命周期里，大家会发现，商品的信息通常被不同的参与方所维护或所拥有。比如生产方、经销商、零售商、物流提供商甚至监管方，这些信息会形成一个一个信息孤岛，各方都是割裂的。这就使得供应链溯源一直是比较令人头疼的事情。

区块链技术使得供应链溯源成为一种可能。比如，最近我们跟上海外高桥自贸区核心区的酒类商品展示交易中心达成了合作意向，用唯链平台对红酒，尤其是进口红酒建立溯源体系。最大的特点是，我们会从红酒的源头——国外的酒厂开始，让各方都参与，在整个红酒的供应链环节进行数据维护、更新，同时给消费者一个单一入口，他们只需要通过智能手机和互联网连接，扫一扫就能知道红酒的供应链产品信息，给消费者最大的权益保证。而且，由于这些信息来自多方，这也可以获得消费者最大的信任。

另外一个我们在研究、探索的案例，跟今天的主题很契合，是贸易仓单真实性的审查和公示，也是非常典型的区块链应用场景。比如，仓单真实性的数据输入方来自多方，有交易平台、仓储数据提供方、海关、清算数据等。同时，信息获取方也来自多方，有交易各方、提供金融服务的金融机构、海关、监管部门等。这就是一个非常典型的区块链应用平台。区块链可以让多方数据实时、及时传递到每个需要这些信息的各方，最大程度上使提供金融服务的相关方能获取最及时、最真实的信息。

所以，总的来说，区块链给我们带来的是一种新的技术，从而带来一种新的思维模式，进而有可能根据这些思维模式，产生一些新的商业模式的变化，或者监管思路的变化。它使得多方协同的效率提高、企业成本或政府监管成本下降，从而带来一些新的商业模式和监管服务模式。

当然，区块链技术还处于发展早期阶段，各方面都需要进一步完善。衷心希望社会各界、政府部门、各个企业，都能拥抱这种新技术，给予它支持，并愿意进行更多的尝试。只有通过不断的应用尝试和应用落地，才能反过来对区块链技术的完善提供更好的建议，推动技术进一步发展。

提升上海投资环境

季瑞达
上海美国商会会长

　　根据纽约咨询公司荣鼎集团的研究报告，过去十五年，美国在华投资额达到2 280亿美元，中国在美投资额同期也达到了640亿美元。值得注意的是，美国对华投资很大一部分集中在上海。

　　中美经济比以往任何时候都更唇齿相依，而且双方投资的发展前景依然广阔。然而，我们从美国大选可以看出，不少美国人认为他们并未从双向贸易投资中获得好处。我们需要向他们解释我们的确从中获利了，比如投资可以创造就业并提高生活水平。

　　上海为企业提供了良好的商业环境。我们十分欢迎和赞赏今年的签证制度改革以及政府在自贸区行政手续简化、清关时间缩短和货币兑换中所做出的努力。我们的会员对上海到2020年成为国际金融中心和2030年成为科技和创新中心的目标表示支持。

　　上海的投资环境美名远扬，对外企具有巨大的吸引力。企业也不断地在这片热土上持续投资，建立地区总部。有两个例子众所周知，迪士尼乐园员工数千名，投资超过55亿美元，通用汽车公司的凯迪拉克上海工厂投资也超过12亿美元。

　　虽然上述成就喜人，但是有一点我们不能忽视，那就是外企在中国仍然面临很多法规条例和制度性交易成本的钳制，这将限制外企在华的投资和贸易的发展。比如说，下面的例子虽然决策权在中央政府层面，但是我希望上海地方政府能尽其所能，向中央施加影响力：

　　一是外汇管制使得资金流通复杂化。最近的外汇政策导致外资银行和金融服务公司在华运营和发展变得困难，同时也使在沪的地区总部难以有效地将资金流动到海外。这些限制也会抵消掉上海为在2020年建成国际金融中心所作出的努力。

　　二是新政策的实施还有很多不确定性。在一些情况下，政策的实施因地而异。我们呼吁中国政府消除政策在实施过程中的地区间差异。通过开展关于新政策如何实施的介绍会和报告会将会有助于消除地区差异。包括我们上海美商会在内的组织也会竭力协助开展上述活动。

同时，在上海市地方政府权责内，我提出以下两个问题，希望可以引起关注，寻求解决方案。

第一，成本上升：跨国公司，特别是制造业跨国公司，正面临着上海乃至整个长三角地区成本上升的严峻挑战。我们呼吁地方政府通过对大中型公司减税或帮助公司寻找低成本替代品等方式帮助公司降低成本。

第二，助力研发：上海市政府鼓励公司在沪建立研发中心以助于将上海打造成科技和创新中心。外国研发中心在上海跻身世界创新城市的征程中扮演着重要作用。众多公司一方面对建立研发中心充满兴趣，另一方面却受到其他方面的限制，削弱了这一方面的能力。（1）我们的《2016 年商务环境调查》显示，知识产权的执法不力抑制了近半数公司对研发中心和创新的投资。（2）用于药品研发的生物材料进口受到严格的限制。生物制药产业是上海七大新兴产业之一。但对于很多生物制药和诊断行业的研发中心来说，用于药品研发和诊断所用的试剂进口很不容易。特别是含有动物和人体成分的化学品，由于一系列技术层面的原因很难进口。我们希望上海政府能够出台新政策，为他们开绿灯，在上述试剂的进口的清关和商检过程中为他们提供协助。（3）政府研发基金的获取受限。从中央到地方都有一批政府基金项目用来资助新兴产业或者如半导体等重点产业的研发。然而一部分基金仅针对本土企业，或者对外企条件苛刻。在这方面政府的协助将对公司建立研发中心大有帮助。

我希望，上海美商会能与上海市政府发展研究中心和上海市政府齐心协力、合作共赢，一起解决上述问题，同时为上海建成金融中心以及科技和创新中心添砖加瓦。

打造全球整合企业——IBM 在跨国投资贸易中战略并购的经验分享

郑 军

IBM 大中华区副总裁及华东华中区总经理

全球整合和跨国贸易显然不是什么新鲜事物，它们早在罗马帝国成立之前就一直是经济推动力。但是，在过去十年，全球化步伐实现了巨幅增长。兼并与收购（并购）成为了支持企业战略实现和快速成长的重要途径。尤其在经历了全球经济下滑后，企业更需要关注价值、发掘机会、快速行动。并购可以帮助企业提升核心竞争力、增加市场份额、获得规模效益、扩大市场区域覆盖，或者通过业务剥离使企业更专注于核心业务，从而创造更多的股东价值。

其中一个主要原因是通信技术的长期革命，这个革命浪潮将继续大幅度降低贸易和交易成本，并且进一步延长互动距离。实际上，1995—2007 年间，跨国公司的数量增加了一倍多，从 3.8 万家到 7.9 万家，外国子公司的数量增长了近两倍，从 26.5 万家骤增至 79 万家。同期，跨国并购交易数量增长了一倍多，从 390 次到 889 次，但这一趋势——与许多其他趋势一样——在 2008 年都出现了下滑。

对于企业领导人来说，此类变革在优化全球资源和资本生产力方面给他们创造了巨大机会。然而，通过并购实现企业战略目标并非坦途。据统计，全球范围内的企业跨国并购只有 25% 左右达成既定目标，中国企业的成功率更低。

因此，企业的并购活动需要准确的战略聚焦、合理的目标选择和有效的整合实施，以正确的方式做正确的交易，从而降低并购风险，实现交易价值。

新兼并的业务单位与整体运营战略脱节，一直是企业并购重组后企业效率的阻碍因素。在当今的全球环境中，并购后，业务单位或各个区域之间各自为政会阻碍企业实现其潜力。近 20 年，许多企业在投资贸易中，不断地发现在应对新地区、新客户、新员工和新技术方面存在着不必要的繁琐和低效流程。对这些企业来说，采用"全球整合企业"运营模式是一种出路，走在"全球整合企业"转型之路上的企业所实现的优秀业绩足以证明这一点。这条转型之路漫长又艰苦，需要花费数年时间，而且要求持续的转型。对于在全球开展业务的企业来说，整合是一个不容忽视的主题：在未来十年内，这有可能成为优胜者和其他企业的区分因素。

世界正持续变得更小、更加困难重重。因此，许多企业发现，它们置身于一个全球环境中，可采用的运营模式却是为更加受限的范围而设计的。孤立的运营、缺乏客户驱动的愿景以及不一致的沟通导致兼并后运营效率低下和资源浪费，并且极大地限制了全企业和 / 或整个生态系统内的统一协作。

许多企业正在通过向全球整合企业（GIE）转型而寻找上述问题的解决方案。全球整合企业将全球运作效率与市场响应能力结合在一起，应对全球化经济为企业及其所在行业带来的挑战和机遇。GIE 运营模式来自 20 世纪 90 年代整个世界的重大社会经济变革，包括互联网的出现和更多跨国企业在全球展开业务。

全球整合型企业需要由内而外的全球转型，优化整个生态系统，从而在并购企业后，更快地整合、管理、运营并购来的企业，提高生产效率、整合资源以进行创新和发展，使并购交易的价值最大化。

IBM 在实施全球整合企业（GIE）方面的经验来自 IBM 自身十余年的转型经历。十年来，IBM 通过积极追求全球整合而实现了自身的转型。通过采用通用的共享支持功能、企业级流程，有力的治理体系，并且利用全球技术和能力，提高了客户价值，显著提高了生产力，并将解放出来的资源用于业务增长和创新。

从 2001 年至今，IBM 已经收购了 120 多家公司。其中 2010 年以前并购的 80 多家公司大多数都充实到以 Websphere、IM、Tivoli、Rational 和 Lotus 为主的品牌软件中。而 2010 年后 IBM 的收购，则更加强调了人工智能、智慧地球、商业智能和分析、云计算、服务器和网络存储优化、企业治理合规与安全等六大热点领域及方向，意在布局未来，掌握市场的先机。尤其在被广泛认为是下一个科技革命的人工智能领域，IBM 在近一两年来动作不断，积极寻找并购目标。从 2010 年初至今，IBM 已经花费了超过 120 亿美元完成了 40 多家公司的并购。

近年来，IBM 的收购把更多目光投向了初创的技术公司，而非已经发展较为成熟的企业。在技术变革十分快速的今天，要想把握先机，必定需要押注那些站在技术开发前沿的团队和人才，这虽然要冒一些投资风险，但是如果等到这些初创企业成熟了再进行并购，往往已经错失了最好的时机，收购成本也大相径庭。

IBM 并购目标也十分国际化，除了大量美国企业，还有许多来自欧洲，如以色列、英国等地。目的都是未来寻找全球范围内最顶尖的技术团队。

如此复杂的并购，IBM 是如何实现整合运营的？这其中全球整合企业

（GIE）的经验功不可没。

为了了解企业如何接受 GIE，以及在应用这种运营模式时的表现（多好以及多快），IBM 商业价值研究院调查了全球 1 000 多位高管。调研由 IBM 研究合作伙伴牛津经济研究院提供支持；在线分发并管理；涵盖 12 个国家；超过 68% 的受访企业在 6—50 个国家开展业务。

高管职位包括 CIO、CFO、CHRO、首席战略官和其他首席领导层，分管战略、财务、供应链管理、人力资源、技术、营销 / 沟通、销售的（高级）副总裁、部门主管和总监。

全球化影响着几乎每家企业，无论是处在哪个行业中。通过分析调查答复，我们发现企业在 GIE 转型进程中多数都遵循了"由内而外"的轨迹。在 GIE 转型过程中，第一步是着眼于企业内部。随着企业通过并购（M&A）扩展产品 /服务范围、能力和技能，它们必须"重新平衡"其业务运作，以满足不断变化的市场和客户需求。最棘手的并购工作并不是交易本身，而是保证运作、技术、人员和文化的整合。这种"平衡"需要新的数字化能力，以支持供应链、财务、人力和端到端的产品生命周期。这些企业从后端办公室、共享服务职能（例如信息技术、销售支持、财务、供应链 / 运营、人力资源）和跨职能流程（例如从订购到付款、从订购到收款）开始。随着转型不断推进，企业逐渐接受了更加外向的观点，并且将关注的焦点转向优化整个生态系统。

我们还发现，一组业绩优秀的企业在这个方面取得了更大的成绩。它们当前的关注点是通过营销和面向客户的举措在供应链中开展合作——同时持续关注改进和创新客户体验。业绩优秀的企业创造了一种创新文化，而且据调研显示，它们的表现明显优于同行。

通过对这些业绩优秀的企业进行分析，并根据 IBM 自身的经验，我们发现GIE 转型包括：

• 由内而外优化全球运作——企业开始跨职能部门和端到端流程而将业务运营向全球整合服务转型。它们通过简化和自动化的手段实现全球流程和网络的优化。它们为业务运营和专业技能创建了卓越中心。它们与其生态系统（业务伙伴、员工和客户）的流程和沟通也得到了优化。

• 利用分析激活信息，获得预测洞察力——业绩优秀的企业利用大数据获得可执行的洞察力，以提升竞争优势。它们开发了广泛使用的分析卓越中心，利用先进的分析实现业务决策的自动化，并且将基于事实的洞察转变为实时行动。它们通过预测和规范分析实现创新，以预测客户的响应和反应。

• 利用创新文化提高企业敏捷度——企业必须应对技术、运营模式 / 流程改进和组织／文化方面的快速变化。它们应通过转变领导方法推动进步，领导者必须制订并推动变革议事日程。它们必须使全球运作与战略意图及业务目标保持一致。它们应努力参与并激发员工的士气——将社交媒体计划嵌入企业的沟通战略中，实现员工协作。

实现 GIE 转型的企业可能成为行业领导者。未接受转型愿景的企业可能在收入、效率、客户忠诚度以及最终的生存能力方面面临着严峻的考验。

最后，我们将提供一些关于如何在 GIE 转型之路上取得进步的建议，因为我们认为这是一个持续的转型历程。有些企业刚刚起步，而有些已经在这一过程中取得了巨大进展。对于全球整合企业，持续转型势在必行，因为任何一家企业在市场中的地位都不是一成不变的。

优化全球运作：

（1）企业将业务运作转变为全球整合服务。首先注重内部创新和整合（M&A、供应链）而创造全球性的影响，然后转向价值链和竞争优势（改造销售／客户支持职能，并协调新兴市场的运作）。影响包括更高的投资回报、复合年增长率、利润率和收入增长。

（2）优化全球流程和网络。注重更高价值、协作流程（销售和运作计划与业务伙伴参与）。优化劳动力、成本和数据。利用全球整合服务扩展到新的新兴市场和高增长市场。划分业务领域，以满足当地客户和市场要求。

（3）向由外而内的客户运营模式转型。开发卓越中心，用于整合技能和资产，以最佳的方式与客户交流并为客户服务。将工作转移到执行效果最好的地点。优化劳动力和交付模式，以降低成本，同时将资源集中用于高价值的支持领域。

激活信息和分析：

（1）通过创建卓越中心来开展业务分析，为所有业务部门服务，进而获得潜在的竞争优势。这使企业能够降低成本，提高生产力，优化运营绩效。利用分析还可以提高销售和营销效率、助力产品／服务开发、识别未来市场机遇，从而增强企业在市场中的竞争优势。

（2）将分析融合到全球运营中，以获得业务洞察。这是高管团队提出的自上而下的要求，并且要求对已经转型的共享服务、跨职能流程和客户／业务卓越中心实现自动化和优化。

（3）在所有职能中使用分析，并且从趋势和历史分析演进到预测和规范解决方案。确定用于规范分析的客户信息的优先级。利用分析可以识别新兴市场风险，从而采取主动的行动。

提高企业敏捷度：

（1）通过转型领导力而激发士气。未来的转型包括具有更高分析能力的大数据、云等新技术、新运营模式和自动化流程。转型领导者必须负责变革议程。创建一种管理系统，将不同地区和产品部门的领导者整合在一起，以便将精力集中在业务绩效协调和客户上。

（2）建立一种接受持续变革的企业文化。基于对实际洞察的关注，通过建立一种严格的创新文化，从而协调技能并部署通用的方法和工具，确保整个组织准备就绪、全员参与和价值创造，从而增强业务成效。启动变革管理卓越中心，为领导者提供组织变革管理咨询服务。

（3）与人员交流并且激励这些人员。将社交媒体计划融入沟通战略。采用协作工具以互动方式讨论员工计划、新技术和运营模式变革。利用云技术实现快速扩展和自助服务。

我们再次强调，全球整合应该从关注由内而外的方法开始，即首先从内部开始，随着能力的增加，再扩展到整个生态系统。对于希望通过全球并购帮助企业提升核心竞争力、增加市场份额、获得规模效益、扩大市场区域覆盖的企业，向全球整合企业的运营模式转型不仅值得一试，而且正在迅速成为势在必行的举措。

贸易和投资：上海发展的基石

琼安娜
欧盟商会上海代表处总经理

去年，我们展望 2050 年的上海，期待它成为一座全球城市。今年，我们聚焦现实，探讨如何通过贸易和投资便利化实现这一宏大的目标。我很荣幸能够代表中国欧盟商会近 1 600 家会员企业以及常驻上海的 600 家企业参与此次峰会，分享他们对贸易和投资便利化的想法和期待。

上海成为卓越的全球城市，建设"四个中心"以及科创中心离不开外商的参与，因为这些规划的核心恰恰是贸易和投资便利化。作为欧洲在华企业的代表，我们希望就这个问题分享以下四个观点与各位探讨。

首先，欧洲商界期待上海在外商投资管理体制改革方面起到更强的引领作用，为欧洲在华投资者带来更多市场机遇。

我们很高兴地看到最近外商投资管理体制改革取得了一些积极进展。在市场准入负面清单制度在全国推广之后，外商投资企业注册登记制度也随之由审批改为备案，"外资三法"也进行了相应修订。然而，我们仍然没有看到新版负面清单的出台，而且今年 10 月 1 日颁布的实施细则仍然提到外商投资指导目录会继续施行。

当中国外商投资准入制度改革似乎停滞的同时，中国对欧的企业并购正在高速增长，2014 年到 2015 年增速达到 44%，而 2016 年上半年增速更快。这些企业并购的案例涉及包括银行业、汽车零部件、机器人和农业科技行业在内的广泛领域，与欧洲投资者在华遇到的种种壁垒形成显著的反差。我们认为，只有中欧双方在市场开放度方面保持平等互惠才能够防止欧洲市场保护主义倾向抬头，助力欧洲保持市场开放和贸易投资的自由。

负面清单制度是上海自贸区引入并试点的最重要的概念。在其公布之初，欧洲商界体现出了极大的热情。然而，之后两批自贸区相继成立，上海自贸区对外国投资者的吸引力逐步减弱。作为在沪欧洲商界的代表，我们希望看到上海能够对其他自贸区保持竞争力，在改革进程中起到更加积极的推动作用，为中外投资者带来更多的市场准入机遇。

第二，一个好的投资环境离不开健康、开放和强健的金融市场，而这也是上海建设全球金融中心的关键。

我们很高兴地看到上海最近提升金融基础设施的努力，而这也使得上海在第十九期全球金融中心指数排名由 2015 年的 21 位上升到 2016 年的 16 位。

然而，若要同香港和新加坡在内的其他金融中心竞争，上海仍需要继续和中央政府保持协调，呼吁资本市场的进一步改革和开放，比如全面的外汇可兑换和自由的跨境汇款。

我们也认为股票市场应该更加开放，这样中外企业，特别是中小型企业，能够更容易地获得成长所需的资金。上海市政府提出的成立国际板和战略新兴产业板的计划让我们倍受鼓舞，但是在去年股市波动的影响下，计划并未实现。我们欢迎在适当的时机能够重启这一计划。

第三，上海是中国最大的集装箱港口和空运枢纽，其国际贸易地位的进一步提升需要各部门间更紧密的合作。

欧盟商会及其会员企业高度赞赏上海在改善物流基础设施和贸易监管环境方面做出的努力。我们最近的几个会员调查显示，分别有超过 37% 和 58% 的受访企业认为上海自贸区的自由化改革在物流和海关两方面服务水平达到或者超出了他们的预期。

然而，当和其他一些发达国家相比时，上海在通关效率方面仍有进一步改善的空间。中国的通关监管涉及多个部门，即便"单一窗口"已经大大简化了通关流程，并且"信息互换、监管互认、执法互助"的"三互"通关也在部门间形成合力，但是更紧密的部门内和跨部门协作仍可以进一步加强，以保证高的通关效率和统一的执法力度。

最后一点，上海的硬件条件与全国其他地区相比处于领先地位，在执法环境、知识产权保护、行政效率和产业集群等方面都利好初创企业的成长。但是，上海在吸引投资的软环境方面仍需克服一些障碍，以赶超其他国际都市。

欧盟商会赞赏上海正努力解决外国人才和国内异地人才来沪就业所面临的挑战，但是这些努力仍然远远未能营造对中外人才，特别是年轻人才，具有吸引力的国际环境。

欧盟是中国最大的贸易伙伴，贡献了中国贸易额的 15%。中国和欧盟互相都需要对方的支持。作为欧洲商界在华代表，我们深深体会到一个繁荣的贸易和投资关系对于中欧双方的重要意义。中国欧盟商会上海分会和我们的会员将一如既往地致力于促进中欧关系的发展，不仅造福两国企业，更惠及双方消费者和更广泛的人民。

中国欧盟商会第二版上海建议书将于四天后发布。我们今天所讨论的许多问题也正是我们会员企业提出的问题。我很愿意给各位分享本建议书，并进一步交流对话。

系统集成、协同创新：上海自贸试验区改革应该处理好的几组关系

张 湧
中国（上海）自由贸易试验区管委会政策研究局原局长

郑海鳌
中国（上海）自由贸易试验区管委会政策研究局副局长

　　三年来，上海自贸试验区按照"大胆闯、大胆试、自主改"的要求，坚持以制度创新为核心，努力在浦东新区一个完整的行政区域内设计改革方案、落实改革举措，形成了以开放倒逼改革、以改革创新促进转型发展的良好局面，为全国范围内的自贸试验区建设和面上的改革提供了一批可复制、可推广的经验做法。展望未来，要始终不忘自贸试验区的改革初心，进一步对照中央要求、对标国际规则、对接企业需求，使自贸试验区成为五大发展理念的最佳实践区，成为更高水平双向开放的桥头堡，成为服务"一带一路"等国家建设的重要基地，成为供给侧结构性改革的重要平台，以归零心态、满格激情在更高起点上续航破冰。为此，我认为上海自贸区改革要处理好九组关系。

　　第一，贸易与金融、投资、政府改革的关系。上海自贸区不仅仅做贸易，最大亮点在于金融改革、金融创新，以及投资和商事制度领域的改革。贸易便利化的推进，离不开外汇管理的改革；贸易形态的升级，会引发企业全球供应链布局的变化，也会对外资"引进来"和国内资本"走出去"产生积极影响；而贸易、投资、金融的更大开放，对政府的治理能力和风控水平提出了更高的要求，为此要更好地深化政府自身的改革。

　　第二，28 平方公里、120 平方公里与 1 200 平方公里的关系。上海自贸区包括了 28 平方公里的保税区片区和 92 平方公里的陆家嘴、张江、世博和金桥。保税区片区完全是物理围网的海关特殊监管区，整个 120 平方公里里面最大的开放度应该体现在这 28 平方公里，尤其是洋山保税港区因其独特的天然优势，完全可以成为一个真正的自由港。扩区到比较发达却没有剩下多少可供开发土地的陆家嘴等区域，显示了上海并没有把招商引资、土地开发作为自贸区的首要目标，

而是想真正沉下心来做制度创新。这92平方公里给我们提供了大量的改革可以试验的东西，因为那里有几万家十分成熟的企业样本，包括一大批金融机构、研发机构、创新企业，它们的需求诉求恰恰就可能构成自贸区改革的命题。再从整个浦东看，2015年4月上海自贸区管委会与浦东新区政府实现合署办公，实质上是让1 200平方公里的浦东新区与占其1/10的自贸试验区一体化运作，可以起到一石多鸟的作用：一是可以让自贸区改革经验率先在全浦东复制推广；二是通过合署办公实现行政资源高度整合、主体责任切实到位，浦东新区成为自贸区建设的主力军和先锋队；三是可以用自贸区理念改造一级地方政府，让浦东新区的干部都具有自贸区思维、自贸区理念，并以此指导推进面上的各项工作。

第三，开放、改革和发展的关系。现在的开放是双向的开放，不仅是外资引进来，研发也要引进来，事实上我们更希望自贸区能够成为创新的高地、资源配置的中心。自贸区开放后要跟国际规则相结合，要在深入研究TiSA、TPP等高标准投资贸易规则的基础上，改进我们自己的管理方式。这体现了开放倒逼改革。封闭起来不容易发现自身存在的差距，更大的开放会发现政府的管理模式、组织架构和能力水平等方面与国际高标准相比的确存在一些差距，缩短差距就是重要的改革命题。

至于发展，上海自贸区不太直接也不太多讲GDP、税收、速度等数字，讲得比较多的一直是制度创新。如果可以通过制度创新的突破、营商环境的改进，自贸区的经济发展能够取得比过去更大的进步，这是我们所追求的。今年一季度以至于上半年，浦东的地方财政收入增长处于历史高位水平，这里面应该有自贸区制度改革的贡献。

第四，政府、市场和社会的关系。自贸区改革必须厘清政府和市场的边界，究竟政府干什么、市场干什么、社会干什么。负面清单告诉我们"法无禁止皆可为"，其实质是让市场来决定负面清单以外的事情，就是给市场提供了足够大的创新空间。

现在政府管理的方式正在发生根本性的转变，核心是从过去的审批制为主改成了现在的备案制为主，随之而来的是政府正在从过去的管制型政府变成了今天的服务型政府。政府服务首要的是要维持一个公平透明的市场环境，既要扶持真创新，又要打击"伪创新"。随着经济活动越来越复杂和社会发育越来越成熟，光靠政府一头是难以承担全部的市场监管、社会管理等职责的，必须发动全社会的力量，让市场主体做到守法经营、自我约束，让行业协会等业界做到自治自律，让各种社会力量共同实行监督，最终形成一个以多元治理、综合监管为基础，以多维度、全方位政府专业监管为支撑的事中事后监管体系。

第五，"放管服"的关系。本质还是要处理好政府和市场的关系，"放"就是通过政府瘦身和简政放权，真正让市场在配置资源中起决定性作用；"管"就是更好而不是更多发挥政府作用，特别是在市场运行、社会管理、公共服务、环境保护等领域强化事中事后监管，确保不发生系统性、区域性风险。"服"是保障。自贸区更大的"放"对更好的"管"提出了更高的要求，这种要求是一种压力测试。自贸区需要在压力测试中发现漏洞、不足和短板。我们的重要经验是不仅要总结自贸区能够干什么，也要总结出什么事情不能干。

第六，供给侧改革与自贸区试验的关系。上海市市长杨雄在今年全国两会上指出，自贸区是上海推进供给侧结构性改革的平台。所以，我们要分析制度的供给和企业的发展之间的关系。供给侧改革就是压缩低端供给，提升高端供给，高端供给必定要靠企业来创造。高端的供给要以科技创新为动力，要以人才为支撑。企业的动力和活力要靠政府制度创新的供给和政府对营商环境的营造。所以，政府在供给侧改革中一定能够发挥重要的作用，自贸区试验就是围绕着供给侧的改革想方设法降低制度性交易成本，金融、投资、贸易改革等无一不是这样考虑的。

第七，国际规则、国家试验和地方实践的关系。对标国际规则非常重要。上海自贸区从 2009 年研究，一直到 2013 年才正式获批，一个重要的背景是国际经济格局的深刻变化，尤其是美国在 BIT 谈判中希望中国承诺对外资实行"准入前国民待遇＋负面清单"，而上海自贸区正是作为一个局部的地区代表国家向国际社会做出了一种开放的姿态，其实也是一种承诺。我们的使命是要代表国家对标国际规则、参与国际竞争，这是一个落在地方实践的国家试验。

第八，重点突破、单兵突进和顶层设计、系统集成的关系。顶层设计和系统集成一直是我们追求的一个重要方面。一些人批评上海自贸区改革的系统性不够、逻辑性不强，有些碎片化，这的确需要不断加以改进。同时，没有过去的许多单项改革包括自贸区之前的试点，没有一些企业和部门的首创精神和单兵突进，没有一批已经取得了重要突破的改革事项作为铺垫和积累，今天谈顶层设计和系统集成也就缺乏基础。为此，下一步既要高度重视串好"珍珠项链"，特别是重视做好三周年之后的改革整体谋划，又要鼓励企业和部门在改革的总体框架下继续实现逐个击破。

第九，自贸区与"四个中心"及科创中心的关系。没有自贸区的时候，上海国际金融中心其实只是国内金融中心。有了自贸区，金融中心的国际化就有了支撑、方向和路径。上海自贸区金融开放的一个发明就是把保税区的物理围网变成了资金流动的"电子围网"，这就是自由贸易分账核算单元体系。上海自贸区正在建设的原油、黄金、股票、债券、外汇等面向国际投资者的各式金融交易市场，其关键是引入了贸易领域"一线放开、二线管住"的理念。最后，科创中心和自贸区之间构成了"双自联动"的关系，让科技创新、制度创新、金融创新、开放创新这四个创新能够"四缸驱动""四轮联动"。我们希望通过自主创新示范区和自由贸易示范区的联动，让上海真正成为全球创新高地，让全世界的精英人才包括科学家、企业家都能够为我所用。

提升上海在新经济领域的
投资和贸易便利性

李广宇

麦肯锡全球资深董事合伙人、全球基础设施与

政府业务联席负责人

　　随着中国经济融入全球化体系的程度进一步加深，中国的国际贸易结构近些年来也产生了深刻的变化，传统的加工贸易所占比重持续下滑，高技术含量、高附加值的贸易比重迅速上升，这也对中国的实体经济带来了巨大冲击。

　　在这一背景下，上海作为中国经济的重要引擎和开展国际贸易的标杆性城市，如何更好地适应新的经济环境和未来国际贸易的发展趋势，关乎其开放型经济的建设和产业结构的转型升级。在政府众多的政策性目标中，如何提升投资和贸易便利化水平便是当下值得深入探究的议题。

1. 发展趋势：高技术、高附加值的货物贸易和服务贸易将成为主力增长点

　　我们看到，未来30—40年世界贸易将迎来爆发性增长，预计2050年全球贸易额将是2010年的8倍。其中新兴市场，尤其是亚洲的新兴市场所占份额将显著提高至近50%。

　　在这种趋势下，国际贸易格局将会发生深度调整。首先，货物贸易增长将更偏向高技术、高附加值的产品。我们看到，交易额增长率前五的制造业在2010年前后分别是船舶制造、药品生产、化学制品、医疗设备和合成纤维化工行业；而预计到2030年前后，将由先进机器人、自动汽车、可穿戴医疗设备、新一代基因药物、高复合新材料等高技术、高附加值的制造业主导。其次，我们通过横向对比发现，我国在2007年到2012年的服务贸易出口年复合增长率接近10%，远高于美国（6%）、德国（4%）、英国（0.7%）等发达国家的水平。当然，我们也应意识到，从服务贸易出口的绝对值来看我们国家（5 660亿美元）与美国（22 980亿美元）、德国（11 960亿美元）和英国（10 140亿美元）等西方发达经

济体还有着不小的差距，服务贸易升级和追赶先进水平的潜力和空间还很大。特别是咨询服务、金融服务、研发外包服务等知识型服务贸易。

2. 上海未来产业格局展望：塑造新型产业生态体系

当前，上海的产业格局呈现出以电子信息、汽车、成套设备、石油 / 精细化工为主导的制造业，加之以金融、批发零售、房地产、信息科技产业为主导的服务业双轮驱动的格局。

但在未来十年，上海的产业格局变化将由科技创新激发，呈现出三大关键趋势：（1）更高技术含量的制造业：通过聚焦高技术产品和生产链的关键环节，提升制造业整体的科技含量水平。（2）更高附加值的服务业：服务贸易占贸易整体比例提高，附加值大幅提升；高端服务业，特别是高人力资本含量的服务业（如研发外包、工业设计等）进一步发展，专业化水准持续提升。（3）科技创新推动跨界融合：通过科技创新把不同的行业通过不同的方式连接起来，推动跨行业及跨产业链的融合，服务业和制造业的边际开始变得模糊。

围绕这三大趋势，我们预计到 2025 年，上海将形成以科技服务、金融服务、文化娱乐、医疗健康服务、新一代信息技术、生物医药、高端装备、新材料、新能源汽车等产业为核心的新型产业生态体系，完成从传统产业向新型产业的转型升级。

3. 营商环境的改进升级：从"硬件设施便利化"到"软性环境便利化"

针对新经济和新产业格局的特点，上海需要重新定义"投资与贸易"的便利性，创造更人性化、透明化、便捷化的营商环境。

总体来看，为了实现更加与时俱进和与国际接轨的"投资与贸易"的便利性，上海需要从传统的以提供"硬件设施"的便利性为主进化成为为企业和其他经济实体提供"软性环境"的便利化。经过成立三年多来的积极探索，上海自由贸易试验区目前已经在投资管理、贸易便利化、金融、服务业开放等软性环境领域实现了一定的便利化，向未来实现更加全面的软性环境便利化迈出了坚实的一步。但与此同时，在一些方面还存在着明显的短板亟待补齐，主要体现在：在整体对外开放程度上，突破性的新政策较少，放宽标准型的政策较多，服务业尤其是高端服务业的开放程度较低；在政策配套和法规支持方面，现有的政策和法规令出多门，覆盖面有限，缺乏整体性。例如，中资非五星船舶沿海捎带业务，交通部已经出台文件予以明确，且中海、中远等企业已经试点操作，但该政策涉及海关、检验检疫、港务集团等多家部门，还需要研究制定配套方案①；在政府办事效率方面，中央和地方层面上，政府权力分配没有理顺，地方政府在开展自贸区的改革试点时被授权不充分。上海自贸区总体方案曾提出"研究完善适应境外股权投资和离岸业务发展的税收政策"，上海自贸区管委会已和中央财税部门进行了深入研究，但迄今为止尚无方案出台②。在地方政府内部层面，目前上海实行的单一窗口服务覆盖的部门有限，可实现的功能不多，无法形成整体性优势。同时，单一窗口的目标模式的选定以及数据元标准化的工作也非常滞后③；在风险控制和监管效率方面，仍然主要依靠人工来进行风险控制工作，缺乏信息整合和信息透明度，多头监管导致效率低下。例如，在海关实行无纸通关的情况下，税务部门继续要求提交纸质单据，加上数据格式不统一，没有与国际接轨，通关便利整体上大打折扣，也增加了国际合作的难度④。

具体来看，上海应致力于几项关键的贸易便利化举措：（1）与国际接轨的贸易便利化法律基础；（2）更加便捷的预裁定、预审查、后审计、提前放行等通关流程；（3）基于标准数据元的、一体化协作的政府单一窗口电子政务体系；（4）对企业、货物的分类监管机制；（5）更加富有弹性和吸引力的金融税收制度；（6）更便捷的跨境投融资等资本流动方式；（7）更加人性化的签证、居住和执业政策；（8）完善的风险参数维护、风险预警、风险管控体系；（9）更开放多元的国际文化空间；（10）更包容创新"试错"的舆论环境；等等。

4. 领先实践：突破常规，创造贸易便利化新模式

国际上的领先实践往往敢于突破常规做法，敢于启用并应用新型技术，创造出促进新经济投资贸易便利化的新模式。其中新加坡、美国纽约和爱尔兰是三个非常典型的成功推动投资贸易便利化落地的地区。

（1）新加坡：电子政府便利企业服务。

从 20 世纪 80 年代起开始致力于电子政府的构建，现已成为世界上电子政务开展最发达的国家之一。在 90 年代，新加坡计算机委员会实施了三项国家信息

---

① 王孝钰：《上海自贸区促进投资贸易便利化相关政策措施梳理汇总》，上海市人民政府发展研究中心博士后工作站。
② 周师迅、张明海：《对接国际贸易新规则，加快自贸试验区改革实践》，上海市人民政府研究中心。
③④ 周师迅、谭旻：《从相关协议标准看上海自贸区贸易便利化存在的问题》，上海市人民政府研究中心。

化技术计划，为政府办公实现信息化奠定了良好的基础。

新加坡的电子政府不仅实现了数据共享、政府与公民及企业服务的电子化，更是搭建了政府职能整合电子平台（OBLS），提高了政府的服务效率。网上商业执照服务（OBLS）平台则大大缩短了商业执照的申请时间（最快仅1天），并为政府节省了上千万美元运营成本。新加坡贸易网络系统（Trade Net）是当今世界成熟运作的"单一窗口"办公体系的代表，也是世界上第一个用于贸易数据审理的电子数据交换系统。它的特点是"系统集成，机构分散"，将新加坡税务、海关等35个政府部门链接起来，形成国际投资贸易的单一窗口，可以实现对文档的自动处理。同时，新加坡政府还非常彻底地简化了海关流程。比如只对4类商品征收关税；在新加坡6个自由贸易区的货物向市场出售前，无需向海关申报，大大提高了通关效率。

（2）美国纽约：数据开放激发商业创新。

2012年2月29日，纽约市通过了《开放数据法案》，3月7日由市长迈克尔·布隆伯格签署后正式生效，这是美国历史上首次将政府数据大规模开放纳入立法。凭据开放数据法案，到2018年，除了涉及安全和隐私的数据之外，纽约市政府及其分支机构所拥有的数据都必须实现对民众开放。而且政府明文规定，使用这些数据不需要经过任何注册、审批程序，数据的使用也不受限制。

各类公开的政府数据成为纽约年度"大数据创新竞赛"灵感来源，在纽约的数据开放一年左右的时候，围绕着开放数据平台而形成的应用开发团队已有几百个之多。他们可以利用各个区划的行人交通数据帮助中小企业制定营销策略；利用区域内的住户、商户数据帮助初创企业布局起步战略，降低投资的门槛。纽约通过将政府数据大规模开放纳入立法范畴，以实现社会运行效率的提高、激发潜在商业价值的创造，最终实现打造"智慧城市"的愿景。

另一个可类比的例子是GPS（全球定位系统）的开放。1983年，美国将原本用于军事的卫星定位系统GPS向民众开放使用，而且在2000年后取消了对民用GPS精度的限制。从汽车导航、精准农业耕作到物流、通信等，GPS开放后不仅服务了生产和生活，同时还创造了大量就业岗位。据估算，仅美国国内就有约300万的就业岗位直接或者间接依赖GPS。

（3）爱尔兰：全程服务促进招商引资。

2008年，受全球金融危机的影响，爱尔兰政府采取了一系列的政策措施，以前瞻性的眼光，战略性地选择了以智能经济为主题的未来重点发展产业。2013年《福布斯》杂志将爱尔兰评为"全球最适宜经商的国家"；2014年，Oracle Capital Group公布的"2014年全球最适宜创业的国家"排行榜，爱尔兰排名全球第七，欧洲第一。在这背后，爱尔兰政府鼓励高科技和智能经济的政策保持长期的一致性和确定性起到了重要的作用。

爱尔兰政府认为，大批初创公司的崛起能增加就业机遇，带动出口，从而促进整体经济的发展。所以政府成立爱尔兰工业发展署，扶持高潜力增长的公司。这支有着超 700 人的团队目前已在 30 多国设立分支机构。

同时，爱尔兰政府还根据重点发展的产业构建了专门的"项目部门"，提高服务企业的专业性，全程跟踪重大投资者，时刻了解企业需求，并提供有导向性的人才对接和政策对接服务。以人才招募为例，爱尔兰的工业发展署为解决科技企业入驻遇到的人才瓶颈，在全球访谈了 300 位爱尔兰籍工程师，选出 85 位优秀候选人，成功助力科技创新企业解决人才问题。

5. 结 语

根据国家"十三五"规划，到 2020 年，上海要基本建成国际经济、金融、贸易、航运中心，以及具有全球影响力的科技创新中心。并明确提出提高自由贸易试验区建设质量、深化服务业开放、提高贸易便利化程度、推动金融开放创新等具体要求。未来五年，上海在经济发展和科技创新领域责任重大。

展望 2040 年，上海将成为卓越的全球城市，一座令人向往的创新之城、人文之城、生态之城。上海应积极发挥引领作用，牢牢把握新经济和未来产业格局的发展，充分借鉴领先实践，在机制体制上锐意创新，进一步提升投资和贸易领域的便利性，打造适合新经济发展、符合国际标准、更富吸引力的整体营商环境。

全球标准，中国速度——关于提升上海投资贸易便利化的建议

周　园
波士顿咨询公司全球合伙人兼董事总经理

李剑腾
波士顿咨询公司合伙人兼董事总经理

当前，全球经济出现反复与波折，以美国与欧盟为代表的发达国家保守主义抬头，贸易保护措施急增，"双反"政策频出。新一届的美国总统特朗普是贸易保护主义的拥趸者，都说"新官上任三把火"，他的第一把火就即将浇灭跨太平洋伙伴关系协定（TPP）；而发展中国家增长开始放缓，我们可以看到金砖国家中的俄罗斯、巴西、南非的经济增长均呈现历史新低，经济高度自然资源化和市场严重外部化的结构性问题凸显。

全球经济的不确定性在增强，但中国在自身开展深度改革的同时，向世界不断传递出构建开放型经济的坚定决心和明确信心。国家主席习近平在今年举办的二十国集团工商峰会（B20峰会）开幕式的主旨演讲中表示，"我们将继续深入参与经济全球化进程，支持多边贸易体制。我们将加大放宽外商投资准入，提高便利化程度，促进公平开放竞争，全力营造优良营商环境"。与此同时，"一带一路"、亚投行与自贸区建设也开展得如火如荼。通过"丝绸之路经济带"和"21世纪海上丝绸之路"，我国已与沿线60多个国家建立全球新型发展伙伴关系，大力推进政治互信、经济融合与文化包容；亚投行至今年年底，成员将超过90个，将为促进亚洲区域的建设互联互通化和经济一体化做出突出贡献；而自贸试验区自2013年上海首个设立以来，已两次扩围至11个，不断扩大开放领域，提升开放能级，接轨国际贸易投资新规则。这无一不在向世界传递着中国对共同构建开放透明的全球贸易和投资治理格局的坚定信念。

在我国经济发展与对外开放的新格局中，上海可谓是秉承中央厚望，充分发挥改革开放排头兵、创新发展先行者的作用。根据上海市城市总体规划，上海将剑指"卓越的全球城市"，到2040年建成国际经济、金融、贸易、航运、科技创

新中心和文化大都市。我们可以看到，继"十二五"之后，上海再度强调其作为国际贸易中心的地位，对投资贸易领域的重视程度可见一斑。

回顾过去，上海一直是我国对外开放战略的先行者，在国际投资与贸易活动中取得了不菲的成就。

1984年，上海作为首批沿海开放城市，获准放宽外资引入的规模与形式限制。1990年，设立外高桥保税区，是全国启动最早的保税区，首个"国家进口贸易促进创新示范区"。2005年，设立洋山保税港区，是全国第一个保税港区，成为实行自由贸易区政策的初始样板。2013年，成立上海自贸试验区，是中国境内第一个自由贸易区，是通关便利化和投资自由化的先驱者。

在对外投资与贸易活动中上海始终领跑全国，2015年上海进出口总额达4 492亿美元，外商直接投资实际利用额达184亿美元，超过北京、深圳与广州等一线城市。在全球市场中，上海也开始占据一席之位，2015年上海口岸货物进出口总额占据全球3.4%，超越香港、新加坡等国际贸易中心城市。

但与此同时，相较于成熟的国际贸易大都市，上海也面临外商总部投资不足、服务贸易占比偏低的发展挑战。

跨国公司地区总部的经济拉动效应强劲，是外商投资企业中的佼佼者。上海自2002年起开始鼓励外资在沪发展总部经济，但就数量与能级上仍与国际大都市存在一定差距。2014年，上海跨国公司总部机构数量为470家，少于同样作为亚太地区重要城市的东京（531家）、香港（1 389家）与新加坡（4 200家）。同时，在总部能级方面，我们发现近三分之一的财富500强企业在新加坡设有地区总部，且多为亚太区综合职能总部；而在上海，仅7%为亚太区总部，其他多为中国区总部或单一职能总部（如研发中心）。

服务贸易方面，与全国其他省市相比，上海的工作推进一直较为领先，但仍存在服务贸易占比相对较低、内部结构不合理等问题。2014年，上海服务贸易进出口额占GDP的比重为50%，仍与香港（62%）、新加坡（92%）有一定差距。同时，运输、旅游等劳动密集型服务占比逾七成，为服务贸易的主要贡献领域；而金融保险服务、文化服务、专业服务等创新性强、附加值高的高端服务业占比较低，发展较为滞后。

我们认为究其根本，是因为上海在投资贸易中的市场准入、边境管理、与运营环境三方面仍存在便利化不足。

（1）市场准入上，投资开放程度有限。现行的2015年版负面清单较长，仍保留122项特别管理措施，而国际标准基本为短清单模式，如美国BIT范本仅为20余项；金融、互联网服务、文化娱乐等高端服务业尚未得到突破，在参股比例、经营年限等方面限制较多；部分特殊管理措施的限制条件描述不足，如评级服务、大型主题公园均为限制类，但却缺乏具体的限制条件、限制程度的描述。

（2）边境管理上，商务人员流动措施待加强。商务人员作为国际贸易的主体，其流动效率与程序简易程度是考验投资贸易便利化水平的关键内容之一。但目前上海的边境管理措施多集中于提高进出口货物的通关效率，在简化跨境手续、促进人员流动方面制度建设不足。

（3）运营环境上，金融服务自由化不足。金融机制受限，对资金运营与跨境业务的支撑力度有待加强，如利率市场化推行缓慢，汇率形成机制与资本项下可兑换改革的落地时间尚不明朗。而已推行的金融创新适用范围有限，尚未在上海大规模推广，如自由贸易账户（FT 账户）的开立主体资格，局限于上海自贸区内，区外企业难以享受金融创新福利。

为切实应对挑战，提升投资贸易便利化水平，我们建议上海市政府从以下三方面切入，全面释放城市竞争力。

（1）推动负面清单进一步"瘦身"，重点扩大更高层次的服务业开放，并推动清单的规范化与透明化。

建议负面清单减少禁止与限制外商投资的产业数，我们发现欧美发达国家对外资限制较少，仅将有关国防与国土资源安全的行业位列负面清单中。重点开放证券、保险等非银行金融业务、商务服务、专业技术服务、教育、医疗、文化娱乐等高端服务业，助推上海服务业与服务贸易的发展。同时，可以考虑采取基于互惠条款的限制措施，如在美国的 BIT 范本中，有七项基于互惠原则，即若 BIT 缔约伙伴国向美国开放该领域投资，美国也会向伙伴国投资者相应开放。

特别管理措施的描述中应增加政府级别、法律依据的阐述，与国内法相衔接，提升规范化与法制统一化需求。具体描述中限制条件需进一步细化，做到让投资者一目了然，增加可操作性。同时，提高负面清单透明度，在制定过程中应当允许各种不同利益主体参与，提供充分发表意见的渠道。

（2）提供便利的商务人员签证制度，并提升一站式手续办理与英语电子政务服务能力。

以自贸区为试点，为符合一定条件的商务人员发放区内特有的商务旅行卡，延长容留期限。可效仿亚太经合组织在各成员间推行商务旅行卡计划，持卡人凭有效护照和旅行卡在三年内无须办理入境签证，并且享有特殊的快速出入境通道。同时，制定灵活的商务签与工作居留签的转换制度，为人才的出入境提供便利。

简化就业许可手续，适当放宽就业许可证的期限规定，如放宽至三年或劳动合同期。目前外国人就业证、外国人居留证、上海市居住证等证照的办理机构不同但申办材料较为相似，可适当进行整合，统一申办。如在新加坡，外籍人士工作居住只需持有就业或创业准证，且办理机构单一，由新加坡人力部统一颁发。

提升英语电子政务服务能力。上海各政府机构的网站已经提供多个网上办事选项，但提供的英文网站或所具备的功能较少。建议上海市政府基于已有的电子政务系统，提升外语服务能力，提供外籍人才便捷的网上办事通道。

（3）充分发挥上海自贸区的"试验田"作用，进一步深化金融创新，并将成功经验推广至全上海，提升面向企业的金融服务能力。

充分利用上海自贸区作为金融改革的试验田。有步骤地推进利率市场化改革，进一步扩大利率市场化的标的与额度，有序下调存款准备金率；大力推进银行存款保险制度，以增强银行体系的市场约束，稳定金融市场秩序。同时，建立多元化融资方式，加强对企业的金融服务能力，如加快推动熊猫债在上海自贸区的发行，提供较为低廉的融资选项，并推进人民币国际化进程；加快自贸区大宗商品衍生品交易平台的建设，为自贸区企业打通国际大宗商品贸易融资、套期保值的交易通道。

推动上海其他区域衔接与复制自贸区的成功改革经验。如加快自由贸易账户（FT账户）向境内区外企业与以外籍人才为代表的个人用户开放。以帮助企业更为便利地开展跨境本外币结算、境外融资、跨境大额存单等，增强资本流动性，降低优化融资成本；并帮助人才通过账户享受到财富管理、境外医疗保健、子女教育等跨境金融服务，以更好吸引海外人才。其他成功经验包括跨国公司外汇资金集中管理、跨境双向人民币资金池、取消融资租赁对外债权业务审批、取消对外担保行政审批等。但同时，需加强监管与风险防范，避免大规模推广带来大量热钱涌入与资本套利行为。

展望未来，希望上海能比肩甚至超越纽约、伦敦、东京等国际大都市，向"卓越的全球城市"迈出坚定的步伐。

新全球化趋势下，从服务企业角度看上海发展新机遇

余煌超
凯捷中国首席执行官

钱敏毓
凯捷中国首席运营官

由于在外商投资服务企业从业多年，见证了全球 IT 服务业的两波转型，结合本次论坛的主题"提升上海投资贸易便利化水平"，我还是回到我的本行，从上海科技和创新服务配套如何促进贸易发展的角度，来谈谈新全球趋势下的贸易便利化。

过去的十年，中国作为发展中国家是全球化的受益者之一。从产业升级、金融和科技创新、到"一带一路"国际合作，上海凭借自身优势和智慧，打造独特的城市竞争力。但是伴随着全球一些地区地方贸易保护主义的抬头，地域区块化开始显现，这个趋势对很多依赖贸易驱动的开放型经济体形成冲击，比如新加坡政府在 11 月将 2016 年经济增长预测下调 1—1.5 个百分点。

地方贸易保护主义虽然是贸易全球化进程的挑战，但作为第二大全球经济体的中国正在以积极主动的姿态走向世界，很多发展中国家地区和组织也形成新的利益共同体。在这个变革时期，唯有资质优良者更有发展之基础，对于有着历史沿革、地缘优势且海纳百川和高度国际化的上海，新全球化趋势也意味着新机遇。

这个新机遇要回到中国"一带一路"发展构想来看。"一带一路"构想联结亚欧大陆沿线 60 多个国家，是"丝绸之路经济带"和"21 世纪海上丝绸之路"，新的全球化蓝图构想。"一带一路"会重新构建陆地和海洋之间的权重关系。中国与欧洲互为最重要的贸易伙伴，处于"一带一路"的两头，共同承担着此次"新平衡"的重任。两个大经济体之间在新形势下的共赢，需要长期不懈的沟通、磨合、试错和调整。这种开放的心态和勇于创新的能力，并非所有"一带一路"的沿途城市都能够一蹴而就便具备。在中央政府的大方向指导之下，龙头城市的示范和带动作用尤为关键。上海身处"一带一路"的地缘交汇点，数百年来积累的海纳百川务实创新的核心气质和商务能力，正是龙头城市的不二之选，是"一

带一路"的所有沿途口岸城市所需要跟随的榜样。

企业是实现贸易的载体，如果说上海必然是"一带一路"的龙头城市，那么企业总部必然就是拉动贸易行为的一个个小火车头。在中国与欧洲之间，在上海与巴黎／柏林之间，有无数的跨国企业在急切地摸索如何适应新格局。凯捷集团作为欧洲最大的管理咨询和技术服务公司，集团总部在巴黎，中国运营超过 20年，大中华区总部在上海。在上海和欧洲之间，凯捷是一座无形的桥梁，通过高科技和创新服务，帮助欧洲企业"引进来"，帮助中国企业"走出去"。这是凯捷对于客户的承诺，这是凯捷对于上海的承诺。

1. 新型总部经济的发展

过去的几十年，上海一直也在提倡总部经济。但是面临全球产业升级和转型的竞争压力，结合联结亚欧的"一带一路"建设机遇，我们需要把有限的高端人才资源和宝贵的政策扶持投入到哪里？我们看到的思考点主要集中在以下两个方面：

第一个是在提升贸易质量和维持贸易稳定发展的前提下，什么样的地区总部应该加大引入的力度？基于对中国消费市场的乐观预测，以及上海"四个中心"的定位，总部经济引入可以更多侧重在两方面：一方面是金融、娱乐、健康、教育等与民生消费相关的领域，另一方面是高科技研发创新，供应链控制等与"一带一路"贸易带动作用相关的领域。在吸引企业总部的形式上，也可以更加多样，相比于以往重投资长周期准备的进入形式，可以有更多敏捷的方法，例如善用自贸区的便利，通过整合数字贸易相关的企业服务，引入更多欧洲高端服务与消费品牌，以及科技品牌，强调上海"品质承诺"的形象，并帮助这些企业以一种低试错成本、快速便捷的方式进入中国市场，迅速调整，站稳脚跟。

第二个是现有的以及在上海落户的地区总部如何转型升级。首先以凯捷这个高科技服务业企业自身为例，工业化规模化发展，以及数字化企业创新是我们的两大发展引擎。上海的整体生活成本上升，对青年人才有一定的挤出效应，在工业化和规模化上，企业会选择向周边辐射。在数字化企业创新领域，我们有强烈的开放创新平台和全球顶尖人才的需求，综观我们辐射和服务的汽车、消费品零售、医药和金融企业，数字化创新同样是一个重要的话题。这部分的思考我会在后面第三部分详细阐述。

2. 外资企业的中国创新全球化

中国本身作为巨大的消费市场，已经成为很多跨国企业最大的收入来源。以汽车行业为例，2014年中国首次成为奔驰汽车的最大单一市场，2015年戴姆勒中国营收为147亿欧元，在集团整体营收中占比9.8%。在医药、连锁零售、IT软硬件和娱乐等行业，很多跨国企业在中国的收益已经超过本土或者其他全球市场。而中国互联网技术的快速发展，也使得民生消费领域的传统霸主面临了前所未闻的竞争者，拥抱变化和新科技，成为在中国运营企业的关键词，而这些都催生了"中国创新"的产生。

创新并不是一个新话题，在成熟的欧洲市场凯捷和设计、生产和销售汽车零部件的法雷奥公司曾经合作推出"Mov'InBlue ™"应用，面向机构和企业车队提供汽车短租服务，其中法雷奥提供了一项基于云平台的，能够使用智能手机开启汽车的专利技术，以及源自合作伙伴网络的各类数字化服务，使整个租赁体验无缝便捷，无需更多实体门店，这个创新为法雷奥在欧洲带来了商业模式的变化。十七年以来凯捷《汽车在线》报告追踪全球汽车市场发展趋势，中国一直是重要市场，2016年研究热点是网上售车，这也是中国市场重要趋势。我们在市场上看到很多汽车企业除了接入几大互联网电商平台，也在积极构建自己的电商系统。根据我们的观察，由于中国市场的规模和多样性，部分跨国企业在中国市场的实施经验已经输出到集团的其他国家。汽车行业是由蓬勃的国内消费市场激活的外资企业创新的典型例子，更进一步，在工业4.0主题下智能制造，物联网相关的技术创新改善生产效率或者用户体验，都有很多的市场发展机遇。

过去我们谈到从中国创新到中国制造，更多的是与中国企业"走出去"关联。但是伴随着中国消费品市场的发展，外资企业的中国创新也显露头角，这类创新有着天生国际化的基因，它的产生能够通过企业自身的网络迅速蔓延和影响全球。而这种影响，将为上海建设新型总部经济，吸引"一带一路"沿线企业投资打下良好基础。

3. 服务大型企业，从人才引进到全球开放创新社群

商业、新科技创新的成功以人为本，从卓越的领军人才到创新的环境缺一不可。相比于传统的人才引进带动科技发展，在新型总部经济和中国创新走向全球的大环境下，上海对创新型人才的需求更上一个台阶。

但是全球顶尖型人才的体量本身很小，而且此类人才的流动意愿相对较低，例如本身在研究和商业领域非常成功的专家，通常已经在特定的国家定居。对于这类专家的交流需求，通常是通过院校之间短期的学术交流，或者在上海地区举办大型的国际论坛，以嘉宾形式出席发言。这类知识交流形式的特点是时间周期短，停留在知识交流层面不涉及经济或商业合作，可持续性效应短，由民间组织发起社会辐

射效应有限。这种类似的人才资源应用深度和广度对开放式创新来说是远远不够的。

开放式创新是 19 世纪后叶被提出的一个概念，特指组织通过内外部的知识交换来拓展组织内部创新，并能够引入外部创新为己用，从而扩大市场份额。在我们习惯的创新领域中，企业和组织是通过招募专才，建立实验室，激发全员试错和项目奖励来鼓励创新发展。这个需求放大到政府和社会层面，就演变成了人才引进机制。但是在开放式创新中，组织需要更关注创新平台的建设，通过对合作伙伴重新定义，激发组织外部整个创新生态系统的活力，而组织则能够从充满活力的系统中获取更好的创新技术、流程和商业模式。

那么组织可以如何构建开放式创新生态系统呢？以凯捷的"应用型创新平台"构想为例，来看企业如何自主建立创新平台。此前，凯捷在各个国家的组织根据自身需求，建立很多不同的创新实验室和卓越中心，但是国家之间的资源共享和复用性存在问题，重复投资、发展能力受地域限制等问题明显。因此从 2015 年初，集团以首席技术官牵头，建立了一套"实用型创新平台"机制，标准化了治理架构、外部共创生态系统管理、创新智慧资产管理、创新方法论。平台建立了全球专家资源库，不仅仅包含企业内部的专家，也囊括了整个创新系统的外部专家，通过项目制整合专家资源。平台以认证实验室的形式在各个国家落地，成为凯捷帮助跨国企业客户在商业模式、管理流程和客户体验领域实现创新的孵化器。比如凯捷帮助法国国家铁路公司设计的车站智能机器人服务系统，通过智能眼镜以及投影设备实现的远程大型机械设备诊断应用等，都可以通过实验室孵化。凯捷的企业开放式创新平台获得了各国政府的大力支持，比如新加坡的凯捷"实用型创新"实验室，获得了新加坡经济发展局（EDB）的大力投资。

目前在上海在创新 2.0 时代有十分成功的众创空间发展经验，根据 2015 年《上海众创空间建设与发展报告》，上海已有创业苗圃 71 家，累计预孵项目 5 300 多个，孵化器 149 家，在孵企业有近 7 000 家。众创空间的发展战略，换一个角度看，也可能是帮助大型外商投资企业实现"中国创新"走出去的利器。我们看到国内一些领先的科技和互联网已经依托政府支持设立了孵化器，对接国内创新。但是很多跨国企业还是依托总部的创新机制，或者在中国市场上独立摸索，分散投资试水，走了一些弯路。同样，我们在帮助中国企业进入欧洲的过程中，也看到中国企业和国外创新体系对接的困难，包括从本地化、体制、伙伴关系、战略协同等角度，也面临创新的水土不服问题。

从以上现状来看，在全球化的大背景下，建立一个对接全球主要创新体系，联结国内外创业企业和独立专才的社群网络，善用国际人才的碎片化时间，提供符合大企业需求的共创服务体系，配套的金融和商业机制，是帮助企业"引进来"和"走出去"，打造商业、科技和人文创新竞争软实力的重要方向。

提升上海投资贸易便利化水平——自贸区创新与全球科创中心建设的高效对接

刘明华

德勤中国华东区主管合伙人

新世纪以来全球化推进迅速，中国自 2001 年加入 WTO 以后，成为全球化的最大受益者，随着进出口规模和结构的提升，中国的产业升级也受益匪浅。但是，从 2008 年金融危机爆发之后，全球发达经济体经历了长时间的经济衰退，今年夏天英国退欧和美国大选之后 TPP 名存实亡都表明全球化进程逐渐发生了逆转，可以预见在未来较长的时期内，贸易壁垒高立，地缘政治风险高企。在这样的国际格局下，我们认为探讨促进投资贸易便利化的命题意义重大。

从 2013 年李克强总理力促成立中国（上海）自由贸易试验区至今三年有余，在此期间，自贸区成为了上海乃至全国的制度创新桥头堡。随着体制机制创新的落实，审批流程的优化，自贸区的开放效应进一步凸显，外商投资对于自贸区投资信心不断增强，投资效率与成效也不断提升。从功能范围上，自贸区已经从最初成立时的 28 平方公里扩容到现在的 120 平方公里，陆家嘴金融片区、金桥开发片区和张江高科技片区都被纳入自贸区范畴。同时，上海自贸区还带动广东、福建和天津复制了"改革开放试验田"。

中国经济进入新常态，经济转型迫在眉睫。"十三五"规划中明确提出"科技创新是第一生产力"。在"大众创业、万众创新"的战略指引下，除了实现原先的既定目标，如何将上海自贸区已经形成的制度优势和生态优势与上海全球科创中心的目标进行有机结合，成为了上海自贸区进一步发挥带动效应的新课题。

上海市政府于 2015 年 11 月 25 日公布加快推进上海自贸区和张江国家自主创新示范区联动发展的实施方案，提出通过发挥两大国家战略叠加区域的核心优势，加快建成具有强大原始创新能力的综合性国家科学中心，着力打造创新环境开放包容、创新主体高度集聚的科技城。这个被称为"双自联动"的方案旨在通过制度创新解决科技发展问题，围绕创新机制，吸引机构落户，带来资金、技术和人才的汇集。

德勤认为，上海具备建设全球科创中心的优势。第一，上海及周边的长江三角区是中国最为富裕和发展最快的区域；第二，上海具备很好的国际营商环境，形成高效透明的政府办事机制；第三，上海基础设施发达，同时有完备的商业配套、服务配套和融资配套；第四，上海对于全球顶尖人才吸引力不断增强；第五，上海依然是跨国公司总部和研发中心落户最多的城市。这些跨国公司集聚在智能制造、生物制药、互联网信息科技和文教服务等支柱行业，是行业生态的核心，同时也是技术创新的沃土。

众所周知，科技创新是系统工程，除了技术的孕育和开发，便利的融资渠道、畅通的货物/服务贸易、完善的知识产权保护和健全的法律环境同样重要。我们发现，目前上海科技创新生态系统的营造主要面临五大挑战。

（1）融资方式单一。目前科技创新企业的资金来源以财政拨款、政策性借款及商业银行贷款为主，缺乏多元化的投资手段与主体，缺乏大规模风险投资资金和创业投资资金的介入。

（2）法制环境不完善。与知识产权保护等相关的法律法规并不完善。

（3）专业服务欠缺。技术咨询、科技金融等专业服务机构在上海科创生态链中较为缺乏，相关的财税、保险、资产评估等服务也缺乏相应的标准和高质量的机构。

（4）科创人才政策缺乏国际竞争力。现有户籍管理政策、外籍员工签证居留政策、税收政策等还缺乏国际竞争力。

（5）企业研发创新成本较高。企业在商事程序制度性成本、人才成本，以及税费成本等方面高于新加坡等地，而在鼓励科研创新的立法政策方面，针对性和有效性仍具有提升的空间。

对标国际上几个成熟的科技创新中心的发展（表1），我们发现政府的引导扶持和创新机制的保障带来了资金、人才和技术等核心生产要素的高效流动（双向），由此产生了极佳的创新落地和技术转化，提高了这些国家在全球价值链分工中的地位。

目前，上海全球科创中心的建设以张江高科技片区为依托，具备先天优势去嫁接和借力上海自贸区的相关鼓励政策、制度创新、流程优化和有效监管，"有放有收"，促进科创中心稳步快速发展。针对目前上海科技创新生态系统面临的主要挑战，借鉴国际成功经验，德勤认为自贸区与科创中心高效对接，提升上海贸易投资便利化水平，可以从以下几个方面尝试推进：

（1）促进创新要素的流动。资金和人才是科技创新的关键要素。从国际上成功的科创中心经验看，政府是协调创新资源的顶层设计者，应鼓励在自贸区内设

表 1

以 色 列	美国硅谷	德国巴符州	新 加 坡
创新企业密度最高国家 • 创新企业以中小型企业为主 • 隔行杂交式创新 • 循环创新 • 开放式创新，鼓励全球领先企业投资建立研发中心，促进企业间国际合作 • "国内创新企业＋海外资金市场"发展 • 军工创新能力和产业化能力向民用领域推广 • 政府主动参与创新创业实践	拥有世界上最大、最密集、最具有创造性的高科技产业集群，其特点主要表现在以下几个方面： • 构建多渠道的金融服务体系（例如，硅谷银行） • 大学和研究机构集聚 • 政府开放的人才政策 • 大学灵活有效的科研人员创业政策	根据 2015 年彭博全球创新指数，德国被列为世界排名第三的创新国家。 • 巴符州创新联盟体系 • 创新联盟包括大学、研究所、科研机构等 • 产业转移平台 • 集咨询服务、研究开发、国际技术转移和人力培训等于一体	政府在提倡创新，以及促进产学研结合方面有丰富的经验值得借鉴 • 政府成立专门引导市场创新的机构，聘请企业界、科学界、学术界专家参与政策制定 • 完善的知识产权保障制度 • 鼓励跨国企业设立创新中心 • 鼓励海外名校商学院设立分校，积极与海外学府联合办学

立分行的银行进行金融创新，并尝试将上海自贸区在金融创新方面举措的受益者扩展至全市的科技创新企业及个人。同时，积极调动跨国公司作为科技研发优势资源的平台功能，引导跨国公司参与到科技初创企业的孵化中，从资金、技术和运营等多个层面提供支持。

（2）降低企业科技创新成本。企业任何创新行动的发起和进行都需要进行成本收益的评估。从德勤历年来对全球和中国高科技高成长企业的跟踪调查可以看出，成本是企业进行科技创新的重要挑战之一。政府应对目前上海科技创新的支柱行业和重点企业进行有针对性的了解，探索是否可以将企业生产销售环节的一部分放置自贸区内进行，充分利用自贸区制度创新为企业带来的成本便利。比如，目前生物医药和集成电路是张江高科技园区的重点产业，也是跨国公司总部聚集最多的行业。充分研究这类企业在生产资料／设备进口中遇到的问题，比如化合物进口归类问题，CPU 测试样品进口征税问题，设备异地使用问题等，切实降低企业有关研发和科技创新所引发的生产和流通成本。

（3）提升服务贸易便利化。从全球范围来看，提升服务贸易便利化都是自贸区的重要课题。高科技企业和研发型服务企业是服务贸易的重要载体。要充分了解这一类企业跨国经营和跨国研发外包的服务贸易业态，以及由信息技术的快速发展而带来的服务贸易业态的转变，将针对高科技企业服务贸易便利化的举措纳入自贸区整体服务贸易便利化的制度创新。可否借鉴货物贸易"单一窗口"的思路，针对与科技创新相关的服务贸易也进行"单一窗口"管理和服务，聘请专业技术人员对相关服务贸易项目进行审批和监管，提高科技创新企业服务贸易的流转效率。

（4）完善知识产权保护。完善知识产权保护法律建设是促进科技创新和提升贸易投资便利化水平的有力保障。自贸区是知识产权保护纠纷的高发区，因此，自贸区司法部门对于知识产权保护纠纷的处理可以适当对标国际标准，把自贸区当作知识产权保护法制建设的试验田。

将自贸区与全球科创中心进行联动发展将促进优势要素的聚集，盘活和整合"碎片化"的资源，发挥跨国公司总部和研发中心的溢出效应，提升上海科创企业在全球服务贸易价值链中的地位，加速科技创新成果的转化和知识产权保护，整体提升上海的投资贸易便利化水平。

打造数字化政府平台，推动投资贸易便利化

吴 琪

埃森哲全球副总裁、大中华区副主席

未来 20 年，两大因素将深刻影响全球经济和中国的发展：全球化和数字化。全球化处在西方不亮东方亮的转折点上。西方风起云涌的反全球化浪潮正在改变二战后的全球化共识，国际贸易和国际商业合作将受到极大挑战。而另一方面，在"一带一路"倡议之下，中国将主力推动新的区域贸易协定，推动地区性基础设施投资，降低投资和贸易壁垒，形成全新贸易和投资格局。与此同时，数字化正在改变经济和贸易方式，推动服务贸易和跨境电商的跨越式增长，由此重塑全球贸易。

上海作为金融、贸易、供应链和港口中心城市，在这个大趋势中扮演领先角色具有先天优势，可以成为全球贸易和投资中心。抓住这个历史机遇，上海市政府需要进行突破性的制度创新，转型政府职能，成为服务型和平台型政府，为企业投资、贸易和创新提供最便利便捷的基础设施和环境。

埃森哲从全球贸易趋势、中国在贸易和投资便利化方面存在的主要问题、以及领先国家在贸易和投资便利化的制度举措三个方面进行分析，并在此基础上提出了我们给上海的方向性建议。

1. 关注服务贸易和数字技术将重塑全球贸易格局两大趋势

目前，国际贸易正处于 2008 年金融危机以来的深度调整期。经历了 2010 年和 2011 年的反弹后，受世界经济不振、金融市场动荡以及贸易保护主义复苏等因素的影响，全球商品与服务贸易的增速逐年下降，已经远低于金融危机前的平均水平。在全球需求普遍疲软的情况下，亚洲贸易情况更不乐观，近两年甚至低于 GDP 增速。而根据世界贸易组织（WTO）今年 9 月发布的贸易展望报告，2016 年全球货物贸易量进一步萎缩，增速由 4 月份预测的 2.8% 下调至

1.7%。

尽管全球贸易形势严峻，在过去几年的贸易量停滞不前，但服务贸易均占比逐年提高，全球服务贸易占贸易总额的比例从 2000 年的 19% 增加到 2015 年的 23%，在亚洲，这一比例从 17% 增加到 22%。2015 年，除旅游（25.5%）和交通（18.2%）外，包括研发、咨询、技术和贸易相关的服务占 21.5%，通信、计算机系信息技术占 9.8%，金融服务占 8.6%，知识产权收费占 6.2%。自 2011 年以来，中国的服务贸易的年增长速度已经连续超过贸易增长速度，2015 年，中国服务贸易的进出口全球排名已经跃居世界第二位，仅次于美国。

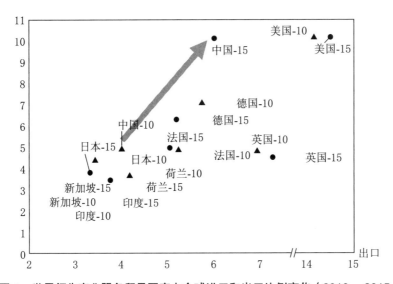

图 1　世界领先商业服务贸易国家占全球进口和出口比例变化（2010vs.2015）

值得注意的是，信息技术对服务贸易发展的推动作用日趋明显，特别是由数字技术推动的服务贸易，正逐渐成长为贸易增长的重点领域。进一步分析我们发现，在 2014 年，全球将近一半（48%）的服务贸易是由数字技术驱动的，在 2000 年这一比例只有 41%。这说明，数字化正在重塑全球贸易格局。一方面，由于互联网、移动互联网和即时通讯等技术发展，原先跨境运输成本较高的服务（非贸易品）变为贸易品，以线上服务的形式进入国际贸易领域。知识密集型服务业受益最为明显，这包括法律服务、会计与税务咨询、审计、市场调研、管理咨询、建筑工程咨询、技术测试和分析、广告等。另一方面，数字技术促使虚拟商品贸易逐步取代实物贸易。CD、DVD 和游戏光碟的消亡，以及在线音乐电影下载和游戏 app 的兴起，就是最好的例证。

在数字技术驱动贸易增长的浪潮中，跨境电商的蓬勃发展不容小觑。埃森哲研究表明，全球跨境 B2C 电商市场规模将于 2020 年达到近 1 万亿美元，年均增长高达 27%；跨境 B2C 电商消费者总数也将于 2020 年超过 9 亿人，年均增幅超过 21%。在数字技术的驱动之下，跨境 B2C 电商改变了全球贸易模式：物联网和数据分析实现跨境货物流的集约化和全程监控；电商平台和社交媒体实现跨境信息流的数字化和便捷化；移动技术和支付平台实现跨境资金流的个人化、便利化与移动化。①

展望未来，数字技术将进一步促进国际贸易一体化，为跨国商业合作带来巨大机会。第一，物联网和数据分析技术将提升生产制造和物流效率，促进全球货物贸易发展，助力企业全球化。全球产业链将进一步细分，中间产品进出口增加，产品设计、生产制造、运输、销售等各个环节即使处于不同的地理区域，也能够实现信息互通、协作优化。第二，服务业将大规模数字化，服务贸易在全球贸易中的比重继续提升。届时，金融业、教育业、医疗产业等将纷纷转型为在线金融服务、线上教育平台和在线医疗，吸引国际消费者。第三，中小企业和创业公司将深度参与国际竞争，提升全球商业合作的活跃度和创新性。3D 打印技术将帮助小企业实现小批量、定制化生产，满足日趋多元化的国际市场；众筹平台将解决小企业融资难题；电商平台将帮助更多的小企业对接国际市场。

2. 识别中国与发达国家和地区在贸易和投资便利性方面的差距及根源

由于缺乏城市层面的贸易和投资便利化的有关调研数据，我们先将中国作为一个整体与先进国家和地区进行比较作为分析的基础，重点研究中国贸易和投资便利程度的现状和世界先进国家（特别是亚洲）和地区的差距，并对导致这些差距的原因进行研究。为此，埃森哲选取了世界银行和世界经济论坛发布的四项权威报告，采用了国家竞争力指标、商业开展指数、贸易评价指标以及物流评价指标来建立了一个综合评估体系。该绩效衡量体系涵盖了影响一国的贸易和投资发展的内部和外部因素，而且有利于通过对相关具体指标子项的比较来识别相应的根源和差距，为了选择对上海有借鉴意义的国家或地区，埃森哲选择了新加坡、中国香港、日本和韩国作为参考对象，而在具体差距的因素分析时，我们选择了新加坡和中国香港作为对标的参考对象，因为从上海的"四个中心"的建设目标、城市发展的总体定位等方面来看，新加坡和香港对上海的参考价值最大。

---

① 埃森哲：《全球跨境 B2C 电商市场展望：数字化消费重塑商业全球化》，2015。

表 1　相关指标比较

国家／地区	国际竞争力世界排名	商业开展指标世界排名	贸易评价指标世界排名	物流评价指标世界排名
中　国	28	78	54	27
新加坡	2	2	1	5
中国香港	9	4	2	9
日　本	9	34	13	12
韩　国	26	78	30	24

资料来源：国际竞争力指标源自世界经济沿坛 2016—2017 报告；商业开展指标源自世界银行 2017 年报告；贸易评价指标源自世界经济论坛 2014 年报告；物流评价指标源自世界银行 2016 年数据。

从对比分析的结果来看，中国的贸易和投资便利程度与先进国家和地区相比依然存在着比较明显的差距。在国际竞争力、商业开展、贸易和物流四个方面，中国在全球的排名分别是第 28 位、第 78 位、第 54 位和第 27 位。而新加坡和中国香港在亚洲乃至全球都处于领先的地位。其中差距最大的分别是商业开展和贸易，而这两个指标在很大程度上反映出中国在整体上在投资和贸易便利化方面依然存在很大的提升和改善空间。

为了进一步深入分析存在差距的原因和根源，埃森哲又分别对商业开展指标和贸易评价指标进行了更加深入的分析的比较。

（1）商业开展指标。

世界银行在评价商业开展指标体系包括了以下的十个维度：公司设立、建筑审批、电力配置、不动产登记、信贷取得、小投资者保护、税赋、跨境贸易、合同执行以及破产清算（图 2）。

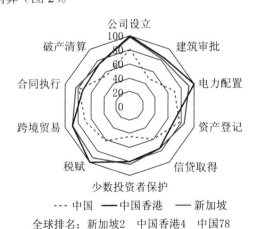

全球排名：新加坡2　中国香港4　中国78

说明：

1　商业开展指标为世界银行 2017 年报告

图 2　商业开展指标 DBR（世界银行）

｜ 提升投资贸易便利化水平，构建开放型经济新体制根据世界银行 2017 年报告提供的数据的对比分析的结果看，中国在反映投资和贸易便利程度的公司设立、建设审批、小股东利益保护、税赋、跨境贸易方面明显落后，其中很重要的原因是流程过多、耗时过长、在效率方面缺乏竞争力。以建设仓库为例，中国需要审批流程有 22 个，大致需要 244 天；而新加坡仅需要 9 个流程，大致需要 48 天。在税赋方面，企业在中国报税所需的时间为每年 259 个小时，平均税赋占企业利润的 68%；而新加坡所需时间仅为 67 小时，平均税赋占利润的 19%。再以进口报关为例，在中国的每次报关成本为 777 美元，每次报关所需的时间为 66 小时；而新加坡的每次报关成本只有 220 美元，所需时间仅为 3 小时（图 3）。

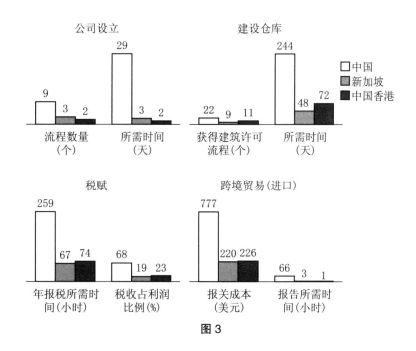

图 3

（2）贸易评价指标。

根据世界经济论坛（World Economic Forum）的《2014 全球贸易促进报告》，中国在 138 个国家的贸易评价指标（Trade enabling index）排名中仅列 54 位，在边境管理服务、信息通信技术和运营环境等方面尚有较大提升空间。该指标体系具体包括：国内市场衔接、国际市场衔接、海关监管和透明度、物流基础设施水平、物流服务水平、信息技术应用水平以及监管环境，共七个维度（图 4）。

在反映贸易便利性的贸易评价指标方面，中国的差距也是全面性的。值得注意的是，中国在提供进入国内市场和国际市场的便利性方面，与新加坡和中国香港的差距巨大，这势必削弱中国巨大的国内市场和制造业大国所带来的吸引

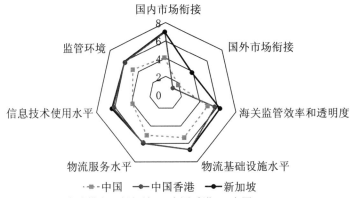

图中标注：
国内市场衔接
国外市场衔接
监管环境
海关监管效率和透明度
信息技术使用水平
物流基础设施水平
物流服务水平

····中国 ─●─中国香港 ─●─新加坡

全球排名：新加坡1　中国香港2　中国54

说明：贸易评价指标源自世界经济论坛 2017 年报告

图 4　贸易评价指标 /ETI（世界经济论坛）

力，妨碍中国今后的投资和贸易的发展。究其背后的原因，除关税因素外，流程效率低、信息技术应用不足、金融服务种类不够丰富以及政府服务不足是最重要的问题。例如，中国在关税水平方面，仅仅排在全球接受调研的 138 个国家和地区的 114 位；出口所需的单证数量和所需天数方面分别名列 108 位和 90 位；在信息技术应用于 B2B 交易和政府的在线信息服务水平方面，名列第 64 位和 59 位；此外，在可提供的金融服务和对贸易争端的解决效率两方面，排名也比较落后（图 5）。

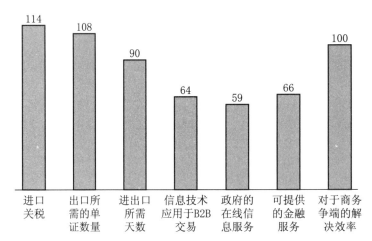

图中柱状数据：
进口关税 114
出口所需的单证数量 108
进出口所需天数 90
信息技术应用于B2B交易 64
政府的在线信息服务 59
可提供的金融服务 66
对于商务争端的解决效率 100

图 5　中国缺乏竞争力的主要方面（在调研的 138 个国家地区的排名）

新加坡在贸易评价指标排名中已经连续六年排名第一，无论市场准入还是运营环境以及基础设施，新加坡都是上海对标的理想对象。新加坡通过一站式信息门户，把税务、海关等 35 个政府部门链接起来，形成了一个国际贸易投资的单一门户。新加坡还开发了多套网络系统，形成了国家航运中心信息平台。新加坡是政府功能和服务平台化的经典案例。

结合中国存在的主要问题和差距，尽管在税收和关税等方面的问题，靠上海单方面是难以解决的，但上海市政府未来的贸易和投资便利化，应该以新加坡和中国香港作为标杆，遵循"以服务企业为中心"的理念，整合和简化与贸易、投资相关的流程，并借助数字化手段和提高信息化应用水平来打造智慧化、创新型的服务型政府，全面提高政府效率、提供更高质量、更丰富的增值服务，打造国际先进水准的监管环境，创造与上海未来城市和经济发展更为匹配的环境。

3. 借力数字化和平台经济，加速贸易和投资便利化，进一步将上海打造成最具吸引力和竞争力的全球经贸中心

数字化方兴未艾，正在深刻改变企业组织的工作方式和人们的生活方式。智能制造、平台经济、数字供应链、跨境电商和物联网等基于数字技术的新商业模式正在重塑行业版图和城市经济结构。"十三五"规划将建设数字经济，推动"互联网+"和智能制造作为国家战略。中国的区域中心城市都在试图抢占数字经济的制高点。建设一个富有创新精神、数字化和平台化政府，将是未来上海城市魅力和竞争力的核心。

埃森哲在 2016 年对 11 个世界主要国家数字经济的研究表明：在未来五年里，中国经济将可以从推动数字化和智慧化的投资中获益，实现数字化红利，并释放出巨大的增长潜力。我们估计到 2020 年，数字化将为中国的 GDP 带来 3.7% 的增长，相当于 5 270 亿美元，增长规模居 11 国之首。

根据埃森哲战略的研究，提高劳动人口中数字技能、增加数字化资本投入和培养良好的数字化市场发展环境可以加速经济增长，可以加速释放经济中的数字化红利。在上述条件得到优化的前提下，到 2020 年，美国经济有望新增 4 210 亿美元，占整个 GDP 的 2.1%。同样，如果中国大力并合理提高这些条件，数字化将给中国经济带来 5 270 亿美元新增产出，占 3.7%，其新增产出位居各国之首。

上海的教育水平和城市吸引力以及投资环境非常有利于提高城市经济的数字化水平，为上海的创新发展提供坚实的人才基础和物质基础。

"创新发展"也已成为时代主旋律和推动中国新一轮经济增长的决胜力量。习主席在刚刚结束的全国科技创新大会上提出"到 2020 年，使中国进入创新型国家行列"的总体战略目标。2015 年，中国政府在"互联网+"战略中提出："推动移动互联网、云计算、大数据、物联网等与现代制造业结合，促进电子商务、

工业互联网和互联网金融健康发展，引导互联网企业拓展国际市场。"中国是数字化人口大国，互联网金融和电子商务在规模和创新能力上均成就显著。

我们认为，从产业升级发展层面，提高全要素生产率，发展数字平台经济是主要推手。根据埃森哲 2015 年的物联网研究，如果采取进一步措施，如改进科研生态系统，优化市场环境，预计未来 15 年产业物联网将为中国 GDP 带来 4 970 亿美元的增长。

传统制造业强国德国意识到数字技术对未来制造业的深刻影响，制定和启动了"工业 4.0"计划，其内涵主要是通过数字技术和平台将实体世界与虚拟世界相结合起来，建立网络—物理融合生产系统和网络化世界，实现智能设备相互通信和交互。

基于上海已有的产业结构、基础设施条件、地理位置特点等资源禀赋基础，参考全球以及中国新常态下的发展特征和趋势，我们认为：上海未来应该考虑应用创新的"平台化""生态化"的思维理念，在长三角地区率先打造智慧化的城市平台，以此来推动产业升级、科技创新，并助力上海城市生态建设，抢占发展先机。通过实现数字化（"互联网＋"）的红利，构建上海新一轮跨越发展的核心优势，在城市智慧化的竞争中能脱颖而出，将是上海提升自身发展实力、抢占未来发展先机、展示城市发展成就和魅力的最佳战略选择。

4. 推动政府服务"平台化"

2016 年 11 月，上海市政府发布了《上海市电子政务云建设工作方案》，旨在运用云计算、大数据等先进理念和技术，以"云网合一、云数联动"为构架，建成市、区两级电子政务云平台，实现市政府各部门基础设施共建共用、信息系统整体部署、数据资源汇聚共享、业务应用有效协同，开展政务大数据开发利用，为政府管理和公共服务提供有力支持，提高为民服务水平，提升政府现代治理能力。

这个目标与我们的建议不谋而合。我们建议上海应该将智慧政府打造、产业升级与创新、智慧城市建设视为有机整体进行总体设计，统筹推进和实施，其关键在于在上海率先建设相互关联的三个核心平台：

（1）创建基于数字技术的智慧化政务平台。通过智慧政府建设和创新服务模式建立等，形成高效的政府与企业间的界面，为企业创造最为便捷的营商环境，降低企业交易成本、提高效率，促进本地企业发展并吸引更多优质企业的落户。最终使政府通过先进的数字化技术手段和自身的职能转变，接近世界领先城市的政务能力、水平和效率。

建立政务平台的核心目标是，构建一个政府、市场、社会共同参与、彼此互动、相互协同的开放性服务体系。平台的建立需要具备四个特征：以用户为中心，安全可靠，单一整合平台以及适应未来技术发展。

以用户为中心："以用户为中心"是推动政府服务和功能"平台化"的核心理念。围绕社会公众和企业的实际需求，对外建立与相关贸易投资伙伴国家贯通的平台，基于大数据手段，建立智慧化贸易和投资联动促进模式；对内梳理各部门业务事项，充分挖掘和整合服务资源，为用户提供高质量、个性化的服务。同时，提升政府平台的开放和互动程度，关注公众和企业的动态需求，通过多方参与的方式不断提升服务质量、实现政府与公众的良性互动。

安全可靠：随着数字化程度的加深，政府网站在运用数字技术为民众提供更便捷服务的同时，在安全性和可靠性方面也遇到了越来越大的挑战。政务平台聚集大量政府、重要行业和个人信息资源，保障和维护信息安全尤为重要，需要建立高水平的信息交换安全和保障。

单一整合平台：政府各部门在提供服务的过程中都沉淀了海量的数据，这些数据与社会经济、公民生活密切相关，具有数量庞大、涉及面广的特点，是宝贵的资源。但如果彼此割裂，数据无法做到共享，资源使用效率将大大极低，也会导致各部门的重复投入。打破数据孤岛，加强整合各部门资源，建立贯穿不同政府职能的、无缝的流程衔接，在降低资源浪费、提升已有政务服务质量和效率的同时，更有利于政府部门运用大数据技术对海量数据开展跨领域、跨渠道的综合分析，深入挖掘政务服务需求，不断优化资源配置，丰富服务内容，变被动服务为主动服务，另一方面促进服务模式和服务形态的创新，这将极大推动竞争力和治理水平的提高。

（2）构建产业创新支持平台，推动上海核心产业升级及战略新兴产业创新发展。该系统一方面可支持上海现有产业体系的数字化创新和升级发展，另一方面还将支撑上海整体创新系统的形成，使上海能够吸引更多的具有高技术含量、具有高成长性的初创企业落户。在这方面，全球有很多可以借鉴的模式，比如，埃森哲帮助新加坡政府和力拓集团在新加坡建设和运营的物联网创新及应用中心，就是上海可以借鉴的世界一流实例。

（3）打造智慧化市民服务平台，以满足市民安全、便捷、健康、教育、绿色等方面的需求。这个平台一方面使市民能够享受到现代数字化技术带来的全方位便利从而提高生活质量，另一方面也会成为未来吸引外部优秀人才落户的独特"卖点"。

适应未来技术发展：技术的不断进步将给政府提供更多的工具进行服务优化和创新。要把握技术发展带来的巨大机会，从技术层面看，政府需要建立灵活的数字化技术架构；从管理层面来讲，政府作为平台，需要秉承"开放"的理念，将政府、企业、创业者、非政府组织与公众都连接起来，共同创造一个具有持续创新活力的生态体系，形成"大众创业、万众创新"的巨大合力，实现政务平台的持续创新。

建立基于云计算、大数据等数字技术的智慧化政府政务平台，推动贸易和投资便利化，打造城市的核心竞争力和吸引力，这将是一个长期工程。厘清这个长期工程，可以分为四个阶段。第一个阶段，要实现政府在数据方面的集成和整合。数据是一切平台的基石，打破数据孤岛，集成来自政府职能部门和商业部门的数据，将是政府数字平台的生命源泉。第二个阶段，政府流程的数字化和移动化。第三个阶段，大数据分析，没有分析就没有洞察，数据也将毫无意义。建设分析能力将是政府数字化平台的核心价值和能力。第四个阶段，人工智能。设想未来的政务活动和贸易投资流程处理可以依托于人工智能，那么政务效率和贸易投资便利将极大的提高。

未来可以想象。作为面向亚太的世界性城市，上海具有独特优势和独特地位，抓住全球化和数字化的历史性机遇，推动向服务型和创新型政府转型，上海就是未来全球贸易、金融投资和创新的中心城市。

基于"电子口岸"推进贸易便利化和供应链互联互通

姚为群

上海 WTO 事务咨询中心经济学研究员

随着区域生产网络的形成,处于不同发展阶段的 APEC 成员经济体在区域价值链上的相互联系已经越来越密切。同时,诸如"云计算""大数据"和"物联网"等信息通信技术的引入和应用,为改善亚太地区内部及外部供应链的互联互通,提供了新方法、新手段和新工具,"电子口岸"就是其中的最成功、最成熟的实践。

2010 年举行的 APEC 第 18 次领导人非正式会议明确指出,贸易便利化和供应链互联互通是支撑亚洲太平洋地区实现平衡、包容、可持续、创新和安全增长,从而保证所有人能持久和广泛地分享区域增长和经济一体化的福利目标的主要动力。2012 年 APEC 第 20 次领导人非正式会议承诺"通过消除在亚洲太平洋供应链中货物和服务流动上的障碍……以实现在 2015 年前亚太地区供应链绩效提高 10% 的目标"。2013 年 APEC 第 21 次领导人非正式会议再次强调"推进监管整合和衔接,消除不必要贸易壁垒在实现加强区域经济一体化,保证产品安全和供应链完整共同目标上的重要性",由此,推进贸易便利化和供应链互联互通是亚太地区实现自由、开放贸易和投资的关键因素。为此,如何在战略与实务层面有效地基于推进贸易便利化和供应链互联互通,成为 APEC 的工作重点。

1. 上海"电子口岸"的实践与经验

2001 年 10 月在上海举行的 APEC 第 9 次领导人非正式会议期间,中美两方达成合作探索建设"电子口岸"的意向。2004 年,在上海市政府与海关总署共同牵头下,上海口岸 18 个利益攸关方,包括中国电子口岸、上海海关、上海出入境检验检疫局、上海出入境边防检查总站、上海铁路局、上海海事局、人民银行上海分行、上海市国家税务局、上海市发展与改革委员会、上海市经济与信息化委员会、上海市商务委员会、上海市财政局、上海市交通运输和港口管理局、上海市口岸服务办公室、上海国际港务（集团）股份有限公司、上海机场（集团）有限公司、上海市信息投资股份有限公司，共同组建了上海"电子口岸"建设联席会议。2005 年，上海"电子口岸"挂牌运行。目前，上海"电子口岸"提供的平台服务，涵盖监管、贸易、物流、支付等四大领域，基本功能包括：为各利益攸关方，如口岸监管部门、生产贸易企业、货代企业及陆海、空运输仓储物流企业，提供了一点式接入，服务覆盖上海所有海空口岸、出口加工区、保税区、保税物流园区、保税港区、综合保税区等监管区域；实现海关货物申报、检验检疫申报、船舶申报、危险申报、船图、舱单、装箱单、订舱、提货、进出门等 218 类数据的交换与共享；提供面向 B2G 和 B2B 的电子支付服务，与国内外 22 家银行互联，海关税费支付服务覆盖全国全部 42 个关区；其他增值数据服务，包括贸易管理、舱单、订舱、集装箱管理、关务协同等集成化应用，提供统一用户管理、应用发布、监控、计费、支付等"云服务"。

2. "电子口岸"的定义、特点、机制、功能和作用

从上海的实践看，"电子口岸"的基本定义可直观地解释为，一个基于供应链生态系统，由口岸运营方、监管方和使用方等共同建设的"多利益攸关方"口岸社区体系，融合在线与离线业务的虚拟枢纽型口岸。

从上海的实践看，"电子口岸"的基本特点有：（1）"电子口岸"是建立在"口岸社区体系"之上，服务于枢纽型口岸的第三方信息通信技术基础设施和"一门式"公用服务平台，由口岸各利益攸关方共建共营，而不是由单一行政机构建设和运营。（2）"电子口岸"涵盖"单一窗口"，"单一窗口"只能解决海关无纸清关。（3）作为信息通信技术基础设施，"电子口岸"提供满足枢纽型。口岸贸易和物流等增值活动，获取"一门式"服务的应用需求。

从上海的实践看，"电子口岸"具有以下四大机制：（1）融合、交互、共享口岸各利益攸关方在线与离线业务信息的机制。（2）跟踪、配置、监管包括商流、物流、信息流及资金流在内的供应链在线与离线数据的机制。（3）口岸社区体系的公共信息通信技术基础设施的机制。（4）包括"单一窗口"功能在内的公用服务平台的机制。

从上海的实践看，"电子口岸"的基本功能有：（1）为实现从有纸贸易到数据捆绑无纸贸易，提供有效的信息通信技术基础设施的解决方案。（2）整合诸如"单一窗口"等贸易便利化措施形成"一门式服务"等供应链互联互通方式。（3）

在实现政府层面机构内、机构间和跨境机构间的协调，为跨境供应链管理提供制度保障的同时，通过多利益攸关方社区机制，将包括政府、企业、行业协会、消费者和其他利益攸关方在整合在"电子口岸"框架下，共同参与贸易便利化和供应链互联互通的发展、运行和实施。

从上海的实践看，由于"电子口岸"从市场出发，以服务导向，"电子口岸"的基本作用是：（1）一门式：物流需要的全面解决方案、与多式运输（海运、空运、铁路运输、公路运输）数据对接的能力，而不仅是"单一窗口"和基于信息通信技术的口岸服务。（2）可操作性：可以在不取代现行系统的情况下实现数据连接，从而解决数据一致性的问题。（3）基于诚信的透明度：接受来自政府和其他公共利益攸关者的多方监督，从而确保数据的隐私和安全。（4）为所有人服务：通过第三方信息通信技术基础设施，整合在供应链上碎片化信息，同时，降低包括中小企业的参与成本和门槛。（5）跨领域：实现机构内部和部门内部的数据共享与合作。（6）拓展性：探索通过基于"云计算"的信息通信技术平台，为企业提供更好的服务，同时拓展电子口岸系统的用途，降低进入门槛。

3. APEC 推进贸易便利化和供应链互联互通的举措

APEC 成立 27 年以来，在兼顾各成员经济体经济、社会发展水平的差异，以"茂物目标"作为促进成员经济体之间实现贸易、投资自由化的基本框架，持续推进贸易投资自由化，商业便利化和经济技术的广泛合作。APEC 采取了一系列扎实有效的举措，推进贸易便利化和供应链互联互通。20 世纪 90 年代，APEC 向各成员经济体推介涵盖关税支付、报关通关和与贸易相关文件的"无纸贸易"；2007 年，APEC 提出了发展使出口商和进口商能通过一个单一接口一次性向政府机构提交通关文件的"单一窗口"的体系框架。2009 年，APEC 通过了《供应链互联互通框架和行动计划》，将提升供应链绩效作为推动贸易便利化和经济增长的核心关注点，确定了实现贸易便利化和供应链互联互通而需要解决 8 个瓶颈：

（1）在影响物流监管事务方面，缺乏透明度和全局意识；在影响物流部门的政策方面，缺乏政府机构间协同的意识和行动；在物流问题上缺失一点接入或领率机构。（2）运输基础设施低效或不足，跨境硬件连接缺失（如道路，桥梁等）。（3）地方或区域物流分包能力不足。（4）海关货物清关低效，边境机构间缺乏协调，尤其是与在边境上的与管制货物清关相关的事项上。（5）海关文件和其他程序（包括优惠贸易）繁琐。（6）多式联运能力不发达，航空运输、地面运输和多式联运连接低效。（7）跨境标准和货物、服务和商务旅行者移动规则多变。（8）缺乏区域性跨境海关和转运安排。

APEC 各成员经济体间实现贸易便利化目标和供应链互联互通最具实践意义的第一步就是完善信息通信技术基础设施，这一目标的实现，需要各成员经济体相互信任与理解，需要融入多边生态体系，需要完善各利益攸关方之间的伙伴关系，需要实现供应链，需要提高与供应链相关政策的透明度，需要关注与供应链互联互通的信息通信技术的能力建设。为此，在保障数据安全和隐私的前提下，探索建立信息共享平台，以提供"一门式服务"信息通信技术基础设施——"电子口岸"作为解决方案，通过全面高效的公私伙伴关系，探索 APEC 成员经济体实现贸易便利化和供应链互联互通的可操作方案。

4. 亚太示范电子口岸网络

2013 年 11 月，在印度尼西亚巴厘岛举行的世界贸易组织部长级会议就《贸易便利化协定》达成共识，2014 年 11 月举行的世界贸易组织临时总理事会批准了《贸易便利化协定》，截至 2016 年 11 月 20 日，世界贸易组织已有 98 个成员方接受了《贸易便利化协定》。《贸易便利化协定》以"透明、简便、一致、规范"为四大支柱，以"单一窗口"为主要路径，以"无纸贸易"为基本目标。

作为推进贸易便利化和供应链互联互通的最积极推手，2014 年 11 月 11 日 APEC 第 22 次领导人非正式会议宣言《北京纲领：构建融合、创新、互联的亚洲太平洋》中明确：同意建立"亚太示范电子口岸网络"，欢迎 APEC 成员经济体提名的首批示范电子口岸，批准《亚洲太平洋示范电子口岸网络工作大纲》，同意该网络运营中心设立在上海示范电子口岸，要求官员们为贸易便利化和供应链互联互通做出更多贡献。目前，已有 9 个 APEC 成员经济体的 12 个枢纽型口岸或电子口岸加入了网络。

该网络的愿景是，在 APEC 框架下，形成经济体枢纽型口岸间通过第三方公共信息通信技术基础设施，实现信息共享和交互的平台，推进经济体之间以及公私利益攸关方之间的互联互通，使枢纽型口岸作为推动区域或次区域以公共信息通信技术基础设施为导向的服务发展的主要推动力，满足公私部门在"一门式"的基础上的各种服务需求，提高供应链效率和整体经济效益，最终通过以信息通信技术为基础的"一门式服务"，实现亚太地区供应链／价值链的一体化。

该网络的运行机制是结果导向的多利益攸关方关系，真正实现各利益攸关方间的愿景和效果的一致性，制定在整个供应链中执行的标准和协议，整合平台服务形成总体分析和展开实际应用，用市场化方式推动方案的执行；在保障利益攸关方隐私和安全权益的同时，通过提升供应链数据透明度，实现生态系统监管。

该网络的可能收益有消除亚太地区供应链互联互通中存在的阻塞点；在"电子口岸"的基础上，建设互联的"单一窗口"体系，进而形成亚太区域性"一门式"服务网络，强化口岸监管跨境合作推进，提升贸易便利化和跨境供应链无缝互联互通水平；实现跨境多式联运物流智能化；提高公私部门间系统连接性与信息互用性，全供应链可视化程度；提高供应链在效率、质量与安全全方位的绩效；加强供应链安全与跨境执法合作，解决货物安全、知识产权、假冒伪劣、走私等问题；促进物流、贸易与供应链无纸化进程；使公私部门能够在可承受的范围内使用最新信息技术手段；提升区域价值链一体化水平。

对于网络成员而言，其可能收益还可表现为：通过信息共享、合作和能力建设，改善网络成员信息通信技术基础设施，提高服务能力和质量；为网络成员所在口岸政府，提供参与 APEC 合作进程的机会。在操作层面上，借助于基于口岸多利益攸关方社区体系，第三方公共信息通信技术基础设施和"一门式"公用服务平台，满足跨境供应链生态系统中所有利益攸关方的需求；实现所有的利益攸关方的数据可视性，提高供应链效率，整合亚太地区供应链；为落实世界贸易组织《贸易便利化协定》，提供新思路、新方法和新路径；提高企业信息通信技术服务的增加值，包括运输、物流、供应链、贸易和生产等部门；通过新兴信息通信技术的应用和供应链关键数据的接入，降低发展中经济体和中小企业的进入中观层面价值链的门槛。

上海应成为全球性的数字城市

黄　昱

高风咨询高级顾问

1. 数字化是最本质的变革

数字化是本世纪以来最重要的科技发展方向。在数字化的浪潮下，互联网、移动互联网、物联网、大数据、人工智能等都有了长足发展，并深刻地改变了许多行业。

数字化对全球的投资和贸易产生了巨大影响。以贸易为例，全球有多达 3.5 亿商家会开始通过数字商务的方式出口产品和服务。这种转变将为全球贸易提供自经济衰退以来首个强劲的助推剂，并带来"投资和贸易的数字革命"。

受全球化经济和创新技术的影响，数字化在中国进入了井喷式的发展，以 BAT 为代表的企业所构建的数字生态，对中国整个商业格局造成了极大的影响。数字化不仅仅让普通消费者受益，对中国企业和整体经济都起到巨大的推动作用。我们的生活方式以及企业的生产模式也在数字化变革中迭代、更新。

在中国，不少融合了数字技术和新型商业模式的企业，业务蒸蒸日上，在短时间之内，价值超过了历史悠久的传统企业。我们也看到所谓传统企业和新兴企业的界限也会越来越模糊。通过数字化技术，建立以客户为中心的商业模式，增加与生态系统内的所有合作伙伴间的亲密度，缩短彼此之间的距离，这些新举措将会为传统产业带来根本性的变化。

2. 上海有条件成为数字领域的世界城市

上海作为国际性的大都市，是全球性的国际经济、国际金融、国际贸易和国际航运中心。并且在"十三五"期间，上海将致力于加强信息枢纽功能和国际门户枢纽地位、中心城市的创新经济驱动和服务辐射带动功能等三大方面。同样非常重要的是，上海应该在未来成为数字领域的世界城市，使用数字技术为上海的产业，贸易和投资服务。

上海应该在智慧城市、金融科技和云服务方面建立世界级的能力。

（1）运用数字技术建设智慧城市。

上海提出 2020 年初步建成泛在化、融合化、智敏化的智慧城市。建设所谓智慧城市就是运用信息和通信技术手段感测、分析、整合城市运行核心系统的各项关键信息，从而对包括民生、环保、公共安全、城市服务、工商业活动在内的各种需求做出智能响应。其实质是利用先进的信息技术，实现城市智慧式管理和运行，进而为城市中的人创造更美好的生活，促进城市的和谐和可持续成长，也为上海整体投资、贸易的便捷提供保障。

（2）金融科技技术将助力金融中心的建立。

2020 年，上海将建成国际金融中心，但与纽约、伦敦金融中心相比，我们在金融服务水平、金融产业集群、基础设施等方面还有提升和发展的空间。为加强上海金融中心竞争力地位，除了货币政策等方面的改革进程，上海更需要积极参与前沿技术变革，为未来金融中心布局。

被认为是继蒸汽机、电力、信息和互联网科技之后最有潜力触发第五轮颠覆性革命浪潮的区块链技术，是目前金融科技领域中重要的进步。区块链通过采用共识机制、去中心化、分布式的共享账本或数据库。以及密码学加密技术，确保账本或数据库的数据通过公开、通明、一致、安全的方式为相关方所利用，大大改善了金融服务的便捷性和可靠性，为现有的金融服务提供了有力的工具。

区块链技术将对全融行业产生的重大影响体现在以下几方面：

• 交易模式的变革：变革现有的交易模式，特别是在清算和结算系统中使用区块链技术，能够降低交易的复杂性，并进行有效监督。区块链技术带来的变革，使得纽约和伦敦交易中心地位可能发生改变，上海应把握时机，鼓励技术创新，加快区块链技术的发展和应用，驱动新型金融交易模式的诞生和发展。

• 金融机构的变革：传统金融机构的核心地位将被更加开放民主的自由交易市场替代。上海应以更开放的理念营造优化的商业环境，吸引更多金融机构、资本和创新人才。推进与区块链技术公司与金融机构合作，持续扩大区块链研发投入，在全国金融机构总起到引领性作用。

• 金融的监管：区块链技术可以从根本上改变金融机构的 IT 系统运行模式，并可形成可量化的自我监管平台，有效降低欺诈行为，提高监管的效率。上海应积极争取在区块链数据部署上的先行先试，逐步开放部分金融数据资料，实时观察读取数据，并作出反应，提供相对应的政策，有效防范金融市场中的系统性风险。

（3）积极推进云服务建设。

为打造上海成为国际经济、金融、贸易和航运四个中心，提高上海国际化城市核心竞争力地位，政府应从行业发展和企业自身痛点出发，在未来数字化技术领域提前布局，在适当的时候推出一系列数字化服务，为企业的投资和贸易保驾护航。云服务是其中非常重要的一环。

云服务是未来城市基础建设的一部分，也是上海竞争力的再提升。云服务会大幅度降低企业的数字化成本，并使得他们在全球竞争中占得先机。

3. 利用自贸区提供针对投资和贸易的数字化服务

上海有着自贸区的得天独厚的优势，应通过数字化大力提升自贸区的服务水平，进一步确立自贸区在中国经济发展中的重要地位。

上海自贸区应在资本项目可兑换，物流，投资和政府监管等方面积极推进。同时，上海也应借力自贸区，在跨境投资服务平台的支持下，推动国家"一带一路"建设，成为主动承接国家战略的先行者、领跑者。自贸区有一系列数字化手段来提升投资和贸易的便利性。

（1）数字物流。物流服务在贸易活动中有着重要的支撑作用，而作为在中国贸易发展中被给予厚望的上海自贸区正在推动物流业渐进式发展，在探索建立货物状态分类监管模式中，数字化管理信息系统的作用至关重要。

（2）货物追踪。RFID管理（电子标签、射频识别），如RFID仓储物流系统可选择性用于采购、存储、生产制造、包装、装卸、运输、流通加工、配运、销售到服务的各个业务环节和流程。能够实时地、精确地掌握整个供应链上的商流、物流、信息流和资金流的流向和变化。

（3）跨境支付。由多家国内外银行搭建的大宗商品跨境金融服务平台10月在自贸区启动（新加坡星展银行、马来西亚联昌国际银行和上海银行等国内外主要银行开展试点）。这个创新的支付生态系统平台也是自贸区数字化变革的重要举措。该平台将上海自贸区打造成无现金贸易中心的革命性典范。

（4）无纸化。银行及客户在传统贸易结算方面一直面对繁琐的纸质归档程序的不便。新型平台能将结算流程的数字化和一体化变为现实。

我们正处在一个被数字化颠覆的时代，信息技术以前所未有的速度在传播，企业和企业之间不再是竞争而更多的体现在竞和、分享，并在生态系统上链接更多伙伴。上海市把握这个战略性的机遇，更具有前瞻性地在数字化领域布局，通过打造升级版的数字基础设施，提升投资和贸易的便利性，使上海成为更具竞争力的全球领先的数字城市。

变化中的世界与跨国并购

范德尚
北京大学全球治理研究中心副主任兼秘书长
乔　倩
北京林业大学经济管理学院
张　琦
中国海洋大学经济学院

1. 变化中的世界及其原因

（1）世界的变化。

当今世界正在发生广泛而深刻的变化。从 2008 年开始的华尔街次贷危机、西方国家主权债务危机，到全球金融、经济危机，从阿拉伯世界的动荡，到查理周刊凸显出的价值观念的冲突，从占领华尔街运动到伦敦骚乱，从英国脱欧公投，到川普胜选引发的美国游行示威、社会撕裂，全球化进程中的世界同时又是一个充满动荡、不满、冲突和对立的世界。由宗教文化和社会分化等因素引发的冲突和对立日趋复杂，整个世界政治、经济形势风诡云谲，复杂多变。

与此同时，科技变革日新月异，推动着人类社会政治、经济和社会呈现出新的变化，面临新的机遇和挑战。从人类社会科技进步的历史来看，人类社会采取什么样的政治权力分配模式，经济生产采取什么样的方式，社会阶层如何分化，大都与人类社会所处时代的科技发展水平有着密切的关系。

农业社会阶段，人类的科技发展水平主要体现在农牧业方面。人类科技创新主要体现在动植物的培育和对季节气候变化的认识和把握。与人类农业社会科技发展水平相适应，社会的经济生产方式主要是以手工业和以家庭为单位的自给自足的生产方式；在政治权力的分配模式上，国王和贵族掌握了国家权力，维持社会秩序和公平正义，典型政治权力模式是君主制。社会阶层的划分为国王、贵族、自耕农和手工业者。

随着蒸汽技术、电气技术出现，人类社会步入工业化社会。人类社会政治、经济、社会阶层的划分随着科技变革又出现新的变化。人类社会的经济发展方式由家庭手工业和自给自足自然经济开始步入工业化大机器生产时代。社会阶层开始分化，科技变革带来的大机器生产把传统的家庭手工业和自给自足的自然经济冲垮，破产的自耕农和手工业者被迫到了掌握机器、技术的资本家工厂里，整个社会日益分裂为两大对立阶级：掌握矿山、资本、机器的资产阶级和无产阶级。针对工业时代变化，马克思敏锐地将社会阶层分析为两大阶级，即资产阶级和无产阶级。在政治权力的分配方面，随着资产阶级的兴起，资产阶级要求在国家权力运行过程中获得对其利益保护的发言权。政治权力的分配变化在英国和法国分别以不同的方式实现了由君主制向资产阶级共和制的转变。

以信息技术为核心科技变革正在对当今人类社会政治、经济、社会阶层分化带来深刻影响。经济发展方式由工业化大机器生产进入深度融合知识、技术和信息的智能化生产时代。传统行业在科技变革的影响下或走向衰落或被迫转型升级，依托高层次人才的新的研发型企业的开始出现。科技的变革同时造成社会贫富分化和社会问题。以美国为例，美国汽车制造产业的工人在20世纪随着美国制造业外迁开始失去工作。奥巴马总统上台以后，致力于让美国的制造业回归，解决产业工人的失业问题。不幸的是，融合了智能、信息和自动化技术的智能机器人永久地取代了美国产业工人的岗位。

（2）当今世界深刻变化的原因。

面对当今世界纷繁复杂的表象，人们从不同视角探究当前世界深刻变化的原因。从根本上讲，全球化和科技变革是推动当今世界变化的两大根本性力量。

• 全球化。中国的改革开放和苏东剧变消除了东西方之间的政治壁垒，使得西方的资本技术在更大地理空间内寻找投资机会，20多亿人口融入全球经济体系，成为西方资本和商品的消费者。这种全球化力量一方面在很大程度上造就了2008年前世界经济繁荣时代，另一方面也因为资本技术、制造业等外迁，使得西方国家大量的中产阶层收入陷入停滞或失去工作。西方国家的社会结构因此开始发生变化，越来越多的人因收入停滞或失业陷入贫困，中产阶层在社会结构中所占比例大幅下降。全球化时代失落者要求通过变革改变现状的诉求从占领华尔街，到伦敦骚乱，从英国脱欧公投到特朗普当选美国总统充分地显现出来。

• 科技变革。全球化力量在深刻地塑造改变当今世界的同时，以信息技术为主的科技变革日新月异，对当前世界政治、经济、社会等产生持久而深刻地影响，人类社会面临着新的机遇和挑战。关于科技变革对美国社会的深刻影响，美国总统奥巴马曾在2011年1月25日的国情咨文中认为："但那个世界已经发生改变。对于许多人而言，这种改变有些痛苦。当我看到曾经繁荣一时的工厂如今已经关门倒闭，当我看到曾经熙熙攘攘的商业街如今已门可罗雀，我就体会到这种变化。当我看到薪水缩减或被迫下岗的美国人的失落之情，我就感受到这种变化。对于这些自豪的美国人而言，他们感觉游戏规则已发生了改变。他们的感觉是正确的，规则已经发生改变。在一代人的时间里，技术革命已经使人们生活、工作和做生意的方式发生彻底改变。曾经需要 1 000 名工人的钢铁厂如今只需要 100 名工人即可完成等量的工作。今天，在任何有因特网连接服务的地方，任何公司都可以开设商店、雇用员工以及销售产品。"

（3）社会贫富分化问题凸显。在世界发生深刻变化的背景下，贫富差距问题显得尤为突出。全球化一方面使得全球投资设厂的财富所有者因更大投资回报而变得越来越富有，另一方面使得因制造业外迁而失去工作的产业工人陷入贫困。科技变革在造就少数因专利技术、商业模式创新而一夜暴富的技术新贵的同时，科技创新和新的商业模式使得传统产业工人、传统商业领域的服务人员永久地失去了工作。根据瑞信研究院 2016 年 11 月 22 日公布《全球财富报告》，最惊人的发现在于，全球财富金字塔底层的 35 亿成年人人均拥有的财富不到 1 万美元，他们拥有的财富仅占全球总财富的 2.4%，而 3 300 万的百万富翁，仅占全球成年人口的 0.7%，却拥有全球 45.6% 的财富，这意味着贫富差距在日益扩大。

正是基于对 2008 年华尔街金融危机的反思，美国总统奥巴马早在 2009 年 1 月 21 日的国情咨文中提到贫富差距的问题，他认为"市场究竟是好是坏？这是一个无需争论的话题。它创造财富、扩展自由的能力无与伦比，但这场危机同时提醒我们：如果缺乏监管，它的力量就有可能失去控制，而一个国家如果一心偏向其中的富裕阶层，就不可能保持长久的繁荣。我们国家经济的成功从来都不只是单纯依靠扩张国内生产总值规模的结果，而是依靠普遍的繁荣；依靠我们让每个心存希望的公民公平享有成功机会的能力——这并非善心所致，而是因为它们是实现共同繁荣的必由之路"。"我们今天提出的问题并不是我们的政府是大是小，而是它是否运转有效——它是否能够帮助美国家庭获得薪酬体面的工作，负担得起的保障以及享有尊严的退休生活。凡是有利于实现上述目标的事，我们都将不断推进；凡是不利的，我们誓要把它画上句号。"

作为大西洋彼岸的盟国，英国在脱欧公投之后开始了对全球化和科技变革时代社会贫富差距扩大带来的问题的深入反思。英国新任首相特雷莎·梅就职演讲中说道："我知道你起早贪黑，我知道你竭尽全力，我知道生活有时是一种挣扎。我领导的政府不会被少数特权者的利益所驱使，而会为你的利益而呼吁奔走。我们将竭尽所能让你更好掌控自己的生活。当我们做重大决定时，我们想到的不是那些有权人，而是你们。当我们通过新的法案时，我们倾听的不是那些有势者，而是你们。当政府收税时，我们优先照顾的不是那些有钱人，而是你们。当政府创造提供机会时，我们不会保护那些少数富人的利益。"从上述就职演讲可以看出英国的反思和教训正如变化的世界一样深刻。

令人遗憾的是，英国脱欧公投后的反思和教训并没有为大西洋彼岸的美国所汲取。从占领华尔街、英国伦敦骚乱，到英国脱欧公投，全球化和科技变革时代失落者曾多次通过示威和数人头的民主政治表达要求变革的诉求。特朗普的胜出正是因为他"听到了其他人没有听到声音"（美国众议院发言人 Paul Davis Ryan 选后反思），变革的诉求在美利坚土地上再次唱响。

2. 当前时代变革背景下跨国并购的思考

跨国并购是指跨国兼并和跨国收购的总称，是指一国企业（又称并购企业）为了达到某种目标，通过一定的渠道和支付手段，将另一国企业（又称被并购企业）的所有资产或足以行使运营活动的股份收买下来，从而对另一国企业的经营管理实施实际的或完全的控制行为。

面对当今世界纷繁复杂而又深刻的变化，深入分析当今世界变化可能带来的结果和原因，能够将跨国并购风险尽可能降低，并为跨国并购战略选择和实施提供支撑。为此，在深刻变化的时代背景下，跨国并购需要从多层面、多因素展开综合分析。

在全球高度相互依存世界里，多层面分析是指为实现跨国并购的目标，需要从全球、区域和国家三个层面展开分析。

（1）全球层面。

全球政治经济层面的深刻变化构成了跨国并购的宏观背景，影响着跨国并购面临机遇和挑战以及并购战略的选择。稳定繁荣的政治经济形势能够为跨国并购提供更多战略机遇和选择，复杂动荡的政治经济形势则为跨国并购带来诸多需要深入分析研究和防范的风险和不确定性。20 世纪 70 年代末中国的改革开放和 90 年代苏东剧变是全球政治经济层面重大变化，这种变化消除了东西方、西方与苏东地区间诸多制度性壁垒，20 多亿人口的市场向西方开放，推动了西方资本技术向这些地区的流动。全球政治经济层面这一变化在很大程度上造就了 2008 年前全球经济繁荣。

（2）区域层面。

区域内的政治、经济、社会形势对跨国并购具有重要影响。区域内的政治、经济、社会形势分析是当今世界深刻变化背景进行跨国并购不可缺少的重要层面。自 2008 年全球金融经济危机爆发以来，一些国家、地区和区域的政治、经济、社会形势动荡加剧，这给跨国并购造成更为复杂多变的风险和不确定性。

2010 年 12 月 17 日突尼斯的小商贩默罕默德·布瓦吉吉自焚事件成为突尼斯局势突变的导火索，并相继造成北非、中东地区动荡。摩洛哥、埃及、利比亚、也门政权多米诺骨牌式相继垮塌，许多国家在该地区投资损失惨重。这些国家都具有相似的政治经济社会背景，政治方面多为独裁、物价居高不下，失业率高涨，民怨沸腾。这一事件说明，在当今深刻变化的世界中，在政权性质、经济社会乃至宗教文化相似的地区或区域，一个看似微不足道的事件能够造成巨大的动荡，给跨国并购或投资带来巨大的挑战和潜在风险。因此，区域层面的政治、经济社会形势分析成为跨国并购风险分析不可或缺的层面。

（3）国家层面。

跨国并购目标国政治、经济、社会情况是跨国并购风险分析的根本。并购目标国的最高国家权力的行使、运用和分配从根本上影响着跨国并购的战略选择。独裁政权相对于民主政权来说具有极大的不稳定性，不稳定的独裁政治环境不利于跨国并购的实施，稳定的民主政治环境则会为跨国并购提供良好的法治环境。同时，跨国并购所涉及两种或多种不同的政治制度和宗教文化，则可能会为并购实施造成难以克服得障碍。随着我国经济实力不断增强，一些视中国为潜在威胁的西方国家四处宣扬所谓的"中国威胁论"，常常以"经济威胁"和"经济安全"为由，对我国企业跨国并购进行政治干预和阻挠。五矿收购诺兰达因加拿大政府的干预而失败，中海油收购美国优尼科石油公司遭遇美国国会的反对而功亏一篑。

跨国并购目标国经济发展状况和社会状况是跨国并购风险评估和制定并购战略的重要参考。并购目标国社会关系和谐稳定是实施并购战略的重要条件。在当前世界深刻变化的背景下，美国等发达国家民粹主义情绪、社会贫富分化是跨国并购战略需要考虑的重要因素。这些社会问题将会对并购产生的影响有待于深入分析。

多因素综合分析是指为实现跨国并购的目标，需要从政治、经济、社会、文化、技术进步等因素及其相互影响展开跨国并购综合分析。面对当今世界复杂而深刻的变化，政治、经济、社会、技术变革等因素所带来的影响日益交织在一起，单一视角分析已不能有效识别跨国并购的潜在的风险。正如前文所述，特朗普胜出不是黑天鹅事件，而是人类社会在全球化不断深化、科技变革飞速发展带来的结果。特朗普的胜出既有经济全球化深化造成贫富差距扩大、社会分化的因，也有科技变革带来更多的失业和贫穷的果。经济全球化、科技变革、社会分化等多方面因素最后结出了美国政治中一位叫特朗普的果。因此，在一个深刻变化的世界里，跨国并购目标的实现需要综合政治、经济、社会、宗教文化、技术变革等多因素及其相互影响展开全面深入的分析。

提升上海投资贸易整体竞争力

欧　文

美中贸易全国委员会上海首席代表

美中贸易全国委员会（USCBC）支持中美两国稳固的互惠互利的商贸关系。在过去的三十多年里，中美关系在两国政府、商业团体及其他各方的共同协作努力下取得了诸多积极进展。贸易与投资为两国经济带来了巨大的利益，同时也是中美关系的根基。

美中贸易全国委员会感谢上海一直以来给予美国公司的支持。上海一直是吸引外资方面的"领头羊"，鼓励中美两国之间的贸易与投资。美中贸易全国委员会的会员公司同样支持上海逐步向外资开放的目标，我们希望能和会员公司一起继续为上海实现这一发展目标贡献绵薄之力。

上海一直致力于促进在华投资和贸易。通过出台一系列的措施，如建设上海自贸区、放宽许可程序、制定透明的政策制定和执法体系等，上海在促进外商投资贸易方面处于全国领先地位。美中贸易全国委员会一直与上海市政府保持密切合作，为上海特别是上海自贸区出谋划策，使外商投资更具吸引力，我们提出的许多建议均适用于继续提高整体贸易投资竞争力的过程。

由于上海不断完善相关政策，以促进经济合作，并给予外国公司的激励政策，营造优良的企业发展环境，许多美国公司选择上海作为其在中国运营、研发投资、人才培养和与中国企业合作的所在地。

随着中美经贸关系的进一步发展，上海将继续在其中发挥重要作用。以下建议是基于美中贸易全国委员会建言献策文件，包括 2016 年董事会声明，希望上海能加以改善，从而促使未来上海与外国企业在投资贸易方面的合作更加顺利。

我们对提升外国企业投资贸易便利化水平的建议主要包括以下几个方面：

1. 继续对外国企业开放并提供竞争环境

（1）减少对外资所有权的限制。上海在为外资提供新的投资机会方面处于领先地位，但是中国仍在多个行业中保有对外资所有权的限制，包括制造业、服务业、农业和资源类行业。当即减少外商投资所有权限制而不是推后行动将有助于美国和外国公司更好地为中国实现经济改革和经济再平衡目标做出贡献。

（2）确保在中国的外企技术公司和产品受到同等对待。技术和创新在推动建立适应 21 世纪经济发展的商业环境中起到了至关重要的作用。对于市场中技术企业的监管方式需要体现企业所维系的全球价值链的复杂性，并且该行业的法规应完全建立在良好的商业和技术因素的基础上，达到这两点要求非常重要。

2. 减少贸易壁垒，实行全球公认的贸易规则

（1）保证法律法规在各地的执行一致。作为其经济改革的一项内容，上海市政府已经在全国范围内简化并下放许多设立和进行商业活动的审批程序。虽然这些措施广受欢迎，但是各地对于法律法规的执行仍存在差异，这些差异导致问题的产生。

（2）对在中国市场销售的产品和服务，更多使用透明的国际通用标准。在中国使用国际通用标准，能够确保中国消费者及终端使用者获得最好的产品与服务，同时让中国产品和服务能受到国际认可并更具国际竞争力。上海应采取更加科学、公平、平等、透明、以市场为主导的方式来制定和发展标准，对所有公司开放，不分国别，包括国内企业、外资企业和国外的生产企业。

（3）解除进口壁垒以鼓励消费、促进经济再平衡。中国对多种消费品征收高额进口关税和税费。这些高额关税和税费抑制了中国经济的再平衡，导致中国消费者选择在海外购买此类商品。减少或免除消费品关税和税费可以简单而强效地刺激国内消费。

（4）不分所有权性质，确保在政府采购中公平对待中国境内所有法人实体。中国尽快完成《政府采购本国产品管理办法》的修订，考虑在终稿中采纳美中贸易全国委员会提交的修改意见，确保在政府采购过程中，不分所有权性质，公平对待在中国境内所有法人实体的产品和服务。如按照我委员会建议对《管理办法》做出相应修订，中国的政府采购规则将与中国企业在美国适用的相关法律法规基本相同。

3. 确保竞争中立并提高透明度

上海一直致力于提高监管环境和市场的透明度，以帮助所有公司提升投资能

力，但是我们仍然建议可以在以下方面做出改善：

（1）确保行政许可的平等对待。行政许可壁垒在过去十年里一直是我委员会年度会员公司调查结果反映的美国公司受到歧视待遇最多的领域之一。这些行政许可包括经营许可、分支机构许可、产品许可、进口许可，以及在银行、医疗保健、保险、建筑、法律和增值电信业务（如数据中心）等行业的许可和审批。在许多情况下，中国公司都能够免受外企或外商投资的企业所面临的限制或延滞获得许可。上海已简化许多外商在沪运营的许可要求。我们鼓励中国进一步努力减少许可壁垒，并确保在许可审批和批复的过程中平等对待所有企业。行政许可和其他政府批复决定都应无歧视地对待任何所有权制度的企业，并且不受竞争方的影响。

（2）进一步提高政策制定的透明度。在过去的几年中，上海在起草与对外贸易便利化相关的法律和政策过程中，提供了许多透明化的平台，以提高政策制定的透明度。在未来的日子里，我们希望上海能继续致力于提高政策制定的透明度，并和中央政府共同在政策制定过程中公示所有与贸易和经济相关的法律、行政法规和部门规章的草案，确保公示征求意见期满 30 天。同时也应考虑进一步在指定网站发布征求意见稿，并给予公众 60 天至 90 天的公开征求意见期。

（3）政策实施。执法部门在执行相关新的政策时，希望能给企业提供相应的培训或详细的政策解析，以方便企业能更好得配合相关政策的执行和实施。在新旧政策替换期间，能够给企业至少 30 天的通知期，以便企业消化理解以及按照新的相关规定做部署。

4. 加强知识产权保护，坚持互惠互利的创新政策

（1）继续加强知识产权体制建设与知识产权执法。加强有力的知识产权保护对中美双方互利。上海应该通过更新相关法律法规继续完善知识产权体系以更好地反映当前知识产权保护和实施现状的发展的要求。上海应继续致力于加强知识产权保护执法，并采取更强有力的惩罚措施来打击侵犯知识产权行为。

（2）加强对网络假冒伪劣和盗版产品的执法。网络平台正成为造假者销售假冒伪劣产品和盗版内容流通的一个新兴途径，因而成为产权持有者和执法人员共同面临的特殊挑战。上海应加大互联网相关的知识产权执法力度，确保法律法规及执法行为涵盖诸如网上商标使用、商标有关的域名注册，以及使用网站、互联网服务及应用程序作为假冒和盗版产品平台等领域。在平衡知识产权合法权利人

及互联网中介机构需求的同时，这些法规与执法应该建立起一个促进法律责任的框架。

（3）加强商业秘密保护。商业秘密保护是创新型经济的核心组成部分。上海可以采取积极的措施，鼓励创新，加大力度解决商业秘密保护相关问题，包括制定商业秘密法，在司法程序中更广泛地使用初步禁令和证据保全令，更明确地规定政府机构应保护在审查过程中收集到的企业机密信息，并减少原告在商业秘密案件中所面临的过重举证责任。

5. 人才政策

对于企业来说，能否借上海经济快速发展以及上海自贸区政策的东风大幅提升业务的关键，在于能否吸引有实际操作经验并且具有国际视野的人才来具体实施上海最新政策带来的商业机会。吸引、保留、培养高端人一直是外资企业面临的挑战之一。

（1）核心人才年龄限制。对于确属核心人才的外籍人士签证年龄限制放宽到65周岁。根据现有的签证政策，年满60岁的外籍人士的工作签证将一年一审。

（2）引进人才政策。上海市的人才引进政策对一些高科技的人才落户提供了很大的便利。但是对于一些企业较为核心岗位的人才，比如高端销售人才或业务发展人才，按照现在的人才制度还是很难落户上海。

（3）外籍就业审批。放宽和进一步简化外籍人员来华就业的行政审批事项。例如之前外国人就业证的审批时间为递交申请材料后5个工作日即可取证书，按照相关新的政策已经延长至15个工作日。据国家法律规定，外国人持工作签证入华后必须在入境的30个工作日内办理居留许可。但是由于办理体检、就业证等时间均较长而有可能导致无法及时办理居留许可。因此希望相关部门能相应缩短相关审批的时间。

6. 关于行政许可制度

（1）审批时限。明确统一的审批时限有助于确保审批过程的透明度。某些许可过程往往没有执行审批时限，这显著拖延了企业在中国的投资进程。为了提高政府审批的透明度和可预见性，我委员会建议政府应制定明确的指导方针要求各机构向申请者提供更多和更及时的信息更新。假如某政府机构的审批错过了截止日期，应向申请方解释行政审批推迟的原因。

（2）审批程序标准化。与地方政府部门合作，建立全国标准化的许可审批程序，以确保申请程序在跨司法管辖区一致性。所有的申请要求，应在当地政府网站全文发布并且在这些机构对外办公地为企业提供纸质的文件。

（3）统一负面清单。实施全国统一的市场准入负面清单将有助于阐述哪些领域对外国投资开放，同时也确保地方政府和省级政府执法的连贯性。

展望更加开放和公平的贸易环境——日本企业对于投资贸易便利化的期望

小栗道明

日本贸易振兴机构（JETRO）上海代表处首席代表

据 JETRO 测算，2015 年世界货物贸易出口额为 164 467 亿美元，比 2014 年减少 12.7%，是近六年来首次出现下降。中国的进口额同比也出现了大幅降低，减少了 18.4%，对世界货物进口额增长的贡献度为 −1.9%。

2012 年后，世界经济增长率与贸易规模的扩张速度相比，停滞不前，即所谓的贸易低增长。与 GDP 实际增长率相比，货物贸易的实际增长率比率只有 0.5。特别是在以中国为首的新兴国家和发展中国家中，贸易低增长现象更为显著。

低迷的投资影响贸易发展势头，进而导致贸易持续低增长。构成设备投资要素的资本商品、中间产品的贸易增长在 2012 年以后呈现世界性减速，在中国尤为明显。按商品类别观察中国的进口动向可以看出，消费品进口额在 2010 年以后得以稳健增长，但是消费品在中国进口额中占比只有 9.1%，而占比 53% 的中间商品和占比 15.9% 的资本商品的进口却显著地减少了。

另一个是结构性原因，即推动世界贸易扩大的全球价值链的发展速度降低了。造成这种显现的因素包括中国作为世界工厂内部生产化越来越明显，亚洲主要地区的区域内贸易比率增高，地区间的成本差缩小等等。特别是中国国内供给能力的提高对贸易增长产生了重要影响。之前中国是从周边国家进口零部件组装成产品，再出口到各地。但是，近年来随着技术能力的提高，加工贸易的进口在进口额中占比下降，国内制造业的附加价值不断提高。中国内部生产化趋势不断加强，使得中国进口和世界贸易整体增长停滞。

在这样的背景下，2012 年后上海对外贸易的低增长倾向也非常显著。按国别贸易来看，对日贸易仅次于美国排名第二，但近年的低增长也十分明显。

此外，2008 年上海外商实际投资额达到 100 亿美元并保持持续增长，其中 2013 年 9 月成立的中国（上海）自由贸易试验区起到了很大的推动作用。

上海自贸区进行了多方面的尝试，比如负面清单管理、企业成立登记制度的简化、贸易制度的便利化等均结出了硕果。但是仍有许多日本企业反映"实际没怎么感受到改革的恩惠"。

近年来，上海在服务业、金融业开放和投资贸易便利化上的努力受到高度评价，但从国际水平来看，还不能说"公平性得到了保证"以及充分构筑起"高透明度"的商业环境。

"十三五"期间，中国政府不断深化改革以完善市场体系，推动行政管理体制改革，完善对外开放新体制。上海一如既往走在前列，日本贸易振兴机构期待上海有进一步发展。

我们希望上海能吸收日本企业的意见，推动发展更加完善公平的商业环境。在投资、贸易便利化方面，具体包括：

1. 积极向日本企业提供信息

2013年后，日本企业对上海的投资，仍出现负增长，2015年更是比前一年大幅减少了60%。JETRO发布的日本企业调查（2015年）结果显示，在参与调查的在沪日本企业中表示今后会扩大规模的企业所占比例虽然略高于全国平均水平（38.1%），但仍处于38.5%的历史新低，今后会维持现状的企业占比为55.2%。

日本企业如此慎重的原因在于，上海推进改革和商业机会的信息未能充分地传达到日本企业，而近年来如中国投资和商业环境的负面信息成本上升和经济减速等这几年却引起了日本企业的注意。

为了消除这些负面印象，我们希望上海继续深化惠及在沪日企的改革措施，并更加积极地通过各种渠道向日本企业宣传上海的改革进展和商业机会。

2. 投资：消除内外差别，对接国际标准

在外资企业对中投资中，制度运营中的不透明性会带来风险。希望政府在可预见的问题上作一些改善，如统一法律制度解释，制度变更时提供充足的准备时间，手续办理简略化、便捷化，以及完善申请咨询的书面答复。

我们高度评价负面清单的推广以及清单中的产业种类的逐渐减少。但有一些特定的产业仍然内外有别。比如100%外资控股的建筑企业可承包施工范围，虽在自贸区有所让步，但限制依然存在。还有在电信行业，外商独资或外商控股

仍不能获得营业许可。希望今后能够针对在这些特定的行业修改政策，使内外无别。

3. 经营资产整合手续的便利化

日本企业很早就进入上海市场。随着市场经济化的推进和投资环境的急剧变化，企业不得不进行资产重组也是大势所趋。但目前，企业的关停及营业网点的整合手续太过繁琐、税务审查时间过长，耗费了大量的人力、物力。我们迫切希望缩短税务调查的时间，使企业资产重组过程中的手续更加简单。采取这些措施也能带动产业构造的合理化。

4. 贸易和通关：提升自由化水平

通过建立上海自贸区，上海贸易通关制度的效率化、透明化及服务水平等的不断提高得到了高度评价。不过，在 2015 年 JETRO 进行的日本企业调查中，依然有很多企业认为"通关手续繁琐""通关太费时间"是企业经营中的难题。

例如，同一产品的 HS 编码、原产地证明等相关制度，在进口申报时仍存在着解释不同的问题。希望今后能通过加强培训、制定更详细的手册来提高执法的统一性。

当然，有关 HS 编码的提前公示制度，最好是能在全国统一实施，让企业能够灵活运用，并公开关于归类商品的详细解释资料。这样不但为企业带来便利，也能减轻政府相关部门的工作负担。

随着上海自贸区"先入区，后通关"等制度的导入及改革的深化，便利化水平也不断提高。不过，虽然口岸实施了电子自动化，但检查仍无法在海关及检疫人员下班后（下午 5 点后）进行，导致货物还是无法尽快通关。期待口岸建立 24 小时值班制，或为深夜出关货物提供绿色通道。

从保税区将拼箱货物再出口时，海关指定的拼箱货物仓库费用较高、对货物的损伤风险也较大，希望今后拼箱货物仓库的使用可以更加自由化。

近年来，中国政府为推进贸易自由化，积极向世界各国、各地推行自由贸易协定。我们对此表示欢迎。早日实现中日韩自由贸易协定、区域全面经济伙伴关系等协定，能促进关税、非关税措施的废除及阶段性取消，也使现阶段贸易的制度更加自由化、便利化，我们衷心希望能尽快签署这些协定。

5. 放宽日本食品的进口限制

现在，中国消费者对安全高品质的日本农产品及食品表现出了很强的购买欲望，日本食材也博得了中国游客的好评。但由于进口限制，很多食材无法进入中国市场，比如因口蹄疫病毒受影响的乳制品，因口蹄疫、疯牛病受影响的肉类，非指定厂生产的精米及熏蒸仓库处理的大米和无进口记录的苹果、梨等水果。

我们认为放宽进口限制，不仅能给中国人民带来丰富的日本食材，充实饮食文化、提高生活水准，还能增加进口税收并激发潜在的消费需求。

上海在全国率先设立了自贸区，为了贸易和投资环境达到国际水平，正在开展进口货物入区手续和检验检疫手续的简化改革，以作为试行改革的一环。我们希望能够放宽或者废除对日本商品的限制。

6. 促进对外投资和手续便利化

近年来，中国企业的对外投资在急速增加，对日投资也在慢慢扩大。中国企业的对外投资相关手续也在愈发简便，但是在资金汇款方面仍然存在很高的壁垒。希望上海促进双向投资的发展，对中国企业的海外投资给予更多支援，让相关手续更加便捷化。

Blockchain: New Technology, New Idea, New Model

Sunny Lu

Co-Founder & COO, BitSE

Recently I heard a very interesting *Hindering Theory*. Any evolutional technologies were invented from the hinders of society development. For instance, the transportation tools were developed from the challenges that humankind want to travel across the world freely; the birth of Internet technology is from the hinders that people faced during the global communication and collaboration. Nowadays, we are facing new hinders again with highly developed social division of labor and global collaboration, which are information asymmetry, disconnected information mobility and nontransparent trust. Hence, Blockchain as a new disruptive technology is born.

Blockchain technology has been considered as one of very essential components of Fintech. Even though Blockchain technology was born from finance industry and many of people believe which could be the technology infrastructure of the next generation of Fintech, we believe Blockchain will have many impacts and influences to every industry other than just finance industry.

The entire human world has been speeding up the digitalization process with enormous development of Internet technology and increasing collaboration needs. For example, "One Belt One Road" Initiative raised up by China requires close cooperation to break the borderline between regions, countries and cultures. Under this specific proposition, the biggest barrier is just the Information Island, inconsistent information mobility and expensive cost of building trust. Blockchain technology is exactly the answer to all of the above concerns. Such new disruptive technology will bring us a brand new pattern to think. It will bring the new changes to the existing models. The traditional thinking logic is about "What can I do" or "Can I bring something new to this circle as a single party or regulator". However, Blockchain could lead us to think in another level such as what we can do from the perspective of the whole industry or the entire society.

Let's think about a typical application scenario for Blockchain by asking such a question—what kind of data or operation model can be running on Blockchain systems? Firstly, either data or operation should be valuable; secondly, they are required to be public, transparent but anonymous with privacy protection; the third, they shall be able to be accessed and operated by multiple participants; last but not least, data and operation can't be tampered or manipulated so as to guarantee the integrity and security. Any data or operation fitting the above conditions makes a typical application scenario for Blockchain technology.

A typical example is the unique & universal ID for products. Unique ID existed in many enterprises for long time. For example, series number for most of equipment is a kind of unique ID. But most of series numbers are not universal which means any player other than enterprise who manufactures the equipment can't recognize it. Blockchain technology make this happen to generate a unique but universal ID.

VeChain as our primary BAAS (Blockchain As A Service) platform is a feasible platform for product management through the entire supply chain based on unique and universal ID running on Blockchain.

Supply chain management is one of the promising application scenarios for Blockchain. The flow of goods and materials, the flow of information and the flow of funds are the three most essential elements of supply chain. Despite nowadays, the flow of goods and materials are quite mature relying on the high level of corresponding technology and services, the information flow usually presents inconsistent and/or unresponsive, which is the biggest challenge to efficiency and cost in supply chain.

In the entire lifecycle of the commercial products, the product information is usually owned and managed by different participants in the different stages such as manufacturer, distributor, retailer, logistic provider and regulator. The product information maintains actually disconnected like Information Islands. That's why the ultimate traceability in supply chain is usually quite complex and difficult to achieve.

Blockchain technology can make this traceability realized. Recently, we have achieved an MOU (Momentum of Understanding) with D.I.G. to build up traceability system for imported wines on VeChain platform. Comparing to the existing solution, this traceability system will start from the original source of wines—the winery oversea and allow multiple participants to contribute the data creation and maintenance of wines through the entire supply chain process. In the end, a mobile App will be provided to consumers as the single portal to provide all of the traceability information simply by using a smart phone and Internet connection. That traceability information coming from multiple players enhances the credibility and integrity giving the maximum protection of consumer interests with customer trust as return.

Another case that we have been working on quite matches what we are discussing today—how Blockchain can help on the publicity and investigation of Trading Warranty. Actually it's a typical business scenario for Blockchain Technology. In this case, the data input which is expected to verify the integrity of each warranty includes ones from multiple participants such as traders, financial institutions who provide financial support, logistic providers like forwarders and warehouse providers, regulators like customs etc. It's a classic use case for Blockchain to make a platform to connect to all of those players which can enable information transfer and exchange in time among all of the information receivers. It will provide most accurate, genuine and timely data supporting to who need.

In general, Blockchain is a newly born technology to the world that brings the new pattern to think, and links to the new business model furthermore, even the probability of new changes from regulators. Blockchain is committed to enable higher efficient collaboration and cost optimization of enterprises and government departments leading to new business model and regulation services.

Nevertheless, Blockchain is still in a very early stage as a new technology with many places to be expected to optimize continuously. We wish the whole society and industries including enterprises and government departments will embrace such disruptive technology with generous supporting and willingness to explore and adventure. Blockchain will be developed to more and more advanced version with continuously trial and use case deployments.

Enhance the Investment Environment in Shanghai

Kenneth Jarrett

President of the American Chamber of Commerce in Shanghai

According to a study by the Rhodium group, a New York consultancy, in the past 15 years, US investment into China reached $228 billion and Chinese investment into US during same period reached $64 billion. Much of that US investment is here in Shanghai.

The US and Chinese economies are more integrated than ever, but there is still room for investment to grow on both sides. However, as the recent US presidential election demonstrated, many American people feel that they have not benefitted from trade and investment. We need to do a better job of explaining the benefits, such as how investment creates jobs or improves living standards.

Shanghai has done an excellent job of developing a friendly business environment. We welcome new visa reforms introduced this year and efforts in the FTZ to simplify administrative procedures, decrease customs clearance time, and support more foreign currency exchanges. Our members support Shanghai's goals of becoming an international financial center by 2020 and science, technology, and innovation center by 2030.

Foreign companies have responded to SH's attractive investment environment by increasing investment here and establishing their regional headquarters in this great city. Two notable recent US examples are the opening of the Shanghai Disney Resort, with an investment of over $5.5 billion, which now employs thousands of people, and the opening of a $1.2 billion Cadillac automobile plant by GM.

Despite those milestones, we must also acknowledge that foreign companies continue to face significant regulatory and operational challenges in China that limits investment and trade. Let me highlight a few, which are issues determined at the national level by the Central Government. I mention them today in the hope that Shanghai can have some influence:

First, We are seeing an increase in restrictions and policies that complicate the repatriation of capital from China. These new regulations make it difficult for foreign banks and financial services firms to operate and expand in China, and make it difficult for companies headquartered in Shanghai to efficiently move money overseas. These restrictions also undermine Shanghai's efforts to become an international financial center by 2020.

Second, There is still too much uncertainty on how new regulations and policies will be implemented. In some cases, implementation differs depending on geographic location. We urge the government to minimize the gap between policy implementation by providing more briefings and reports on how new policies should be implemented. Organizations such as AmCham Shanghai can help to organize these efforts.

I would also like to raise two areas of concern where Shanghai has more ability to provide solutions:

1. Rising Costs: MNCs, particularly those in manufacturing, face costs challenges as the cost of doing business in Shanghai and the YRD continues to increase. We urge local governments to consider taking more measures to lower costs such as reducing the tax burden on middle-sized and large enterprises or helping companies find lower cost options for their operations.

2. Supporting R&D: The Shanghai government has encouraged companies to establish more R&D centers as a part of its efforts to develop a science, technology, and innovation center. Foreign R&D centers play an important role in Shanghai's endeavor to be a world innovative city. Companies are interested in establishing more R&D Centers, but a few factors prevent or limit their abilities in this area. (1) According to our 2016 business climate survey, lack of IPR enforcement has constrained nearly half of respondents from investing in innovation and R&D. (2) There are importation restrictions on biological materials for drug development: Bio-pharmaceuticals is one of 7 emerging industries for Shanghai, but for many R&D centers in bio-drug or diagnostic business, the import of reagents used for drug development and diagnostics, specifically those containing animal ingredients and human ingredients, is very difficult due to a number of technical reasons. We hope that Shanghai can introduce a new import approval procedure for such R&D materials to clear Customs and CIQ and hope

that certified foreign R&D centers will be granted with more assistance in this regard. (3) Access to Government R&D Funds: There are special government funds and programs at the local and central level that encourage R&D in emerging or prioritized industries such as semiconductors. Some of these funds are only available to local companies or foreign companies must meet certain requirements that are impossible for them. Assistance in this area would go a long way in encouraging companies to establish more R&D centers.

I hope that we can continue to work with the SDRC and the Shanghai government on these issues and help Shanghai reach its development goals.

Striving Towards a Globally Integrated Enterprise—IBM's Experience in Strategic M&A in International Investment and Trade

Zheng Jun

Vice President, Enterprise Business Unit, East & Central China

Global integrationa and international trade are not something new. They have long been the economic engine before the Roman Empire was founded. Nevertheless, in the past decade, it is mergers and acquisitions (M&A) that have played a major role in serving enterprises' strategies and fast growth, because globalizaiton was moving on at a much faster pace. Particularly, in the wake of global economic slump, enterprises are expected to shift more attention to values, opportunity discovering and quick responses. Through M&A, enterprises are able to develop core competencies, increase market shares, gain economies of scale and enlarge market coverage. And through business spin-off they can focus on core business to boost shareholder value.

It is partly because of the long-lasting Information and Communication Technology (ICT) revolution, which will continue to dramatically cut down trade and transaction costs, and further expand interaction scope. During the period of 1995—1997, the number of multinationals doubled from 38 000 to 79 000, and the overseas subsidiaries trippled from 265 000 to 790 000. In the same period, international transactions of M&A increased two times from 390 to 889. But the trend slowed down in 2008 like other economic trend.

The revolution has also generated vast opportunities for business leaders to optiimize global resources and capital productivity. However, the path to realize enterprise strategies through M&A is by no means smooth. According to statistics, only some 25% enterprises in the world succeed in M&A activities, and much fewer Chinese companies achieved their goals.

So in M&A activities, enterprises need to set up accurate strategies and appropriate goals, implement effective consolidation measures, and make deals in a correct way, so that they can reduce risks and get realize the value of trading.

Newly acquired individual business units, or functional silos, that are insulated from an overarching operating strategy have long been an inhibitor of efficiencies. But in today's global environment, individual fiefdoms among business units and geographies can keep enterprises from realizing their potential. In the last 2 decades, a number of enterprises found themselves troubled by red tapes and low-efficient procedures when dealing with new regions, clients, employees and technologies. The answer for many is to adopt a "globally integrated enterprise" operating model. The results can be significant, as demonstrated by the high performers already on this journey. The path can be long and tough, taking years and requiring continuous transformation. But for those companies with a global footprint, integration is a topic that can no longer be ignored: it is likely to separate the winners from the rest in the coming decade.

The world continues to get smaller and bumpier. As a result, many companies find themselves functioning in a global environment with an operating model designed for more limited scope. Insulated operations, lack of customer-driven vision and inconsistent communication combine to create inefficiency and waste and greatly inhibit concerted, company-wide and/or ecosystem-wide collaboration.

Many companies are finding solutions to these issues by transforming into globally integrated enterprises (GIE). A globally integrated enterprise combines global efficiencies with market responsiveness to address the challenges and opportunities that a global economy brings to an organization and its industry. The GIE operating model emerged from massive socioeconomic changes that occurred throughout the world in the 1990s, including the emergence of the Internet and the increased global footprint of multinational companies.

To develop as a GIE, enterprises need to focus on inside-out global transformation to optomize the entire ecosystem, so that after M&A, they can integrate, manage and run acquired businesses faster, improve productivity and integrate resources for innovation and fevelopment, and maximize values deliverd by the deal.

Our experience in becoming a globally integrated enterprise (GIE) comes from over a decade of transforming IBM. For over a decade, IBM has been transforming itself through aggressive pursuit of global integration. By adopting common shared-support functions, enterprise-wide processes, a strong governance system and leveraging global skills, the company has improved client value and driven enormous productivity, freeing up resources to invest in growth and innovation.

Since 2001, we have acquired over 120 companies. Most of the 80 companies acquired before 2010 have been successfully integrated into the development of the softwares including Websphere, IM, Tivoli, Rational and Lotus. After 2010, IBM focused more on six areas, i.e. AI, Smarter Planet, Business Intelligence and Analysis, cloud computing, server and NAS optimization, and legal compiance and security in corporate governance. To do so, we can draw roadmmap of future, and grasp the market opportunities in future. Particularly, we have been playing an active role in seeking M&A targets in the area of AI which is widely believed will spark the next techologial revolution. We have spent over $12 billion in acquiring some 40 companies since the beginning of 2010.

In recent years, IBM has shifted more attention to technology start-ups rather than relatively mature companies. As technology is evolving rapidly, we are supposed to bet on the groups and talents who are standing at the forefront of technology R&D so that we can grasp decisive opportunities. Though we need to take some investment risks, if we carry out M&A activities only after the start-ups grow into well established companies, we will miss the golden time and have to spend more.

Our M&A targets are from all over the world, including not only a number of American enterprises, but also many others in European countries like Israel and the UK. By doing so, we intend to seek the most prestigious technical teams in the world.

Our M&A deals are very complex, how can we realize integrated operation? Our experience in transitioning into a GIE ensure our success.

To learn about how companies are embracing GIE and how well (and quickly) they are adopting this operating model, the IBM Institute for Business Value surveyed more than 1, 000 executives around the world. The survey supported by IBM's research partner, Oxford Economics; distributed and administered online; geographic representation from 12 countries; more than 68 percent have a physical presence in 6—50 countries. Executive titles included CIO, CFO, CHRO, Chief Strategy Officer and other C-suite executives, Senior Vice President/Vice President of Strategy, Finance, Supply Chain Management, Human Resources, Technology, Marketing/ Communications, Sales, heads of departments and managing directors.

Globalization impacts nearly every organization, no matter what industry.

Through analysis of survey responses, we found that companies generally progress in their GIE journey in an "inside-out" manner. The first step in the GIE transformation is to look inward of the company. As organizations expand their product/service footprints, capabilities and competencies through mergers and acquisitions (M&A), they must "rebalance" their operations to meet shifting market and customer needs. The most daunting M&A work is not the deal itself, but how to ensure integration of operations, technologies, people and culture. The "rebalancing needs" new digital capabilities to support Supply Chain, Finance, Human Resources and the end-to-end product lifecycle. They start with back-office, shared-services functions (e.g., Information Technology, Sales Support, Finance, Supply Chain/Operations, Human Resources) and cross-functional processes (e.g., order to pay, order to cash). As they progress on their journey, they tend to take a more external view and shift their focus to optimizing their entire ecosystem.

We also found that a group of high performers take this even further. Their focus today is on partnering across their value chains through marketing and customer-facing initiatives—with constant attention to improving and innovating the customer experience. The high performers create a culture of innovation that, according to our study, greatly surpasses that of their peers.

From the results of these high performers, as well as from IBM's own experience, we have found that GIE transformation is about:

• Optimizing global operations from the inside-out—Companies begin to transform operations to globally integrated services across functions and end-to-end processes. They optimize global processes and networks by simplifying and automating them. They create centers of excellence for business operations and specialized skills. They optimize processes and communications with their ecosystem (business partners, employees and customers).

• Activating information with analytics for predictive insights—High performing organizations use big data to get executable insights that can drive competitive advantage. They develop an analytics center of excellence for widespread use. They apply advanced analytics to automatic business decisions and bring fact-based insights to real-time actions. They innovate through prediction and prescriptive analysis to anticipate customer responses and reactions.

• Accelerating organizational agility with a culture of innovation—Companies must respond to rapidly developing changes in technology, operating model/process improvement and the organization/culture. They should inspire progress through transformational leadership—leaders must own and drive the change agenda. They must align global operations with strategic intent and business objectives. And they should strive to engage and energize people—embedding social media programs into their communications strategy for employee collaboration.

Those that accomplish the GIE transformation are likely to be the industry leaders. Those companies that do not embrace the transformation vision are likely to face an uphill battle for revenue, efficiency, customer loyalty and, ultimately, survival.

Finally, we will offer recommendations about how to progress along the GIE journey, which we think of as an ongoing, continuous transformation. Some companies are just beginning, while others have taken significant steps along the way. For a globally integrated enterprise, continuous transformation is an absolute must, since no company's position in its market is permanent.

Optimizing operations globally:

Recommendation 1: Transform operations to globally integrated services. Start with creating global impacts that have an internal innovation and integration focus (M&A, supply chain) and then move to those for value chain and competitive differentiation (restructuring sales/customer support and aligning operations in emerging markets). Impact includes greater return on investment, compound annual growth, profitability and revenue growth.

Recommendation 2: Optimize global processes and networks. Focus on higher-value, collaborative processes (sales and operations planning and business partner enablement). Optimize labor, costs and data. Leverage the globally integrated services to scale in new emerging and growth markets. Segment operations to meet local customer and market requirements.

Recommendation 3: Shift to an outside-in customer operating model. Develop centers of excellence to concentrate skills and assets to best engage and serve the customer. Move work to where it can be best performed. Optimize labor and delivery models to reduce costs while focusing resources on high-value support areas.

Activating information and analytics:

Recommendation 1: Gain the potential for competitive advantage by developing a center of excellence for business analytics serving all business units. This enables the organization to reduce enterprise cost, improve productivity and optimize operational performance. Analytics enhances competitive advantage in the market through sales and marketing effectiveness, product/service development and bringing insights to identify future market opportunities.

Recommendation 2: Put analytics into global operations for business insight. This is a top-down mandate by the senior executive team and requires automation and optimization of previously transformed shared services, cross-functional processes and customer/business centers of excellence.

Recommendation 3: Use analytics in all functions and advance from trend and historical analysis to predictive and then prescriptive solutions. Prioritize customer information for prescriptive analytics. Analytics can be applied to identify emerging market risks to enable proactive actions.

Accelerating organization agility:

Recommendation 1: Inspire through transformational leadership. Future transformation includes big data, with improved analytical capabilities, new technologies, such as cloud, new operating models and automated processes. Transformation leaders must own the change agenda. Create a management system that integrates leaders across geographies and products to focus on business performance alignment and customers.

Recommendation 2: Foster a culture that embraces continuous change. Improve outcomes by establishing a rigorous culture of innovation with attention on real insights, aligning skills and deploying common methods and tools to ensure organizational readiness, engagement and value. Launch a change management center of excellence to provide leaders with organizational change management advisory services.

Recommendation 3: Engage and motivate people. Embrace social media programs into the communication strategy. Utilize collaboration tools for interactive discussions about employee programs, new technologies and operating model changes. Leverage cloud technologies for rapid scaling and self-service.

To recap, global integration begins with an inside-out focus; it begins internally and, as capabilities grow, extends across the entire ecosystem. For those global companies that wish to enhance core competency, increase market shares, gain economies of scale and expand market coverage, the transformation to the globally integrated enterprise operating model is not only desirable, it is rapidly becoming a necessity.

Trade and Investment: Cornerstones for Shanghai's Future

Ioana Kraft

General Manager of Shanghai Chapter, European

Union Chamber of Commerce in China

Last year, we envisioned Shanghai as a global city in 2050. This year, we are zooming into the closer reality and discussing how to achieve this ambitious goal through trade and investment facilitation. It is my honour to represent the European Chamber's 1 600 members, about 600 of which are based in Shanghai and to share their opinions on and expectations for trade and investment facilitation.

Shanghai's advancement towards a city with global excellence as well as the home of the "Four Centres" and Innovation Centre cannot be realised without foreign participation since the core of these initiatives is exactly trade and investment facilitation. As the representative of the European business in Shanghai, we would like to share the following four points to help Shanghai achieve its goals.

First of all, European business would like to see Shanghai leading a bolder reform in terms of foreign investment administration to grant greater market access for European investors in China.

We were happy to see that China's foreign investment administrative regime has gone through several positive developments recently. Following the introduction of the *Market Access Negative List* nationwide, the corresponding change from business registration to filing and the amendments of the three FIE-related laws were made. However, no new negative list for foreign investment was promulgated and the implementing regulations issued after 1st October only indicate that the *Foreign Investment Catalogue* will continue to apply.

While China's reform on market access for foreign investment seems to have stalled, China's outbound M&A into Europe in 2015 increased 44% year-on-year

提升投资贸易便利化水平，构建开放型经济新体制

from 2014 and even more dramatically in the first half of 2016. The M&A cases cover large varieties of industries ranging from banking to auto components, from robotics to agricultural technology. In contrast, European investors in China are facing far more restrictions. The European business expects a more equal treatment and a shorter *Negative List* to boost investors' confidence in continuing investing in China. Only reciprocity in openness will prevent fuelling protectionist tendencies in the European market and offer much needed support to advocates of free trade and investment in maintaining open markets.

The Negative List mechanism is the most important concept introduced by Shanghai FTZ. European business was excited about it when it was first released. However, after the launch of the other two batches of FTZs, Shanghai FTZ may gradually lose its attractiveness for foreign investors. As European business in Shanghai, we would like to see Shanghai FTZ keep its competitiveness against the new FTZs and create better market access opportunities for both domestic and foreign investors by playing a bolder role in driving China's reform agenda.

Secondly, a good investment environment needs to be nourished by a healthy, open and robust financial sector and it is also the key to establish Shanghai as a global financial centre.

We are pleased to see Shanghai's recent improvement in financial infrastructure and this has been reflected in its rise up the *Global Financial Centre Index 19* from 21st place in 2015 to 16th in 2016.

However, to increase its competitiveness against other financial centres such as Hong Kong and Singapore, Shanghai will need to continue coordinating with the Central Government and advocating for further reforms in the capital market, such as full currency convertibility and free cross-border money transfer.

We also see the necessity to open up the stock market so that both domestic and foreign companies, particularly small and medium-sized enterprises, could have more access to capital to expand their business. We were encouraged to learn Shanghai Government's plan to establish an international board and a strategic emerging industries board. However, due to last year's stock market routs they have not materialised. We would welcome the resumption when time is appropriate.

Thirdly, as the largest container port in China and a rising airfreight hub,

Shanghai needs greater synergy among different departments to facilitate international trade.

Shanghai's effort in improving logistics infrastructure and trade regulatory environment is highly appreciated by the European Chamber and its member companies. Our recent surveys show that over 37% and 58% of the respondents believe that liberalization in Shanghai FTZ reform in logistics services and customs services have either met or exceeded their expectations.

However, when compared with some more developed countries, there is still room for improvement in terms of clearance efficiency. Clearance management in China involves many stakeholders. Even though the Single Window scheme has significantly simplified the clearance procedures and the so-called "three mutuals" — "mutual exchange of information, mutual recognition of supervision and mutual assistance of law enforcement" —is set for better synergy, cross-departmental and inner-departmental coordination could be further strengthened to ensure more efficient clearance and consistent law enforcement.

Shanghai is in a leading position compared with other regions in China when it comes to the so called hard ware. Law enforcement, IPR protection, administrative efficiency and the building of industry clusters that may favor start-up businesses rank high when compared with other cities and regions in China. Nevertheless, there are still obstacles that Shanghai need to overcome to create a favorable environment for investment, compared with international metropolises in areas that are generally referred to as software.

The European Chamber appreciates Shanghai's effort to reduce administrative challenges to talent mobility for both foreigners and local talent without a Shanghai *hukou*. However, these are not yet far reaching enough to create a welcoming international environment that would increase Shanghai's attractiveness for top local and global talent, especially as young talent is concerned.

As China's largest trading partner, the EU represents about 15% of the country's trade. China needs the EU as much as the EU needs China. As the representative of the European business in China, a thriving trade and investment relationship between EU and China is at our heart. The European Chamber Shanghai Chapter as well as our members will continue contributing to making this relationship successful not only to the benefit of both European and Chinese companies but also to that of consumers and more widely citizens of both China and EU member states.

I would like to take this opportunity to announce that our 2nd version of *Shanghai Position Paper* will be released in four days. Many of the issues we discuss today are exactly the issues raised by our members. I'm happy to share a copy with you and have further discussion.

System Integration and Coordinated Innovation: Some Relationships That Should be Dealt With for the Reform of China (Shanghai) Pilot Free Trade Zone

Zhang Yong

Former Director-general of the Policy Research Bureau of

China (Shanghai) Pilot Free Trade Zone Administration Office

Zheng Hai'ao

Deputy Director-General at the Policy Research Bureau of China (Shanghai)

Pilot Free Trade Zone Administration

In the last three years, guided by the principle of "active exploration, bold attempt and independent reform", China (Shanghai) Pilot Free Trade Zone has been focusing on institutional reform and trying to design reform plans and implement reform measures for the whole administrative division of Pudong New Area, thus creating a promising situation in which opening-up drives forward government reform, and reform and innovation pushes forward economic transformation and development, and providing many replicable and applicable experience for the construction and reform of other free trade zones in China. When looking forward, we should bear in mind the fundamental goals of the reform in China (Shanghai) Pilot Free Trade Zone, and continue to follow the guidance from the central government, abide by international rules and meet companies' needs. In this way, China (Shanghai) Pilot Free Trade Zone will become the best practice zone of Five Development Concepts (innovation, coordination, green development, opening up, and sharing), will be a higher-level bridge head for two-way opening-up, will function as an important base serving "the Belt and Road" initiative and other strategies, and will turn into a significant platform for supply-side structural reform. We also should be modest and behave like a beginner to continue our voyage of making breakthroughs with full passion. In this process, we need to deal with nine relationships in the reform in China (Shanghai) Pilot Free Trade Zone.

First, the relationship between trade and financial, investment and government reforms. Shanghai Free Trade Zone is not just about trading. Its highlights lie in financial reform and innovation, and reforms of investment and commercial affairs system. Promoting trade facilitation should be accompanied by foreign exchange reform. Trade pattern upgrading can lead to the change in the enterprises' layout of global supply chain, and will have positive impact on attracting foreign capitals and our overseas investment. Expanding the opening in trade, investment and financial areas require more on government's governance and risk management ability, so the reform of government should be intensified.

Second, the relationship between three figures, i.e. 28 sq.km, 120 sq.km and 1, 200 sq.km.China (Shanghai) Pilot Free Trade Zone integrates 28 sq.km bonded zone and the other 92 sq.km areas including Lujiazui Financial and Trade Zone, Shanghai Jinqiao Economic and Technological Development Zone, the World Expo Zone and Zhangjiang Hi-Tech Park. The bonded zone is a customs special supervision area with physical fences. And it enjoys the highest level of opening-up in the whole 120 sq.km free trade zone. In particular, Yangshan Free Trade Port Area has all the possibilities of becoming a free port area in real terms thanks to its inherent advantages. The expansion of China (Shanghai) Pilot Free Trade Zone to Lujiazui and other wealthy areas where little land is left for development indicates that Shanghai prioritizes institutional reform of the free trade zone, rather than foreign investment attraction or land development. A number of reform measures can be implemented in the 92 sq.km area, where lots of mature companies including financial institutions, R&D organizations and innovative businesses are based. Their demands are connected with the reform of China (Shanghai) Pilot Free Trade Zone. Set Pudong New Area as a whole, the Administration Office of China (Shanghai) Pilot Free Trade Zone has been co-located with Pudong New Area People's Government since April 2015. This integration of the operation of 1 200 sq.km Pudong New Area and that of the free trade zone taking up 1/10 of the area can generate several effects. Firstly, it enables the replication and application of the reform experiences in China (Shanghai) Pilot Free Trade Zone. Secondly, co-location greatly integrates administrative resources, ensures the main body shouldering due responsibilities and make Pudong New Area take the lead in the construction of China

(Shanghai) Pilot Free Trade Zone. Thirdly, it can help to reform the local administration system at the next higher level with the idea implemented in China (Shanghai) Pilot Free Trade Zone so that officials of Pudong New Area will absorb the new idea and use it to guide and propel their work.

Thirdly, the relationship between opening-up, reform and development. At present, opening-up now is a two-way activity, in which we need to attract both capitals and R&D from abroad. What we aspire more is to develop China (Shanghai) Pilot Free Trade Zone into a breeding ground of innovation and the center of resource allocation. The opening-up of China (Shanghai) Pilot Free Trade Zone should conform to international rules, so we are supposed to improve our administration mode on the basis of in-depth study on TiSA, TPP and other demanding investment and trade rules. This reflects that opening-up can advance reform. If we isolate ourselves from the outside, hardly can we find how far we lag behind others. In contrast, expanding opening enables us to realize the remaining gap between us and best practices in the world in terms of government's administration mode, institutional structure, ability and etc. To narrow the gap, we need to carry out reforms.

When it comes to development, China (Shanghai) Pilot Free Trade Zone does not focus much on GDP, tax revenues, growth rate or other figures, but emphasizes a lot on institutional reform. If we can attain achievements through institutional reform and improve business environment, the economic development in China (Shanghai) Pilot Free Trade Zone will be much better than the past. This is what we are pursuing. From the first quarter to even the first half of 2016, the growth of Pudong's fiscal revenue has been at the record high. This is partly contributed by the institutional reform of the China (Shanghai) Pilot Free Trade Zone.

Fourth, the relationship between the government, market and society. In the reform of China (Shanghai) Pilot Free Trade Zone, we should clarify the boundary of the government and the market, so that each side is cleat about its responsibility. The negative list tells us that "we can do whatever as long as they are not banned by the law". The essence of the concept is to let the market make decisions on all that have not been prohibited by the list, and provide adequate space for the market to launch innovation.

The government's administration mode is changing fundamentally, which is mainly reflected by the shift from approval system to filing system. Following that, the

提升投资贸易便利化水平，构建开放型经济新体制

government is transforming from regulation-oriented to service-oriented. The priority of government service is maintaining a fair and transparent market environment. The government should crack down "fake innovation" while supporting real innovation. As economic activities are increasingly sophisticated and the society is more mature, the government alone is not able to fulfil all the responsibilities. For example, market regulation and social management need the effort of the whole society. We should let the market players run their business legally and restrain themselves, let trade associations and other organizations realize autonomy and self-discipline, let all social forces participate in regulation, and ultimately, set up an in-process and post supervision system which is based on polycentric governance and comprehensive regulation, and is supported by multi-level and all-round government regulation.

Fifth, the relationship between simplifying, administration and safeguarding. The essence is to handle the relationship between the government and the market. "Simplifying" means do more to streamline administration and delegate more powers to lower-level governments and to society in general. This is to let the market play a decisive role in resource allocation. "Administration" means the government should play its role better instead of more. In particular, the government should enhance its in-process and ex post administration on market operation, social management, public services, environmental protection and other areas to avoid systemic and regional risks. Greater simplification in China (Shanghai) Pilot Free Trade Zone requires more on improving regulation. This is a stress test. In the test, China (Shanghai) Pilot Free Trade Zone needs to find out its weaknesses. What we should do is drawing experience not only about what the zone can do, but also what it can't.

Sixth, the relationship between supply-side reform and China (Shanghai) Pilot Free Trade Zone. In this year's National People's Congress (NPC) and the National Committee of the Chinese People's Political Consultative Conference (CPPCC), Yang Xiong, the then Mayor of Shanghai pointed out that China (Shanghai) Pilot Free Trade Zone was the platform for Shanghai to promote the supply-side structural reform. So we need to analyze the relationship between system supply and enterprise growth. The supply-side reform is to reduce the supply of low-end products and increase that of high-end products, which depends on enterprises. The supply of high-end products is driven by scientific and technological innovation and is supported by talents. Enterprises' vigour and impetus come from government's institutional reform and the improvement of business environment. Thus, the government can play a major role in supply-side reform. All the pilot programs in China (Shanghai) Pilot Free Trade Zone are serving the reform by cutting down institutional transaction cost. This can all be found in financial, investment and trade reform.

Seventh, the relationship between international rules, national pilot projects and regional practices. Conformation with international rules is of great importance. Study on China (Shanghai) Pilot Free Trade Zone was started in as early as 2009, but the approval has not been granted until 2013. One of the main reasons for the establishment of China (Shanghai) Pilot Free Trade Zone is the dramatic change in the international economic landscape. In the BIT negotiation, the US expressed its wish that China should pledge to enforce the mode of "pre-establishment national treatment + negative list" for foreign investment. As a regional practice, China (Shanghai) Pilot Free Trade Zone embodies out inclination to open ourselves to other countries. This is the fulfilment of promise. Our mission is on behalf of China, we conforms to international rules and take part in global competition through the national pilot project implemented by local authorities.

Eighth, the relationship between major breakthroughs, one-sided development and top-level design, and system integration. Top-level design and system integration have always been an important part of our goals. Someone criticized that the reform in China (Shanghai) Pilot Free Trade Zone were unsystematic or illogic, and even somewhat fragmented. This is what we need to improve. In addition, we do not have much individual reform experience in the past, including pilot projects launched before the establishment of China (Shanghai) Pilot Free Trade Zone, do not have the initiative and one-sided development which can be found in some enterprises and agencies, or do not have some reforms that have delivered major breakthroughs. Thus, we lack a foundation for top-level design and system integration. When taking next step, we should focus on designing reform plan in a systemic way like stringing pearl necklace. Of a particular note, we need to make a general reform plan to be enforced three years later, and encourage companies and agencies to make step-by-step advancement under the framework of reform.

Ninth, the relationship between China (Shanghai) Pilot Free Trade Zone, "Four Centers", and Sci-tech Innovation Center. Before the establishment of China (Shanghai) Pilot Free Trade Zone, though Shanghai was labelled as an international financial center, it was indeed a domestic one. After the establishment of China (Shanghai) Pilot Free Trade Zone, Shanghai's international finance center is provided with support, directions and means. One of the financial openness innovation in China (Shanghai) Pilot Free Trade Zone is the "electronic fence" that regulates capital flows replacing the physical fence of bonded areas. This is the FTU-Free Trade Accounting Unit. The introduction of the idea of "To ease control on the first line, and to have effective and efficient control on the second line" is the key principle for those diverse financial markets under construction in China (Shanghai) Pilot Free Trade Zone, including crude oil, gold, stocks, bonds and foreign exchange markets that facing foreign investors. Finally, the interaction between the science and technology innovation center and China (Shanghai) Pilot Free Trade Zone enables the interaction between scientific and technological innovation, institutional innovation, financial innovation and open innovation. We hope through the interaction, Shanghai will become a highland for international innovation, and gather scientists, entrepreneurs and other elites all around the world to make their contribution here.

Enhancing Investment and Trade Facilitation for Emerging Economic Sectors in Shanghai

Li Guangyu

McKinsey & Company

As China's economy is further integrated into the world economy, tremendous changes have taken place in its international trade structure in recent years, with continued declines in the share of traditional processing trade and rapid increases in the share of trading activities with high technology contents and high added value. This also has substantially impacted China's real economy.

In such a context, how Shanghai, as a key growth engine of China's economy and an icon for international trading, will better adapt to the new economic environment and the trends of international trade is essential to its building of an open economy and the transformation and upgrades of its industrial structure. Of the many policy targets set by the government, how to enhance investment and trade facilitation is a topic to delve into for the moment.

1. Trends: Trade in Goods and Services Featuring High Technology Contents and Added Value will Become Major Growth Points

It has been observed that the world trade will embrace explosive growth in the next 3—4 decades, with the volume for 2050 expected to be 8 times that of 2010, in which the share of emerging markets, particularly those in Asia, will grow substantially to 50%.

As a result, the international trade landscape will undergo deep restructuring. First, the growth in trade in goods will stem more from products featuring high technology contents and added value. Our observation shows that the top 5 manufacturing segments by the growth of trading value around 2015 were shipbuilding, pharmaceuticals manufacturing, chemicals, medical equipment and synthetic fiber chemicals. In comparison, by 2030, it is expected that the growth will be dominated by manufacturing segments featuring high technology and added value such as advanced robotics, autonomous cars, wearable medical equipment, new generation genetic drugs and high-performance new composite materials. Second, our lateral comparison finds that the compound annual growth rate (CAGR) of trade in services exports in China from 2007 to 2012 was close to 10%, much higher than developed countries such as the U.S. (6%), Germany (4%) and the U.K. (0.7%). Certainly, we should come to beware that China (USD 566 billion) is still far behind the developed Western economies such as the U.S. (USD 2298 billion), Germany (USD 1196 billion) and the U.K. (USD 1014 billion), indicating great potential and room for China to upgrade its trade in services and keep up with the advanced level, especially the knowledge-based trade in services including consulting services, financial services and R&D outsourcing services.

2. Outlook for Shanghai's Future Industrial Landscape: Shaping a New Industrial Eco-system

Shanghai's industrial landscape is currently driven by two wheels: the manufacturing industry dominated by electronic information, automobile, complete-set equipment, oil and fine chemicals, and the services industry led by financial services, retailing and wholesaling, real estate and information technology.

Yet in the following decade, the industrial landscape of Shanghai will present three key trends driven by technological innovation: (1) Manufacturing with higher technology contents: to enhance the technology contents of the manufacturing industry as a whole by focusing on high-tech products and key links of the manufacturing chain. (2) Services with greater added value: as trade in services accounts for a higher share in trade as a whole, the added value will rise dramatically; the high-end services sector, especially those boasting high contents of human capital (e.g. R&D outsourcing and industrial design) will gain ground, with the level of professionalism continuing to rise. (3) Technological innovation boosting crossover integration: various industries will be connected through technological innovation in different ways, boosting cross-industrial and cross-industry chain integration, and blurring the distinction between the services industry and the manufacturing industry.

Given the above three trends, we anticipate that by 2025, Shanghai will witness a new industrial eco-system with technical services, financial services, culture and entertainment, healthcare, new generation information technology, biomedicine, high-end outfits, new materials and new energy automobiles as the core, thereby completing the transformation and upgrades of traditional industries towards new industries.

3. Improvement and Upgrades of Business Climate: From "Hardware Facilitation" to "Software Facilitation"

In view of these features of the new economic and industrial landscape, Shanghai needs to redefine the investment and trade facilitation, creating a business climate that is more humane, transparent and convenient.

Overall, to achieve the investment and trade facilitation that is more aligned with the times and the international level, Shanghai needs to transform the facilitation priorities from providing "hardware facilities" to providing software environment. Since its inception three years ago, China (Shanghai) Pilot Free Trade Zone has made progress in facilitating software environment such as investment management, trade facilitation and liberalization of financial and services industries, which lays a solid foundation for it to realize more comprehensive facilitation of software environment in the future. However, there is still evident weakness to be overcome in aspects as follows: (1) in terms of overall liberalization, there are limited new policies to make breakthroughs but many policies to relax standards, and the services industry, especially the high-end one, features a low level of liberalization; (2) with regard to supporting policies and legislative support, existing policies and regulations are introduced by different authorities and feature a limited coverage, failing to reflect the whole picture. For instance, as for Chinese-invested foreign ships piloting the coastal shipping, the Ministry of Transport has clearly set it out in its documents and companies such as CSCL and COSCO have carried out the pilot program. However, supporting schemes still need to be studied and formulated since this policy involves many authorities such as the Customs, Inspection and Quarantine authorities, and port authorities[1];

---

[1]   Wang Xiaoyu, Summary of China (Shanghai) Free Trade Zone's Policies and Measures for Promoting Investment and Trade Facilitation, Post-doctoral Workstation of the Development Research Center of Shanghai Municipal People's Government.

(3) in terms of administration efficiency, the division of administration powers has not been straightened out between the central government and local governments, and the latter have not been fully empowered in the pilot program of free trade zones. In Shanghai (China) Pilot Free Trade Zone, for example, "to study and refine the tax policy to adapt to the overseas equity investments and offshore business development" was once proposed in its general plan, but no final plan has been introduced up till now[1], although the Management Board has conducted in-depth research jointly with the central finance and taxation authorities. At the local government level, Shanghai now adopts the single window service model, which is unable to create the holistic advantage since only a limited number of authorities could be covered and a few functions could be achieved. Moreover, the city lags far behind in selecting the target model of the single window and standardizing data elements[2]; (4) in terms of risk control and regulatory efficiency, Shanghai is still reliant heavily on human efforts for risk control, with information not integrated or made transparent. The regulatory efficiency is poor due to duplicate regulation. For example, although the municipal Customs has adopted the paperless clearance model, local tax authorities still require submission of written documents. Further, data formats have not been harmonized and failed to meet the internationally recognized standards. As a result, the facilitation of customs clearance has been compromised and international cooperation has become more difficult[3].

To be specific, Shanghai is advised to commit itself to a few key measures for trade facilitation as follows:(1) to form a legal basis well geared to the international standards for the ultimate purpose of trade facilitation; (2) to build a more applicant-friendly Customs clearance system, consisting of pre-determination, pre-examination, post-audit and advanced release; (3) to establish an e-government system based on standard data elements, which features a single window and integrated collaboration;

---

[1] Li Kun et al., Interfacing with New Rules of International Trade and Accelerating the Reforms in Pilot Free Trade Zones, Internal References, Issue 16 for 2016.

[2] Chen Lifen, Problems with Trade Facilitation in China (Shanghai) Free Trade Zone as Observed from Applicable Standards under Pertinent Agreements, Institute of Circulation and Consumption of the Ministry of Commerce.

[3] Chen Lifen, Problems with Trade Facilitation in China (Shanghai) Free Trade Zone as Observed from Applicable Standards under Pertinent Agreements, Institute of Circulation and Consumption of the Ministry of Commerce.

(4) to establish a classified regulatory mechanism for enterprises and goods; (5) to work out a more flexible and attractive financial and taxation system; (6) to cultivate more convenient means of capital flows such as cross-border investment and financing; (7) to introduce more humanistic visa, residence and practitioner policies; (8) to establish a full-fledged system for risk parameter maintenance, risk alert and risk control; (9) to foster a more diversified and open space for fusion of different cultures; and (10) to build more inclusive and innovative public media ambience for trials and errors.

4. Leading Practice: Breaking New Grounds and Creating New Models for Trade Facilitation

More often than not, the global leading practices are bold to break new grounds, and initiate and apply new technologies, so as to create the new models to boost investment and trade facilitation for the emerging economic sectors. Singapore, New York and Ireland are three typical regions that have succeeded in this regard:

(1) Singapore: e-government system facilitates corporate services.

Singapore started to build its e-government system in the 1980's and has now become one of the countries boasting the most advanced e-government functionalities. In the 1990's, the Singapore Computer Society implemented three national information technology programs, laying a solid foundation for the launch of its e-government system.

The e-government system in Singapore not only enables data sharing and e-government services to citizens and enterprises, but also establishes an Online Business Licensing System (OBLS), which ramps up the service efficiency of the government. The OBLS significantly saves the length of time needed to apply for a business license (only 1day at the fastest) and reduces the government's operating costs by more than 10 million US dollars. Singapore's Trade Net is a typical sophisticated office system worldwide that features "single window" mechanism and also the world's first electronic data exchange system used to review trading data. Characterized by "integrated system for scattered institutions", this system connects 35 governmental departments in Singapore, such as tax authorities and custom house, and presents itself as the "single window" for international investment and trade through automated handling of documents. Besides, the Singaporean government has fundamentally simplified the service process of the Customs. For instance, tariff is levied on 4 types of merchandise only; no declaration to the Customs is required for goods in 6 free trade zones in Singapore before they go to market. All these have significantly enhanced the Customs clearance efficiency.

(2) New York (US) : data openness fuels business innovation.

29 February 2012 saw NYC pass the Open Data Bill, and on 7 March, the then mayor Michael Rubens Bloomberg signed this bill into law, which was the first time in the US history that the large-scale opening of government data had been incorporated into legislation. According to the Open Data Bill, all the data obtained by the NYC government and its branches and sub-branches must be opened to the public by 2018, excluding those relating to security and privacy. Furthermore, the government has stipulated expressly that no procedures of registration and approval are required prior to use of such data and that no restrictions will be imposed on the use of these data.

Various types of government data now open for public access have become a source of inspiration for NYC's annual "BigApps" event. Just about one year after NYC opened its data for public access, hundreds of app development teams have been built, all centered on the open data platform. With the passenger and traffic data in relevant boroughs, they can help SMEs formulate their marketing strategies. With the resident and merchant data in the region, they can help start-ups to work out the start-up strategies and reduce the threshold of investment.

By legislating the openness of governmental data on a large scale, NYC aims to enhance the efficiency of social services and fuel the creation of potential business value, in a bid to accomplish its vision to build a "smart city".

Another comparable instance is the openness of GPS. In 1983, the US opened to the public the access to the GPS that was formerly applied as a satellite positioning system to serve the military purposes, and after 2000, the government called off its restrictions on the precision of GPS for civil use. After the access was opened to the public, the GPS has supported production and people's life, ranging from auto navigation and precision farming to logistics and communications, and created numerous employment opportunities. Estimations show that about 3 million job posts in America alone are dependent on GPS directly or indirectly.

(3) Ireland: a full spectrum of services boosts the solicitation for business investment.

Due to the global financial crisis in 2008, the Irish government adopted a series of policies and measures, and selected in a forward-looking way and for the strategic consideration a myriad of industries relevant to the smart economy as the key industries to be developed in the future. In 2013, Ireland was shortlisted in Forbes' Best Countries for Business. In 2014, Oracle Capital Group released its rankings of "Most Entrepreneurial Countries in 2014", of which Ireland was in the 7th place globally and the 1st place in Europe. This should be attributed to the pivotal role played by the long-term consistency and certainties of the Irish government's policies that encourage high technology and smart economy.

According to the Irish government, the mushrooming of start-ups can create more employment opportunities, drive exports and consequently promote the overall economic growth. Therefore, the Industrial Development Agency Ireland has been founded to support the companies with immense potential for business growth. So far, the Agency with more than 700 staff has set up branches and sub-branches in over 30 countries.

Meanwhile, the Irish government has set up project-specific departments relevant to the key industries to be developed to enhance the professionalism of service providers, track major investors all along, understand business demands and provide directional talent and policy interfacing services. In talent recruitment, for example, given the talent bottleneck encountered by technology enterprises in building presence in Ireland, the Industrial Development Agency Ireland has interviewed 300 Irish engineers around the world and selected 85 excellent candidates, successfully helping the technical innovation enterprises overcome the shortage of talents.

5. Conclusion

According to China's 13th Five-Year Plan, Shanghai is expected to grow into an international economic, financial, trading and shipping center by 2020 and also a technical innovation hub with global influences. What's more, the Plan makes it clear that Shanghai should improve the quality of the free trade zone, further liberalize the services industry, enhance trade facilitation, and drive financial liberalization

提升投资贸易便利化水平，构建开放型经济新体制

and innovation. Shanghai will shoulder the significant responsibilities for economic development and technical innovation in the coming five years.

Looking into 2040, Shanghai will grow into an excellent global city, fascinating for its innovation capability, distinct culture and ecological progress. Shanghai should play a leading role for the rest of the country, keeping abreast of the developments of the new economy and industrial landscape, drawing on leading practices, breaking new grounds and forging ahead in mechanisms and systems, and further enhancing investment and trade facilitation, in a bid to build a more attractive business environment that is fit for the development of the new economy and geared to international standards.

Global Standard, China Speed: Recommendations for Investment and Trade Facilitation in Shanghai

Yvonne Zhou

Global Partner and Managing Director, Boston Consulting Group

Leo Li

Partner and Managing Director, Boston Consulting Group

At present, the global economy is going through setbacks and fluctuations. Conservatism is on the rise together with trade protection in the United States, the European Union and other developed countries, as manifested in the anti-dumping and countervailing duty policies launched one after another. The new US President Donald Trump, as an advocate of trade protectionism, abandoned the Trans-Pacific Partnership (TPP) at the very beginning of his administration. Economic growth in developing countries start to slow down as record lows have been witnessed in Russia, Brazil and South Africa, all of which are BRICS countries; and what stands out from such an economic slowdown are structural problems such as heavy dependence on natural resources and serious market externalization.

There are more and more uncertainties in our global economy today, but China, while deepening its domestic reforms continuously, has been conveying its firm determination for and strong confidence in building an open economy once and again to the entire world. In his keynote speech at the opening ceremony of the 2016 B20 Summit, Chairman Xi Jinping said, "We will continue to be fully involved in economic globalization and support the multilateral trading regime. We will expand access for foreign investment, facilitate such investment, promote fair and open competition and create a sound business environment." In the meantime, the Belt and Road Initiative, the Asian Infrastructure Investment Bank and various free trade zones are also making rapid progress. Through the Silk Road Economic Belt and the Maritime Silk Road,

China has established new global partnership with more than 60 countries along the routes, fostering political mutual trust, economic integration and cultural inclusiveness. The Asia Infrastructure Investment Bank, with more than 90 member countries by the end of this year, will make its contribution to the infrastructure connectivity and economic integration in Asia. The Shanghai Pilot Free Trade Zone (the FTZ), established in 2013, has completed two rounds of expansion and now covers up to 11 parts. It aims at incorporating more and more fields, creating greater capacities for opening-up and aligning with the new rules of international trade and investment. With all these moves, China conveys its firm belief in building an open and transparent global trade and investment governance with joint efforts.

In the grand new picture of China's economic development and opening-up, Shanghai gathers high hopes from the central government as a trailblazer for the country in its pursuit of innovation and development. According to the master plan of the city, Shanghai aims to become an "excellent global city" and a major city of the world in terms of economy, finance, trade, shipping, science and technological innovation and culture by 2040. As we can see, following its 12th Five-Year Plan, Shanghai once again emphasizes itself as an international trade center, and this clearly indicates how much importance it attaches to investment and trade.

Over the past decades, Shanghai has always been a forerunner in the opening-up of China and has achieved considerably in international investment and trade.

In 1984, Shanghai, as one of the first coastal open cities of China, Shanghai was allowed to open its doors to larger and more forms of foreign investment. In 1990, the Waigaoqiao Bonded Area became the first of its kind launched in China and the first "national import trade promotion and innovation demonstration area." In 2005, Yangshan Bonded Port Area was established as the first bonded port area across the country and as the first attempt for the implementation of the free trade zone policy. In 2013, Shanghai Free Trade Zone was created, again the first of its kind in China, and it paves the way for customs facilitation and investment liberalization.

In terms of foreign investment and trade, Shanghai has always been in the lead in China. In 2015, Shanghai's total import and export registered USD 449.2 billion, and the actual foreign direct investment reached USD 18.4 billion, surpassing other first-tier cities such as Beijing, Shenzhen and Guangzhou. In the global market, Shanghai has also taken a strong foothold with the port cargo import and export volume accounting for 3.4% of the world's total in 2015, overtaking Hong Kong, Singapore and many other international trade centers.

However, when compared with better-developed international trade centers, Shanghai now faces challenges of insufficient foreign-invested headquarters and a relatively low proportion of trade in services.

The regional headquarters of multinational companies have a strong pulling effect on the economy as a whole and they are the best players among all foreign-funded enterprises. Shanghai has been encouraging foreign investment to develop headquarters economy since 2002, but it still lags behind many other international metropolises in terms of the number and economic strength of headquarters. By 2014, Shanghai hosted 470 headquarters, fewer than Tokyo (531), Hong Kong (1389) and Singapore (4200), which are also major cities in the Asia-Pacific region. Also, in terms of economic strength, nearly one third of the Fortune 500 companies have regional headquarters in Singapore, mostly comprehensive headquarters of the Asia-Pacific region with full functions; while in Shanghai, only 7% of headquarters are Asia-Pacific headquarters and most of the others are China headquarters or headquarters with a single function (e.g. R&D center).

Trade in services has seen better development in Shanghai than in many other regions of China but problems remain. For example, trade in services has a relatively small share and its structure remains unbalanced. In 2014, Shanghai's import and export of services accounted for 50% of its GDP, lower than the corresponding figures of Hong Kong (62%) and Singapore (92%). Meanwhile, labor-intensive services such as transportation and tourism are the main contributors, accounting for more than 70% of the total; while innovative high-end services with high value-add, such as financial and insurance services, cultural services and specialized services, have only a small share in the overall structure with slow development.

Such a situation, we believe, can be attributed to inadequate facilitations in three aspects: market access, border control, and environment for business operation.

(1) Market access: Limited openness for investment. The current negative list of 2015 is long with up to 122 special management measures, while the common practice of the international community is to have shorter lists. The model bilateral investment treaty (BIT) of the United States, for example, has only some 20 items. High-end industries such as finance, Internet services, culture and entertainment are still subject to many restrictions in terms of the proportion of shares held by foreign investors and the

years allowed for business operation, among others, with breakthroughs yet to come. Some special management measures remain obscure with insufficient descriptions regarding restrictions. For example, rating services and large theme parks are restricted business areas, but terms and conditions remain unclear as in what the restrictions are and how strong they will turn out to be.

(2) Border control: Easier customs procedures for businesspeople. Businesspeople are the major part in international trade and how efficient and easy they travel is a major indicator of investment and trade facilitation. However, Shanghai currently aims mainly to promote the efficiency of customs clearance of import and export goods in its effort to improve border control, while fewer measures are taken to streamline customs procedures for the easier flow of people.

(3) Business environment: Inadequate liberalization of financial services. The current financial mechanisms are subject to various limitations and better support is needed for capital operations and cross-border business operations. For example, progress has been slow towards market-based interest rates and the timeline remains unclear for the reform of exchange rate formation mechanism and a convertible capital account. Also, for existing financial innovations, the scope of application is limited, and they are not yet widely used in Shanghai. Free trade accounts (FT accounts), for instance, are available only within the FTZ, while enterprises outside the FTZ cannot have such accounts or enjoy any benefit brought about by this and other financial innovations.

To effectively meet these challenges and to further facilitate investment and trade, we offer the following three recommendations to the Shanghai municipal government to fully unleash the competitiveness of the city.

(1) Shorten the negative list, mainly focus on extending openness towards higher-level services, and make the list standard and transparent.

It is recommended that the negative list should contain fewer prohibited and restricted industries for foreign investment. In western developed countries, the negative list for foreign investment contains only industries related to national defense and homeland and resource security. For Shanghai, the focus should be placed on opening up high-end service industries such as non-banking financial services, commercial services, specialized technical services, education, healthcare, culture and entertainment, so as to boost the development of service industry and trade in services. Meanwhile, restrictions can be based on reciprocity. The model BIT of the United

States, for example, has seven reciprocity-based items, which means if the other party of a BIT opens these fields to investment from the United States, the United States will also do so in return.

Special management measures should contain provisions specifying the level of government authorities in charge and the legal basis. They should be connected and coordinated well with relevant domestic law so as to enhance the standardization and consistency. Restrictions should be described in detail and in a more refined manner so that they are clear to investors and easier to use. Moreover, the negative list should be made more transparent and various stakeholders should be encouraged to participate in the formulation process of such list and fully express their opinions.

(2) Simplify visa application for business people, offer better one-stop services for relevant procedures, and build the capacity for delivering e-government services in English.

Pilot programs may be launched to issue special business travel cards to qualified people to stay within the FTZ and for longer periods. For this purpose, reference may be drawn from the APEC Business Travel Card Scheme. Cardholders with valid passports will not need to apply for visas within three years and will have access to a special fast-track for entry and exit. In addition, there should be a flexible system for the conversion between business visa and work/residence visa to enhance the cross-border mobility of talents.

Application procedures for employment permit should be simplified and the validity period should be extended, perhaps to three years or to as long as the relevant work contract lasts. Currently, similar documents are required for the application for the work permit and residence permit for foreigners and the residence permit for non-Shanghai residents, but applications are handled by different authorities. It may be advisable to integrate the three applications to make things easier. For example, in Singapore, foreigners need only one permit, i.e. job permit or business permit, to live and work in the country, and both permits are issued by the same authorities, the Ministry of Manpower.

The capacity to provide e-government services in English needs to be enhanced. Various government authorities of Shanghai have already offered a number of services online, but there are still few corresponding English websites and where such websites do exist, they usually have fewer functions. We suggest, therefore, that the Shanghai municipal government, based on the existing e-government systems, enhance its capacity to deliver services in foreign languages so as to make it easier for foreigners to go through various administrative formalities online.

(3) Give full play to the FTZ as an experimental field to further deepen financial innovation and promote successful experience across Shanghai so as to enhance financial service capability for enterprises.

Shanghai Pilot Free Trade Zone should be given full play as the experimental field of financial reform. The reform towards market-based interest rates should be advanced step by step, with expanded target scopes and allowances and methodically reduced deposit-reserve ratio. Deposit insurance should be vigorously promoted so as to enhance the market discipline on the banking system and to stabilize the financial market. Also, diverse financing methods should be made available so as to enhance the capacity of delivering financial services to enterprises. This may be done by expediting the issuance of Panda debt in the FTZ, providing more affordable financing options and facilitating RMB internationalization. The construction of a trading platform for commodity derivatives should be expedited so as to open up international trading channels for commodities financing and hedging for enterprises in the FTZ.

Encourage other parts of Shanghai to borrow the successful experience of the FTZ. For example, we may speed up the progress in making FT accounts available to enterprises and individuals (especially foreigners) outside the FTZ so that cross-border settlement of home and foreign currencies, overseas financing, cross-border certificate of deposit and other financial services can be more easily available, capital mobility can be enhanced and the financing costs reduced. Such accounts can also enable foreigners to receive wealth management services, overseas health care, overseas education for their children, and other cross-border financial services, which will enhance the attractiveness to talents. Other successful experiences include centralized management of foreign exchange funds for multinational companies, two-way cross-border RMB cash pooling, cancellation of foreign debt approval for financial leasing business, cancellation of administrative approvals on external security. In the meantime, it is necessary to strengthen supervision and risk prevention so as to avoid hot money inflows and capital arbitrage caused by wide promotion of more financial options.

The prospect is that Shanghai will catch up with or even surpass New York, London, Tokyo and other international metropolises, and advance towards an "excellent global city" with firm steps.

From the Perspective of Service Enterprise to Explore New Opportunities in Shanghai under New Globalization Trends

Cliff Yu

CEO of Capgemini China

Alva Qian

COO, Capgemini China

Our international think tank selects related topics for research and discussion each year. I have served in a foreign enterprise that specializes in investment services for many years, and I have witnessed two waves of transformation in the global IT service sector. As the seminar topic is on "strengthening trade and investment facilitation in Shanghai," I shall return to my own profession to approach trade facilitation under new global trends by discussing how Shanghai's technology and innovative services facilitate the development of trade.

In the past decade, China has been one of the developing countries benefiting from globalization. Shanghai has used its advantages and intelligence to build competitiveness that is unique to the city, from industrial upgrading, financial and technology innovation to the "Belt and Road" international cooperation initiative. However, as trade protectionism gains ground in certain parts of the world, regionalism has begun to emerge. This trend will impact many open economies that rely on trade for growth. For instance, the Singaporean government has lowered the estimate of its economic growth rate for 2016 by 1%—1.5% in November.

Although regional trade protectionism challenges the progress of trade globalization, China is actively advancing into the world as its second largest economy while many developing countries, regions, and organizations have also formed groups for common interest. In this transition period, only the qualified have what it takes for

提升投资贸易便利化水平，构建开放型经济新体制

development. For Shanghai, with its historical development, strategic location, and diversity and internationality, globalization means new opportunities.

A new opportunity lies in China's "Belt and Road" initiative. The "Belt and Road" concept connects over 60 nations in Eurasia and it is a combination of the "Silk Road Economic Belt" and the "Maritime Silk Road" as well as a new blueprint for globalization. The Belt and Road will redefine the relationship between land and sea. China and Europe are each other's most important trading partners and as they are located at the two ends of Belt and Road, they shoulder the responsibility of the "new balance." To ensure mutual prosperity in the new status, the two major economies require sustained long-term communication, negotiation, trial and error, and adjustments. This open attitude and innovation ability are not readily present in all cities along Belt and Road. Under the guidance of the central government, the demonstrative and leading roles of top cities are especially critical. Shanghai is located at the geopolitical intersection where Belt meets Road. Its acceptance of diversity, practical innovative qualities, and business capabilities accumulated throughout centuries make Shanghai the ideal choice for the top city, and an example to be followed by all cities along the Belt and Road.

Enterprises are the vessels for trade. If Shanghai is to be a top city for Belt and Road, then corporate headquarters must be the locomotives for trade. Between China and Europe, and between Shanghai and Paris/Berlin, numerous multinational corporations are scrambling to adapt to the new status. Capgemini is the largest management consulting and IT services provider in Europe. The group's headquarters is in Paris. We have operated in China for over 20 years and the headquarters for the Greater China region is in Shanghai. Capgemini has formed an intangible bridge between Shanghai and Europe that helps European companies enter China as well as help Chinese companies go abroad. This is Capgemini's commitment to clients and to Shanghai.

1. Development of New Headquarters Economy

Shanghai has been promoting the headquarters economy for the past decades. But faced with competition from global industrial upgrades and transformation as well as the opportunities brought forth by "Belt and Road" that connects Europe and Asia, where should we invest our limited supply of high-end talents and invaluable policy support? Our ideas concentrate mainly on the two aspects below:

First, what kind of regional headquarters should we make increased efforts to introduce into Shanghai while ensuring improved trade quality and stabilized trade development? Based on optimistic forecasts in China's consumer market and the positioning of Shanghai's four centers, the introduction of a headquarters economy can help facilitate two broad types of enterprises: The first type includes sectors related to basic consumption such as financial services, entertainment, healthcare, and education; the second type includes sectors related to the promotion of Belt and Road such as high-tech innovation and R&D, and supply chain management. There can be more diversified methods to attract corporate headquarters. Compared to the preparation for long investment cycles required in the past, there are now agile ways such as making use of the convenience of the free trade zone, providing corporate services through integrated digital trade, introducing more high-end services and consumer brands from Europe, and technology brands that emphasize Shanghai's commitment to quality. These methods provide companies with low trial and error costs and allow them to enter the Chinese market quickly and conveniently, make quick adjustments, and secure their places in the market.

Second, how to transform and upgrade the existing regional headquarters that currently resides in Shanghai. Let us first take Capgemini, a high-tech services provider, as an example. Industrialized large-scale development and digitalized corporate innovation are our two engines for development. As Shanghai's overall cost of living rises, it has a certain crowding out effect on young talents. When industrialization and scale-ups are required, companies would opt for nearby areas. In the digitalized corporate innovation sector, we have a strong demand for open innovation platforms and top talents from across the world. Digital innovation remains an important topic for the automobile industry, consumer goods retail, pharmaceuticals, and financial companies we service. My thoughts on the topic will be detailed later in the third part.

2. The Globalization of Chinese Innovation from Foreign-Invested Company

China, the largest consumer market in the world, has become the largest source of revenue for many multinational companies. Take the automobile industry as an example. China became the largest single market for Mercedes Benz for the first time in 2014. Daimler's revenue in China amounted to €14.7 billion in 2015, constituting around 9.8% of the group's overall revenue. In pharmaceuticals, chain retail, IT software/hardware, and entertainment industries, many multinational companies have achieved more revenue in China than in their local markets or any other global markets. The rapid development of internet technology in China has given rise to unprecedented competitors that challenge the traditional hegemonies in basic consumption sectors, and embracing changes and new technology has become the new key words for operation enterprise, all of which have brought about "Chinese Innovation".

Innovation is not a new topic. In the mature European market, Capgemini once worked with Valeo, a designer, manufacturer, and distributor of automotive parts in promoting the "Mov' InBlue™" application that provides institutes and company fleets with short-term car rental services. Valeo provided a patented cloud-based technology that allows smartphones to activate cars and various digitalized services provided by partner networks so as to deliver a seamless and convenient rental experience without the need for physical stores. This innovation has brought changes to Valeo's business model in Europe. Capgemini has tracked the development trends in the global automobile market in "Car Online" for 17 years. China has always been an important market, and the hot topic in 2016 was online car sales, an important trend in the Chinese market. We have seen many automobile companies on the market that tap into major internet e-commerce platforms as well as actively construct their own e-commerce system. We observed that due to the scale and diversity of the Chinese market, many multinational companies have exported their experience in the Chinese market to other countries. The automobile industry is a classic example of foreign enterprise innovation that was activated by a flourishing domestic consumer market. Take a step further, and we shall discover that there are more market development opportunities in the intelligent manufacturing under industry 4.0 and improved production efficiency and user experience through IoT-related technology innovation.

We have talked about innovation in China and manufacturing in China; there are more cases that involve Chinese companies "going abroad". But with the development of the consumer goods market in China, foreign companies' innovations in China have also risen. These types of innovation have inherent international DNA and they can spread and influence the world quickly through their own networks. This influence will create new types of headquarters economy in Shanghai by attracting companies along the "Belt and Road" to their base here.

3. Servicing Large-scale Corporations, from Talents Import to the Global Open Innovation Community

Commercial success and successful innovation of new technologies are based on talents; outstanding leadership and innovative environments are both indispensable. Compared with traditional talents who facilitate technological developments, Shanghai requires a higher level of talents for innovation in face of the new headquarters economy and China's advancement into the world.

But there is a limited supply of top global talents and these types of talents have comparatively lower desire to relocate. For example, experts successful in their fields of study or business often already reside in specific countries. Demand for these types of experts is usually settled through short-term academic exchanges between institutes or by inviting them to speak as distinguished guests in large international seminars hosted in Shanghai. These types of exchanges facilitate only short-term collaborations in knowledge exchange that do not involve economic or business collaborations. The sustainable period is short and private organizations can only achieve limited effects in the society. The depth and magnitude of this type of talent resource applications cannot satisfy demands for open innovation.

Open innovation is a concept that came into play in the second half of the 19th century, and it refers to an organization's external knowledge exchanges for its organizational innovation as well as the ability to adopt new external innovation for its own use and to expand market shares. In the innovation realm that we are accustomed to, enterprises and organizations usually recruit specialized talents, set up laboratories, and encourage staff to make new innovative developments through trial and error as well as rewards in projects. When this demand is magnified to government and social sectors, it evolves into a mechanism for introducing talents. However, in open innovation, organizations need to focus more on the construction of new innovation platforms and invigorate the entire innovation ecosystem of the external organization by redefining partners. The organization can then acquire new innovative technologies, processes, and business models from a vitalized system.

How can organizations construct open innovation ecosystems? Take Capgemini's "Applied Innovation Exchange" concept as an example and observe how companies establish innovation platforms independently. Prior to the establishment of the platform, Capgemini's organization in various countries established many different innovation laboratories and centers of excellence. However, issues in resource sharing and reusability have caused significant problems with repetitive investment and geographical limitations with regard to development capabilities. Therefore, starting from early 2015, the Group's Chief Technology Officer established a set of "Applied Innovation Exchange" mechanisms to standardize the organizational governance structure, external innovation ecosystem management, innovative intelligent property management, and innovative methodologies. The platform established a resource database of global experts and includes not only internal experts of the company but also experts from the entire innovation system, and integrates expert resources through a project-based system. The platform is established in various countries in the form of certification laboratories. They have become Capgemini's incubators for helping multinational companies achieve innovation in business models, management procedures, and customer experiences. As an example, Capgemini has helped the French National Railway Company design an intelligent robotic service system for stations. The long-distance machinery diagnostic applications through smart glasses and projection equipment can be incubated in the laboratories. Capgemini's open corporate innovation platform has won the support of governments in many countries. Capgemini Singapore has received large sums of investments from the Singapore Economic Development Board for the "Applied Innovation Exchange" laboratory.

The current Innovation 2.0 era in Shanghai has enjoyed success in maker space development. According to the 2015 "Shanghai Maker Space Construction and Development Report", there are 71 established business incubators, over 5, 300 of accumulated incubation projects, 149 incubators, and close to 7, 000 incubated enterprises. From another perspective, the maker space development strategy can be a useful tool for helping large-scale foreign companies spread "Chinese innovation". We have seen leading technological and internet companies who have established incubators in the country with support from the government to facilitate domestic innovation. However, many multinational corporations are still reliant on the innovation mechanisms in the headquarters, or they may have diversified trial investments and took the long way around when they explored independently in the Chinese market. At the same time, as we help Chinese companies enter the European market, we also witness their struggles and issues in adapting to innovation they face in connecting with foreign innovation systems including localization, systems, partnerships, and strategic synergy.

In conclusion, under the current status of globalization, the most important tasks include building an innovative system that connects the world, domestic and international entrepreneurs, and independent experts through a social network, making use of the fragmented time of international talents, providing common innovation services that meet the requirements of large corporations, and providing corresponding financial and commercial mechanisms to help companies advance in and out of China in order to create soft power in competition in business, technology, and culture.

提升投资贸易便利化水平，构建开放型经济新体制

Shanghai Set to Promote Investment and Trade Facilitation—Leveraging the Synergy Between Innovation of China (Shanghai) Pilot Free Trade Zone and the Establishment of Global Technological Innovation Center

Liu Minghua

Managing Partner of Eastern China, Audit Partner of Shanghai, China, Deloitte

Rapid progress has been made in globalization since the new century. By joining WTO in 2001, China has become the largest beneficiary of globalization, under which the scale and structure of its import and export have been improved and Chinese industry upgrading has also benefited a lot. However, global developed economies have suffered a long-term recession after the financial crisis in 2008. Both Brexit and the dying TPP after American presidential election indicate that the progress of globalization has been reversed gradually. And it is foreseeable that there will be high trade barriers and huge geopolitical risks for a long period in the future. In light of such international situation, we think it is of great significance to have discussion on promoting investment and trade facilitation.

It has been over three years since 2013 when Premier Li Keqiang urged to establish China (Shanghai) Pilot Free Trade Zone ("Shanghai FTZ"). During this period, Shanghai FTZ has been serving as a bridgehead for institutional innovation in Shanghai and even the whole country. With the implementation of institutional innovation and optimization of approval process, the effect of opening-up in Shanghai FTZ has been further strengthened, leading to stronger confidence of foreign investors and improved investment efficiency and effectiveness. As for its coverage, Shanghai FTZ has enlarged from 28km^2 to 120km^2 after incorporating Lujiazui Financial Area, Jinqiao Export Processing Zone, and Zhangjiang Hi-Tech Park. Meanwhile, Shanghai

FTZ has been regarded as a model by Guangdong, Fujian, and Tianjin to follow its suit.

With Chinese economy entering into a period of new normal, economic transformation has become a matter of great urgency. The 13th Five Year Plan clearly states that "science and technology constitute a primary productive force." Guided by the strategy of "mass entrepreneurship and innovation", Shanghai FTZ will face a new challenge in making a driving effect, e.g. how to integrate its institutional and ecological advantages with the goal of establishing global technological innovation center, in addition to realizing the pre-set goals.

Shanghai Municipal Government has released the implementation plan on accelerating the joint development of Shanghai FTZ and Zhangjiang National Independent Innovation Demonstration Area on November 25, 2016, proposing to utilize the core advantages of the overlapped area for two national strategies to speed up the establishment of a comprehensive national science center with powerful original innovation, and make great efforts to build a sci-tech city featuring open and inclusive innovation environment and highly concentrated innovators. The plan, called "Joint development between Shanghai FTZ and Zhangjiang", aims to address science and technology development issues through institutional innovation and attract organizations to settle down with the help of innovation mechanism, in order to retain capital, technology and talent.

Deloitte believes that Shanghai owns its advantages to establish a global technological innovation center. Firstly, Shanghai and the Yangtze River Delta area are the wealthiest and fastest growing regions in China; secondly, Shanghai is equipped with a good international business environment and efficient and transparent government service mechanism; thirdly, Shanghai enjoys well-developed infrastructure, as well as comprehensive commercial facilities, service facilities and financing facilities; fourthly, Shanghai is becoming more appealing to global top talents; fifthly, Shanghai is still the top choice for multinationals' headquarters and research and development (R&D) centers. Those enterprises are mainly engaged in pillar industries such as smart manufacturing, bio-pharmaceutical, Internet information technology and culture & education service, which are the cores of industry ecosystem and also the driving force for technological innovation.

It is well known that sci-tech innovation is a kind of system engineering.

In addition to the incubation and development of technology, easy financing channels, smooth cargo/service trade, full protection of intellectual property and sound legal environment also matter. We find that the formation of Shanghai sci-tech innovation ecosystem is challenged by the following five factors:

(1) Limited financing method. Currently, the sci-tech innovation-oriented enterprises mainly fund through fiscal appropriation, policy-related loans and commercial bank loans, lack of diversified investment instruments and investors as well as the participation of large-scale risk investment fund and venture capital fund.

(2) Deficient legal environment. There are no well-established laws and regulations in relation to intellectual property protection or so.

(3) Lack of professional services. Professional service organizations engaged in technology advisory, fintech and others rarely appear in Shanghai's sci-tech innovation ecosystem, hence there are no high-quality organizations to deliver services concerning tax, insurance and asset evaluation. Nor the corresponding service standards have been established.

(4) Uncompetitive talent policies. The existing policies in relation to household registration management, visa and residence of foreign employees and taxation are not internationally competitive.

(5) High cost for enterprises' R&D innovation. The institutional cost related to commercial procedures, talent cost and taxation cost are higher than those in Singapore and other countries. And the legislative policies for encouraging scientific research innovation still need to be improved in terms of pertinence and effectiveness.

By benchmarking against several well-established sci-tech innovation centers worldwide (Table 1), we find that it is the guidance and support from governments and the innovation mechanism which brings about efficient bi-directional flow of core production factors like capital, talent and technology, which then boosts excellent innovation implementation and technology transfer and enhance those nations' level in global value chain.

Currently, relying on Zhangjiang Hi-Tech Park and supported by incentive policies, institutional innovation, process optimization and efficient supervision of Shanghai FTZ, the establishment of global technological innovation center, concentrating on key issues and downplaying the unimportant ones, is in steady and

Table 1

Israel	Silicon Valley	Baden-Wuerttemberg (Germany)	Singapore
Israel is characterized by the highest density of innovation enterprise. • Innovative businesses are mainly small and medium-sized enterprises • Cross-industry innovation • Cyclic innovation • Open innovation, encouraging global leading enterprises to invest in Israel to set up R&D centers, so as to promote international cooperation • Development model of "domestic innovation enterprises + overseas capital market" • Extending the innovation and industrialization in military industry into civilian sector • The government actively participating in innovation and entrepreneurship practices	Silicon Valley owns the largest, most intensive and most innovative high-tech industrial cluster, presenting the following features: • Establishing multi-channel financial service system (e.g. Silicon Valley Bank) • Lots of universities and research institutions • Open talent policies from governments • Flexible and effective entrepreneurship policies in universities	According to Bloomberg's Global Innovation Index in 2015, Germany was rated as the third most innovative nation in the world. • Innovation alliance system • Consisting of universities, research institutions and others • Industry transfer platform • Providing consulting service, research & development, international technology transfer and manpower training	The Singaporean government has rich experience in boosting innovation and promoting the integration of production, study and research, which is worth learning. • The government setting up a specific organization to guide market innovation, and hiring specialists in business, science and academia to participate in policymaking • Sound intellectual property protection system • Encouraging multinationals to set up innovation centers • Encouraging overseas prestigious business schools to set up branches in Singapore, and actively conducting joint running of schools with overseas universities

rapid progress. Learning from international successful experience, to address the main challenges facing Shanghai sci-tech innovation ecosystem, we suggest to make the following attempts to achieve synergy between Shanghai FTZ and global technological innovation center through promoting investment and trade facilitation in Shanghai:

(1) Facilitate the flow of innovation factors. Capital and talent are key elements for sci-tech innovation. According to the experience of successful international sci-tech innovation centers, the government plays the top role of coordinating innovation resources to encourage the financial innovation of banks who establish branches in Shanghai FTZ, with an attempt to enable sci-tech innovation enterprises and individuals to benefit from financial innovation measures of Shanghai FTZ. Moreover, the government can mobilize multinationals to function as platforms equipped with superior resources in sci-tech R&D, and direct them to engage in the incubation of sci-

tech start-ups with support of capital, technology and operation.

(2) Reduce enterprises' cost of sci-tech innovation. Cost-benefit assessment is required for enterprises' to initiate and develop innovation. It can be seen from Deloitte's follow-up surveys on global and high-growth and high-tech enterprises for years that cost has been one critical challenge in sci-tech innovation for enterprises. The government shall have special knowledge of pillar industries and key enterprises in Shanghai's sci-tech innovation, and reduce costs for enterprises through institutional innovation by deploying parts of enterprises' production and sales into Shanghai FTZ. For example, most MNCs' headquarters in Zhangjiang Hi-Tech Park are engaged in biomedicine and integrated circuit, which are also key industries in the park. It is necessary to develop researches on issues in importing production materials/ equipment of such enterprises, such as classification of compound import, taxation on CPU test sample import and equipment offsite application, and to lower enterprises' production and circulation costs resulted from R&D and sci-tech innovation.

(3) Promote the facilitation of service trade. Globally, promoting the facilitation of service trade has been a key issue for free trade zones with high-tech enterprises and R&D service enterprises being important vehicles of service trade. The government shall fully understand the formats of service trade in cross-border operations and R&D outsourcing of these enterprises, and the changes of such formats due to rapid development of information technology. It shall also integrate measures targeting the facilitation of service trade by high-tech enterprises into institutional innovation for overall facilitation of service trade in Shanghai FTZ. "Single window" of goods trade may be leveraged for service trade related to sci-tech innovation. Recruit professional technicians to approve and supervise relevant projects of service trade to raise circulation efficiency of service trade of sci-tech innovation-based enterprises.

(4) Improve intellectual property protection. Improving the construction of legal system for intellectual property projection is to ensure driving sci-tech innovation and trade and investment facilitation. As free trade zones are generally areas of disputes over intellectual property protection, the judicial department of Shanghai FTZ may apply underlying international standards appropriately to such disputes and pilot the legal system construction of intellectual property protection in Shanghai FTZ.

Efforts for joint development between Shanghai FTZ and global technological innovation center will accelerate the aggregation of advantages to reinvigorate and integrate fragmented resources through spillover effects from the multinationals' headquarters and R&D centers. These efforts will also elevate Shanghai's sci-tech innovation-based enterprises in global value chain of service trade and facilitate the transformation of sci-tech innovation achievements and intellectual property protection to promote overall investment and trade facilitation in Shanghai.

Establish a Digital Governance Platform to Promote Investment and Trade Facilitation

Wu Qi

Senior Managing Director and Vice Chairman

of Accenture Greater China

In the next decade, global economy and China's development will be profoundly influenced by two factors: globalization and digital technology. Globalization is at a turning point where the east performs well whereas the west does not. The rising anti-globalization sentiment in the rich world is threatening the consensus on globalization reached after the second world war, which in turn is posing a serious challenge to international trade and business cooperation. Besides, with the Belt and Road initiative being launched, China will spare no effort to promote regional trade agreement, expand regional infrastructure investment, and reduce investment and trade barriers, thus developing a new trade and investment landscape. Meanwhile, digital technologies are having an effect on our economy, changing the trade mode, fueling the dramatic development of service trade and cross-border e-commerce, and finally reshaping global trade.

As a hub of finance, trade and supply-chain, and a port city, Shanghai is endowed with unique advantages to take the lead in this development trend, and to become a global trade and investment center. To seize this historic opportunity, the Shanghai Municipal government needs to implement institutional reforms and transform government functions so that the authority will be service-oriented and will provide effective platforms to create the most favorable infrastructure and environment for trade and investment.

On this topic, Accenture has made analysis from three perspectives, based on which suggestions are provided for Shanghai on its future development. The three perspectives are global trade development, challenges facing China in terms of investment and trade facilitation, and policies and measures introduced in leading countries.

1. Pay Attention to Two Major Trends under which Trade in Services and Digital Technologies are Reshaping Global Trade Landscape

International trade has been undergoing dramatic changes since the 2008 financial crush. Despite the economic rebound in 2010 and 2011, global trade in goods and services has been growing at a slower rate year by year, much lower than the average rate before the crisis, due to sluggish economy over the world, volatility in the financial market and the re-emergence of trade protectionism. With demands weak in the world, Asia's trade is performing far worse, growing slower than GDP over the past two years. What's worse, according to the trade outlook report released by WTO in this September, global goods trade will continue to shrink and the organization cut the trade growth forecast from 2.8% in April to 1.7%.

Though the prospect of global trade remains bleak and trade volume has been stagnated, trade in services is growing year on year, accounting for 19% of the total trade volume in 2000 while 23% in 2015. In the Asia, this figure increased from 17% to 22%. In 2015, tourism and transportation were responsible for 25.5% and 18.2% respectively, services related to R&D, consulting, technology and trade contributed 21.5%; communications and IT accounted for 9.8%; financial services

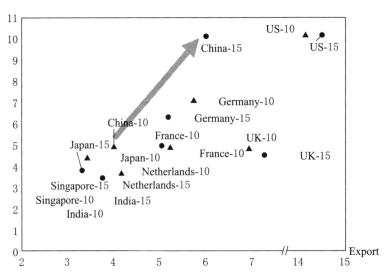

Fig. 1   Proportions of World's Leading Commercial Service
Trading Nations in Global Import and Export (2010 VS. 2015)

提升投资贸易便利化水平，构建开放型经济新体制

took up 8.6%; and charges for the use of intellectual property was responsible for 6.2%. Since 2011, China's trade in services has been growing faster than trade in goods annually. In 2015, China was only second to the US in terms of foreign trade in services.

It is worth noting that information technologies, particularly digital technologies that are serving as the growth engine for trade, are playing an increasingly important role in promoting the development of trade in services. With further analysis, we have noticed that in 2014, nearly half (48%) of the trade in services all over the world was driven by digital technologies. Whereas the figure of 2000 was only 41%. It suggests that digital technologies are reshaping the global trade landscape. Thanks to the development of networking, mobile internet, instant messaging and other technologies, non-tradable services that used to cost a lot in cross-border transport have become tradable and are being traded online in the global market. Knowledge-intensive sectors are benefited the most, including legal services, accounting, tax consulting, market research, management consulting, building engineering consulting, technology test and analysis, and advertising. Besides, with the help of digital technologies, trade in virtual goods are gradually replacing physical trade, best exemplified by the phasing out of CD, DVD and game disks, and the popularity of downloading music and movies online and games apps[①].

In the wave of digital technologies powering trade development, we should not overlook the booming of cross-border e-commerce. As out study reveals, the global cross-border B2C e-commerce market will be worth nearly as much as $1 trillion by 2020 with an annual growth rate reaching 27%. By 2020, the number of cross-border B2C e-commerce consumers will exceed 900 million, increasing by more than 21% annually on average. Driven by digital technologies, cross-border e-commerce are shaking the current model of global trade. internet of things and data analysis help to achieve integrated cross-border transportation and can monitor the whole process. E-commerce platforms and social media make cross-border information flows more efficient, in which digital technologies are employed. Mobile and payment technologies make cross-border cash flow more individual, fast and efficient.

In the future, digital technologies will continue to promote the integration of

---

① Accenture, *Global Cross-Border B2C Electronic-Commerce Market Prospect*, 2015.

international trade, and create remarkable opportunities for transnational business cooperation. First, internet of things and data analysis will enhance the development of global trade in goods by increasing manufacturing productivity and logistics efficiency, eventually helping enterprises going global. Global industrial chain will be further divided. The import and export of intermediates will go up. Product design, manufacturing, transport and selling though are done in different places, information can be shared and these stages will be coordinated. Second, as digital technologies will be widely used in service sectors, trade in services will contribute more to global trade. Therefore, financial sector will provide online services, education sector will offer online platform and medical sectors will provide online services to attract consumers from all over the world. Third, SMEs and start-ups will play an important role in global competition, thus making global business cooperation more vigorous and innovative. With the use of 3D printing, small enterprises can realize small-batch and tailored production to meet the needs in the increasingly diversified global market. Crow-sourcing platforms can help to deal with funding challenges facing small companies. E-commerce platforms will enable more small enterprises to participate in the global market.

2. Identify the Gap between China and Developed Countries and Regions in Terms of Trade and Investment Facilitation, and Figure out the Reasons

Due to the lack of research data on trade and investment facilitation measures from urban areas, we have made a comparison between China as a whole and developed countries and regions. Based on it, we focused on analyzing how and why China lags behind advanced countries, especially other Asian countries in terms of the current situation of trade and investment facilitation. We have studied four official reports issued by World Bank and World Economic Forum, and established a comprehensive assessment system with the use of Global Competitiveness Index (GCI), Doing Business Index (DBI), Enabling Trade Index(ETI), and Logistics Performance Index (LPI). This performance assessment system includes both internal and external factors that can have an effect on a country's trade and investment development. This system also enables us to identify the gap and pertinent reasons by comparing sub-indexes of some metrics. When analyzing factors leading to the gap in certain areas, we chose Singapore, Hong Kong of China, Japan and South Korea as the reference, from which Shanghai could draw lessons. As Shanghai has similar urban development target to Hong Kong and Singapore, and has the strategy of developing Four Centers, these two regions are the best examples to learn from.

Table 1   Comparison of Different Indexes

Country/Region	GCI ranking	DBI ranking	ETI ranking	LPI ranking
China	28	78	54	27
Singapore	2	2	1	5
Hong Kong of China	9	4	2	9
Japan	9	34	13	12
South Korea	26	78	30	24

Source: Global competitiveness index from WEF's report 2016—2017; doing business index from World Bank's report 2017; enabling trade index from WEF's report 2014; and logistics performance index from World Bank's data in 2016.

Through comparison, we have found that China is lagging far behind advanced countries and regions in terms of trade and investment facilitation. China ranks 28th, 78th, 54th, and 27th in terms of global competitiveness, ease of doing business, enabling trade and logistics performance respectively. Whereas Singapore and Hong Kong of China are among the first in Asia and even in the world. The widest gap exists in the ease of doing business and enabling trade. The two indices reflect that China has a lot to do to facilitate trade and investment.

To figure out the more fundamental reasons for the existing gap, we have carried out deeper analysis on the Doing Business index and Enabling Trade Index.

(1) Doing Business Index.

World Bank includes ten factors in the assessment system of doing business. They are: company establishment, building review and approval, power supply, real estate registration, credit availability, protection for small investors, taxation, cross-border trade, contract enforcement, and liquidation (Fig. 2).

Ranking: Singapore 2, Hong Kong of China 4, China 78

Note: Doing Business Report is World Bank's report in 2017.

Fig. 2　Doing Business Report (World Bank)

By looking into the data from World Bank's report in 2017, we concluded that China lags behind in company establishment, building review and approval, protection forthe benefits of minority shareholders, taxation and cross-border transactions. It is mainly because of red tapes that result in time waste and low efficiency. Take warehouse construction as an example. In China, there are 22 steps in the review process, which takes about 244 days. While in Singapore, there are only 9 steps, and only some 48 days is needed. In respect of taxation, it takes companies in China 259 hours to go through tax declaration, and on average they have to pay 68% of their revenues for tax. Whereas in Singapore, only 67 hours is needed, and the tax rate is 19% on average. Take customs declaration as another example. In China, customs declaration costs $777 and consumes 66 hours each time, while in Singapore, companies only have to spend $220 and 3 hours (Fig. 3).

(2) Enabling Trade Index.

In the *Global Enabling Trade Report 2014* published by World Economic Forum, China ranks 54th out of 138 economies in the assessment of Enabling Trade Index. There is a large potential for China to make progress in border administration, information and communication technologies and operating environment. This index consists of seven pillars: domestic market access, foreign market access, efficiency and transparency of border administration, availability and quality of transport infrastructure, availability and quality of transport services, availability and use of ICTs, and regulatory environment

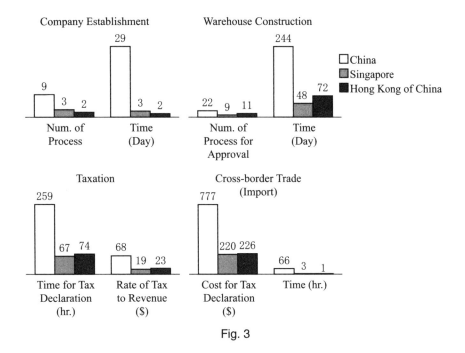

Fig. 3

(Fig. 4).

In terms of the Enabling Trade Index, an indicator of trade facilitation, China lags behind in all regards. In particular, there is a wide gap with Singapore and Hong Kong of China in providing access into domestic and global markets. This will weaken China's advantages created by its large domestic market and manufacturing power, and will in turn impede the country's investment and trade growth in the future. Apart from tariff barriers, low efficiency, inadequate application of ITCs, the lack of diversified financial services, and insufficient government services are to blame. For instance,

Ranking: Singapore 1, Hong Kong of China 2, China 54

Note: Enabling Trade Index is from World Economic Forum's Report 2014.

Fig. 4   Enabling Trade Index (WEF)

China ranks 114th out of 138 respondents with regard to tariffs. To be more specific, China ranks 108th in terms of the number of documents needed for export, 90th for the time spent, 64th for the application of ICTs in B2B transactions, and 59th for the online information service provided by the government. Besides, China is placed way down the list in regard to available financial services and the time spent in resolving trade disputes (Fig. 5).

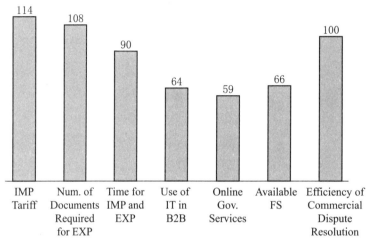

Fig. 5   Areas where China is not Competitive
(Ranking out of 138 Countries and Regions)

Singapore has been ranked the first for six consecutive years in the measurement of Enabling Trade Index. The country is an ideal example for Shanghai to learn from in terms of market access, operating environment and infrastructure. With the use of one-stop information portal, Singapore has established a single window for international trade and investment by connecting 35 government departments, such as the administration of taxation and the customs. It has also developed a national shipping center information platform that consists of many self-developed network systems. In a word, Singapore is a typical example whose government functions and services are based on platforms.

Issues related to taxation and tariffs can be handled by Shanghai alone, but due to existing challenges facing China, the municipal government will have to learn from Hong Kong of China and Singapore to facilitate trade and investment. Focusing on serving enterprises, the government needs to consolidate and streamline trade and investment processes, and rely on digital technologies and improve the capability of using information technologies so that it will turn into a service-oriented government that is good at innovation, and will widely use smart technologies. In this way, the authority will be more efficient, more various and higher-quality value-added services can be offered, and regulations will be consistent with that in advanced countries, thus creating an environment that can better serve Shanghai's urban and economic development in the future.

3. Rely on Digital Technologies and Platform Economy to Accelerate Trade and Investment Facilitation and Develop Shanghai into the Most Attractive and Competitive Finance Center in the World

Digital technologies are gaining momentum, and are exerting far-reaching influence on the work pattern of organizations and people's lifestyles. New business models based on digital technologies like intelligent manufacturing, platform economy, digital supply chain, cross-border e-commerce and internet of things, are reshaping the industry landscape and restructuring urban economy. In the 13th Five-year Plan, the development of digital economy, Internet +, and intelligent manufacturing are regarded as national strategies. Regional hub cities are racing to gain an upper hand in digital economy. So developing an innovation-based government that provides services through platforms and by using digital technologies will be the source of Shanghai's charms and competitiveness.

According to our 2016 study on the digital economy of 11 major countries, by increasing investment in digital and intelligent technologies in the next 5 years, China will harvest economic benefits, gaindigital dividends, and get large potentials for growth. It is estimated that by 2020, digital technologies will account for 3.7% of China's GDP growth, worth $527 billion, the biggest increase among 11 economies.

As our strategy analysis indicates, improving labor forces' digital skills, increasing investment for digital technologies and developing a favorable market environment for digital technologies can help to accelerate economic growth and unleashing digital dividends. In this way, by 2020, America's economy will increase by $421 billion, accounting for 2.1% of its GDP. And with all these attempts done, digital technologies will generate more yields for China than other countries, namely $527 billion, accounting for 3.7% of its GDP.

Shanghai has a well-established education sector, unique advantages, and investment-friendly environment. These are beneficial for developing its digital economy, creating a skilled labor force, and laying a solid physical foundation for the city's innovation development.

Innovation development is the priority in this age and the new engine for China's economic growth. Recently, in the national conference on science and technology innovation, President Xi came up with the overall strategic goal of making China one of the innovation powers in the world. In 2015, the central government raised the "Internet +" strategy, pledging to apply mobile internet, cloud computing, big data, and internet of things in modern manufacturing, to promote the healthy development of e-commerce, industrial internet and internet finance, and leading internet companies going global. As China has more digital technology consumers than any other countries, its internet finance and e-commerce have impressive performance in terms of scale and innovation capability.

We are convinced that to achieve industrial upgrading, improving total factor productivity, and developing digital platform economy should be the priority. According to Accenture's study on the internet of things in 2015, if more measures are introduced, for example to improve the eco-system for scientific research and the market environment, the industrial internet of things will yield $497 billion growth for China's GDP in the next 15 years.

After noticing the huge impact that digital technologies will have on manufacturing, Germany, a conventional manufacturing power has launched the "INDUSTRIE 4.0" initiative. In the initiative, cyber-physical systems (CPS) are developed to enable technologies which bring the virtual and physical worlds together to create a truly networked world in which intelligent objects communicate and interact with each other.

Given the resource endowment like current industrial structure, infrastructure, and geographical advantages, Shanghai needs to understand China's development features in the new normal and follow the global development trend. We believe Shanghai will need to put into practice the ideas of establishing platforms and eco-systems for innovation. The smart urban platform should be set up in the Yangtze River Delta region first to promote industrial upgrading, boost science and technology innovation, and facilitate ecological construction of Shanghai, so that the city can take the lead. Creating digital dividends to develop core advantages for Shanghai to leap forward will make the city stand out when competing with others in the development of smart cities. Therefore, this is the best strategy for Shanghai to improve its competency, seize opportunities and present achievements.

4. Provide Government Services on the Platform

In the *Action Plan for the Construction of Shanghai E-government Cloud* published in November 2016, under the framework of the integration of cloud and internet, and the interaction of cloud and data, the municipal government has decided to rely on advanced technologies like cloud computing and big data to establish e-government platforms at both city and district levels. With this attempt made, government departments in Shanghai can work together to build and share infrastructure, deploy information systems in an integrated way, consolidate and share data resources, provide services in a coordinated manner, and explore and make full use of big data for governance. This in turn will greatly support administration and public services, improve the ability of serving the public, and strengthen governing capacity.

This goal is exactly what our suggestions aim at. The Shanghai government is suggested to design the overall plans for developing an intelligent government, for industrial upgrading and innovation, and for building a smart city from an integrated perspective. When the government is implementing these plans in a coordinated way, it is essential to establish three core platforms that are interconnected.

(1) Set up an intelligent governance platform based on digital technologies. With the development of intelligent government and the establishment of innovative service models, effective connection between the government and enterprises can be realized and the most business-friendly environment can be built. This will cut down transaction cost for enterprises, increase efficiency, boost the growth of local enterprises and attract more well-performing companies to operate in Shanghai. Eventually, with the help of advanced digital technologies and the transformation of government functions, the government of the Pudong New District will be almost as competent as its foreign counterparts in terms of governing capacity and efficiency.

Establishing an intelligent governance platform is mainly to set up an open service system in which the government, the market and the whole society work together, and interact and coordinate with each other. So the platform should be user-oriented, safe and reliable, integrated, and in line with technological development in the future.

User-oriented: Being user-oriented is the key for the government in setting up a platform to provide services and play its role. Based on the needs of the public and enterprises, the government needs to establish a platform that connects the city with trading and investment partner countries. Using big data, the government is able to createan intelligent model to promote interaction on trade and investment. By clarifying the responsibilities that each department is supposed to take, the government can fully explore and integrate their service resources, thus providing quality and individual services for users. What's more, the government needs to make the governance platform more open and interactive, understand the needs of the public and enterprises in a dynamic way, and cooperate with multiple parties to enhance the quality of its services and achieve the interaction with the public.

Safe and reliable: with the wide use of digital technologies on its website to provide more convenient services for the public, the government is encountering tougher challenges to make its portal safer and more reliable. The governance platform has a wealth of information resources concerning the authority, pillar industries and the public. So it is rather important to ensure information security, and realize information exchange done in a perfectly safe way.

Integrated: When providing services, all departments have obtained an ocean of data, from which we can get insight into the economy and people's life. Vast in amount and scope, the resource is valuable. But if each government department works in isolation and fail to share the data, this resource will be used inefficiently and all of the departments may repeat their efforts. By breaking isolation, consolidating resources from all departments, and establishing a seamless connection between different departments, the government can make better use of resources, and improve the quality and efficiency of its services. More importantly, with the help of big data, each department will be able to conduct comprehensive cross-sector analysis through various channels, fully understand the need on government services, improve resource allocation, diversify its services, and serve the public in an active instead of passive way. Innovating the model and pattern of services, the government can greatly improve its competitiveness and governing capacity.

(2) Set up a platform to support industrial innovation, facilitate the upgrading of Shanghai's pillar industries, and power the innovative development of the city's strategic emerging sectors. The system will enable digital innovation, upgrading, and development of the current industrial system in Shanghai. It will promote the establishment of the city's innovation system to appeal to more promising high-tech start-ups to operate in Shanghai. In this respect, there are many examples for Shanghai to learn

| 提升投资贸易便利化水平，构建开放型经济新体制

from. For example, the Center for the Development and Application of Internet of Things Technologies set up in Singapore by the state government and Rio Tinto Group with the help of Accenture is a world-class practice for Shanghai to draw lessons from.

(3) Establish intelligent public service platform to meet people's requirements for safe and convenient life, health, education and green environment. With this platform and modern digital technologies, people can have access to higher-quality life that is convenient in all aspects can provide convenient life in all aspects. This platform will be a unique highlight to attract skilled work force to work in Shanghai.

In line with future technological development: Continuous technological development will create more tools to develop services. To seize the great opportunity brought by technological development, technically, the government needs to set up a flexible framework of digital technology. In terms of administration, the government needs to play a role as an open platform that connects government departments, enterprises, entrepreneur, NGOs and the public together. All parties will cooperate to set up an innovative and dynamic eco-system, entrepreneurship will boom up, and the governance platform will be improved continuously.

It will take a long time to use cloud computing, big data and other digital technologies to establish an intelligent governance platform to facilitate trade and investment, and to build up core competitive capacities and raise charms for Shanghai. This project can be divided into four stages. At the first stage, the government needs to integrate data resources. Data is the brick of all platforms. Breaking isolation and integrating data from public sectors and the business world are essential for the digital governance platform. At the second stage, the government needs to realize digital and mobile process. The third stage is about big data analysis. Without analysis, no insights will be gained, and the vast amount of data will be meaningless. Analysis capability is the essence of the government's digital platform. The fourth stage is about artificial intelligence. Ifthe government affairs, and trade and investment process can be handled by AI, the government will be more efficient, and trade and investment can be better facilitated.

A brighter future is within sight. As a global city located at the Asia-Pacific region, Shanghai has unique advantages and positions. If it can capture the historic opportunities brought by globalization and digital technologies, if the government continues to transform itself into a service-oriented and innovation-based one, without doubt, Shanghai will play the role as a global center of trade, financial investment and innovation.

Promote Trade Facilitation and Supply-chain Connectivity Through E-Port

Yao Weiqun

Economic Researcher at Shanghai WTO Affairs Consultation Center

With the emergence of regional production networks, APEC member economies at different development stage are increasingly connected with each other in regional value chains. Meanwhile, the introduction and application of cutting-edge information and communications technologies such as cloud computing, big data and the internet of things have created new methods, technologies and tools to improve the supply-chain connectivity in and outside of the Asia-Pacific area. The E-Port is the most successful and mature practice.

In the 18th APEC Economic Leaders' Meeting held in 2010, it was declared that trade facilitation and supply-chain connectivity could help to realize a balanced, inclusive, sustainable, innovative and secure growth in the Asia-Pacific region, so that in the long run everyone could be benefited by the driving force behind regional development and economic integration which were for the well-being of the public. In the 20th APEC meeting held in 2012, pledges were made on achieving an APEC-wide target of a ten percent improvement in supply-chain performance by 2015, in terms of reduction of barriers to the movement of goods and services through the Asia-Pacific region. In the 21st meeting hosted in 2013, the commitment was reaffirmed to promote regulatory consolidation and coordination, and eliminate unnecessary trade barriers impeding the realization of the common goals of product safety and supply chain integrity. It means promoting trade facilitation and supply-chain connectivity is essential for free and open trade and investment in the Asia-Pacific region. Therefore, how to promote trade facilitation and supply-chain connectivity in strategy-making and practice is the priority for APEC.

1. The Practice of and Experience from the Shanghai E-Port Project

During the 9th APEC Economic Leaders' Meeting held in Shanghai in October, 2001, China and the U.S. agreed upon the cooperation on exploring into the construction of E-Port. In 2004, led by Shanghai Municipal People's Government and the General Administration of Customs, eighteen stakeholders at Shanghai port set up the Joint Session of Shanghai E-port Construction. The 18 members are China E-port; Shanghai Customs District; Shanghai Entry-Exit Inspection and Quarantine Bureau; Shanghai General Station of Immigration Inspection; Shanghai Railways Administration; Shanghai Maritime Safety Administration; the People's Bank of China Shanghai Branch; the People's Bank of China, Shanghai Headquarter; Shanghai Municipal Office, SAT; Shanghai Municipal Development and Reform Commission; Shanghai Municipal Commission of Economy and Informalization; Shanghai Municipal Commerce Commission; Shanghai Municipal Finance Bureau; Shanghai Municipal Transportation and Port Authority; Shanghai Municipal Office for Port Service; Shanghai International Port Group Ltd.; Shanghai Airport Authority; and Shanghai Information Investment Inc..

Formally established in 2005, Shanghai E-port platform is offering services in four aspects, i.e. regulation, trade, logistics and payment. Its basic functions are as follows: It creates a one-stop access network for stakeholders, such as the port administration; manufacturing and trading companies; freight forwarders; as well as land, sea and air transportation and warehousing enterprises. Its services cover all air and sea ports in Shanghai, and the regulatory zones and areas like export processing zones, bonded areas, bonded logistics parks, bonded port areas and integrated bonded zones. It realizes the exchange and sharing of 218 types of data, such as data of cargo declaration, inspection and quarantine declaration, shipping declaration, hazardous goods declaration, map of ships, shipping bill, container loading list, booking, delivery, as well as import and export message. It provides B2G and B2B payment services, and is interconnected with 22 banks at home and abroad. Its payment of customs taxes and duties covers 42 custom districts all over the economy. It also boasts value-added data services. Integration application such as trade management, shipping bill, booking, container management, and customs affairs collaboration has been provided. Basic services of cloud application such as unified user management, application launching, monitoring, billing, payment etc. is available.

2. The Definition, Characteristics, Mechanisms, Functions and Effects of Shanghai E-port

According to the practice of Shanghai E-port project, E-port obviously refers to a supply-chain ecosystem-based port community system under the joint construction of multiple stakeholders including port operators, regulators and users. As a virtual terminal, it provides both online and offline services.

The characteristics are as follows: (1) Based on the Port Community System, the E-port functions as a third-party ICT infrastructure and one-stop public service platform. It is constructed and operated by port stakeholders in joint efforts, instead of by one single administration. (2) The E-port has a "single window" system, which helps to realize paperless customs clearance. (3) As an ICT infrastructure, the E-port meet the need of hub ports for trade, logistics and other value-added activities, as well as "one-stop service".

There are four mechanisms related to the E-port. (1) The online and offline business information of stakeholders is integrated, exchanged and shared among each other. (2) The online and offline data of supply chain including business, product, information and capital flows as well as other flows are tracked, allocated and regulated. (3) The public ICT infrastructure of the Port Community System. (4) The public service platform with "single window" as one of its functions.

The E-port has these basic functions.

(1) It provides an effective solution of ICT infrastructure to shift from trade with documents to paperless trading on the basis of data. (2) It consolidates trade facilitation measures like the "single window" practice, and provides "one-stop access to services" as well as other ways to promote supply-chain connectivity. (3) It helps to realize coordination in different government level, such as the inner-agencies, inter-agencies, and cross-border agencies coordination. Through multi-stakeholders community system, it offers an institutional guarantee to cross-border supply chain management. Besides, it integrates the government, enterprises, trade associations, consumers and other stakeholders into the framework of E-port so that they will be a real part in

developing trade facilitation and supply-chain connectivity.

As the E-port is market and service oriented, it has these effects. (1) One-stop access: It can provide comprehensive logistics solutions and be interfaced with data of multiple transportation options including ship, air, railway and road transports. It is more than the "single window" system and an ICT-based port service system. (2) Workable: Without replacing the ongoing system, it can still be interfaced with data to realize data consistency. (3) Transparent based on trust: Under the supervision of the government and other stakeholders, the E-port ensures data privacy and security. (4) Serving all: With the help of the third-party ICT infrastructure, it can consolidate fragmented information in the supply chain and lowering the participation cost and threshold for SMEs. (5) Interdisciplinary: It helps to realize data sharing and cooperation between different departments in an organization and that within the department. (6) Developable: Based on the ICT platform of cloud computing, it can provide better services for enterprises and its functions can be developed to lower the entry threshold.

3. Measures for Promoting Trade Facilitation and Supply-Chain Connectivity Undertaken by APEC

Since its establishment 27 years ago, APEC has given consideration to the difference of each member's economic and social development, and used the "Bogor Goal" as a basic framework to promote trade and investment liberalization and extensive economic and technological cooperation. It has also undertaken a package of effective measures to promote trade facilitation and supply-chain connectivity.

In the 1990s, APEC began to introduce "paperless trading" initiative covering customs duty payment, customs declaration and clearance, as well as trade documents handling to member economies. In 2007, APEC put forward the "single window" system whereby importers and exporters can one-off submit documents for customs clearance to government organizations through one single interface. In 2009, it published the *Supply-Chain Connectivity Framework Action Plan*, in which improving supply-chain performance was regarded as the priority in promoting trade facilitation and economic growth. The document also clarifies eight chokepoints that should be resolved so as to realize trade facilitation and supply-chain connectivity.

(1) Lack of transparency and overall consciousness in regulatory issues affecting logistics; Lack of awareness and action of coordination among government agencies on policies affecting logistics sector; Absence of one-stop access or leading agency on logistics matters. (2) Inefficient or inadequate transport infrastructure; Lack of cross border physical linkages (e.g. roads, bridges). (3) Lack of capacity of local or regional logistics sub-providers. (4) Inefficiency in customs' cargo clearance; Lack of coordination among border agencies, especially relating to clearance of regulated goods 'at the border'. (5) Burdensome procedures for customs documentation and other procedures (including for preferential trade). (6) Underdeveloped multi-modal transport capabilities; inefficient air, land, and multi-modal connectivity. (7) Variations in cross-border standards and regulations for movements of goods, services and business travelers. (8) Lack of regional cross-border customs and transit arrangements.

To achieve the goal of trade facilitation and supply-chain connectivity in APEC economies, the first and most practically significant step is to improve ICT infrastructures. Besides, each member should build up mutual trust and understanding, should be integrated into the multi-ecosystem, should improve the partnership with all stakeholders, should have a supply chain, should make polices concerning supply chain more transparent and should focus on developing the capability of the information and communications technology that will impact supply-chain connectivity. Therefore, when protecting data security and privacy, the government has attempted to set up an information sharing platform so as to provide the solution of E-port, an ICT infrastructure that can offer "one-stop service". The government has also explored into feasible plans for trade facilitation and supply-chain connectivity in APEC economies through comprehensive and effective public- private partnership.

4. Asia-Pacific Model E-port Network (APMEN)

In September 2013, consensus was reached on *Trade Facilitation Agreement* in WTO Ministerial Conference held in Bali, Indonesia. In September 2014, the WTO General Council approved the *Trade Facilitation Agreement* in a temporary meeting. By September 20th, 2016, 98 members of WTO have ratified the *Trade Facilitation Agreement* which defines transparency, simplification, consistency and discipline as the four basic elements, "single window" as the main channel, and "paperless trading" as the target.

China has always been an active player in promoting trade facilitation and supply-chain connectivity. In the 22nd APEC Economic Leaders' Declaration, *Beijing Agenda for an Integrated, Innovative and Interconnected Asia-Pacific* published on November 11th, 2014, members agreed to set up an Asia-Pacific *Model E-port Network*, welcome the first batch of APEC Model E-ports nominated by the APEC economies, endorse the *Terms of Reference of the APMEN* and agree to set up the APMEN operational center in the Shanghai Model E-port, and instruct officials to make further efforts to contribute to regional trade facilitation and supply chain connectivity. Up to now, twelve hub ports and E-ports in nine APEC economies have been part of the network.

Through the network, it is hoped that under the framework of APEC, the hub ports in APEC economies can realize information sharing and exchange by using the third-party public ICT infrastructure as the platform, so that the connectivity between different economies and between public and private stakeholders will be strengthened. What's more, hub ports can play a major role in developing public ICT infrastructure-based service in their regions or sub-regions to satisfy the need of public and private sectors for "one-stop service", to improve supply chain efficiency, and to generate more overall economic benefits, thus realizing the integration of supply chain and value chain in the Asia-Pacific region with the help of "one-stop service" provided through ICT infrastructure.

The network is operated on the basis of the result-oriented relationship between stakeholders, and is to achieve their hopes and bring about consistent effects. The network also helps to make operation standards and agreements for the supply chain, consolidate services on the platform for overall analysis and real practice, and promote plan implementation through market-oriented way. It can improve the transparency of supply chain data to achieve eco-system management while protecting stakeholders' privacy and security.

The effect that the network is likely to bring about is that it may eradicate the chokepoints of supply-chain connectivity in the Asia-Pacific region. On the basis of the E-port, the establishment of an interconnected "single window" system followed by the set up of "one-stop service" network in the Asia-Pacific region can help to promote cross-border cooperation on port administration, trade facilitation and seamless connectivity of cross-border supply chain. The network is able to enhance systemic connection and information sharing between public and private sectors, and improve the visualization of the whole supply chain. It can improve supply-chain performance in terms of efficiency, quality and security, step up cooperation in supply chain security and cross-border law enforcement, and resolve the problems about cargo security, intellectual rights, fake goods and smuggling, etc. It can promote paperless logistics, trading and supply chain; provide affordable up-to-date information technologies for private and public sectors; and further integrate regional value chains.

The network can also generate other benefits for its members. Through information sharing, cooperation and ability development, members can improve their ICT infrastructures, service capability and quality. Their port authorities can take part in the cooperation program of APEC. In practice, the need of stakeholders in cross-border supply chain eco-system can be satisfied with the help of the port community system for stakeholders, the third-party ICT infrastructure and one-stop common use service platform. The network can visualize the data of all stakeholders, enhance supply chain efficiency, and integrate supply chains in the Asia-Pacific region. It can help to form new ideas, create new methods and ways, and increase the added value of enterprises' ICT services for the departments of transportation, logistics, supply chain, trading and production, etc. It can also lower the threshold for developing countries and SMEs to enter the value chain in meso-level.

Shanghai Should Become a Global Digital City

Huang Yu

Senior Executive Advisor at Gao Feng Advisory Company

1. Digitalization is the Most Essential Driving Force

Digitalization is the most essential driver of technological development in the 21st century. Under the trends of digitalization, progress has been made in many fields such as the Internet, Mobile Internet, Internet of Things (IoT), Big Data, and Artificial Intelligence, profoundly changing many industries.

Digitalization has a great influence on global investment and trade. Take trade as an example, around 350 million enterprises worldwide will export their products and services via digital business. Such transition is becoming the first boost to global trade since the economic recession.

Influenced by globalization and technological development, digitalization witnessed exponential growth in China. Enterprises in particular the BAT (Baidu, Alibaba and Tecent) have stimulated the digital ecosystem which has significantly impact on businesses in China. Not only is digitalization beneficial to consumers, it also serves to facilitates China's enterprises and economy to leapfrog into new era. This is an era that everything changes, from lifestyle to business practice.

In China, many enterprises that have combined digital technology and new business models have achieved encouraging growth and surpass traditional enterprises in a short period of time. It is also observed that the so-called boundaries between traditional and emerging industries are increasingly blurred. Through digital technology, companies are building customer-centric business models that enhance the intimacy between all collaborative partners in one ecosystem, bringing a fundamental change in traditional industries.

2. Shanghai is Best Positioned to Become a Global Digital City

As a world class metropolitan, Shanghai is a global center of economy, finance, trade and shipping. During the 13th Five Year Plan, Shanghai will focus on three areas: Solidifying its position as international center of information exchange; Generating economic growth as a central city through innovation, and developing strong service industry. Of the same importance Shanghai should also transform itself to become a digital city, and utilize digital technology in providing business, trade and investment services.

Shanghai should build world-leading capabilities in the areas of Smart City, Fintech, and Cloud services.

(1) Building smart city with digital technology.

Shanghai plans to become a ubiquitous Smart City by 2020. To achieve this, Shanghai could utilize information and communication technologies to detect, collect, analyze and integrate key information of the city's core operating systems, enabling quick and dynamic response to the various needs in people's livelihood, environmental protection, public safety, public services, and commercial activities. It is in fact using advanced information technology to implement smarter city management and operation, improve people's livelihood, and ensure the harmony and sustainability of the city. These measures will greatly support the investment and trade activities in Shanghai.

(2) Leveraging fintech in the establishment of financial center.

Shanghai will become an international financial center by 2020. However, compared with New York and London, improvement is still needed in terms of services, industrial cluster and infrastructure. To be more competitive as a financial center, Shanghai should not only speed up the progress in the area of policy and regulation, but also be proactive in exploring new technologies.

Blockchain technology is currently the most cutting edge technology in finance, widely considered as a potential trigger for the fifth round of disruptive technological revolution, previous four of which are steam engine, electricity, information technology and internet. Blockchain is based on consensus mechanism and decentralized, distributed shared ledger or database. By using cryptography, it ensures a public, consistent, transparent and secure tool for users. Blockchain is a powerful tool that improves the convenience and reliability of financial services.

提升投资贸易便利化水平，构建开放型经济新体制

Shanghai government could leverage blockchain technology in following ways:

• Financial transaction: Blockchain changes the way financial transaction is conducted, particularly in areas of payment and clearing system. It will simplify transaction and strengthen the supervision. In light of this, the roles of New York and London as world trading centers might change. Shanghai should seize this opportunity and encourage technology innovation, accelerate the development and application of blockchain technology, and design and implement a new financial transaction mechanism.

• Financial institutions: Traditional financial institutions' fundamental role will be replaced by a more open, democratic and free market. Shanghai should be open-minded and build an optimized business environment that attracts more financial institutions, capital and talents. Collaboration between fintech companies and financial institutions should be fostered, and R&D investment should be encouraged. Shanghai is in the position to lead in shaping the future of financial institutions.

• Supervision: Blockchain technology fundamentally changes the role of IT system in financial institutions, and it promises a measurable self-supervised platform that reduces fraud and improves the efficiency of supervision. Shanghai should continue to explore a more efficient and effective way in regulation and supervision in the context of new technology such as blockchain.

(3) Offering cloud services.

As Shanghai becomes an international center of economy, finance, trade and shipping, providing better services to businesses and enterprises is getting more important than ever. With digital technology in mind, there are a number of venues where Shanghai could exhibit its strength and determination, especially in the areas of investment and trade. Cloud service can play an important role in this effort.

Cloud service is part of the city's future infrastructure and a growth engine for Shanghai's competitiveness. It will not only reduce cost for enterprises but also prepare them well in global competition.

3. Free Trade Zone Is a Corner Stone in Digital Trade and Investment

Having the unique advantage of free trade zone, Shanghai should upgrade its services through digitalization and thus consolidate the essential role of free trade zone in China.

Shanghai should focus on areas such as capital account convertibility, logistics, investment and government supervision. Meanwhile, by leveraging free trade zone and cross-border platform for investment, Shanghai should become the forerunner in supporting the One Belt, One Road national strategic initiative. Free trade zone owns a collection of digitalization initiatives to promote convenience for trade and investment.

(1) Digital logistics. Logistics plays an important role in trade. Driven by the importance of trade development, Shanghai's free trade zone is leveraging information technology and digital equipment in its logistics operations. For example, digitalization management system is becoming vital in cargo routing and supervision.

(2) Tracking. RFID (Electronic label, radio-frequency identification), including RFID storage and logistics system can be applied in purchasing, storage, manufacturing, package, stevedoring, shipping, circulating, distributing, selling and other business segments. It can accurately and in real-time monitor the flow of business, logistics, information and capital.

(3) Cross-border payment. A cross-border commodity financial service platform constructed by domestic and international banks is launched in October, 2016 in free trade zone (experimental phase for DBS Group, CIMB Bank and Bank of Shanghai). This is a remarkable step for digitalization of the free trade zone. The platform marks Shanghai free trade zone as the pioneer of a cash-free trading center.

(4) Paperless. The traditional archive process in paper for the payment and clearing system has always caused inconvenience for banks and clients. A new paperless platform is the realization of digitalization and integration of the clearing system.

In an era of digital disruption, technology is being upgraded at an unprecedented speed. New ecosystem is being formed and instead of pure rivalry, enterprises are sharing, collaborating and developing partnership. It is critical for Shanghai to anticipate these changes and upgrade digital infrastructure to attract and better serve leading enterprises, especially in areas of investment and trade. Shanghai is well positioned to become a leading global digital city.

The Changing World and Cross-border M&A

Fan Deshang

Deputy-Director and Secretary-Genreal of China Center for Global
Governance, Peking University

Qiao Qian

School of Economics and Management, Beijing Forestry University

Zhang Qi

School of Economics, Ocean University of China

1. The Changing World and Its Causes

(1) The changes of the world.

The world is undergoing extensive and profound changes. From the 2008 Wall Street subprime crisis and sovereign debt crisis in western countries to the global financial and economic crisis, from the turmoil in Arabia to the value conflicts highlighted by Charlie's Weekly, from the occupy Wall Street movement to the London riots, from the referendum on whether Britain should remain a member of the European Union or leave to demonstration and social division triggered by Trump's victory, we can see that the world in the process of globalization is also a world full of turmoil, discontent, conflict and confrontation. The conflicts and confrontations caused by religious culture and social differentiation are becoming more and more complex. The whole world's political and economic situation is very changeable and complicated.

Meanwhile, with the rapid development of science and technology, human society, politics, economy and society are facing new changes as well as new opportunities and challenges. From the perspective of human society's science and technology history, the mode of political power distribution, the method of economic distribution, and the differentiation of social stratum, have a close relationship with the science and technology development level of human society at the time.

In the stage of agricultural society, the development of science and technology is mainly reflected in the aspects of agriculture and husbandry. Human science and technology innovation is mainly reflected in the cultivation of animals and plants as well as the understanding and grasp of seasonal climate change. To adapt to human social agricultural science and technology development level, social economic mode of production mainly based on handicraft industry and self-sufficient production in the unit of family; in the allocation mode of political power, the king and the nobility grasped the state power, maintained social order and justice. The typical political power mode is the monarchy. Social stratification is consisted of king, nobles, peasants and handicraftsmen.

With the emergence of steam technology and electric technology, human society has stepped into the industrialized society. And with the development of science and technology, the division of the political, economic and social strata of human society had new changes. From the family handicraft industry and the self-sufficient natural economy, the economic development mode of human society started to walk towards the era of large industrial machinery production. The social stratum began to differentiate. Technology revolution brought big machine production to the society and crushed the traditional family handicraft industry and self-sufficient natural economy. The bankrupt farmers and craftsmen were forced to enter the factories owned by the capitalists with machine and technology. The whole society has split into two opposite classes: the proletariat and the bourgeoisie with mine, capital and machine. In view of the change of the industrial age, Marx categorized the social stratum into two classes, namely, the bourgeoisie and the proletariat. In the distribution of political power, with the rise of the bourgeoisie, the bourgeoisie demanded the right to speak in the process of state power. England and France changed from monarchy to bourgeois republic during the political power distribution.

Science and technology revolution with information technology as its core has been bringing human social politics, economy, social stratification a profound impact. The mode of economic development changed from the industrialized production of large machinery to the era of intelligent production with knowledge, technology and information. Under the influence of the scientific and technological revolution, the traditional industries either went downhill or were forced to upgrade, while new R&D enterprises relying on high-level talents began to appear. At the same time, the transformation of science and technology began to cause social polarization and social problems. In the United States, for example, workers in the American auto industry began to lose their jobs in the last century as the American manufacturing industry moved out. After President Obama came to power, he was committed to the return of American manufacture industry so as to solve the unemployment problem of industrial workers. Unfortunately, intelligent robots that combine intelligence, information and automation have permanently replaced the jobs of industrial workers in the United States.

(2) The causes for the profound changes in the world today.

Facing today's complex world, people explore the causes for the profound changes in the world from different angles. Basically, globalization as well as science and technology revolution are the two fundamental forces that drive the changes in the world today.

• Globalization. The reform and opening up in China and the great changes in Soviet Union and Eastern Europe eliminated the political barriers between the East and the West, making the western capital look for investment opportunities in greater geographical space. Over 2 billion people entered global economic system, became the consumer of western capital and goods. On one hand, to a great extent, this force of globalization created the economic prosperity before 2008. On the other hand, due to the emigration of capital, technology, and manufacturing industry, a large number of people in the western middle-class suffered from income stagnation or even lost their jobs. The social structure of the western countries began to change, and more and more people lived in poverty because of income stagnation or unemployment. The proportion of the middle class in the social structure decreased significantly. Those who failed in the era of globalization began to demand changes through reform. From the occupation of Wall Street, to the London riots, from referendum on whether the UK should remain a member of the European Union or leave to Trump elected as president of the United States, they all fully revealed this demand.

• Science and Technology Revolution. The force of globalization has profoundly shaped and changed today's world. At the same time, science and technology revolution based on information technology has been making changes every day, causing a lasting and profound influence on the present world politics, economy and society. The human society is facing new opportunities and challenges. About the influence in the United States, President Obama, in his January 25, 2011 state of the Union address, said that world has changed. For many, this change is painful. When he sees a once prosperous factory is now closed, when he sees a once crowded commercial street is now deserted, he feels this change. When he see the loss of the Americans who had been cut off or forced to lay off, he feels this change. For these proud Americans, they feel that the rules of the game have changed. Their feeling was right. The rules were changed. In the time of one generation, the technology revolutions have completely changed the way people live, work and do business. Steel mills that once needed 1 000 workers now need only about 100 workers to do the same amount of job. Today, in any place where there is an Internet connection, any company can set up shops, hire employees and sell products.

(3) The prominent issue of the polarization of wealth.

In the context of profound changes in the world, the gap between rich and poor is particularly prominent. On one hand, globalization made the wealth owners who had been investing globally richer with larger investment return. On the other hand, it made manufacturing workers live in poverty because of the unemployment caused by relocation of manufacture industry. Technological revolution created few technology new monies who won their wealth by technology patent and business model innovation. Meanwhile, science and technology innovation as well as the new business model made industrial workers and the traditional commercial service personnel permanently lost their jobs. According to the "World Wealth Report" released by Credit Suisse Research Institute on November 22, 2016, the most surprising finding was that the 3.5 billion adults at the bottom of global wealth pyramid owned less than 10 thousand dollars on average. The wealth they owned only accounted for 2.4% of the global wealth. While the 33 million millionaires, who constitute 0.7% of the global adult population, owned 45.6% of the global wealth. This means that the wealth gap has been widening.

Based on the reflection of the 2008 Wall Street financial crisis, the U.S. President Obama, in "The State of the Union Address" on January 21, 2009, mentioned the issue of the gap between the rich and the poor. He believes that there is no argument about whether the market is good or bad. Its ability to generate wealth and expand freedom is incomparable. But the crisis also reminds them that: with the lack of supervision, they may lose the control of market power. And if a country favors its wealthy class, it is impossible to maintain long-term prosperity. Their country's economic success is never solely relied on the expansion of the GDP scale, but on the common prosperity; relied on their ability to let every citizen with hope enjoy equal chance of success—this is not because of kindness, but its necessity in realizing common prosperity. The question they ask today is not whether their government is big or small, but whether it works—whether it helps families get a decent job, afford insurance, and enjoy a retirement with dignity. Anything that helps to achieve these goals, they will carry forward; anything that counts against the goals, they vow to end it.

As an ally on the other side of the Atlantic, after the referendum on staying in Europe, the United Kingdom began its in-depth reflection on issues brought by a widening gap between the rich and the poor in this era of globalization and also science and technology revolution. In her inaugural speech, Britain's new Prime Minister Teresa May said that she knows people were working from dawn to dusk, she knows people are trying their best, and she knows that sometimes life is a struggle. The government led by her will not be driven by the interest of a few privileged people, but will call for the majority's benefit. They will do everything they can to make their people's life better. When they make big decisions, they do not think about the privileged, but the people. When they pass a new bill, they do not listen to those who are powerful, but the people. When the government collects taxes, it is not the rich that they care for, but the people. When the government creates opportunities, they will not protect the interests of the privileged. It can be seen from the inaugural address that the UK's reflections and lessons are as profound as the changing world.

Unfortunately, the U.S. did not learn from UK's reflection and lessons after the referendum. From the occupation of Wall Street, riots in London, to Britain's referendum on staying in EU, the people who failed in the era of globalization and science technology revolution expressed their demand of reform numerous times through demonstrations and votes. Trump's victory came from "hearing the voice other people did not hear". (Reflection after the election by Paul Davis Ryan, the speaker of the House of Representatives). The demand for change is once again rising on the land of America.

2. Reflections on Cross-border Mergers and Acquisitions in the Context of the Current Era

Transnational merger refers to cross-border mergers and acquisitions of transnational enterprises. It is an enterprise in one country (also known as M&A enterprise) use some method and means of payment to buy all the assets or shares sufficient to exercise operational activities of another enterprise (also known as the merged enterprise) in order to achieve a certain goal, and thus able to actually or completely control the operation of the other enterprise.

Facing the complicated and profound changes of today's world, making in-depth analysis of the possible result and cause of the changes in the world can reduce the risk of cross-border mergers and acquisitions as much as possible, and provide support for cross-border M&A strategy and implementation. Therefore, in the context of profound changes, cross-border M&A need to carry out a comprehensive analysis of multi-level and multi-factor.

In this highly interdependent world, multi level analysis means to achieve the goal of cross-border mergers and acquisitions. It needs to be analyzed from three aspects: global level, regional level and national level.

(1) Global level.

The profound changes in the global political and economic level provided the macro background for cross-border M&A, and it affects the opportunities, challenges, and strategy choices of the cross-border M&A. A political and economic situation with stability and prosperity provides strategic opportunities and choices for cross-border M&A. A political and economic situation with complexity and turbulence causes risks and uncertainties that need in-depth research and preemption for cross-border M&A. The reform and opening-up of China at the end of 1970s and drastic changes in Soviet Union and Eastern Europe at 1990s are major changes in the global political and economic level. These changes eliminated many institutional barriers, opened a market with more than 2 billion people to the West, and pushed the Western capital and technology flow to these areas. The changes in the global political and economic level have greatly contributed to the global economic prosperity before 2008.

(2) Regional level.

The political, economic, and social situation in a region has a significant impact on cross-border M&A. The analysis of these situations is an indispensable and important aspect of cross-border M&A in today's world of changes. Since the outbreak of the global financial and economic crisis in 2008, the political, economic, and social situation in some countries and regions became more and more turbulent, causing even more complicated risks and uncertainties for cross-border M&A.

On December 17, 2010, the self immolation of Tunisian vendor Mohammad

Bouazizi triggered the sudden change of situation, which caused turmoil in North Africa, Middle East, Morocco, Egypt, Libya, and Yemen, made regimes fall like a domino. Many countries with investments in those regions suffered heavy losses. Those regions had similar political and economic social background of autocracy, inflation, and high unemployment. The people there were boiling with resentment. This incident showed that in today's world of profound changes, a seemingly small incident can cause tremendous turmoil in similar regions and bring great challenges and potential risks to cross-border M&A or investment. Therefore, the analysis of regional political, economic and social situation has become an integral part of cross-border M&A risk analysis.

(3) National level.

The political, economic and social situations of the target country are the foundations of cross-border M&A risk analysis. The exercise, application and distribution of the target country's highest state power have a great influence on the strategic choice of cross border M&A. Comparing with democratic regime, dictatorship has great instability, which is not good for the implementation of to cross-border M&A. While a stable political situation can provide a good legal environment for cross-border M&A. What's more, cross-border M&A involves two or more different political systems and religious culture, it may be extremely difficult to overcome barriers to mergers and acquisitions. With China's growing economic strength, some western countries see China as a potential threat, and spread around the theory so-called "China threat". They often use "economic threat" and "economic security" as excuses to interfere the cross-border M&A of Chinese enterprises. China Minmetals Corporation failed to acquire Noranda Inc. due to the interference of Canadian government. And China National Offshore Oil Corporation was unable to purchase Unocal Corporation because of the objection proposed by U.S. Congress.

The political, economic and social situations of the target country are the important references for M&A risk analysis and strategy. The harmonious and stable social relations of the target countries are essential conditions for the implementation of M&A strategy. With the profound changes in today's world, the populist sentiment and social polarization of wealth in the developed countries such as the United States are important factors that need to be considered in cross-border M&A strategy. The impact of these social problems on M&A will need to be further analyzed.

The comprehensive analysis of multiple factors means that in order to achieve the goal of cross-border M&A, it is necessary to carry out a comprehensive analysis from the political, economic, social, cultural, and technological progress factor etc. Facing the complex and profound changes in the world, the impact of these factors are intertwined with all kinds of things, and single perspective can no longer spot the potential risk of cross-border M&A. As mentioned above, Trump's victory was not a black swan incident, but the consequence of globalization and rapid development of science and technology. The former led to social polarization and a widening gap between the rich and the poor, the latter caused more unemployment and poverty, both of which contributed to Trump's victory. Thus, in a world with profound changes, to realize cross-border M&A, we need to conduct a comprehensive in-depth analysis, consider factors such as politics, economy, society, religious culture, technical development, and their interaction.

Remarks on Promoting Investment and Trade Facilitation in Shanghai

Owen Haacke

Chief Representative, Shanghai Office, US-China Business Council

The US-China Business Council (USCBC) support stable and mutually beneficial commercial relations between the US and China. Over the past 30 years, there has been progress in further developing the US-China relationship through government and commercial stakeholders. Trade and investment bring important benefits to both US and China economies and serve as an important foundation of the relationship.

USCBC appreciates the support Shanghai has given to American companies. Shanghai has always played a leading role in encouraging trade and investment between US companies and China and in attracting foreign investment. USCBC member companies support Shanghai's goal to become an increasingly open to foreign trade and investment. We hope that our organization and our member companies can continue to contribute to Shanghai's development goals.

Shanghai is a leader in promoting measures to facilitate trade and investment in China. Through efforts like reforms in the China (Shanghai) Pilot Free Trade Zone, easing licensing processes, and developing a transparent rulemaking and enforcement system, Shanghai has been able to be a leader at the national level. USCBC has worked closely with the Shanghai government on ways to make Shanghai, especially China (Shanghai) Pilot Free Trade Zone more attractive to foreign investment, and many of our recommendations are applicable as Shanghai continues to improve overall trade and investment competitiveness.

As a leader for developing policies to promote economic cooperation, incentives for foreign companies, and a business-friendly investment environment, many US companies have chosen Shanghai as their base for China operations, investing in R&D, talent development, and cooperation with Chinese partners.

As the relationship continues, Shanghai will continue to play an important role. Several areas are listed below based on USCBC advocacy documents including our 2016 Board Priorities Statement that Shanghai can continue to promote to allow for further smooth cooperation with foreign companies in trade and investment.

1. Continue Openings for Foreign Companies and Create a Competitive Environment

(1) Reduce foreign ownership restrictions. Shanghai is a leader in attracting and providing opportunities for foreign investment, but China still maintains numerous foreign investment ownership restrictions across many sectors of its economy, including manufacturing, services, agriculture, and resources. Reducing foreign ownership restrictions now, rather than later would allow American companies to contribute more to China's economic reforms and economic rebalancing goals.

(2) Ensure equal treatment for foreign technology companies and products in China.Technology and innovation play a critical role in creating stronger commercial environments that are capable of meeting the needs of 21st century economies. It is important that companies operating in this space are regulated in ways that reflect the complex, global value chains they maintain, and that regulations governing the sector are based solely on sound commercial and technical factors.

2. Reduce Trade Barriers and Enforce Globally Accepted Trade Rules

(1) Implement laws and regulations consistently across. As part of its role economic reforms, Shanghai has streamlined and decentralized many approvals necessary to establish and operate businesses throughout the country. These efforts are welcome, but implementation of laws and regulations by provincial and local authorities remains uneven and therefore problematic.

(2) Increase the use of transparent, internationally harmonized standards for goods and services sold in China's market. The use of internationally harmonized standards in China will ensure that Chinese consumers and end users have access to the best products and services, and that Chinese products and services are accepted

and competitive internationally. China should adopt more science-based, fair, equal, transparent, and market-led approaches to standards setting and development that is open to all companies regardless of nationality, including domestic, foreign-invested, and foreign-based manufacturers.

(3) Eliminate import barriers to facilitate economic rebalancing and consumption. China maintains high import duties and taxes on a wide array of consumer goods. These high tariffs and taxes inhibit China's economic rebalancing and lead Chinese consumers to purchase such products overseas. Reducing or eliminating tariffs and taxes on consumer goods would be a simple yet powerful stimulant of domestic consumption.

(4) Ensure equal treatment in government procurement for all legal entities in China, regardless of ownership. China should finalize the draft Administrative Measures for Government Procurement of Domestic Products with modifications recommended by USCBC to ensure that goods and services provided by all legal entities in China are treated equally during procurement processes, regardless of ownership. If appropriately revised, the rules would roughly parallel similar rules applied to Chinese companies in the United States.

3. Ensure Competitive Neutrality and Improve Transparency

Shanghai is a leader in improving transparency and the ability for all companies to navigate the regulatory environment and invest in the China market. However, there are several areas we would recommend for improvement:

(1) Further improve rule-making transparency. In the past few years, Shanghai has provided transparent platforms when drafting laws and regulations that would impact foreign trade facilitation. We hope that going forward, Shanghai will continue to have a high level of transparency in the policy-making process, and along with the central government, publish all draft trade and economic related laws, administrative regulations, and departmental rules for a full 30-day comment period. Shanghai can consider going further by posting draft regulations on a designated website for a 60- or 90-day public comment period.

(2) Policy implementation period. We hope that when policies are implemented that enforcement agencies will provide briefings or detailed overview of the policy to allow companies enough time to ensure they comply. When a new policy replaces an

old policy, we hope there will be a minimum of a 30-day notice period.

4. Strengthen Intellectual Property Rights (IPR) Protection and Adhere to Mutually Beneficial Innovation Policies

(1) Continue to strengthen China's IPR regime and enforcement of IPR in China. Stronger IPR protection brings mutual benefits. Shanghai should continue to improve its IPR legal regime by updating laws and regulations to reflect the latest developments in IPR protection and enforcement. It should also continue to expand resources devoted to IPR enforcement and adopt stronger deterrents against IPR infringement.

(2) Improve enforcement against online counterfeiting and piracy. Internet platforms are a growing means for counterfeiters to market and sell counterfeit goods and distribute pirated content, but they present special challenges for rights-holders and enforcement officials alike. Shanghai should increase enforcement of Internet-related IPR to ensure its laws, regulations and enforcement efforts cover areas such as use of trademarks on websites, trademark-related aspects of domain name registrations, and the use of websites, Internet services, and apps as platforms for counterfeit and pirated products. Such rules and their enforcement should establish a framework that promotes accountability while balancing the needs of legitimate IPR holders and Internet intermediaries.

(3) Strengthen trade secrets protection. The protection of trade secrets is a core component of innovative economies. Shanghai can take positive steps to encourage innovation by expanding its efforts to address trade secrets concerns, including the development of a Trade Secrets Law, broader use of judicial procedures on preliminary injunctions and evidence preservation orders, clearer measures requiring government agencies to protect confidential information collected from companies during government review processes, and reducing the high evidentiary burden that plaintiffs face during trade secrets cases.

5. Talent and Visa Polices

As Shanghai's economy rapidly develops and new policies are released to promote openness, such as in the Shanghai Free Trade Zone for example, a key concern for

提升投资贸易便利化水平，构建开放型经济新体制

companies to expand business is whether they will be able to attract talent with practical experience and an international background. Attraction, retention, and developing high-end talents have been one of the challenges faced by foreign companies.

(1) Age requirement on visas for key talent. Liberalize the age limitation on visa application to 65 years old for those who have been considered as key talent. According to the existing visa policy, foreigners who have reached to 60 years old, his/her visa needs to be reviewed by government once a year.

(2) Introduction of a talent policy for Shanghai. Facilitate the process for highly-skilled talent to settle down and acquire a *Hukou* in Shanghai. For key positions in a company such as skilled senior business development personnel, it is still very hard for them to get a local Shanghai *Hukou* according to current talent polices.

(3) Work permit application for foreigners. Streamline the process for foreigner work permit applications. For example, in previous experience work permits will be awarded to foreigners within five working days after submitted all the application materials, but per current policies, it was extended to 15 working days. Foreign companies now need to obtain a residence permit within 30 days once entering China. However, procedures for health check and work permit application are also time consuming, often exceeding 30 days, and this can cause the delay for a residence application. We hope the relevant department will shorten the license approval time and make this process more efficient.

6. Administrative Licensing and Approvals

(1) Ensure equal treatment in administrative licensing processes. USCBC's annual membership surveys cite administrative licensing as a top challenge for conducting business in China, consistently ranking among the top 10 priority issues over the past decade. These licenses include business licenses, branch licenses, product approval licenses, import licenses, and other licenses and permits in sectors such as banking, healthcare, insurance, construction, legal, and value-added telecom services (such as data centers). Shanghai has already streamlined many foreign investment related operating license requirements for foreign business. We hope that China will continue to reduce licensing barriers, and that companies are treated equally during the approval process.

(2) Approval timelines. Clear, consistently implemented timelines help ensure transparency in any licensing process. Companies say that timelines often are not followed in certain approval processes, which creates significant delays in the process of investing in China. To improve transparency and predictability in approvals, USCBC recommends that the government develop clear guidelines requiring agencies to provide more frequent and timely updates to applicants. If the agency misses a deadline, agencies should explain why the approval was delayed.

(3) Approval process standardization. Work with local government agencies to standardize licensing processes across jurisdictions. Align central, provincial, and local regulations to ensure unified regulations across levels of government and agencies.

(4) National negative list. Implementation of a nationwide market access negative list would clarify which sectors are open to foreign investment and ensure consistent enforcement by local and provincial governments.

Looking for a More Open and Fairer Trading Environment—The Expectations of Japanese Enterprises on Investment and Trade Facilitation

Michiaki Oguri

Director-General, JETRO Shanghai

In 2015, the export value of world's trade in goods was 16 446.7 billion dollars (calculated by JETRO) , and was 12.7% less compared with 2014. It has seen the first decline in six years. The import value of China's goods also experienced a sharp decrease of 18.4%, and its' contribution to world trade import was −1.9%.

Since 2012, the expansion pace of trade scale remains stagnant comparing with the world economic growth rate. This phenomenon is the so called "slow trade". Comparing with the actual growth rate of GDP, the actual growth rate of trade in goods is only 0.5. Especially in emerging countries and developing countries led by China, slow trade is particularly significant.

The low level of investment affects the development of trade, therefore caused the extended downturn of trade. The growth of trade in capital goods and intermediate goods, which constitute the elements of equipment investment, has seen a worldwide slowdown since 2012, especially in China. Under the commodity category, China's import trends show that the import of consumer goods in 2010 gained a solid growth, but the proportion of consumer goods in China's imports accounted for only 9.1%; the import of capital goods and intermediate goods, which accounted for 53% and 15.9% respectively, was significantly decreased.

Another possible structural reason for this is that the development of the global value chain (GVC), which has driven the expansion of world trade, has slowed down. The cause of this phenomenon includes the internal production of China, as a world factory, is becoming more and more obvious, the internal trade rate is increasing in major regions of Asia, and the cost difference between regions is reducing, etc. In particular, the improvement of China's domestic supply capacity acts an important role in trade growth. China used to import equipment components and parts from neighboring countries, assemble them into complete set, and then export the products to worldwide. However, with the enhancement of technology in recent years, imports of processing trade accounted for a decline in the proportion of imports, and the added value of the domestic manufacturing industry continues to grow. The increasing trend of China's internal production led to the sluggish of China's import and world trade growth.

Under this trend of world trade and investment, the foreign trade of Shanghai after 2012 has a significant tendency towards slow trade. In the aspect of trade between nations, the trade with Japan, while still maintaining the second only to the United States, is apparently increasing slowly.

In addition, the actual foreign investment in Shanghai reached $10 billion in 2008, and has continued to grow. The establishment of the China (Shanghai) Pilot Free Trade Zone in September 2013 has played a significant role in promoting foreign investment in particular.

China (Shanghai) Pilot Free Trade Zone has made lots of attempts in different aspects and accomplished many achievements, including the management of negative list, the simplification of enterprise registration system, as well as the facilitation of trade system. However, there are still a lot of Japanese companies express that they did not enjoy much actual benefits from the reform.

In recent years, Shanghai has earned excellent comments for its efforts on the service industry, the financial industry, as well as the investment and trade facilitation. However, standing from the international level, it is hard to say that Shanghai has "assured the fairness" and fully established a "high transparency" business environment.

During the 13th Five-Year Plan, Chinese government has been deepening the reform to improve the market system, promoting the reform of the administrative system, improving the system of opening-up. Shanghai, as always, is on the frontline and looking forward to further development.

Thus, we hope that Shanghai can accept the suggestions of these Japanese enterprises, promote and develop a more excellent and fairness business environment. The specific suggestions from Japanese enterprises on investment and trade facilitation are as follows.

1. Actively Provide Information to Japanese Enterprises

Since 2013, the amount of Japanese enterprises' investment in Shanghai changed from growth to decline. In 2015, the investment amount significantly dropped by 60% comparing with 2014. According to the investigation of Japanese enterprises (2015) implemented by JETRO, though the proportion of Japanese enterprises planning to expand their scale in Shanghai is a little higher than the national average (38.1%), it is still only 38.5%, which is the lowest number in history of Shanghai. The proportion of enterprises that will maintain the current status accounted for 55.2%.

The reason why Japanese enterprises are so cautious is that the information on promoting reform and business opportunities in Shanghai has not been fully conveyed to Japanese enterprises. However, the negative information about China's investment and business environment in recent years, such as rising costs and slowing economic growth, has attracted the attention of Japanese companies.

In order to eliminate the negative impression, we hope the Shanghai government can continue to deepen the reform that could bring investment benefits to Japanese enterprises, and also actively provide information on reform progress and business opportunities in Shanghai through various channels.

2. Investment: Eliminate the Internal and External Difference, Match with International Standards

The non-transparency in system operation is often regarded as a risk in foreign enterprises when investing in China. We hope to see some improvement in foreseeable problems such as unifying implementation of the legal system interpretation, providing more preparation time for institutional exchange, simplifying and facilitating various procedures, improving the consultation answering work and so on.

We highly value the promotion of negative list and the decrease of industry types in the list. However there are still differences in treating domestic and foreign enterprises when it comes to certain industries. For example, in China (Shanghai) Pilot Free Trade Zone, there is less restriction in the range of contract construction for 100% foreign invested construction enterprises. But there are still limitations in other areas. And in telecom industry, exclusively foreign-owned enterprises or foreign share holding enterprises still cannot get their business license. We hope that the policies in these specific areas can change and eliminate the difference.

3. The Facilitation of Operating Assets Integration

Japanese enterprises enter Shanghai's market at an early stage. With the fast development of market-oriented economy and the rapid change of the investment environment, it is a trend that enterprises have to carry out asset restructuring. But the current situation is that the closure of enterprises and the integration of business outlets have to go through a very complicated procedure, waiting for a long period of tax review, which consuming too much manpower and resources. We are eager to shorten the time of tax investigation, so that the process of enterprise assets restructuring will be simpler. These measures can also promote the rationalization of industrial structure.

4. Trade and Customs: Expect more Liberalization

Through establishing the China (Shanghai) Pilot Free Trade Zone, there are improvements in enhancing the efficiency, transparency, and service level of the system in the trade and customs aspect. However, in the investigation of Japanese enterprises (2015) implemented by JETRO, there are still lots of enterprises think that the complicated procedures and long time of customs clearance are the difficulties during their operation.

For example, when it comes to Customs review and the legal interpretation of import declaration, there are different explanations from different people about HS code, certificate of origin of the same product. We hope that through strengthening training and making more detailed manuals, we can achieve unification of law enforcement.

Of course, it would be better if the advance publicity system of the HS code can be implemented in the whole nation so that enterprises can use it with flexibility. We also appreciate it if the detailed and specific material about the classification of goods is open to the public. Not only can it provide convenience for enterprises, but also reduce the burden of the government and relevant authorities.

With the introduction of "entry first, clearance second" system and deepening of reform in China (Shanghai) Pilot Free Trade Zone, the level of facilitation is improved. However, even though the port realized electronic automation, the goods still cannot be cleared after 5 p.m., when the customs and quarantine officers are off-duty. We hope Shanghai's port can carry out 24h watch system, or provide green channel for goods at night.

When we re-export less than container load (LCL) from bonded area, the container freight station (CFS) warehouse designated by the Customs is not only expensive but also has a high risk of damaging the goods. We hope that the using CFS warehouse can be more liberalized in the future.

Chinese government has been actively introducing free trade agreement with other countries and regions to promote trade liberalization, which is something we welcome. The early implementation the FTA among China, Japan and Korea, and Regional Comprehensive Economic Partnership (RCEP) can abolish and periodically cancel the tariff and non tariff measures, bring more liberty and facilitation to present trade regulations. We sincerely hope that we can sign this as soon as possible.

5. Relaxing Restrictions on Imports of Japanese Food

At present, Chinese consumers are showing a strong desire to buy safe and high-quality Japanese agricultural products and food. And Japanese food has won a high reputation among Chinese tourists. However, due to import limitation, many foods cannot be imported to China, like dairy products because of foot-and-mouth disease (FMD), meat because of FMD and bovine spongiform encephalopathy (BSE), fine rice produced by unspecified factories and rice without fumigating warehouses' treatment, as well as fruits such as apples and pears because of zero experience in export. I would like to ask for a relaxing in these restrictions. It can provide Chinese people with rich and varied Japanese food, enrich the diet culture, improve the living standards, and also increase the import tax and stimulate the potential of consumer demand.

Shanghai took the lead in the establishment of the free trade zone. In order to achieve an international level of trade and investment environment, Shanghai is carrying out the procedure simplification of the entry of imported goods and inspection and quarantine procedures. We hope that as part of a pilot reform, the restrictions on Japanese goods will be abolished or broadened.

6. Promote Overseas Investments and Facilitate Procedures

In recent years, China's investment abroad is increasing rapidly, and the investment in Japan is also gradually expanding. The relevant procedures for investments abroad are becoming simpler, but there is still a high level of capital transfer barriers. We hope that Shanghai will promote the development of two-way investment, giving more support for the overseas investment of Chinese enterprises, make the relevant procedures more convenient.

ROUNDTABLE DISCUSSION

圆桌讨论

主持人·HOST

黄　佳　Elton Huang
普华永道中国中区市场主管合伙人、上海首席合伙人
Leader of PwC Central China Markets, Senior Partner of PwC Shanghai

互动嘉宾·PANELISTS

申卫华　Shen Weihua
上海市商务委员会副主任
Deputy Director General of Shanghai Municipal Commission of Commerce

李咏今　Li Yongjin
上海市国有资产监督管理委员会副巡视员
Deputy Inspector of the State-owned Assets Supervision and Administration Commission of Shanghai Municipal Government

武　伟　Wu Wei
上海市口岸服务办公室副巡视员
Deputy Inspector of the Shanghai Municipal Office for Port Services

谢秋慧　Xie Qiuhui
上海出入境检验检疫局党组成员、浦江局局长
Member of the Party Committee of Shanghai Entry-Exit Inspection and Quarantine Bureau，Director of Shanghai Pujiang Entry-Exit Inspection and Quarantine Bureau

张　科　Zhang Ke
上海电气集团副总裁
Vice President of Shanghai Electric Group Co., Ltd.

丁嵩冰　Ding Songbing
上海国际港务（集团）股份有限公司战略研究部总经理
General Manager of Strategic Research Department, Shanghai International Port (Group) Co., Ltd.

范　杰　Fan Jie
上海新工联集团总经理
General Manager of Shanghai NIU (Group) Co., Ltd.

陆　扬　Sunny Lu
BitSE 公司创始人兼首席运营官
Co-founder and COO of BitSE

赵　熙　Zhao Xi
德意志银行董事总经理、首席运营官、董事会执行董事
Managing Director, COO, Executive Director of Deutsche Bank, China

诺伯特・梅尔林　Norbert Meyring
毕马威中国区高级合伙人、环球客户部负责人、中国及亚太区生命科学部负责人
Senior Partner, Head of Global Accounts, Head of Life Sciences Division in China and Asia Pacific, KPMG China

邵　枫　Shao Feng
雅培中国政府关系总监
Director of Government Relations, Abbott, China

李俊杰　Li Junjie
中伦律师事务所合伙人
Partner of Zhong Lun Law Firm

邓玲凌　Deng Lingling
泰科电子政府关系经理
Manager of Government Relations, TE Connectivity, China

陈子雷　Chen Zilei
上海对外经济贸易大学教授
Professor at Shanghai University of International Business and Economics

乔依德　Qiao Yide
上海发展研究基金会副会长兼秘书长
Vice Chairman and Secretary General of Shanghai Development Research Foundation

欧　文　Owen Haacke
美中贸易全国委员会上海首席代表
Chief Representative of Shanghai Office, US-China Business Council

小栗道明　Michiaki Oguri
日本贸易振兴机构上海所所长
Director-General of JETRO Shanghai

姚为群　Yao Weiqun
上海 WTO 事务咨询中心经济学研究员
Research Professor of Economics, Shanghai WTO Affairs Consultation Center

黄佳：曾经有人说，现在想讨论城市的发展，包括企业国际化、"一带一路"等话题，可以每天参加这类研讨会，但时间差不多也就用完了。智库则是一个持续的平台。上海的经济分为央企、地方国企、民企、跨国企业四类，这个良好的生态圈给大家创造了合作的平台。假设大家对某一个议题特别感兴趣，我们可以搭一个开放的平台，就这个议题建一个研究小组，明年带过来和大家做更多的分享，这是我的一个倡议。

邵枫：我来自美国雅培公司，我们的问题是：上海要成为世界研发中心城市，其中很重要的一点就是药物的研发，生物制药也是今后除了化学药物以外的一个重要发展方向。雅培公司有诊断方面的需求，其中带有动物原性和人原性生物制剂是研发生物制药的非常重要的原材料，在进口上，上海市的海关和商检有没有更加便利的措施，来帮助企业进口这些材料？特别是面向已经认定为上海市研发中心的研发机构，相关部门是否会出台更加便利的措施？

谢秋慧：我来自上海出入境检验检疫局。刚才雅培公司提了一个很好的问题。事实上为了促进生物医药产业的发展，2015 年上海国检局专门推出了《关于支持上海生物医药产业发展的若干意见》，从转变行政职能、创新监管模式、简化事前审批、加强事中事后监管等方面，帮助生物医药单位破解共性瓶颈，采取相关的措施，大大简化相关流程。我们也做了很多调研和了解，在进口医药所需的时间和各项流程上，制剂卫生检疫审批的相关流程已经从 20 个工作日缩短至 5 个工作日，最快的仅需 3 个工作日。2015 年开始，上海口岸出入境的特殊物品单位已经达到 387 家，出入境特殊物品达到了 27 988 批次，同比增长 46%。

另外，针对生物医药研发单位普遍反映的高风险、特殊物品的入境难、审批手续多步的问题，在上海市政府的协调下，目前审批工作明显减少了流程。2016年7月，上海国检局和上海市卫计委共同发布了《关于做好过渡期间特殊物品出入境卫生检疫管理工作的通知》。从2016年10月1日起，除医疗机构申请用于临床治疗的进口特殊物品，其余由上海出入境检验检疫局直接受理、开展风险评估和检验检疫审批，解决了企业入境高风险、特殊物品时间长、需跑多个部门的困境。企业若需要深入了解信息，可以登录上海国检局的门户网站，也可以查阅特殊物品监管的相关公告。从2016年10月以来，上海国检局已经受理了48个项目的风险评估手续，相关工作顺利有序进行。

黄佳： 我想谈一下自己关于医药方面的感受。我曾经和上海市政府领导沟通，为什么不多开放各层级需求，比如高端医疗领域。他说，不是不开放，而是大家有一个痛点：国外的医生过来也能够拿到执照，但是待一两年都想回去，究其原因在于他们看病无法开国外能够开的药，因为中国没有相关的FDA批复，而一旦暂时用的产品不顺手，他们便只能待两年就离开。还请会后相关监管部门对这个问题进行交流。

丁嵩冰： 我来自上港集团，我的问题是关于海外投资汇率风险方面的。这几年，上港集团在"一带一路"沿线考察了不少项目，客观来说，项目很多，好的项目也不少。然而真正涉及投资的话，一般都比较谨慎，因为面临一个比较现实的问题，投资必须有回报，从逻辑上说，涉及资金的一出一进。上港集团海外的国际信用评级比较高，但是目前我们不能通过把国内货币换成美金去海外投资，而是要在海外融美元或者外资，再将国外货币直接投入到国外市场，将来取得回报之后，资金再通过某种方式回到国内。

这样就出现一个比较尴尬和两难的问题：海外投资有一定的回报期，大型项目的前几年现金流相对较差，海外项目融资还款付息如果不依靠借新还旧，就要通过国内对海外平台增资解决资金来源，在人民币贬值的情况下，还款压力加大。反过来如果人民币升值，集团以人民币为结算货币，海外项目的收益在并回集团母公司的时候会出现项目本身收益正常，但折算为人民币后收益下降的情形。例如，之前汇率水平下，1美元相当于7元人民币。当人民币升值，1美元只相当于5元人民币时，就造成海外经营资产可能增值了，但并回母公司报表时却反映不出增值。

我们认为，自贸区和整个评价考核，应该做一些综合性的考量。不仅仅要考虑回报率，还要考虑海外资产的增值率，从两条线综合评价。

还有一个想法是，现在企业海外发债都要通过发改委的申报流程，我们需要通过上海市发改委，再报国家发改委，一层一层上报。现在我们说要提升上海投资贸易便利化水平，那么在自贸区是否在将来能够争取到政策的先行先试？例如，在一定的政策额度之下，发改委能否允许企业自行决策。这是一个建议，也是一个问题。

黄佳：财务并表的问题，我们可以会下交流。人民币双向流动和汇率波动背景下产生的问题，是近期的热点话题。我想归纳一下刚才上港集团提到的一个重要问题，它们作为大国企，评级比较高，有很强的海外融资渠道，怎样才能让它在资金支持上具有灵活性，或者说使资金双向发挥最大效用？

李咏今：中共十八大以来，在深化改革的顶层设计中，国资委作为资产管理部门，以管资本为主。上港集团作为一个上市公司，国资委只是股东之一，它所有的企业经营决策都是通过董事会决定的。在整个过程中，包括海外战略，国资委实行备案管理，只要符合它的主业，没有任何的特殊要求。

上港集团提出的问题在国资委管理的企业中有一定的普遍性。目前，我们境外的企业大概有446家，资产总额在4 000亿元人民币左右。这两年境外投资比较多，今年境外投资有80多亿美元左右，大约有16家企业8个项目做投资，包括锦江国际等公司在这方面做了很多努力。需要说明的是，董事会做决策，包括汇率风险怎么回避，其实都属于企业决策，而不是国资委来替它们做决策。关于上港集团提出的其他问题，需要我们政府其他公共管理部门一起帮企业解决，国资委会跟企业一起向相关公共管理部门呼吁，帮助企业解决眼前碰到的困难和问题。

乔依德：我从研究者角度谈一点想法。上港集团提的问题很有意义和普遍性，我知道绿地集团也有类似的情况，他们投融资也都在海外，收益也是外币，这种情况下没有汇率风险。第二个情况是海外项目周期较长存在人民币兑换风险，关于这个问题，我记得自贸区有优惠政策，投资额在1亿美元以下只需要备案，至于海外发债，不知道自贸区有没有优惠政策。

首先，企业要做好长远的思想准备，把握好今后的方向，要看到汇率走向浮动的趋势。人民币走向浮动汇率以后，企业要加强研究，特别是对全球的经济和汇率研究。其次，企业需要有研究成本投入，这样企业整体走向不会错。很多企业最后吃大亏，是因为它们觉得自己聪明可以赌一把。

从人民币的角度讲，今后几个月到半年，海外风险比较大，不确定性也比较大，总的来说人民币可兑换还是应当以稳为主，包括汇率方面。这是我从研究者的角度提出的观点。

黄佳：如果说前几年大家关注的是以在华外商直接投资为主，那么现在大家可能更加关注人民币，包括企业"走出去"。

申卫华：对外投资确实面临汇兑风险的问题，外商投资企业、外贸企业，甚至从事进出口涉外业务的企业都会出现汇兑风险的问题。严格意义上讲，这是市场的判断问题。对于中央政府来讲，主要是向国内企业传递汇率的趋势，要根据国家政策相应提出汇兑政策。

从市场经济行为来说，对外投资有很多种保值增值的方法。汇率的变动在国际上经常发生，只是变动幅度大小的问题。如果有时候纯粹不管的话，不一定对你不利，看你如何结算，有时候按照人民币结算有利，有时候美元结算有利，企业做出重大投资决策的时候要进行客观的判断。尤其是长期付款，时间跨度很长，可以采取很多市场的方法。就像绿地投资，杠杆率很高，怎么保证汇率稳定？比如和对方谈收购谈合作，你可以锁定价格，这些都取决于你在收购市场的议价能力有多强。如果企业议价能力弱，受市场波动的风险就大，如果议价能力强，对控制市场风险的能力就强。

市场中确确实实会面临很多风险。有时候随着大宗商品汇率下降，一些航空运输企业会得到很多的利益，但是可以通过锁定利率价格，就像国资委谈到的，这是市场的决策行为。当企业作出重大决策的时候，一定要考虑好汇兑风险，还要考虑国别投资，因为有些企业会在不同国别投资基础设施和港口，比如"一带一路"中的很多港口投资也是将来"一带一路"建设的重点。

这些和汇率、国别以及汇兑风险相关的问题，企业都要进行考虑。风险会一直伴随着企业"走出去"的行为，企业要信息充分，也要多听一些咨询机构对未来的发展趋势，包括汇兑走势的判断，量身定做一个相应的决策方案。

在企业海外发债问题上，由国资委、发改委对企业国外投资进行管理是正确的。不能说管理很严格，而是确实应该加强管理。风险是对企业的多层面提醒，特别在基础设施投资风险非常大的地方。一方面，要加强对当地市场和汇率变动的研判。另一方面，也要多跟相关主管部门，包括国资委、发改委等部门进行充分沟通和汇报，使企业走出去更加顺利、风险更加小，不至于损失太大。

黄佳：一家上海国企在海外并购，在管理汇率风险上坚持自然对冲，当交易是美元对价时没有借美元，反而借英镑。我问财务主管为什么这么做，他说所谓自然对冲就是并购标的公司收入主要来源是在英国使用英镑，那么收入来源和负债自然对冲，这是最低的风险。而一些企业高管会说，人民币贬值这么厉害，当时为什么不借人民币？我的看法是，对大家来说，把控风险是第一位，而不是获利。

张科：上海电气的问题类似于上港集团谈的问题，除了刚才提的问题以外，我再补充几个。

第一，上海电气现在除了海外兼并公司以外，也有很多海外的项目，这些项目理论上来讲是董事会决定哪些项目要做，但是也牵扯到流程的审批，除了上海还要到北京去批，因此我们建议流程可以缩短一点。

第二，融资担保的手续能不能简化。

第三，随着上海电气大量产品"走出去"，其中遇到了一些问题，就是国家之间，或者中国国家标准和国际标准之间不相同的问题。这与国家标委会相关，我们应当怎么来协调这个问题？用中国标准去做对我们来讲非常熟悉，我们的产品不错，但是到了国外需要认证美国标准或者其他地方的标准，整个制造工艺的要求不一样，在这个方面能否做一些工作？

黄佳：这个其实是两个问题，一个是关于工程项目"走出去"的时候涉及地方批和北京批的问题。第二个是关于国内国际标准规范化认证的问题。

欧文：通过对比各国的一些贸易标准，包括 WTO 以及其他国际组织，贸易标准化是非常重要的一个方面。无论中国公司去美国投资，还是美国公司来中国投资，对于美国都非常重要。据我所知，上海，特别是自贸区，会进一步加强贸易和标准化方面的规则制定。

黄佳：谈到企业投资贸易标准的时候，我们会发现美国有大量企业集群性的组织设在中国，例如美国商会。但是现在中国到海外投资的时候，更多的是企业单独去做，并没有非常明显的企业集群。谈到国与国之间的标准准入的时候，经常需要群体做呼吁和倡议，这也是各个企业需要思考的问题。关于上海批和北京批，线下大家可以和部委进行交流。刚刚听到关于中国承包的话题，既然谈到中国企业去海外投资，不妨也听听在建筑方面外资企业到中国投资遇到的问题。比如建筑公司在国内承包工程时，是不是也存在着标准和壁垒的问题？

小栗道明：日本企业进入上海市场比较早，其中包括一些建筑公司。但是现在国外的独资公司在上海开设建筑公司还是有一定障碍的。这几年在华的日本独资企业比较少，订单也减少了，如果能接到中国国内的项目，它们也可以生产下去。日本企业非常希望这方面市场能开放。

黄佳：外商独资企业承包工程的时候，会不会有相应的壁垒问题？

姚为群：建设项目牵涉到两个方面：一方面，现在中日之间没有双边自贸协定，所以现在日资企业要进入中国市场，是按照中国对 WTO 的服务贸易承诺执行的。我们非常希望日本企业、韩国企业能推动中日韩三边自贸区早日实现，在服务业方面有所突破。另一方面，目前中国还不是 WTO 政府采购协定成员，正在谈判加入。由于我们不是成员，当日本企业要进入中国的公共建筑市场的时候，我们只能按照 WTO 中国对建筑业的承诺开放。所以有以下几个方法：一是中国争取早日加入 WTO 政府采购协定，这样日本企业有机会投到中国公共工程项目。二是希望通过中日韩自贸区协定推进中国建筑业市场的开放。

申卫华：刚刚上海电气和日本贸易振兴机构的问题都涉及投资。

上海电气对外投资涉及标准化的问题，这也是对外签承包工程协议时带成套设备需要注意的一个方向。根据很多实践经验，非洲、欧洲，特别是发展中国家的标准迥异。比如俄罗斯有俄罗斯的标准，发达国家有发达国家的标准。国家鼓励并且希望对外承包工程能带动国内的大型成套设备出口。由于成套设备不经常做标准化设备出口，有很多成套设备都是定制化的，涉及改造，不仅仅是火电，甚至核电，都要根据业主要求做。因此成套设备出口会涉及标准不统一的问题，这也会增加很多成本，签订大型成套设备要注意。如果不是总承包，而是分包项目，更涉及这个问题。总包商需要研究标准认证问题，分包商需要多跟国内的总包商接触，看能不能提前做标准认证。包括报价也要注意，因为涉及改造、改标准。上海电气还提到投资路条的问题，时间审批上有长有短。而且涉及国内的互相竞争，这属于协调的问题。需要到商务委和发改委等国家部委协调，实际上也是一个前置性路条的问题。估计在座的很多外资企业不了解，但是国内企业知道，拿路条很难，时间上需要协调。

刚才小栗先生谈到的问题，姚老师从 WTO 的角度来解释，讲得非常正确。

服务贸易开放，首先是严格按照我们加入 WTO 时的承诺，即服务贸易中的商业承载内容来履行相关义务，包括跨境消费、跨境交付、自然人流动等内容。其次，我们会根据签署的双边、多边自贸协定中开放服务贸易的相关内容做一些承诺，这是国家义务，也是正在做的事情。第三，是自主放、自主改。在自贸区内，现在已经开始做准入前负面清单加国民待遇，把外资的准入放开。但是准入后，确确实实出现了一些服务业在运营过程中出现非国民待遇的情况，有些是超国民待遇，也有低国民待遇。按照业务范围，外商承包工程可能只能承接一些中外合作的、国外政府赠款或中国技术无法实现的项目，范围确实很小。还有一些领域，比如教育和医疗机构领域，可以开放，但是因为进入不了劳保范围，选择的人相对较少。针对这一方面，我们正在研究今后在自贸区能不能实行准入后国民待遇。所谓准入后国民待遇就是外商投资企业尽量享受到跟国有、民营企业相同的待遇。我们现在正在进行梳理，外商投资企业进入后在经营过程中还有哪些限制范围，想在自贸区里试着改变。这是自主改、自主放的相关内容。另外，发改委和商务部已做的市场准入，指的是流通或其他准入，还没有完全细化到外商投资企业能不能做的问题，下一步我们会推动这个工作。我们现在正在收集这方面的信息，今天日本贸易振兴机构提供了很好的信息，如果还有其他进一步的信息，希望你们可以提供。不仅如此，我们基本可以做一个服务贸易的负面清单，其他几个类别中，也要体现企业主体有差别待遇的问题。这是自主放、自主改，能放多少、能改多少，还需要进一步跟中央各个部委一起研究，进行推进。

黄佳： 对"路条"一词可能很多人还不理解，我们需要进一步解释。还有现在某些城市在实行"沙盒计划"，在负面清单上要做一些尝试。就是在一个相对封闭的区域或者领域，把现行法规放在一边，允许某些新技术或新模式，比如区块链、服务贸易，进行突破法律法规的尝试，比如在 6 个月的时间内，做一些不涉及触犯当前法规红线的尝试，自由做尝试，然后做反思。

赵熙： 刚刚大家谈进出口贸易，我们非常感兴趣。国内和国际有不同标准，给国内企业"走出去"、国外企业来中国投资造成了一些困难。以我们的经验来说，一些跨国企业来中国运作，在上海和其他城市之间也有很大的地区性差异。从金融行业角度来讲，因为受监管部门的监管，无论是外管局、人民银行，还是银监局、银监会、地方银监会，对我们的监管都非常严格。这也就造成了跨国企业在不同区域运作时，从地区性差异来看，会遇到一些困难。

大多数的跨国企业在向集中运营的模式转化，共享服务中心都设在上海。上海作为中国的最大的金融中心，在政策的统一性、简化性等各方面，都是走在全国前列的。但各个跨国公司只是把总部设在上海，子公司、分公司更多地分布在其他的省市。这种情况下，举一个具体的例子，一个跨国企业总部在上海，开放人民币跨境现金池和跨境对外放款业务时，这个公司的账户开在德意志上海分行。按照上海监管要求，资金对外付款业务不需要登记报备，但是客户子公司所在地的外管局表示，这个业务还需要按照当地要求进行登记、报备、操作。这种情况下，上海作为中国最大的金融中心，在跟国内其他的省市进行法律法规协调统一的方面，能不能起到一个牵头或领导的作用，减少中国内部的区域差异性，为银行、跨国公司在国内的运作提供更有利的条件？

黄佳：曾经有外资企业开玩笑说，在中国做业务就像是在 30 多个国家做业务，这是一些企业的心声。不知道委办局对于加强区域合作、消除区域之间对法律法规解读的差异问题上有没有什么想法，来帮助企业在中国市场运营上有个统一的标准？

申卫华：首先，金融问题涉及整个管理部门，涉及自贸区跨国公司的结算和子公司的结算问题，也涉及政策突破问题。从政策覆盖上说，政策要覆盖到相应的分公司没有问题，但是由于中国是划区域进行管理的，各个省都有外管局，还有相应的管理制度，因此政策覆盖到子公司有一定的困难。但对上海作为跨国公司总部的集聚地来说，这是需要解决的问题。

最主要的，还是跨国公司、母子公司的整合问题。就像德国很少会出现各个州都设一个子公司的现象，但是中国在各个地方都需要设一个子公司。因为从客观角度来讲，分公司的生存和运营没有子公司那么方便。各个省市通过招商引资，对设立子公司的优惠和设立分公司的优惠不一样，对人员的管理也不一样。德国有一个很大的化工企业，作为制造型企业，想要把全国 18 家子公司全部整合为分公司。用了接近 1 年时间，找了很多中介、顾问，最后彻底放弃了这种想法。要想把制造型企业整合为分公司，确实有很大困难，因为中国各个地方的经济发展的特点有所不同。

上海目前也在逐步解决这个问题。暂且不提上海市跟其他省市相比情况如何，仅仅上海一个区到另外一个区，就很难"走得动"。要想把上海某个子公司变成分公司也很难。例如，家乐福为什么要在各个区设子公司，而设立分公司有问题？假设一下，如果家乐福从浦东新区迁到黄浦区，或者把浦东新区的分公司变成子公司，5 年内的税收基数不转移。这个企业贡献 1 个亿的税收，1 个亿的税基不转移，增量部分放到黄浦区，减量部分也是减到黄浦区，也即增是黄浦区的，减也是黄浦区的，这种情况下从浦东新区迁到黄浦区，浦东新区因为保5年内税基不变，而对黄浦区来讲就有压力，要解决税基各方面的转移问题。如果有相关的政策就可以很容易地将区跟区的迁移改成相应的分公司的做法。

但省市之间，这个政策要靠企业不断反映才能逐步解决，这确实会给企业带来很大的运营成本。政策不统一就需要一个独立的运营体系，这又会引发公司治理结构问题。企业的选择不尽相同，有的企业愿意做子公司，有的愿意做分公司，应该由市场主体自己决策公司治理结构如何改变。

我赞同德意志银行的观点，也支持你们呼吁的情况，但是这个改革措施需要各个省市共同协调。比如长三角地区、京津冀地区从今年开始统一协调，其中包括很多公司运营、迁移也涉及税基的问题。说到底就是涉及地方财政收入的问题，这需要统一协调。上海要牵头做法律上的统一，可以先从自贸区尝试，但是这个难度会很大，希望大家理解，这需要一个很长期的推进过程。

黄佳：利益、税制的问题，不是简单的一个政府就能解决的问题。一枚硬币有两面，高交易成本、运营成本之下，我们还能有这么快的经济增长，一旦这些效率得到进一步的提升、释放，潜力其实非常巨大。

刚刚谈了很多关于投资的问题，不妨再回到贸易。小栗所长代表的是日本贸易振兴机构，之前提到了日本农产品和海关的相关问题，不知道有没有问题想问海关、商检、口岸办的相关人员？

小栗道明：目前中国对于日本的农产品进口，由于检验检疫问题，新鲜食品中只有苹果和梨可以进口，水产品可以进口，牛肉、猪肉、鸡肉都因为口蹄疫和疯牛病的关系，禁止进口。我们觉得，日本的食品还是比较安全的，所以我们也希望这方面早日放开限制。

谢秋慧：关于日本农产品、食材、食品进口限制政策的问题，中国采用的是准入制度。目前实行的新品种准入，需要原产国官方的检验部门向国家质检总局提出书面申请，并提供开展风险分析的必要技术资料。我相信日本这方面做得很规范，很严格。国家质检总局收到相关资料后，会组织专家开展风险评估，并根据风险分析结果，确定与我国保护水平相一致的风险管理措施，签订双边的议定书后方可进口。如果出现区域性的疫情或安全质量事件，将影响到进口质量安全的，国家质检总局也会采取应急预案做出停止或加严监管的临时性或阶段性措施，保护国情安全、食品安全。

刚才提到的日本农产品，比如苹果、梨，属于传统贸易，已经获得了国家的准入，一直以来我们对这两种水果没有特殊的监管要求，但是有一部分特殊情况，2011 年 3 月 11 日，日本地震导致核物质泄露以来，为确保日本输华食品安全，国家质检总局对日本农产品提出，需要有日本官方出具的原产地证明。2011 年 5 月、11 月，国家质检总局分别下发了《关于印发日本输华水产品原产地证书和放射性物质检测证明书的通知》和《关于日本输华农产品饲料原产地证明签发机构盖章样本的通知》，要求来自日本农产品提供原产地相关证书。目前上海口岸也是根据总局要求进行监管，因为涉及放射性的相关物体，与日本福岛群岛、东京、千叶等十个县相关。

如果你需要了解进一步的准入条件，可以参考现有流程。我们对进口的水产品、农产品，已经出台了很多便捷措施。比如，对进境的水果、农产品的工作流程都进行了优化，对风险受控的、质量达到要求的产品，24 小时就能进货架，很多商品因为效率高了，售价都下降了 30% 左右。

黄佳：刚刚更多的是从法规、政府和政府间对某些产品的规定来进行探讨。假如说从技术层面看，区块链在食品安全、药品安全和溯源方面，还有很多应用。我们不妨换换气氛，听听技术颠覆在这个行业中是如何应用的。

陆扬：其实区块链这项技术带来的是一种效率上的提升。最主要的原因是它打破了原来各种信息孤岛产生的效率问题或成本问题。比如小栗先生提到的问题，检验检疫局的专家提到要有产品溯源。其实很多时候，溯源、源头信息是存在的，包括源头资料也是存在的，但是如何做到自由流动，或者及时反映给监管和相关部门，实现信息有效传递，是比较困难的。这取决于各个国家或者各个部门、各个企业 IT 系统或数据的流动性。目前来讲，是比较大的障碍。

区块链可以很好地解决这些问题。我们现在正在跟不同的部门、企业做这方面的沟通，其中包括红酒溯源，是一个非常明显的案例，它能实现从源头把信息的每个节点一点一点地分别传递到监管部门和最终消费者。我相信这一定能极大地提高溯源效率，降低溯源成本。原来传统的 IT 技术或数据技术，在对接方面有很多安全顾虑问题，所以才会形成这种障碍。区块链技术，是一个"技术阻碍理论"的诞生品，它一定可以帮助我们跨越这个阻碍。

黄佳：大家一定很关心上海建设全球科创中心的目标。科创中心离不开在上海的企业，无论是国企、民企还是外资企业，大家对技术贸易、技术进出口、包括技术贸易公共平台方面是不是有一些问题？请企业代表泰科电子分享一下他们关心的问题。

邓玲凌：上海市政府在促进服务贸易方面有一系列的努力，过去一两年中，上海也出台了一些政策。作为一家每年将全球销售额 5% 投入到研发领域的企业，我们在上海做了很多技术进出口。

技术贸易有很多种形式，包括技术转让、技术服务、技术资产的进出口等，而监管环境的差异可能对各种技术贸易形式发展有不同的影响。我们有以下几个问题：首先，上海市政府推动技术贸易时，是否会优先支持某类或某几类技术贸易？第二，上海集众力创建了一些公共服务平台，包括技术贸易公共服务平台。现在技术贸易公共服务平台建设的基本情况如何？企业怎样利用这个平台？

范杰：我来自新工联集团。我们企业既有投资业务，也有贸易业务。作为企业，我们对投资贸易便利化的期待主要是两个方面，一个是降低成本，另一个是提高效益。投资上，新工联集团响应上海自贸区发展，在上海自贸区成立了一个融资租赁公司，运作了三年多，体会到了投资便利化的实效。但是在贸易便利化方面，企业的成本降低不明显，有时还会略有提高。

我有一个建议，希望多从企业的角度出发，研究投资贸易便利化对企业成本降低和效率提高的实效。这是企业最关心的问题，或者是产业链中最终链的结果。过去上海市统计局有一个成本调查队，专门针对企业成本做过一些调查。由于没有做过这方面的统计，我只从企业代表的角度来说，如果能从宏观或者中观层面，分析企业的成本、利润等要素，这对于今后研究和出台投资贸易便利化政策，会起到非常好的作用。

黄佳：新工联集团提出了一个很好的倡议，降低交易成本、进行成本优化是企业最基本的问题。拿上海跟新加坡比较，不算货运成本，每个集装箱单体通关过程中发生的费用，上海是 300 欧元左右，新加坡是 100 欧元左右，几年前就已经有这样的差距。普华永道曾与上海市政府沟通过如何缩短这一差距的问题。这个问题对于每个企业来说，都是显性的。其他问题，包括跟政府相关的劳动力成本、土地成本、企业交易成本，还有跟供给侧结构性改革密切相关的如何提升效率，用创新、技术驱动整个效率的问题，这些问题不妨作为智库的重要研究题目和推动方向。

申卫华：大家今天提出来的问题跟商务委有或多或少的联系，包括日本小栗先生讲的植物和水产品、食品的进出口检验检疫各方面的问题。我先做一个简单的补充，替检验检疫局的同志从另外一个角度说几句。

商务委接待过很多国外代表团，他们也专门提到了这个问题。现在中国改革开放要对接高标准的国际贸易投资规则。请问在座所有企业，每个人都应该有切身的感觉，从《卫生和植物卫生措施协议》（SPS）动植物检验检疫的规定来说，究竟是国外管得严，还是中国管得严？《卫生和植物卫生措施协议》（SPS）保护人身安全、动植物的唯一性，是世界各个国家追求的共同目标。在有些分类管理中，对动植物的检验检疫过程确实比较长，但是这个政策制度还是要坚持做。

我是一个消费者，也是一个普通市民。选择食品的时候，我会选择稍微贵一点的国外进口食品。有时候我们希望价格能降低一点，但管理不能弱化。不过管理的流程、双认证的方式方法可以改革。比如区块链技术能不能解决国外认证的问题？利用新的技术和新的认证来解决，这是在自贸区、在上海可以改革的。技术上可以改进，流程上也可以改进，但不能为了逃避监管，为了方便，而减少、弱化监管的程序。

比如小栗先生，您在上海吃了多少日本牛肉？您吃的牛肉是哪国牛肉呢？我们知道，检验检疫局把控国门，监管非常严格，不然小栗先生就不会提到这个问题了。在洋山港和浦西，我们设置了很多水果进口的点；在长宁高岛屋，也在做进口食品协调。但还是这个理念，管理还要加强，不能放松。

另外，关于技术贸易我给你一个官方的说法。技术贸易进出口没有偏向性，只要是企业做技术贸易，无论是专利还是专有技术，或者是外观设计，包括计算机的集成电路布图，只要客户有需求、且纳入到技术贸易范围之中，所享受的各方面的进出口政策都应该是一样的。在技术登记的时候，也是按照相关的情况进行登记的。但有没有优先？有，因为技术确实有高低、有先进之分。这也是有依据的，比如《上海系统推进全面创新改革试验加快建设具有全球影响力的科技创新中心方案》提到重点领域是信息技术、生命科学、生物医药、高端设备、智能制造、新能源和质量技术等。在技术贸易领域，商务部和相关部门刚刚公布了服务贸易创新发展试点，出台了相关领域的重点支持政策，涉及技术贸易中的云计算、大数据、移动互联网等相关技术贸易，上海是试点城市之一。

相应的技术贸易公共服务促进平台有很多，各个区也不一样，有大有小。像软件，有服务外包的贸易促进交易中心，在张江还有软件业联盟；技术促进交易方面，科技部、上海市政府和知识产权总局、商务部，共同设立了上海市技术进出口交易中心，每年上交会就是他们举办的，作为一个技术交易平台，有很多这类技术交易。上海市本身也有一些技术转移中心，各个委办局有相应的接口和相应的资金支持，比如对科创中心的支持有创新型企业基金，事实上起到的就是平台的作用。

谢秋慧：我也是从事技术研究的。各个部门都在努力实现贸易便利化，商务委努力了很多年。检验检疫的贸易便利化是什么概念？在管理部门上，大家说到"便利"，总是同时提起检验检疫局和海关。检验检疫局和海关同为执法部门，但是专业分得很细。我检验检疫局现在也在有关促进电商发展，降低企业成本，促进贸易便利化的课题。按照我的理解，下一步要推进的贸易便利化，是差异化的。从企业来说，最担心的情况类似于，一个人生病，所有人都必须吃药，为了保障安全，导致全部检查，管理成本非常高。但是严格意义上，法律法规对所有企业都是一视同仁的。未来我们想推进的，是一种差异化的、两维的贸易便利化概念。在风险的基础上实施分类管理，通过风险分析，实现管理能力、质量提高，降低能力较强的企业的抽查比例，提高通关效率和资源使用效率。我们想把有限的资源投放到质量保证能力比较差、风险比较高的企业上面。简单地根据法律法规一刀切很容易，差异化的管理却有一定的困难，我们正在做这方面的探索。

针对在自贸区形成可复制可推广的经验，我认为，很多可复制、可推广的经验，是有条件的。一项制度 A 可以做，并不代表 B 就可以做，而是 B 需要具备这个能力，要创造条件。不然全国只要有一个法规就可以了，不需要在自贸区先行先试。在这个方面，需要企业配合，提升企业自身的能力。所以我再次呼吁相关的企业跟我们合作。一方面，我们可以合作研究；另一方面，在风险可控的情况下，我们会有针对性地探索一些贸易便利化的做法。简单说，是"一二三四五"："一"是差异化；"二"是两维，分类分析、分类管理；"三"是分三类，高、中、低类风险；"四"是四类管理；"五"是五种监管模式，有信用监管、验证监管、一般监管、特别监管、加严监管。现在国内检验检疫是不合格假定，所以偏慢。今后我们针对五种监管模式，会设置合格假定和不合格假定，通过这种形式探索贸易便利化。

关于贸易中的标准认定问题，我们国家有 90% 以上的标准已经跟国际接轨。但是这些接轨的标准怎么宣传灌输到企业？待我们有机会再跟各位汇报。

黄佳：谢局长提到一个非常重要的观点，就是为什么上海自贸试验区的技术贸易平台需要企业的配合。其实企业的能力，以及企业构成的生态圈的能力和成熟度，是自贸区一些新做法和新尝试的重要基础，这就是为什么我们是一个双向或者多元化的生态圈。促进技术贸易、自贸区发展，企业要有强烈的参与意识，这并不是单向的委办局的一个任务。

武伟：刚才很多企业谈到贸易便利化的问题，我代表口岸办参与讨论。

首先声明一点，从现在海关、检验检疫、海事、边防检查以及其他的相关口岸部门来讲，所有的政策和监管，完全是按照一个标准执行的，没有任何针对某个国家的特殊标准，当然战争的特殊区域除外。但对待企业，我们会有不同标准。海关、检验检疫局都是实行风险分级、分类监管。如果企业产品风险小，监管就更简便；如果企业以前有不诚信的不良记录，监管就更严格。我从事经济贸易工作十几年，现在为止没有发现我们政策有专门针对某个国家或者某个企业的。我们的市场是公平、公开、透明的市场。这是我的一个体会和感想。

第二，市场开放的问题。市场开放最核心的一个问题，是双边对等。中美有BIT谈判，中日没有BIT谈判，如果中国进口日本牛肉，那日本进口中国的什么产品？这需要对等。所以不是一个简单的"日本牛肉好不好"的问题。我建议小栗所长回去以后，把日本有关的牛肉企业或想进入中国市场的大企业集合起来，先跟日本政府谈，你们向中国出口什么产品，同时日本对中国放开哪些产品。这是一个双赢的通道。美国和日本在农业、农产品方面分歧很大就是这个道理。

第三，建筑行业的问题。我在陆家嘴工作了四年半，其中三年是管规划建设。在建筑设计方面，中国是开放的。日本著名的建筑设计家矶崎新设计了芳甸路、龙阳路的证大喜玛拉雅中心。但是有一个问题就是必须和中国的建筑设计院合作。据我所知，在这方面，中国的开放程度比日本高多了。我们希望中外企业在中国发展，在上海发展。口岸部门，包括商务委，都在尽心尽力为大家创造良好的条件。

第四，通关成本问题，可以在国际贸易"单一窗口"查看，我们已经公布了海运、空运、水运的通关流程。比如海运集装箱货物的通关流程，以及每步流程所用的时间均已公布。同时，上海市政府为了降低企业通关成本，已经开始采用政府购买。在洋山港，如果企业集装箱被海关查验，而查验结果没有问题，这个单谁由来买？是由上海市人民政府的财政经费来出；如果查验有问题，是不良或者违法行为，才由企业自己买单。这个政策是不分国别的，在有问题的情况下，无论哪个国家的企业都需要买单。这个政策今后可能还会在外高桥、机场、上海港全面推开。这是我们比较重视的。

还有一点，企业要注意通关过程。在此，我为海关、检验检疫局、海事的同志们多说几句话，并不完全是他们造成了企业通关时间长。通关是全流程的，从船到岸或申报一直到最后一个环节，其间要经过很多过程。海关现在可能放行一票载货少的船只只需几秒钟，90%以上速度都很快，但如果涉及查验，时间会稍微长一点。检验检疫大多数情况下也是很快的，但如果涉及法检货物，比如进口红酒，速度就会放慢一些。检验的过程和企业信誉也有关系。

如果大家是从事进出口业务的企业，我要提醒一下：企业有时候单听报关、业务代理、船代或货代的说法，内心要再斟酌。因为可能就是他们把材料报错了，或者是报材料时将A商品报成B商品，海关系统最后检查发现是B商品，于是从电子渠道进入人工渠道，导致通关流程时间大大加长。遇到这种情况，业务代理、船代或货代会说是海关的问题，但实际上是报关有问题。在实践中，我们发现了很多这样的具体的案例。

第五，标准问题，不同国家有不同标准。在食品方面，欧盟的标准大大高于美国的标准，美国人要用美国标准，欧盟人要用欧盟标准，于是大家通过TTIP谈判。作为企业，要将产品出口到国外，那就要执行外国的标准。

今天峰会的主题是关于提升上海投资贸易便利化水平，口岸办、海关、检验检疫等部门愿意听企业的意见，也愿意竭诚为企业服务。企业呼声比较强的话，我希望能专门找几家典型性企业，口岸办可以带着海关、检验检疫的同志过去了解情况；口岸办也可以自己内部来听听企业的想法。但我们也有一个要求，就是开会之前，企业要找几个典型案例，具体是哪年哪月哪日哪票货，事情的来龙去脉都讲清楚。如果反映的问题确实属实，相关部门肯定会查。我们不怕困难和问题，但大家提出的问题、困难要具体和客观，不要带有情绪色彩、感情色彩。我们需要数据和典型的、具体的案例，当然更需要你们向我们提出建设性的解决方案。或许其他国家有好的路径，但他们的路我们不一定走得通。他们的国情跟中国不一样，政府机构设置不一样，法律法规也不一样，但是我们可以借鉴其他国家的优秀方法。

诺伯特·梅尔林： 最近两年来，外资在中国和上海投资收入和利润率进一步下降，在中国已成为跨国企业重要市场的情况下，这形成了巨大压力和挑战，引起了众多全球CEO们的担忧。因此，如何说服全球企业的CEO，投资中国、投资上海？中国和上海特殊的地方在哪里？尤其现在中国经济增速下降，将对贸易造成什么影响？外资跨国企业继续在中国和上海投资的新的增长点和利润点在哪里？

黄佳：跨国企业将中国视为不可忽视的市场。为什么要投资中国和上海，这是一个非常好的题目。刚才在座各位谈到，通过政府和企业的共同努力，能够解决成本优化和提升效率这两件事情。面对中国未来3—5亿比美国人口都多的中产消费群体，这个问题不是仅仅是为什么要在中国、在上海投资的问题，而是如何深耕中国、深耕上海，取得全球竞争力的问题。

李俊杰：过去四五年来，中伦律师事务所一直帮助中国企业"走出去"进行海外投资。这一块业务活跃，政府也很支持，但最近由于方方面面的国际和国内的经济情况，包括人民币外汇储备的情况，这一块有收紧的感觉，是不是在现在对一个对外投资的项目审批时间比原先有所延长？

黄佳：这个问题涉及的部门比较多，包括发改委、商务委、外管局等，还涉及国资委对相关国企的审批，我建议把这个问题留到会后进一步探讨。

陈子雷：我来自高校，不是最接地气的。今天的上海国际智库峰会，出席嘉宾包括国际知名智库、企业负责人以及政府职能部门。今天借这个机会和大家沟通。

第一，大家提到的问题，例如制度性的障碍，是上海自贸试验区需要突破的地方。当然，力度会不断加大，但绝对不是一蹴而就。

第二，我们在什么形势下谈这个问题？投资贸易便利化，反映了全球贸易走向公平的趋势。经济全球化发展到现在，总的来说是从追求贸易效率的时代，走向趋于追求贸易公平时代。在这个背景下，我们再谈投资和贸易便利化的问题。中国政府，甚至上海市人民政府在这个问题上体现出了制度改革、改革开放的决心。

自贸区建设不同于传统的建设，也不同于保税区建设。上海自贸区建设主要体现为体制机制的创新，它聚焦的核心是投资目录的负面清单。与此同时，正面清单向负面清单转变的过程中，政府的职能也不一样，因此政府的监管职能需要改变。从过去的事前审批向事中事后监管转变，意味着政府要简政放权，放权过程产生的问题和纠纷，需要通过法制化建设加以解决。

反过来，中国的特色在哪里？我们传统的制造业属于加工贸易，从现在的贸易规模来看，虽然加工贸易比重不断下降，但是还是产生了国际贸易顺差。这个情况下，产业结构转型要求我们开放服务业。服务业的开放涉及很多部门，以及体制机制上的问题。那么如何开放？先开放哪些领域？我们要先从优势上开放，因此提出生产型服务业的概念。在这个领域，我们有底气可以着手。接下来还有很多领域需要开放，当中最难的是金融服务业的开放。因为金融服务业开放的背后有来自汇率和贸易上的压力，必须解决这两个问题。上海自贸区要真正建设成为"四个中心"，包括具有全球影响力的科技创新，金融功能要非常突出。这还涉及今后改革的方向和路线图。

上海市人民政府推出新举措、新政策绝非易事，相信中国政府有能力进一步推动深化改革。从上海建成第一个自贸区，中国自贸区的数量和规模不断在扩大。上海的特色是什么？李克强总理说，要有壮士断臂的决心。今天与会的企业的代表，很多是现代服务业的跨国公司，也反映了上海这座城市本身在转型，外商投资结构也在转型。

关于成本问题大家都能理解。纽约的成本不低，东京的成本也不低。我对日本东京的研究比较多，东京 GDP 产值的 80% 是服务业。结合上海城市功能转型，未来如何体现投资贸易便利化改革的方向，是需要解决的问题。

Elton Huang: As it is said that to explore such issue of city development as internationalization of enterprises, and "Belt and Road" Project, we are given the opportunity to attend seminars every day, but most of time will be spent on it if we do so. However, the think tank is a sustainable platform. The enterprises in Shanghai can be divided into four categories: state-owned enterprises, local state-owned enterprises, private enterprises, and international enterprises. All of them have helped to form a favorable eco-system that creates a platform for cooperation. So I think in case everybody has common interest in a specific issue, we can establish an open platform and a research group for it, and the research results should be shared among us here next year.

Shao Feng: I come from Abbott. Drug R&D is one of the essential areas that Shanghai should focus on in the construction of global R&D center. Apart from chemical drugs, biopharming is another important direction in drug R&D. As diagnosis is one of our focuses, and biological preparations including animal origin and human origin are essential raw materials in biopharmaceutical R&D. Our question is: Do Shanghai Customs and Shanghai Entry-Exit Inspection and Quarantine Bureau have any policy to facilitate the import of these materials, particularly the policy for those that have been recognized as the official R&D institutions in Shanghai?

Xie Qiuhui: I am from Shanghai Entry-Exit Inspection and Quarantine Bureau. Abbott has put forward a very good question. Actually, in order to promote the development of biopharmaceutical industry, Shanghai Entry-Exit Inspection and

Quarantine Bureau published the "*Opinions on Supporting the Development of Shanghai Biomedical Industry*" in 2015. We have tried to transform the administrative function, innovate the regulatory model, simplify the review process, and strengthen regulation in process and afterwards, so as to break the common bottlenecks for biomedical organizations. We've also carry out several steps to achieve streamline some procedures. After researching on the time span and procedures that are needed to import medical products, we have found quarantine of preparations takes 5 workdays, if not as short as 3 workdays, much less than the 20 workdays in the past. Since 2015, the number of organizations that import or export special products through Shanghai's ports has increased to 387, and the batch of special imports and exports has risen to 27988 with a year-on-year growth of 46%.

Moreover, biomedical R&D institutions have complained that it is hard for them to import high-risk or special medical products, and they have to go through complicated review process. To deal with this problem, we have remarkably streamlined the process under the coordination of the municipal government. According to the "*Notice on the Entry-Exit Quarantine Management of Special Items During the Transition Period*" jointly released by Shanghai Entry-Exit Inspection and Quarantine Bureau and Shanghai Municipal Commission of Health and Family Planning in July 2016, the Entry-Exit Inspection and Quarantine Bureau is endorsed to directly execute risk analysis, inspection and quarantine on special items except those for clinical treatment applied by medical organizations since October 1st, 2016. This measure prevents enterprises from spending too much time or visiting too many departments to import high-risk or special items. For further information, enterprises can log on Shanghai Entry-Exit Inspection and Quarantine Bureau's website, or access to relevant notices on special items supervision. Since October 2016, Shanghai Entry-Exit Inspection and Quarantine Bureau has carried out risk analysis on 48 projects. All of the work were done in a smooth way.

Elton Huang: I would like to share my experience. I have discussed with a leader from the municipal government about why not open up more areas to meet various needs, for example, the high-end medical area. He replied it was not because they didn't want to, but due to a pain point. Foreign doctors can be licensed to provide medical services in China, but they will only stay here for less than one year because they can't prescribe medicines that are available abroad due to China's lack of FDA approval for the using of these drugs. This leads to inconvenience for foreign doctors who thus will leave China in one or two years. After the meeting, we kindly request discussions on the issue among relevant departments.

Ding Songbing: I am from Shanghai International Port (Group). My question is about exchange rate risk facing overseas investment. In recent years, we have investigated many projects in the "Belt and Road" region. Objectively speaking, there are lots of projects, and many of them are very good. But investment projects are not all ambitious enough, because of the realistic concern over return. It is logical to assume that investment should be rewarded with profits. Though our company is highly rated by international agencies, we are not allowed to exchange RMB for dollars for overseas investment. We can only directly invest into overseas market after getting funded in the US dollar or other foreign currencies at abroad. When we gain profits, we will transfer the capital to China in certain ways.

This put us into an awkward dilemma. Overseas investment has a payback period. Large projects have cash flow inadequacy in the first few years. If you do not rely on new loans to pay for the interest, you will have to finance at home to get more capital. On the one hand, RMB depreciation will add more pressure on debtors. On the other hand, RMB appreciation will be another problem. If we use RMB as the settlement currency, and returns from overseas projects are converted into RMB in the report of our parent company, we will find the income decreased. Put it into perspective, in the past, $1 could be exchanged for 7 yuan. After RMB appreciation, $1 is worth only 5 yuan. This will result in the increase in the overseas operating assets, which however cannot be reflected in the balance sheet of the parent company.

We believe assessment on China (Shanghai) Pilot Free Trade Zone and other projects should be carried out in a comprehensive way. Not only should we take the return rate into consideration, but also should have a look at the appreciation ratio of overseas assets.

Besides, when enterprises are to issue bonds offshore, they have to apply to Shanghai Municipal Development and Reform Commission and then the National Development and Reform Commission. As the government is focused on investment and trade facilitation in Shanghai, will some favorable policies be piloted in China

(Shanghai) Pilot Free Trade Zone? For example, will Shanghai Municipal Development and Reform Commission introduce policies to give some autonomy to enterprises over the issuing of bonds overseas?

Elton Huang: The issue of consolidated financial statements is suggested to not to be covered during the meeting. Concerns related to the two-way flow of RMB and exchange rate volatility have been under the spotlight. Shanghai International Port (Group), a highly-credited large-scale state-owned enterprise have adequate access to funds from offshore. According to its question, the company is concerned about how to provide financial assistance in a flexible manner, and make the best of two-way fund pool.

Li Yongjin: Since the 18th National Congress of the CPC, in accordance with the top-down design to deepen reforms, the State-owned Assets Supervision and Administration Commission (SASAC), an asset management department has been focused on asset management. Shanghai International Port (Group) is a listed company with the State-owned Assets Supervision and Administration Commission of Shanghai Municipal Government as one of its shareholders. All of its business decisions are decided by the board of directors thereof. These decisions including overseas strategies only have to be recorded for management by us, as long as they are related to the company's major businesses.

Shanghai International Port (Group)'s problem is shared by the enterprises under the administration of the State-owned Assets Supervision and Administration Commission of Shanghai Municipal Government. At present, we have some 446 offshore enterprises with assets totaling 400 billion Yuan. Over the past two years, we have invested a lot in overseas projects. This year, the outbound investment is more than 8 billion dollars with 16 companies participating in 8 projects, like Jinjiang International that have made a lot of attempts. It should be noted that it is the board of directors rather than us that make business decisions, including how to avoid exchange rate risks. To resolve other problems put forward by Shanghai International Port (Group), we need joint efforts from the government and public authorities. On behalf of the company, we call for public authorities to join us to solve the problems and difficulties facing them.

Qiao Yide: From the perspective of a researcher, concerns raised by Shanghai International Port (Group) are very meaningful and commonly seen. Greenland Group has encountered a similar problem. They invest and finance abroad, and get returns in foreign currency. This makes them immune from exchange rate risk. But due to the long cycle of overseas projects, they are faced with risks in RMB conversion. According to my knowledge pool, there are favorable policies in China (Shanghai) Pilot Free Trade Zone. An investment project will only have to be recorded if it is worth less than $100 million. But I have no idea if there are any preferential policies for the issuing of bonds overseas.

Firstly, enterprises should take long-term preparations, grasp the trend and understand the pattern of exchange rate fluctuation. Once the RMB becomes a freely floating currency, enterprises should strengthen the research, especially research on global economy and exchange rate. Secondly, enterprises need to invest in research, so that they will not move out of the track. Many companies have suffered tremendous losses because of their complacency that drove them to take unnecessary risks.

In the offshore market, there will be more risks and uncertainties in the next few months if not half a year. As a researcher, I think the government should take a stable approach in terms of RMB convertibility and the exchange rate.

Elton Huang: Over the past few years, we mainly focused on foreign companies' direct investment in China. But now we have shifted our attention to the RMB, and enterprises going abroad, which has a lot to do with the Shanghai Municipal Commission of Commerce. Is there any suggestion for enterprises?

Shen Weihua: True, outbound investment faces currency risks, which are inevitable for foreign-investment enterprises, foreign trade enterprises and even enterprises with foreign investment or foreign trade, even companies engaged in foreign-related matters for import and export. In the strict sense, it's up to the market to make the decision. The central government should inform domestic enterprises of the trend of exchange rate, and introduce currency policies on the basis of national policies.

In terms of market economy, there are many ways to preserve and increase the value in foreign investment. Exchange rate fluctuation is common in global market, but the amplitude matters. Sometimes if we give it a free rein to the market, we may not be benefited, because different currencies are used for settlement will deliver different results. In other words, sometimes settlement in RMB can be more beneficial than in the dollar, but sometimes not. So enterprises should make objective analysis when making a big investment decision. In particular, when it comes to long-term payment, there are many options for enterprises to take. A stable exchange rate is important for greenfield investment that has a high leverage rate, we need to know how to guarantee it. In negotiation on acquisition or cooperation, whether you can stick to a certain price depends on your bargaining capability. If the capability is weak, the company will be more likely to be greatly influenced by the market shockwaves. Vice versa.

Indeed, enterprises in the market will face many risks. Sometimes when commodity price drops, a group of air transport enterprises will be benefited a lot. Enterprises can try to manage risks by locking in a certain interest rate. As the State-owned Assets Supervision and Administration Commission of Shanghai Municipal Government suggested, this is up to the market to make the decision. When making big decisions, enterprises must be careful about currency risk, and take the situation of the country to which investment will go into consideration. Because some companies have decided to invest in the infrastructure and port of various countries, and many port investments in the "Belt and Road" Strategy are the priority.

All of these issues should be paid attention to. When enterprises are going global, risks will always be there. So they should collect sufficient information, listen to consulting agencies over development trend, such as the prediction on the change in exchange rate, so that they can tailor an individual solution.

Concerning enterprises' issuing of bonds overseas, it is necessary for SASAC and the Development and Reform Commission to regulate their foreign investment. The regulation is not strict enough, and thus should be strengthened. Risks ring alarm bells to enterprises, particularly huge risks in infrastructure investment. So on one hand, enterprises need to reinforce the research and analysis on changes in the local market and the exchange rate. On the other hand, they should further communicate with and report to SASAC, the Development & Reform Commission and other departments, so as to make the going-out course smoother with less risks and losses.

Elton Huang: A Shanghai-based state-owned enterprise likes to use natural hedge to manage currency risks in outbound M&As. When trade is done in dollars, they instead borrow pounds. When asked the reason, its financial executive responded that the target company made profits in pounds. As profits were the natural hedge against debts, the use of the natural hedge could minimize risks. While other executives doubted why not borrow yuan as the currency continued to depreciate. In my opinion, risk control is the first priority rather than profit-making. Shanghai Electric Group, a high-profile SOE is present here.

Zhang Ke: The problems we face are similar to that of Shanghai International Port (Group). Besides, there are some other concerns.

First, Shanghai Electric Group is not only involved in outbound M&As, but also many overseas projects. Theoretically, participation in these projects was decided by the board. But in practice, we have to go through review procedures to gain approval from the authorities in Shanghai and Beijing. So we suggest the procedures be streamlined.

Second, the procedures for financing guarantee are expected to be simplified.

Third, when we are selling products abroad, we have encountered with many problems resulting from the different standards of different countries, or the difference between China's standards and the international's. To deal with the problem, we need help from the Standardization Administration of the People's Republic of China (SAC). We are familiar with China's standards, and our products are quality. However, in the foreign market, we are required to get certification from their standard system which is different from ours like in terms of production techniques. Can you help us to deal with it?

Elton Huang: He raised two problems. One is about the requirement on approval from local and central authorities for projects going global. The second is related to the difference between domestic and foreign standards and certification.

Owen Haacke: By comparing trade standards of many countries, and of international organizations like WTO, I have noticed the importance of trade standardization. The two-way investment between China and the US is essential to us. As far as I know, Shanghai, especially the China (Shanghai) Pilot Free Trade Zone, will enhance rule-making for trade and standardization.

Elton Huang: When it comes to standards on business investment and trade, we can see that the US has set up a lot of company unions in China, such as the American Chamber of Commerce. But due to the lack of Chinese company unions abroad, Chinese enterprises can only rely on themselves when going global. To handle market entry standards, companies should be represented by an organization to express their views. This problem is worth thinking of. As for the complex approval system, you can discuss with government officials after the meeting. Just now someone talked about problems facing Chinese contractors investing abroad. Now let's shed light on difficulties facing foreign companies investing in China in construction area. For example, when foreign constructors are to contract projects in China, will they encounter any challenge caused by standards and barriers?

Michiaki Oguri: Japanese companies like construction companies entered the Shanghai market very early. But due to obstacles preventing sole foreign-funded enterprises from setting up construction companies in Shanghai, less Japanese-owned companies have been established in China over the past few years and orders for us have also decreased, though we are capable of completing projects in Chinese market. So we hope China can further open the market for foreign-owned enterprises.

Elton Huang: Is there any barrier impeding sole foreign-funded enterprises in project contracting?

Yao Weiqun: In terms of construction projects, there are two problems. First, due to the lack of bilateral free trade agreement between China and Japan, Japanese companies will need to act in accordance with China's commitment on service trade made for in WTO if they are to go into Chinese market. So we hope Japanese and South Korean companies will work together to promote the trilateral FTA between us three countries. Second, China is not a member in the WTO Agreement on Government Procurement (GPA), and the membership negotiation is under the way. So Japanese companies need to go ahead with China's commitments made in WTO when attempting to access into China's construction market. There are two approaches that can help to address the issue, either to include China in the GPA as soon as possible or to further open China's construction market by setting up the FTA between China, Japan and

提升投资贸易便利化水平，构建开放型经济新体制

South Korea.

Shen Weihua: The problems facing Shanghai Electric and JETRO are all related to investment.

In foreign investment, Shanghai Electric is encountering challenges from standardization, which is what we should pay attention to when signing contractor agreement that includes the provision of complete sets of equipment with foreign partners. According to practices, countries are different from each other in terms of standards, particularly developing countries. Chinese government encourages the export of home-made complete sets of large equipment through contracting projects overseas. But usually the exported complete sets of large equipment are tailored, so we have to modify the equipment, for example for the coal-fired power plant and even nuclear power plant, to meet clients' needs. Difference in standards lead to the increase in the cost of exporting complete sets of equipment. This problem is particularly tricky for subcontractors. The general contractor is responsible for analyzing standard authentication, while subcontractors need to keep contact with the general contractor at home to see if authentication can be done in earlier. Subcontractors also need to be careful in quoting, because the cost will go up due to equipment modification and standard adjustment. The problem related to approval mainly lies in the uncertainty of the time span of review. The intense competition in the domestic market results from the lack of coordination between companies.

Shanghai Municipal Commission of Commerce and Shanghai Municipal Development & Reform Commission need to negotiate with national ministries to advance the approval on outbound investment. Many of the foreign companies present here are unfamiliar that getting project permit is not easy and negotiation is time-consuming, which Chinese companies know quite well.

In the context of the WTO, Mr. Yao well answered the question raised by Mr. Michiaki Oguri. Firstly, when realizing free trade in service, China will strictly follow the commitments we've made when joining the WTO, on cross-border consumption, cross-border delivery, movement of human capital and other business matters. Secondly, we will deliver promises based on free trade in service included in the bilateral and multilateral free trade agreements we signed. This is our country's responsibility and what we are working on. Thirdly, we should open up and reform independently. China

(Shanghai) Pilot Free Trade Zone has started to practice pre-establishment negative list and national treatment to widen the access for foreign capital. But surely after the entry, some service sectors received non-national treatment in operation, of which some were beyond-national treatment and the others were below-national treatment. In terms of the scope of business, foreign contractors may only be allowed to undertake Chinese-foreign cooperative projects, or projects funded by foreign governments, or projects that are technologically impossible for China to complete. The scope is very limited. There are some other areas like education and medical service are open to foreign companies, but they are not popular due to the lack of labor protection for foreign companies. To deal with it, we are thinking the feasibility of post-establishment national treatment in China (Shanghai) Pilot Free Trade Zone. In post-establishment national treatment practice, foreign investors will be offered almost the same treatment as Chinese companies. We are trying to figure out the limits facing foreign-invested enterprises in Chinese market, and will attempt to lift them in China (Shanghai) Pilot Free Trade Zone. This is part of the independent opening-up and reform. In addition, the market access policy introduced by National Development and Reform Commission and the Ministry of Commerce only tells us about the flow of goods and service, as well as entry to other areas, but does not detail on the negative list for foreign companies. We are collecting information on it. Today JETRO provided great information for us, and we look forward more from you. We can establish a basic negative list for service trade. In other negative lists, we need to differentiate companies in terms of treatment according to their status. In this independent opening-up and reform, the extent of which should be negotiated with state ministries.

Elton Huang: Many people may not be familiar with the idea of project permit. We need to further explain it. Several cities are implementing Sandbox project and pilot projects on the negative list. It means in certain regions or fields, laws and regulations that are in force will be put aside to give it a free rein for the development of edge-cutting technologies and new models, like the block chain and service trade. For instance, within 6 months, on the condition of legal compliance, relative parties are given freedom to try new things and then do reflection.

Zhao Xi: We are very interested in the issue of foreign trade. China has different

提升投资贸易便利化水平，构建开放型经济新体制

rules on trade from other countries. This makes it hard for Chinese companies to go global and for foreign companies to invest in China. According to our experience, regional difference also causes challenges for multinational companies to operate in China. Strict regulations on the financial sector from regulators like the State Administration of Foreign Exchange, People's Bank of China, BRSA, CBRC, and local CBRC add to the difficulties facing multinationals.

Most multinational companies are in the transformation to the model of centralized operation, and have set up their shared service center in Shanghai. Shanghai, the largest financial center in China, is pioneering in unifying and simplifying rules. But multinationals only set up their headquarters in shanghai. Their subsidiaries and branch companies are located in other cities. Put it into perspective, a multinational is headquartered in Shanghai, and has opened an account in Deutsche Bank's Shanghai Branch for cross-border RMB cash pooling and cross-border financing. The company does not have to register and file their payment overseas to Shanghai regulators, while the subsidiaries have to report to local exchange regulators for the business. So to make it more convenient for banks and multinationals to do business in China, will Shanghai take the lead in coordinating with other local governments to unify laws and regulations so as to reduce regional differences?

Elton Huang: There was a joke by a foreign-funded enterprise that doing business in China was like doing business in 30 countries. Actually, this is the concern of many enterprises. Shanghai authorities, do you have any suggestion for enhancing regional cooperation, reducing regional differences on laws and regulations and unifying rules to facilitate the operation of foreign companies?

Shen Weihua: First, financial problems are related to the whole regulatory department, to the settlement of multinational companies in China (Shanghai) Pilot Free Trade Zone and their subsidiaries, and are also related to policy-making. In terms of the scope, polices can have its impact on branch companies, but hardly on subsidiaries, because each province has its own administration of foreign exchange and local regulatory institution. This problem needs to be resolved as Shanghai is the magnet for multinationals to set up headquarters.

The main problem lies in the consolidation of parent company and subsidiaries.

It's unusual to establish subsidiaries in all states in Germany, but it is common in China. Objectively speaking, running a branch company is more difficult than running a subsidiary. When provinces are to attract foreign investors and companies, they will have differentiated favorable polices for branch companies and subsidiaries, and will introduce distinctive rules on staff management. A large Germany chemical manufacturer attempted to consolidate its 18 subsidiaries in China into a branch company. They spent almost one year and had turned to many consulting firms for help, but finally they gave up. Because economic conditions vary throughout China, it is challenging to consolidate manufacturing subsidiaries into a branch company.

Shanghai is trying to solve the problem step by step. But it is almost impossible to consolidate subsidiaries in Shanghai, let alone consolidating companies in Shanghai and companies in other areas. It is also difficult to convert a subsidiary in Shanghai into a branch company. For example, why Carrefour established subsidiary companies in different districts of the city, and what problems may this move result in? Let's imagine a scenario. Carrefour relocates itself from Pudong New Area to Huangpu District, or turns its branch company at Pudong New Area into a subsidiary, but its tax base remains to be calculated at Pudong New Area in the next five years. Put it into perspective. Carrefour pays the tax of 100 million yuan, and a corresponding amount of tax base on which the tax is determined remains to be calculated at Pudong New Area. If the taxable income is higher than the certain tax base, the increment should be transferred to Huangpu District. But if the taxable income is smaller than the base, the gap should be filled by Huangpu District. This will put huge pressure on Huangpu District. To deal with this problem, policies should be introduced to replace the transferring of tax base between districts with the transferring between branch companies.

To implement this policy in all cities and provinces, companies have to consistently express their concerns to governments, which will hike the operation cost for them. The lack of unified policies result in the establishment of an independent company, which will in turn cause problems in the corporate governance structure. Different companies have different choices. Some prefer to be set up as a subsidiary, while some prefer branch company. Market players should have a say in changing corporate governance structure.

I agree with the point made by Deutsche Bank, and share your concerns. But this reform needs the coordination between all provinces. For example, since this year, the Yangtze River Delta region and Beijing-Tianjin-Hebei Metropolitan Region will coordinate on the tax base issue facing many companies during operation and relocation. Indeed, coordination is needed to deal with the problem concerning local governments' fiscal revenues. In taking the lead in unifying laws, Shanghai will start pilot programs in China (Shanghai) Pilot Free Trade Zone. As the unification is not something easy, we hope you can understand that the process will be very long.

Elton Huang: The issues of returns and taxation system cannot be solved by a government alone. Every coin has two sides. Though the transaction and operation costs are very high, the economic growth remains to be fast. So once efficiency is improved, larger potential for growth can be created.

We've talked a lot about investment. Let's shift attention back to trade. Mr. Michiaki Oguri, on behalf of Japan External Trade Organization, you've expressed your concerns about agricultural products and customs. Do you have any question for Shanghai Customs, or Shanghai Entry-Exit Inspection and Quarantine Bureau, or Shanghai Municipal Office for Port Services?

Michiaki Oguri: At present, due to restrictions on inspection and quarantine for agricultural products, apart from apples and pears, and aquatic products, other fresh food from Japan is forbidden from being imported into China, such as beef, pork and chicken, which are not allowed to be imported out of the concern for foot-and-mouth disease and bovine spongiform encephalopathy (BSE). But we are convinced that Japanese food is safe, these two types of fresh food from Japan can be imported into China, and aquatic products are allowed of Japanese agricultural product, only fresh apples and pears can be imported into China, and aquatic products into Chinese mainland. Due to the foot-and-mouth disease and mad cow disease, beef, pork and chicken is forbidden to import into China. We do think that Japanese food is relatively safe, so we hope these restrictions can be lifted.

Xie Qiuhui: China is practicing the market access system to restrict the import of Japanese agricultural products, food ingredients, and food. To export new varieties into China, the government of the producing country needs to apply to General Administration of Quality Supervision, Inspection and Quarantine of the People's

Republic of China (AQSIQ), and submit technical document on risk analysis, in which Japan is doing very well. After receiving the documents, the Administration will organize experts to carry our risk assessment, based on which it will introduce risk management measures that are in line with China's protective capability, and will sign up bilateral agreement for the import. If epidemics or food safety incidents take place regionally, and may have an impact on the imports, the Administration will take emergency measures to suspend food import or strengthen regulation to ensure national security and food safety.

The import of Japanese agricultural products like apples and pears, is traditional trade, and has gained market access permit. We have no special regulatory requirements on these two kinds of fruit, but there are exceptions. Due to the nuclear leaks caused by the earthquake on March 11, 2011 in Japan, the AQSIQ has required that Japanese government should provide the certification of the place of origin for their agricultural products to ensure food safety. This requirement is stated in the *Notice on the Issuance of the Certification of the Place of Origin for the Fishery Products of Japan Imported into China and the Certification of Safety Level of the Radiating for the Fishery Products of Japan Imported into China*, and in the *Notice on the Seal Sample of the Authority Issuing the Certification of the Place of Origin for the Feed of Japan Imported into China*. These two documents were circulated in May, 2011 and September, 2011 respectively. Based on the rules implemented by the General Administration, Shanghai Municipal Office for Port Services is regulating Japanese imports, because some imports from ten Japanese prefectures like Fukushima, Tokyo, and Chiba are likely to be contaminated by radiation.

If you want to know more about requirements on market entry, you can refer to the existing entry process. We have implemented a lot of measures to facilitate the import of fishery and agricultural products. For example, procedures for importing fruits and agricultural products have been streamlined, quality products whose risks are under control can be put on the shelf within 24 hours. Thanks to the higher efficiency, the selling prices of some products have dropped by some 30%.

Elton Huang: The discussion we just had is mainly about laws and regulations for introduced by governments for certain products. Now let's shift to the application of technologies in these areas. For example, block chain is being widely used for food and

　　　提升投资贸易便利化水平，构建开放型经济新体制

drug safety, and origin tracing. Let's talk about how the technology is disrupting these areas.

Sunny Lu: Actually, what block chain has brought is the increased efficiency, mainly because it has resolved the efficiency and cost problems caused by Information Island. For example, both Mr. Michiaki Oguri and experts from Shanghai Entry-Exit Inspection and Quarantine Bureau have raised the problem related to product traceability. In fact, the source can be traced and the information can be found, but there is the lack of free movement of information, and it is hard to efficiently share information with regulators. This is a great challenge. The free flow of information depends on the IT system of the country, government departments and enterprises, as well as data liquidity.

Block chain can solve these problems very well. We are negotiating with multiple departments and enterprises on products traceability. Tracing to the source of wine is a typical example. All wine-related information from the source is shared with regulators and end-consumers. I believe this will greatly increase efficiency and reduce cost for traceability. Due to security concerns over the use of traditional IT and data technologies, information does not flow freely. This challenge can be resolved by block chain, an outcome of disruptive innovation.

Elton Huang: All of us must be interested in the goal of developing Shanghai into a Global Science and Technology Innovation Center. To realize it depends on enterprises in Shanghai, including SOEs, private sectors and foreign companies. As for the questions related to technology transactions, foreign trade in technologies, and associated public platforms, we'd like to invite TE Connectivity to share their ideas.

Deng Lingling: The Shanghai Municipality has been carrying out a range of measures to promote trade in services. Over the past few years, the government has introduced some policies. Each year, we invest 5% of our global sales into R&D. We have also made a lot of attempts in the import and export of technologies.

There are many forms of technology transactions, including technology transfer, the import and export of technical services and technical assets. But the difference in each country's regulatory regime has a different impact on the development of various kinds of technology transactions. My questions are as follows. First, when trying to promote trade in services, will the Shanghai municipal government prioritize certain forms of technology transactions? Second, Shanghai has set up many platforms for public services through joint efforts, particularly the platform for technology trade. How's the progress of the development of the platform, and in what ways can companies use it?

Fan Jie: I come from Shanghai NIU (Group). When doing investment and trade, we have two expectations on investment and trade facilitation. They are cost reduction and benefit improvement. Following the development of China (Shanghai) Pilot Free Trade Zone, we have established a financial leasing company in the zone. During three-year's operation, we have been benefitted a lot by measures to facilitate investment. But in terms of trade facilitation, measures to reduce cost for companies are not effective, and sometimes even counter-effective.

I suggest that from the perspective of companies, the government should analyze the tangible benefits that companies can get from measures to facilitate investment and trade in terms of reducing costs and improving efficiency. This is what companies are concerned most about, and is important to support the industrial chain. Shanghai Municipal Statistics Bureau used to have a research group studying enterprise cost. I have never done this research, so I can only share my opinions on behalf of a company that analysis on enterprise cost and revenues from macro and meso perspectives can help a lot in studying and introducing policies to facilitate investment and trade in the future.

Elton Huang: The Shanghai NIU(Group) made a very good suggestion. How to reduce transaction cost and optimize cost are the fundamental concerns for enterprises. Let's make a comparison between Shanghai and Singapore. In Shanghai, with the freight cost excluded, a container unit costs about 300 euros in customs clearance, while the cost in the Singapore is 100 euros. This gap has existed for years. PwC has discussed with the Shanghai government on how to reduce the gap. This is a significant problem for all companies. There are other issues, like the labor cost, land cost, companies' transaction cost, which are relevant with the government, and efficiency improvement associated with supply-side structural reform and driven by innovation and technologies. I think all these issues can be regarded as an important subject for think tanks to pursue.

Shen Weihua: I am from Shanghai Municipal Commission of Commerce. Questions discussed today are partly related to us, including the inspection and quarantine of agricultural and fishery products, and food, the question raised by Mr. Michiaki Oguri. First, I'd like to add some new information from the perspective of colleagues from the Shanghai Entry-Exit Inspection and Quarantine Bureau.

The foreign delegates we received have pointed out the question specifically. In reform and opening-up, China has been trying to be in line with demanding international trade and investment rules. All companies present here fully aware that whether China has stricter rules on animal and plant inspection and quarantine than foreign counterparts. Agreement on the Application of Sanitary and Phytosanitary Measures (SPS) is to protect people's health and the uniqueness of animals and plants. This is the shared goal of the world. In classified management, the process for inspection and quarantine on animals and plants are time-consuming, but this is what we have to do.

As a consumer and citizen, I prefer imported food, though it is a bit more expensive. Sometimes we wish the price could be lower, but regulatory rules should remain strict. The process of regulation and the approach of double certification need to be improved. For example, block chain technology may be reliable to solve the problem related to foreign certification. New technologies and new certification approaches can be piloted in China (Shanghai) Pilot Free Trade Zone and even in Shanghai as a whole. Regulatory process can be improved, but should not be weakened just for convenience.

I'd like to ask Mr. Michiaki Oguri, do you like beef? Which country's beef do you prefer? As is known to all, Shanghai Entry-Exit Inspection and Quarantine Bureau strictly regulate the import of beef. That's the reason why Mr. Michiaki Oguri has this concern. At Yangshan Port and Puxi, we have set up many organizations to deal with the import of fruits. Takashimaya Shanghai Store at the Changning District is coordinating with the government in food import. But we should keep in mind that regulation should be strengthened, not otherwise.

Besides, I'd like to give you the official explanation on technology transactions. No enterprise can get favorable treatment when doing technology trade. As long as the transaction is technology transaction, either on patents or proprietary technology or appearance design like integrated circuit layout in computers, enterprises can only have access to the same foreign trade policies. But some technologies are given the priority in registration. For example, according to the *Plan for Shanghai to Systemically Promote the Pilot Program of Comprehensive Innovation and Reform and Accelerate the Development of Globally Influential Science and Technology Innovation Center*, many areas are attached importance to, including information technology, life science, biomedicine, high-end equipment, intelligent manufacturing, new energy, and quality engineering. The Ministry of Commerce and other ministries have unveiled pilot programs on service trade innovation in some cities, including Shanghai, and have introduced supporting policies for various kinds of technology transactions, such as trade in cloud computing, big data, and mobile internet.

There are many public service platforms to facilitate technology trade. Each district in Shanghai has its own platform, either large or small. There are trade promotion centers for the outsourcing of software services. In Zhangjiang Hi-Tech Park, there is an association of software industry. To promote technology transactions, the Ministry of Science and Technology, Shanghai Municipal People's Government, State Intellectual Property Office (SIPO), and Ministry of Commerce have jointly established Shanghai International Technology Exchange Center, which holds China (Shanghai) International Technology Fair every year. On this technology trade platform, a number of technology transactions have been done. Shanghai itself has developed many technology transfer centers funded and managed by Shanghai authorities. For example, the Shanghai Technology Innovation Center is serving as a platform and supported by the innovative enterprise fund.

Xie Qiuhui: I am also a technology researcher. Every department is trying hard to realize trade facilitation, like Shanghai Municipal Commission of Commerce that has been investing efforts for years. But what is trade facilitation in terms of inspection and quarantine? When it comes to facilitation, we will immediately think of the regulators, the administration of inspection and quarantine as well as the customs. They are both law enforcers, but have difference due responsibilities. Shanghai Entry-Exit Inspection and Quarantine Bureau is focused on how to enhance the development of e-commerce, reduce the cost for companies, and promote trade facilitation. In my opinion, we need to carry out differentiated measures to facilitate trade in the future. I want to use an analogy to describe companies' concerns. If you are ill, you will have to take medicines. But for your good, you'd better go through a general health check-up, which will cost you a lot. This is the same to companies that will be faced with high management cost. Strictly speaking, neither do laws nor regulations discriminate or favor anyone. But we would like introduce differentiated and two-dimensional measures to facilitate trade. Through risk analysis, we can improve our management capability and quality, and implement classified management so as to make it less likely for competitive companies to be selected for inspection, and to increase customs clearance efficiency and resource efficiency. In this way, we can also make full use of limited resources by focusing on companies that are less able to assure quality of products and are subject to risks. It is easy to enforce laws and regulations in a clean-cut way, while differentiated management is difficult to be done. This is what we are exploring.

I think the so-called replicable experience gained in China (Shanghai) Pilot Free Trade Zone can only be practiced in other areas when certain pre-conditions are met. Put it simple. A program may be effective in Place A, but not necessarily in Place B. To implement the program, Place B needs to develop certain capabilities and create some conditions. Otherwise only a universal law is needed throughout the country, and projects don't have to be piloted in China (Shanghai) Pilot Free Trade Zone first. To introduce differentiated measures to facilitate trade, we need efforts from companies that are expected to develop themselves. We call for companies to work with us. We can cooperate in research, and work together to explore measures to facilitate trade on the condition that risks are under control. These measures should be differentiated. In the two-dimensional trade facilitation system, both analysis and management are classified. Risks are categorized into three groups. There are four management approaches and five regulation models, namely credit regulation, verification regulation, general regulation, special regulation and tightened regulation. Nowadays in China, before inspection and quarantine, products are assumed to be disqualified, so the whole process is very slow. In the future, both approaches of qualification assumption and disqualification assumption will be implemented in accordance with the five regulation models, so as to facilitate trade. 90% of our country's standards are in line with international standards. It's important to clarify these standards to companies. In the future, if we had the chance, we would elaborate it to you.

Elton Huang: Mr. Xie shared a very important insight, explaining to us why companies need to be engaged in the technology trade platform in China (Shanghai)

Pilot Free Trade Zone. Companies' capability, as well as the function and maturity of the eco-system developed by companies lay an important foundation for new attempts in China (Shanghai) Pilot Free Trade Zone. That's reason why the eco-system is two-way and diversified. Promoting technology trade and the development of free trade zone requires the companies to play an active role. It is not the sole responsibility for authorities.

Wu Wei: Many enterprises have shared their ideas on trade facilitation. On behalf of the Shanghai Municipal Office for Port Services, I'd like to share our opinions.

First, we should make it clear that the customs, the administration of inspection and quarantine, maritime affairs administration, frontier inspection office and other departments in charge of port services all implement policies and regulations based on the same standard. We apply the same standards to all countries, except war zones. But we have different standards targeting different companies. Both customs and inspection and quarantine bureau are conducting risk classification and classified regulation. If a company's product is low-risk, the regulation will be simple, whereas a company will undergo strict regulation if it has a bad credit record. Having worked on the area of economics and trade, I have never noticed any policy that is aimed at any country or company. I am deeply convinced that our market is equal-footing, open and transparent.

Second, I'd like to talk about opening the market. The key issue is bilateral reciprocity. China has BIT negotiations with the US and Japan respectively. In terms of the import of beef, China and Japan should have reciprocal relations. It's not just about the quality of beef. So I think after the meeting, Mr. Michiaki Oguri can organize all Japanese beef traders who want to enter Chinese market to discuss with your government about what products that you want to export to China and what Chinese products that are allowed to be imported into your market. This is a win-win relationship. But this is also where the US and Japan have huge disagreements on agriculture and agricultural products.

Third, the construction industry. During the four-year-and-a-half work in Lujiazui, I was responsible for planning and construction for three years. China opens the area of architectural design to foreign countries. For example, Mr. Arata Isozaki, the famous Japanese architect designed Zendai Himalayas Center on the Fongdian Road and Longyang Road. The only requirement is that foreign architects have to cooperate with Chinese architecture design institutes. But to my knowledge, China is more open than Japan in this area. We are always looking for the growth of domestic and foreign companies in Shanghai and in other places in China. Therefore, departments in charge of port services, like Shanghai Municipal Commission of Commerce are sparing no effort to create a favorable environment for everyone.

Fourth, the cost of customs clearance. On the Single Window of international trade, we have published the customs clearance process for ocean shipping, air freight, and water transport, such as the process for ocean container shipping. Meanwhile, to reduce costs for companies, the Municipal Government has undertaken the cost of customs clearance. For instance, at the Yangshan port, if the cargo is inspected by the customs, the cost will be paid by the Shanghai government. But if quality problems are found, or enterprises are involved in illegal trade, it will be the company that should make the payment. This policy discriminates or favors no country. Whatever countries should pay the cost, if problems are found. This policy is given priority to and will be introduced to Waigaoqiao, airports, and Shanghai port.

Besides, companies need to make it clear about customs clearance process. It is not the customs, the inspection and quarantine administration or maritime affairs office that make the whole process time-consuming. Customs clearance starting from the arrival of cargo, including customs declaration involves many procedures. But at least 90% of the cargo are cleared very quickly. Only when inspection is needed, the process will be prolonged a little bit. Inspection and quarantine will be finished very rapidly. But when legal inspection is required for some goods, like imported wine, more time will be needed. How long the process will last also depends on the company's credit.

If you are engaged in import and export business, I will have to remind you that you'd better be careful about words by customs broker, shipping agent and freight forwarder. Because sometimes it is these agents that submit the wrong documents to the customs or mistaken product B for product A in declaration. After the customs notice the mistake, the cargo will have to be inspected by the officials instead of inspected in the e-channel, which will greatly prolong the whole process. In this situation, agents will blame the customs. But in fact, it is because of their mistakes in customs declaration. In practice, cases like this are usual.

Fifth, the standard. Different countries have different standards. The EU has higher food standard than the US. Americans stick to their own standards, while the EU citizens insist on their own. So the sides agree on TTIP. If a company intends to export products, they will have to follow the standards of the target market.

In this summit under the theme of Promoting Investment and Trade Facilitation in Shanghai, departments including port services office, the customs, and the inspection and quarantine administration are looking forward to the concerns from companies, and are ready to help you. If companies have many to say, I think we can pick out some typical companies and officials from the port services office together with officials from the customs and the inspection and quarantine administration should go to have a visit. A private meeting with the port services office alone can be held. But there is one request that companies need to select some typical cases before the meeting, and provide as many details as possible, like the date, and information related to the cargo. If it is a true story, competent department will investigate into it. Problems and difficulties cannot deter us away, but your complaints should be objective and concrete. We need data as well as typical and detailed cases, and more importantly your constructive suggestions. Some approaches are effective in other countries, but may not be viable in China, we have different conditions, different government apparatus and different legal system. But we can learn from their impressive practices.

Nobert Meyring: In recent two years, foreign companies have witnessed the decrease in their investment yield and profit margin in Shanghai and even in China as a whole. This puts huge pressure on foreign companies and has become a great challenge, as China has become an important market for multinationals. A number of CEOs are very concerned about it. Thus there are many questions to be answered. How to persuade CEOs of global enterprises to invest in China, and in Shanghai in particular? What is the uniqueness of China and Shanghai? What impact that China's economic slow will have on trade? What are the new engines for growth that China and Shanghai can provide for foreign-funded multinationals?

Elton Huang: China is an indispensable market for multinationals. It is important to figure out why it is necessary for multinationals to invest in China and Shanghai in particular. Just now we have concluded that with the joint efforts from the government and companies, we can optimize the cost and improve efficiency. As China has a 300 million to 500 million middle-class consumers, larger than America's population, it is important to know not only why to invest in China, particularly Shanghai, but also how

提升投资贸易便利化水平，构建开放型经济新体制

to invest in this country to be competitive in the world.

Li Junjie: Over the past four or five years, Zhonglun Legal Firm has been helping Chinese enterprises to "go global" and invest abroad. Chinese companies are actively engaged in it, and it is greatly supported by the government. But due to economic issues at home and abroad, for example the contracting of China's foreign exchange reserve, it seems that the review process for outbound investment project takes more time than the past. Is it correct?

Elton Huang: Many departments are involved in this issue, like the Shanghai Municipal Development and Reform Commission, Shanghai Municipal Commission of Commerce, State Administration of Foreign Exchange, and even the State-owned Assets Supervision and Administration Commission of the State Council which is responsible for the review and approval for state-owned enterprises. So I think we can further discuss it after the meeting.

Chen Zilei: As a teacher in the university, I don't have much first-hand knowledge on this issue. In the Shanghai International Think Tank Summit attended by world-renowned think tanks, companies' representatives and officials from functional departments, I feel it a great opportunity to share my ideas with you.

First, problems in China (Shanghai) Pilot Free Trade Zone raised by you, such as institutional restrictions need to be resolved. More efforts will be invested, but they can't be dealt with overnight.

Second, we need to understand the circumstance under which the issue is raised. Investment and trade facilitation reflects that global trade tends to be more equal-footing. The development of economic globalization is the shift from the pursuit of trade efficiency to fairness. It is in this context that the issue of investment and trade facilitation is being discussed. The central government and even the Shanghai Municipal People's Government have expressed their commitment on improving institutions, and reform and opening-up.

The development of free trade zone is different from that of traditional projects and bonded area. The construction of China (Shanghai) Pilot Free Trade Zone features in institutional innovation and focuses on the negative list for investment. What's more, the shift from positive list to negative list should accompanied by the change of government roles, so the government needs to improve its regulatory policies. Transforming from prior review and approval to regulation in process and afterwards requires the government to rely on the legal system to deal with the difficulties and disputes that are emerging in streamlining administration and delegating power to the lower levels.

We also need to find out China's uniqueness. Traditional manufacturing is doing processing trade. In current trade landscape, the proportion of processing trade is dropping, but it still helps to result in international trade surplus. In this circumstance, we need to open up the service industry for industrial structure transformation. The opening-up of service industry is involved with many departments and will be faced with institutional challenges. So how to open this industry, and what sectors should be opened? We can open up the sectors where we have advantages. That's why the term of producer service sector has been coined. In producer service sector, we have competitive edges. After opening the sector, more service sectors will have to be opened up. Among them, the most difficult one is the financial service sector. The opening-up of it will face pressure from exchange rate and trade. These two challenges must be solved. If Shanghai is to become "four centers", namely global economic center, global financial center, global shipping center and global trade center, China (Shanghai) Pilot Free Trade Zone should have a global influence in science and technology innovation, and should be able to provide impressive financial services. This should be taken into account for the direction and roadmap of future reforms.

It is not easy for Shanghai Municipal People's Government to carry out new measures and new policies. But I believe that the Chinese government is capable of further deepening the reform. Since China's first free trade zone was established in Shanghai, the number and size of free trade zones in China have been growing. So we need to find out the uniqueness of Shanghai. Premier Li Keqiang said we should have the determination to cut the wrist like brave warriors. Many of the companies present here today are multinationals from the modern service sector. This suggests that Shanghai is experiencing transformation, as well as foreign companies' investment structure.

All of us are well aware of the issue of cost. New York is expensive. So is Tokyo. I have done a lot of research on Tokyo where the service industry accounts for 80% of the city's GDP. We need to find the direction for improving investment and trade facilitation to serve the transformation of Shanghai.

SUMMARY
STATEMENT

总结发言

黄 佳 Elton Huang

普华永道中国中区市场主管合伙人、上海首席合伙人

PwC Central China Markets Leader，

Shanghai Senior Partner

回应刚才一位外商提到的问题：为什么选择上海？因为上海给了大家更多的宽容性。

刚才我们提到很多负面的东西，就像黑天鹅，人类大脑对负面的东西总是特别关注。比如我们批判一个比较极端的领导，却没有庆贺世界上大多数领导都没有那么极端；我们都说今天发生了一场车祸，却没有说这之外的每天都生活在很安全的环境当中。

我们今天生活的社会可谓是人类历史上最美好的时代，最近十年也是人类历史上战争最少的十年。上海的人均寿命已经接近世界先进水平。曾经有预言，科学家每多活一年，人类平均寿命将往前推进大约半年到一年。这意味着在座的各位生活到 120 岁、150 岁都不是梦想。这么美好的世界下，我们应当共同为上海创造更美好的未来。

我曾经跟上海各种企业家讨论，梦想中的上海是什么样的。"二维"的上海能够像纽约一样解决很多交通的问题，能够把工作和办公半径设计到同一城区，解决两地奔波的问题；"三维"的上海可以实现空中住宅，通过各种无人机解决交通问题；"四维"的上海能实现全球领先的数字流；"五维"的上海有国企、民企、央企和外企构成的丰富生态圈，产生创新的火花；"六维"的上海则是能实现在每个阶层、不同人群当中有最平等、最丰富的机会，能产生阶层之间的流动，给整个社会注入最美好的未来。

祝贺 2016 年上海国际智库峰会取得圆满成功，让我们共同期待明年再聚于智库峰会，衷心祝愿上海这个城市前景更加美好！

First I would like to respond to the question raised by a foreign investor: why to invest in Shanghai? Because Shanghai is very tolerant.

Today, we have talked a lot about negative issues that are like black swans. People are particularly concerned about negative things. For example, we accuse a leader of being extreme, but never celebrate that this leader is only the few. We will be very upset because of a traffic accident one day, but will not be happy for the other days when we are safe and sound.

This is the best of times. The last decade is a period with least wars ever. Shanghai ranks among the first in terms of life expectancy. It is predicted that if scientists live one year more, human average lifespan will extend by six months to one year. It means living to be 120 or even 150 years old is not a distant dream for us. In this beautiful world, we are supposed to work together to create a brighter future for Shanghai.

I have discussed with many entrepreneurs in Shanghai about how their ideal Shanghai looks like. A two-dimensional Shanghai should be like New York that is able to deal with transportation problems. Office buildings and living areas are built in the same district, which makes it unnecessary for people to commute from place to another every day. In a three-dimensional Shanghai, houses will be built in the air, and drones will be used to reduce traffic congestion. A four-dimensional Shanghai will take the lead in the world in terms of digital stream technology. A five-dimensional Shanghai will be dynamic in innovation thanks to the eco-system consisting of SOEs, private sector, local SOEs, and foreign companies. In a six-dimensional Shanghai, people from all works of life can have equal access to abundant opportunities. Thus social mobility can be achieved and the most prosperous future will be created.

Finally, congratulations on the success of the 2016 Shanghai International Think Tank Summit! Look forward to the summit next year. Wish Shanghai a brighter future!

CONFERENCE REVIEW

峰会综述

2016 年 12 月 9 日，由上海市人民政府发展研究中心主办，普华永道中国、上海发展研究基金会、上海国际智库交流中心联合承办，举办了以"提升上海投资贸易便利化水平"为主题的第三届上海国际智库峰会。来自国际知名智库和企业的专家共同探讨了投资贸易便利化新趋势以及上海在这些领域存在的突出问题，对上海提升投资贸易提出了一些具体建议，为自贸区积累更多经验并为未来上海参与国际投资、贸易谈判和规则及标准的制定有参考意义。

1. 上海服务贸易滞后于香港新加坡

智库和企业专家肯定了上海在提升投资贸易上的努力和成效，也指出了存在的不足。波士顿咨询的专家概括了上海在全球投资贸易中的位置：上海仍然滞后于亚洲主要城市。2015 年上海服务贸易额总额是 GDP 的 51.2%，同期，香港、新加坡分别占 62% 和 92%，其中，上海劳动密集型服务（运输、旅游等）占到七成以上；创新性强、附加值高的高端服务业（金融保险、文化服务、专业服务等）占比较低。

2. 上海投资贸易便利化存在的三个问题

智库和企业专家集中提出了政府管理服务过程、金融部门服务能力和宏观改革政策趋势等三个方面的问题。

（1）地方政府在公共服务上的作为不够。

智库和企业专家认为，上海在提升投资贸易方面还有许多领域有待开拓。雅培制药的专家提出了动物原性和人原性生物制剂进口海关商检效率低下、关检程序和措施不利生物制药研发、不符合上海建设具有全球影响力的科技创新中心目标；他们认为，在推动便利的专业关检制度上，还有更多可作为的空间，在促进各地政策法规的统一上，上海也远没有发挥应有的作用，制约了其在全国投资贸易上的影响力。[①] 同时，雅培制药的专家还提出了生物制药领域资产重组的行政审批程序繁琐和周期长等问题。

（2）金融部门提供金融支持的能力不强。

智库和企业专家非常关注人民币汇率波动的影响，主要集中在企业的投资贸易汇兑和记账损益及其进行有关投资决策等方面的影响。上港集团的专家认为，上海金融机构和市场的创新能力仍然不足，未能充分开发创新海外投融资汇率避险工具。

欧盟商会的专家认为，上海在提升投资贸易和跨境业务上，没有发挥出金融中心的作用，金融支撑力度和能力不足，不能满足日益增强的投资贸易需求。

（3）宏观层面投资贸易改革开放有所放缓。

智库和企业专家认为，宏观投资贸易改革开放步子有所放缓，行政限制积繁难简。上海电气的专家提出，国企海外项目或发债过程中，要经过中央和地方双重审批。跟国企海外投资相关，上港集团的专家提出，目前许多国企国际信用评级较高[②]，海外融资成本低，但现有政策限制了国内使用海外融资的渠道和领域。

欧盟商会的专家认为，利率和汇率改革放缓，改革政策落地长期拖延，实现资本可兑换遥遥无期，资本市场的国际板和战略新兴板搁浅；上海自贸区自由贸易账户有效范围狭隘，因此，推进金融改革非常紧迫。

3. 探索积累提升上海投资贸易便利化的政策建议

智库和企业专家对上海提升投资贸易提出了建议。

（1）加强国内投资贸易规则的创新，发挥上海的影响力。

智库和企业专家认为，在国际投资贸易出现暂时颓势的情况下，自贸区要加快探索国内投资贸易规则，把自贸区创新和实践的国际贸易规则，运用到国内投资贸易中来，推进改革，消除各地区之间的投资贸易壁垒和障碍。雅培制药的专家特别强调了上海要推动统一各地投资贸易政策法规，发挥在国内制度安排上的作用和影响力。

---

① 目前，许多跨国企业的中国业务，采取了在上海设立地区总部或管理中心、在其他地方设立子公司的布局方式。但是，这个布局方式受到了不同省市费税和社保等政策法规较大差异的制约。
② 上港集团标普评级 A+，穆迪评级 A1。

（2）把握投资贸易趋势，选择突破领域。

麦肯锡的专家强调，上海要关注投资贸易领域正在出现的三大趋势：服务贸易成为投资贸易主力、颠覆性的创新决定贸易主动权和数字化推动投资贸易转型升级；投资贸易发展的重点要聚焦在新的商业模式、制造业服务化和跨境消费高端化等带来的服务和贸易上，要发展有高技术含量的实物贸易。

凯捷公司的专家提出，上海要依托"一带一路"、自贸区建设和数字化创新趋势，加大对数字贸易企业服务的整合，推动总部经济转型，重点吸引消费相关领域、高科技研发创新和供应链控制领域的企业。上海电气和上港集团的专家建议，在自贸区"先行先试"，放宽企业规定额度下对外投资的权限，拓展海外融资在国内使用的领域，把握国企海外投融资的趋势。

BitSE 公司的专家强调了金融科技带来的投资贸易机遇，建议关注和开发区块链在信息溯源、审查和公示等供应链管理的应用前景。①

（3）对标投资贸易国际惯例，改善公共服务。

波士顿咨询的专家认为，坚持向国际惯例靠拢，是推动投资贸易的重要路径，要缩短负面清单，开放非银行金融服务（证券、保险等）、商务和专业技术服务和高端服务（教育、医疗、文化娱乐等）；要落实与其他国家签订的互惠条款②，加强这些互惠条款规定与国内有关特别管理措施之间的衔接，提升相应投资贸易环节操作的规范化和可操作性。同时，建议在自贸区试点，向符合条件的商务人员实施国际通行的商务旅行卡计划并对滞留期限作适当延长③。

埃森哲咨询的专家认为，改善公共服务对提升投资贸易至关重要。因此，可以结合智慧城市建设，率先在全国建设三大智慧化公共服务平台：一是政务服务平台④，基于数字技术、针对企业需求，建立政府与企业间互动界面，提升营商环境；二是创新服务平台，推动产业数字化创新和升级发展，对整体创新体系提供支持，吸引初创高科技企业落户；三是市民服务平台，满足城市人群对生活、安全、健康等服务的需求，提高生活质量，吸引优秀人才。

---

① 区块链是一个多方共同接入、安全的全球总账本型的通用型平台，完整记录所有可数字化的物品、用户信息和相对操作行为，形成连贯、及时的信息流。

② 如在美国的 BIT 范本中，有七项基于互惠原则，即若 BIT 缔约伙伴国向美国开放该领域投资，美国也会向伙伴国投资者相应开放。

③ 商务旅行卡是 APEC 成员经济体之间商务人员出入境的惯例。根据这个计划，商务旅行卡持卡人在三年内凭有效护照和旅行卡无须办理入境签证，享有特殊的快速出入境通道。

④ 可分四个阶段推进：（1）实现政府在数据方面的集成和整合；（2）政府流程的数字化和移动化；（3）大数据分析；（4）引进人工智能。

On December 9th, 2016, the 3rd Shanghai International Think Tank Summit, themed on "Promote the Investment and Trade Facilitation in Shanghai", was hosted by the Development Research Center of Shanghai Municipal People's Government (SDRC), co-organized by PwC China, Shanghai Development Research Foundation, and Shanghai International Think Tank Exchange Center. Experts from leading international think tanks and enterprises discussed about the new trend of investment and trade facilitation and the key issues of these fields in Shanghai. They proposed specific suggestions on promoting investment and trade in Shanghai, which provides more experience for the free trade zone and gives a reference for Shanghai's participation in international investment, trade negotiations, and the formulation of rules and standards in the future.

1. Shanghai's Trade in Services Trade in Lags Behind Hong Kong and Singapore

Experts from think tanks and enterprises approved the efforts and accomplishments that Shanghai has made in promoting investment and trade facilitation. They also pointed out the existing shortcomings. The expert from Boston Consulting Group (BCG) outlined Shanghai's position in global investment and trade: Shanghai is still lagging behind the major cities in Asia. In 2015, Shanghai's total service trade accounted for 51.2% of GDP, while in Hong Kong and Singapore, the proportion is 62% and 92% respectively. In the total trade of services, labor intensive services (transportation and tourism) accounted for more than 70%; high-end services with strong innovation and high value-added (finance and insurance, cultural services and professional services, etc.) accounted for a relatively low proportion.

2. Three Problems of Investment and Trade Facilitation in Shanghai

The experts from think tanks and enterprises pointed out problems from three aspects: the process of government management, service capability of financial departments, and tendency of macro reform policy.

(1) The Inefficiency of Local Government on Public Services.

The experts from think tanks and enterprises believed that there are many investment and trade promotion fields in Shanghai waiting to be explored. The expert from Abbott pointed out several problems in customs inspection, including low efficiency in importing animal origin and human origin biological preparations. Abbott thought that the procedures and measures are unfavorable to biopharmaceutical research and development, and they are not in accordance with the goal of Shanghai constructing a global Technology Innovation Center. Abbott also thought that there is lots of work to do in promoting customs inspection facilitation, and Shanghai is far from playing its role in promoting unification of policies and regulations throughout China, which in turn has restricted its influence in national investment and trade.[1] Apart from the above, the expert pointed out an issue about the complicated and tedious examination procedure on asset restructuring in the biopharmaceutical industry.

(2) The Weak Ability of Financial Sectors in Financial Support.

The experts paid close attention to the impact of the RMB exchange rate fluctuations, especially the enterprise's investment, trade, exchange, accounting profits and losses, related investment decisions, and other aspects of the impact.The expert from Shanghai International Port (Group)believed that Shanghai's financial institutions and market innovation capacity is still inadequate, and failed to fully develop innovative overseas investment and financing, exchange rate hedging instruments.

The expert from European Chamber of Commerce in China thought that Shanghai did not play the role of financial center in promoting investment, trade and overseas

---

[1] At present, the China operation of many multinational enterprises adopted the layout of setting regional head quarters or management centers in Shanghai and subsidiaries in other places. However, this layout is restricted by the difference of taxes, social security and other policies in provinces and cities.

service. The financial support intensity and capability is inadequate, and cannot meet the growing demand of investment and trade.

(3) The Reform and Opening up of Investment and Trade Have Slowed Down on Macro Level.

The experts from think tanks and enterprises believed that the pace of reform and opening up in investment and trade sector on the macro level have slowed down, and administrative restrictions are too complicated. The expert from Shanghai Electric pointed out that state-owned enterprises have to go through the double approval of central and local authorities during the overseas project or issuing process. The expert from Shanghai International Port (Group) said that many state-owned enterprises have higher international credit rating[1] and lower overseas financing costs at present, but the existing policies restricted the use of overseas financing channels and fields.

The expert from European Chamber of Commerce in China believed that the interest rate and exchange rate reform has slowed down, the implementation of reform policies has been delayed for a long period, realizing capital exchange is not in the foreseeable future, and the international board of capital markets and the emerging strategic boards are stranded; the domain of account validity in Shanghai Pilot Free Trade Zone is narrow. Therefore, promoting financial reform is very urgent.

3. Policy Proposals to Promote Investment and Trade Facilitation in Shanghai

Experts from think tanks and enterprises offered suggestions for Shanghai to promote investment and trade.

(1) Strengthen the Innovation of Domestic Investment and Trade Regulations, Fully Exert the Influence of Shanghai.

The experts believed that under the current temporary decline in international investment and trade, the free trade zone needs to speed up the exploration of domestic investment and trade regulations, and apply its innovation and practice to domestic investment and trade so as to deepen the reform and eliminate the investment and trade barriers and obstacles between different areas. The expert from Abbott stressed that

---

[1] Shanghai International Port (Group) S&P rating is A+, Moody's rating is A1.

Shanghai should promote the unification of policies and regulations on investment and trade across the country, and play a role in the domestic institutional arrangements and influence.

(2) Grasp the Trend of Investment and Trade, Choose the Areas to Breakthrough.

Expert from McKinsey&Company pointed out that Shanghai needs to pay attention to the three emerging trends in the investment and trade sector: service trade has become the main trade investment, disruptive innovation decides trade initiative, and digitalization promotes the transformation and upgrade of investment and trade; The focus of investment and trade development should be the service and trade brought by new business models, servitization of manufacturing, and high-end cross boarder consumption, etc. Shanghai needs to develop high-tech visible trade.

The expert from Capgemini China proposed that Shanghai should rely on "The Belt and Road initiative", free trade zone strategy and the new digital innovation trend, increase the integration of digital trade enterprise services, promote headquarters economy transformation, and focus on attracting consumer related, high-tech research and innovation related, and supply chain control related enterprises. The experts from Shanghai Electric and Shanghai International Port (Group) suggested that the government could start from the free trade zone, loosen the overseas investment restrictions under the enterprise specified amount, expand the use of overseas financing in our country, and grasp the trend of overseas investment and financing of state-owned enterprises.

The expert from BitSE stressed the importance of investment and trade opportunities brought by financial technology. He suggested that Shanghai could pay attention to and further explore the application prospect of Blockchain in supply chain management (such as information origin tracing, censorship and publicity)[1].

(3) Benchmarking International Practices in Investment and Trade, Improving Public Services.

The expert from BCG thought that adhering to international practice is an important path to promote trade and investment. Shanghai should shorten the negative list, and open non-banking financial services (such as securities and insurance, etc.),

---

[1] Blockchain is a general platform with multiparty access and secure global ledger. It can fully record digital items, user information and relative operation behavior to form a coherent and timely information flow.

business and professional technical services, and high-end services (such as education, health, culture and entertainment, etc.). Shanghai should also implement the bilateral provisions signed with other countries[1], strengthen the connection between bilateral provisions and therelated domestic special management measures, and enhance the standardization and operability of the corresponding investment and trade operation. Meanwhile, it was suggested to implement international business travel card to qualified business personnel in the pilot free trade zone, and appropriately extend the duration time[2].

The expert from Accenture believes that improving public services is crucial to boosting investment and trade. Therefore, combined with the construction of smart city, Shanghai can take the lead in establishing three intelligent public service platform nationwide: the first one is government service platform[3]. Based on digital technology and the needs of enterprises, this platform provides an interactive interface for the government and enterprises, can advance business environment; the second one is innovation service platform. It can promote digital innovation and upgrading of the industry, provide support for the whole innovation system, and attract newly established high-tech enterprises to settle; the third one is citizen service system. It satisfies citizens' demands of services such as livelihood, security, and health etc., enhance the quality of life, and attract talented people.

---

[1] For example, in the U.S. Model BIT, there are seven items based on the principle of reciprocity, which means that if a BIT partner opens a field for U.S. to invest, U.S. would also open a corresponding field for the partner.

[2] Business travel cards are the practice of entry and exit of business personnel between APEC member economies. According to this plan, the business travel card holder can enter a country with only the card and a valid passport. He or she does not have to apply for an entry visa, and enjoys a special fast entry and exit channel.

[3] It can be carried forward by four stages: (1) to realize the integration of government data; (2) to digitize and mobilize government processes; (3) to analyze big data; (4) to introduce artificial intelligence.

ATTACHMENTS

附　件

上海企业对外投资合作发展
回顾与展望（2015—2016）

上海市商务委员会

安永（中国）企业咨询有限公司

摘　要

随着"走出去"战略步伐的加快，近年来中国对外直接投资规模发展迅速，投资主体和方式日趋多样化。商务部统计显示，2015 年度我国对外非金融类直接投资创下 1 180.2 亿美元 [①] 的历史最高值，同比增长 14.7%，实现中国对外直接投资连续 13 年增长态势。中国资本大规模进军国际市场，已经成为全球投资市场引人瞩目的现象。

伴随着"一带一路"（"丝绸之路经济带"和"21 世纪海上丝绸之路"）和国际产能合作政策的进一步推广，以及"中国制造 2025"等国家战略的推进落实，以基础设施建设和产能优化为主题的"一带一路"投资合作正在兴起。提升"中国制造"的国际影响力正迎来历史新机遇。

作为全球领先的专业服务机构之一，安永有幸受邀连续于 2015 年以及 2016 年两年为上海市商务委员会撰写《上海企业对外投资合作年度发展报告》。通过两年的编写，我们对近年来中国，特别是上海的对外投资情况有了深入了解，也对企业"走出去"过程中常见模式与可能遇到的风险有了一定程度的认识。为了更进一步向广大投资者提供参考，为上海对外投资工作起到更好的支持作用，本文将基于连续两年的研究分析与访谈调研，从以下几个方面汇总阐述近年来中国与上海对外投资情况：

（1）中国与上海对外投资合作现状与趋势：从大数据掌握近年来中国与上海对外投资动向。

（2）中国与上海对外投资政策：对于中国与上海的对外投资合作政策及公共服务体系提供了概览。

（3）上海企业对外投资合作问卷调查结果分析：通过调查与分析展示包括投

---

① 除特别标注，本文中涉及的观点与数据均来自：上海市商务委员会《上海企业对外投资合作年度发展报告（2015）》以及《上海企业对外投资合作年度发展报告（2016）》。

资主体，投资领域以及投资风险等重要信息。

（4）上海企业"走出去"模式与案例分析：按照对外投资合作驱动因素以及战略定位的不同，归纳总结了上海企业"走出去"模式与案例分析，其中将重点分析股权基金投资模式。

（5）对外投资合作风险评估与应对建议：根据问卷调查与访谈中的发现，归纳总结了"走出去"企业目前面临的六大对外投资合作风险，并从企业自身风险防范与应对措施的建立健全提出了不同风险下的应对建议。

（6）有效的投后整合帮助中国企业在海外并购中取得成功：通过对正在实施海外并购的上海企业进行调查，探究企业在并购后整合过程中面临的普遍挑战以及分享成功经验。

1. 中国与上海对外投资合作现状与趋势

在国内产业转型需求与"一带一路"政策的推进下，越来越多的中国企业正在实现从全球制造者到全球投资者的角色转换。2014年，中国实际对外投资总额首度超过利用外资规模，成为全球投资市场引人瞩目的焦点。根据过往两年于《上海企业对外投资合作年度发展报告》的分析，中国投资者足迹已经遍布全球156个国家和地区，随着中国经济转型升级和中国企业的发展壮大，投资目的从早期的获取资源等生产要素逐渐转变为获取先进技术和品牌，以增强企业国际竞争力及满足国内日益增长的消费需求。在此驱动下中国海外投资目的地日趋多元化，中国企业的足迹从亚非拉等资源型国家扩展到欧美等发达国家。中国企业的主要对外投资行业除了传统的商业、房地产业及制造业外，电信、媒体和科技（TMT）、汽车和运输以及金融服务三大行业的占比与增速也体现了中国海外投资方向的多元与高端化。

作为中国面向世界的窗口，上海凭借其优越的地理位置和"四个中心"（即国际经济中心、国际金融中心、国际航运中心、国际贸易中心）的战略定位，成为了中国吸引外资和对外投资的生力军。近两年来上海市实际对外投资额逐年增长，2015年已达到166.36亿美元，同比增长382%，占全国同期境外投资的比重超过14%，位列全国第一。从投资总额来看，民营企业占总体投资比重逐年上升，成为对外投资的绝对主力。私募股权投资为上海企业对外投资提供引领与资金支持，而自贸区则成为上海以及其他省市企业出海的首选平台。从投资目的地和热点行业来看，上海企业境外投资的区域布局更趋多元，投资足迹不仅遍布美国、大洋洲和欧洲等发达国家与地区，在"一带一路"建设的号召下，新加坡、印度尼西亚、哈萨克斯坦、泰国等"一带一路"沿线国家与地区也成为投资热点。根据过往两年于《上海企业对外投资合作年度发展报告》的分析，上海企业的主要对外投资行业包括租赁和商务服务业、房地产业、批发和零售业、制造业，以及信息传输、软件和信息技术服务业等。

2. 中国与上海对外投资政策

国家为推动"走出去"战略的实施，不断简政放权以激发对外投资活力，通过多方位支持以完善对外投资服务体系。中国对外投资合作政策包括推行"一带一路"的建设、资源开发、产业和金融合作，推动中国资本输出；简政放权，简化审批流程、拓宽融资渠道、健全服务体系，推动企业出海，促进制造业和金融业向中高水平迈进；完善对外投资服务体系，包括权益保障、投资促进、风险预警等。

表 1 列示了 2015 年 4 月以来中国政府出台的部分对外投资有关的重要政策。

表 1

颁布时间	政 策 内 容	意 义
2015 年 4 月	国家税务总局服务"一带一路"发展战略十项措施	充分发挥税收协定作为国际税收关系与税收合作的法律基础作用，提高税收确定性，避免双重征税，维护纳税人的合法权益
2015 年 5 月	国务院发布《中国制造 2025》	这是我国实施制造强国战略第一个十年的行动纲领，部署全面推进实施制造强国战略
2015 年 5 月	国务院发布《国务院关于推进国际产能和装备制造合作的指导意见》	提出了推进国际产能和装备制造合作的指导思想和基本原则、目标任务、政策措施，是当前及今后一个时期推进国际产能和装备制造合作的重要指导性文件
2015 年 6 月	国家税务总局发布《关于境内机构向我国银行的境外分行支付利息扣缴企业所得税有关问题的公告》	减轻银行业"走出去"的税收负担
2015 年 8 月	商务部印发《境外经贸合作区服务指南范本》	为进一步做好境外经贸合作区建设工作，推动合作区做大做强，发挥其境外产业集聚和平台效应
2015 年 10 月	国家发展和改革委员会发布《标准联通"一带一路"行动计划（2015—2017）》	主动适应经济发展新常态，积极培育国际竞争新优势，紧密围绕"政策沟通、设施联通、贸易畅通、资金融通、民心相通"的总体要求，不断深化与"一带一路"沿线国家标准化双多边合作和互联互通，大力推动中国标准"走出去"，加快提高标准国际化水平，全面服务"一带一路"建设
2016 年 4 月	国家发展改革委关于修订《境外投资项目核准和备案管理办法》的决定（公开征求意见稿）	• 取消了中方投资额 10 亿美元及以上项目的国家发改委核准要求 • 取消了中方投资额 20 亿美元及以上，并设计敏感国家和地区、敏感行业的境外投资项目，需由国家发改委提出审核意见并报国务院审核的要求 • 进一步简化行政审批，放宽权限

资料来源：政府部门公告、安永整理。

同时上海市各级政府亦从制定规划思路、营造政策环境、培育市场主体以及构建服务体等方面，有效助推企业"走出去"：2015年9月，中国（上海）自由贸易试验区境外投资服务联盟正式成立；2016年2月上海市发展和改革委员会发布的"十三五"规划，明确上海在"十三五"中将拓展"走出去"新空间，将全面参与"一带一路"国家战略；上海市商务委员会以"走出去"战略作为核心，构建包含信息服务、投资促进、人才培训、风险防控等全方面的服务体系，为企业"走出去"提供坚实的后盾。

3. 上海企业对外投资合作问卷调查结果分析

安永与上海市商务委员会根据过往两年于《上海企业对外投资合作年度发展报告》的分析，针对正在进行或存在对外投资合作活动意向的上海企业通过问卷调查的形式，统计了上海主要走出去企业的实际情况和发展方向。

问卷调研取得的反馈中，民营企业正更加积极的参与对外投资合作活动。根据过往两年于《上海企业对外投资合作年度发展报告》的分析，上海有较多的投资性公司正在积极参加对外投资活动，除了传统制造、商业、建筑房产等行业外，预计未来期间在信息传输、软件和信息技术服务业、科学研究和技术服务业等科技相关领域会更加活跃。对于对外投资合作活动，企业普遍持有谨慎乐观的态度，预计未来对外并购活动会进一步增加。

对外投资合作的主要驱动因素包括海外市场开拓，品牌影响力提升，国内竞争力增强和上下游产业链发展。上海企业的国际化水平，尤其是在国际化整合、国际营销能力、品牌声誉和市场占有率方面有待进一步提高。上海企业普遍认为精准的国际化战略与行业判断，和高效的海外团队是海外投资合作取得成功的重要因素。调查结果显示，受访企业认为在对外投资合作活动中主要存在三大风险分别为海外政治经济及法律风险，企业对于国外市场、法律、税收环境缺乏了解以及企业面临并购投资后的企业文化整合障碍。

4. 上海企业"走出去"模式与案例分析

本章节中我们根据公开信息与管理层访谈，撰写了相关案例分析，总结了上海企业四种主要的"走出去"模式：

（1）产业链、供应链上下游整合推动产业升级转型的对外投资模式。

企业积极寻求先进国际技术、力争获取自主知识产权，并且获得海外优质资源与品牌，大力发展上下游产业链，实现产业升级转型，进一步提升国内外市场竞争力，满足国内外市场需求。

以光明集团为例，从最初的对国外投资环境不了解、到后来的低调处事、友好公关、准确把握并购价格，并寻求政府支持及寻找并购同盟者，光明集团在海外并购中不断进步。2012 年 5 月，光明集团宣布以 12 亿英镑的价格收购英国维他麦 60% 的股份，成为中国食品行业最大宗的海外收购。①

（2）优化生产布局、开拓海外市场和转移富余产能的对外投资模式。

该模式下的上海企业既致力于以独资、合资或合作等方式开拓海外市场、转移富余的生产能力，也积极优化海外生产布局，同时配合收购国外技术、品牌、渠道等实现全球销售和资源优化配置的国际战略布局。

上汽集团充分利用自身产业链整体竞争优势，通过国内市场的领先地位，一方面在并购国际先进技术获取核心自主知识产权的基础上，通过自主研发体系进行进一步创新并应用于国内市场。另一方面，以国内成熟品牌为导向，积极开拓海外销售渠道。②

（3）利用国内先进行业经验和项目运作能力的海外资源投资和基础设施建设模式。

在该模式下，走出去企业利用其成熟的行业经验和先进的管理水平，在全球范围内寻求投资或合作机会，创造业务和收入增长点，开拓海外市场或资源，同时提升企业自身的品牌影响力。

以上海建工集团为例，其成功完成了一大批国内外标志性建设项目，并且通过承建当地的标志性建筑，创出"上海建工品牌"；同时，立足于丰富的海外项目经验，上海建工目前已能充分了解到海外项目可能存在的风险点，可以通过合理有效的风险管理进行控制。③

（4）股权投资基金引领产业互动发展的对外投资模式。

近年来，中国产业投资人跨境并购中较多以国内协同效应为出发点，旨在将发达国家的先进技术、知名品牌带回国内，或通过并购拓展自身上下游产业链，增加国内细分市场份额。基于相似的战略出发点，立足中国国内市场需求，股权投资基金带有战略意图的主导或参与跨境并购的交易数量亦呈现逐年增长的态势。股权投资基金具有丰富的投资与交易经验、技术及资金资源，正在积极物色

---

① 来源：《2015 走向全球的十大中国企业》，福布斯中文网，http://www.forbeschina.com/news/news.php?id=40149，2015 年 1 月 15 日。

② 来源：《上汽通用五菱在印尼建厂生产"五菱"车》，中国汽车网，http://auto.china.com.cn/news/corp/20150202/648116.shtml。

③ 来源：上海建工集团海外事业部网站公开信息，安永整理，http://www.cscgoversea.com/。

具有"中国视角"的海外资产，与中国企业实现双赢局面。

股权投资基金参与海外投资的模式主要包括：股权投资基金独立 / 主导收购；股权投资基金联合产业投资人协同收购；财务投资基金为海外投资提供资金支持；其他特殊投资模式。其中，股权投资基金联合产业投资人协同收购包括：股权投资基金与中国企业组团进行海外并购，以及股权投资基金与中国企业共同设立并购基金，进行跨境并购。

目前，中资跨境股权投资基金通常具有以下特点：

• 高效的筹融资能力：股权投资基金通过非公开方式向特定投资机构或个人定向募集资金，借助基金管理人的资源和灵活的融资结构安排可以更有效地解决并购交易所需要的资金。

• 丰富的投资运作与管理经验：通常而言，股权投资基金在行业分析、目标企业估值方面经验丰富，并且具有灵活的谈判技巧，对于物色合适标的并促成交易方面起着积极的作用。

• 避免商业、文化及政治敏感性：股权投资基金作为专业投资机构，在并购时与投资目标企业进行直接接触，可以依靠积极的态度与专业的立场，较大程度上减少来自不同方面的顾虑，获得当地政府的审批，以及并购对象股东及管理层的支持。

2014 年以来，国内股权投资基金呈现出更为清晰的战略目标和更为独立的运作模式。股权投资基金以独立或主导并购的方式，或者与中国企业组团联合进行海外并购的交易频现。与早年单一的财务投资人身份相较，中资跨境股权并购基金的战略意图日益明显。例如，2014 年 7 月，弘毅投资收购英国休闲餐饮公司 Pizza Express[1]，以及中信资本收购美国牙科器材及服务公司 DDS Lab[2]。2015年 7 月渤海华美与中航工业汽车联合收购美国瀚德公司[3]，中民投收购斯诺国际保险集团[4]，武岳峰创投收购芯成半导体（ISSI）[5] 等。

上海作为全国金融中心，聚集了诸多专业服务机构和国际化人才，并提供了自贸区的制度创新平台以及高效的行政效率。以上海为依托，中资股权投资基金及中国企

---

[1] 《弘毅近百亿收购英国比萨店或为上市获利》，新浪财经，http://finance.sina.com.cn/chanjing/gsnews/20140714/015919690126.shtml。

[2] 《中信资本宣布完成收购美牙科器材公司 DDS LAB》，经济网，http://www.ceweekly.cn/2014/0702/86040.shtml。

[3] 《李祥生揭秘收购美国瀚德公司始末》，晨哨网，http://www.morningwhistle.com/website/news/5/46923.html?bsh_bid=955468482。

[4] 《中民投 140 亿元全资收购美国再保险巨头斯诺集团》，观察者，http://www.guancha.cn/economy/2015_08_17_330910.shtml。

[5] 《武岳峰击败赛普拉斯，成功收购芯成》，集微网，http://toutiao.com/a4639287601/。

业在跨境并购方面取得了显著成就。TMT（科技／媒体／通信）、汽车制造业、房地产、批发和零售业及生物医药等行业日益成为股权投资基金对外投资的热点行业。

5. 对外投资合作风险评估与应对建议

诚如前文问卷调查结果分析所述，走出去企业在落地的过程中面临着诸多风险。我们总结了以下六大对外投资合作风险，并从企业自身风险防范与应对措施建立的角度提出了应对的建议。

（1）东道国政治风险：建立防范应急机制，承担企业社会责任，照顾多方利益关系，利用海外投资保险。

（2）缺乏清晰的战略定位：做好行业市场调研，加强技术品牌建设，立足整体协同效应，寻求战略合作联盟。

（3）风险防范意识和能力欠缺：完善内控管理制度，重视投前尽职调查，适当使用商业保险，积极防范外汇风险。

（4）跨文化整合能力弱与公信力不足：制定详尽整合方案，尊重当地文化习俗，增加企业信息透明，加强有效沟通宣传。

（5）国际化人才匮乏：尊重当地劳动环境，构建良好雇主品牌，调整全球人才配置，优化人才激励机制。

（6）法律、税收等制度风险：遵守东道国法律法规，充分利用国际规则，加强政府中介沟通，完善融资税务筹划。

6. 有效的投后整合帮助中国企业在海外并购中取得成功

并购后整合是跨国并购成功的关键因素，成功的整合，能够使收购方和被收购企业的资源均得到充分利用，实现双方的业务协同、运营提升，最大化双方企业价值和股东价值。同样，我们根据问卷调查对投后整合进行了探讨并总结了一系列具有针对性的对策：

（1）建立有效的公司治理架构，防范管控风险：对被并购企业利益关联方的权力进行划分，明确权力运作机制，是实现对被并购企业组织与管理整合的重要前提。

（2）激发核心团队积极性，确保业务及团队稳定：对收购方而言，了解核心团队流失风险以及留任要素，是实现对其保留与激励的基础。

（3）明确财务管理要求，及时获取相关信息：成功实施整合的企业通常会通过评估分析并购双方的财务管理体系，向被并购企业明确提出财务管理要求，使被并购企业的财务管理体系符合企业的战略目标和管理需要。

（4）重视沟通及文化整合，渐进实现团队融合：成功实现海外并购的中国企业会建立有效的内外部沟通机制，协调好文化背景各异的利益关联方之间的关系，逐步实现团队融合。

（5）稳妥推进业务协同，逐步获取协同效应：在并购后整合中，通过整合品牌营销、客户资源、销售渠道和网络、采购模式、研发体系等，形成协同合力，从而提升并购双方企业的核心竞争优势。

（6）加快中方国际化人才队伍培养，扩大外派人才库：国际化人才是支持企业跨国经营活动的重要保障。成功企业会非常重视企业内部国际化人才的培养，扩大外派人才库，同时加强对外派人员的管理。

结　论

以优化产业布局与经济转型升级为发展主旨的中国企业，在全球化 4.0 的浪潮下，必将更积极地参与到海外投资合作活动中去。放眼未来，中国和上海企业的对外投资将继续保持高速增长。中国经济的进一步转型包括上海全球科创中心的建设，将带动更多的上海企业投资到高科技、高端制造、高端服务等产业链上游领域；同时，立足于国内市场需求进行的消费导向性全球产业整合，也将成为上海企业未来投资合作的重要方向；在"一带一路"战略政策的引领下，可以预见基建和高端制造业等将迎来向沿线国家转移富余产能的良好时机；而作为国际金融中心的上海，以金融资本带动多元化投资的方式也必将继续作为上海企业对外投资的重要方式之一，帮助上海资本走向全球，重塑世界经济版图。

我们相信在政府针对"走出去"企业配套政策和服务不断推进与日益成熟的基础上，依靠社会专业服务机构对于海外投资合作的经验指引，以及企业自身海外投资经验的积累，上海企业的"走出去"之路会愈发顺畅。同时，在连续两年的报告编制过程中，我们也欣喜地看到多数"走出去"企业已能够积极充分地评估海外投资合作过程中可能遇到的问题与风险，并协同政府与社会服务机构积极地寻找应对措施。

不断变化的国际市场既充满机遇也遍布风险。根据过往两年于《上海企业对外投资合作年度发展报告》的分析，我们清醒地认识到绝大多数中国企业还处于国际化的初级阶段，不少企业仍缺乏长远战略规划和风险意识，对东道国投资环境和文化不够了解，也欠缺海外投资管理经验和国际化人才。在此衷心希望越来越多的企业在合理战略规划和风险管控下加入到"走出去"行列中，引进先进技术，推动产业链升级，助力中国完成经济转型。

孟买—上海对话：姊妹城市多模式合作远景

马德武

印度工业联合会上海代表处大中华区负责人兼首席代表

1. 介绍

中国和印度既是亚洲两大巨头和友邻，同时又是世界上两大发展最快的经济体。即将到来的亚洲世纪将建立在两国是否能够共同努力，处理发展性的挑战的基础上。习近平主席和莫迪总理对加强加深两国双边合作都给予了高度的重视，两国合作与融合的新局面正在迅速崛起。

2014 年 9 月中国国家主席习近平对印度进行国事访问，这对于两国具有深远的意义，其中双边举措中一项重要的内容就是提出了缔结两国之间友城关系。其间，确立了上海与孟买，艾哈迈达巴德与广州的姐妹城市关系，以及古吉拉特和广东的姐妹省邦关系。2015 年 5 月莫迪总理访华，通过建立省邦领导人论坛，加强区域层面的合作关系，进一步巩固了中印双边合作的这一愿景。省邦政府领导之间的互访越来越频繁，合作机会也在不断被挖掘。

在这样的整体框架里，孟买与上海的姐妹城市关系具有特殊的重大意义，可视作整体双边合作发展的重要驱动力。

上海和孟买是中印两大经济体中发展最为蓬勃的中心城市。双方均具有丰富的商业历史、发展的前景、多样化的行业布局和强健的基础设施，同时也是各自国家的金融中心。结合了金融领导力与强劲的外力，拥有分布广泛的内陆连接，这两大城市中心俨然成为了各自国家最大的港口城市。它们已经承担起促进出口、吸引外资，以及连接世界的重要角色。这两大城市拥有大量且多样化的人口，代表了崭新的思想与观念、文化特色的领导力、创造力和创新力，并且是蓬勃发展的娱乐与传媒行业全球中心。

孟买在中国的历史上扮演着微弱却特殊的角色。在 18、19 世纪，孟买的商人就已经成为第一批冒险进入中国市场的人，他们从事船务运输和棉花交易等商业活动。许多孟买人，或是来自孟买的印度人曾经在中国的广州、香港甚至上海，参与建设基础设施和大学的工作。与孟买有着强大联系的一大批印度人居住在香港，成为了孟买和中国内地之间强有力的联系。孟买居民 David Sassoon 和之后的 Victor Sassoon 在孟买和上海建造了许多标志性的建筑物。

孟买和上海象征着两个怀揣远大抱负的国家的梦想，双方都是各自国家的增长中心和经济、文化、政治、体育，以及技术等多重领域的领航者。作为姐妹城市，这两大城市必能成为亚洲新世纪的主要连接者，带动拥有庞大人口的两个生机勃勃的新兴经济体朝着互相理解，友好合作的目标不断前进。

2. 孟买—上海对话

2014 年 9 月习近平主席访印后，提出了建立孟买与上海姊妹城市关系，旨在进一步加强两国人文交流，促进理解。作为印度最重要的行业机构，印度工业联合会（CII）的目标是促进这一伙伴关系的建立，为两大城市的民众建立更加紧密的联系。因此，我们提议设立孟买—上海对话机制，以论坛的形式将来自工商业、艺术与文化等不同领域的利益相关者聚集到一起，共同谱写合作的篇章。

通过加入产业的经济元素，孟买—上海对话将确保广泛的综合交流项目的实施，覆盖日常生活的不同维度和民众的关注。

印度工业联合会（CII）为孟买—上海对话做了如下四个主要方面的设想，来加强姊妹城市关系：
- 经济，工业和基础建设
- 可持续城镇化
- 教育和文化关系
- 旅游和体育

印度工业联合会（CII）将通过其在新德里总部和分设在上海与孟买的办事处，在两个城市的领导和管理者的指导、鼓励和支持下，努力推动姊妹城市缔结项目的发展和实施。我们规划了针对上述四个方面为主题的一系列近期和中长期的交流会，旨在建立持久的合作伙伴关系。对于两个城市之间的合作潜力，CII 感到非常的兴奋，并将推动两大邻国之间的紧密友好关系。

3. 孟买和上海经济概览

上海，坐落于长江口，是中国主要的金融中心和最大的港口。它占地 6 340 平方公里，拥有 18 个区和一个县。作为中国四大直辖市之一的上海，2014 年其人口数量达到 2 425 万。

2014 年，上海的人均收入达 97 370 元（相当于 15 000 美元）。作为中国重要的工业中心，上海最大的制造业包括汽车、计算机、通信和其他电子设备、化工材料与产品，以及机械设备等行业。

上海吸引着来自各行各业的大型跨国公司，拥有 320 家投资企业，402 个研发中心和 558 家跨国公司的区域总部。上海的金融行业发展良好，目标是成为全球金融中心。上海自由贸易区成立于 2013 年，是一个卓越的创新中心，自由贸易模式参考香港，享有宽松的对外投资政策，人民币完全可兑换。

孟买，一座拥有 4 350 平方公里的大都市，是印度最开放的城市，印度门是其著名的地标性建筑。很多知名印度企业的总部都设在孟买，它吸引着很大一部分的印度对外投资和合资企业。对大部分外国游客来说，孟买机场是他们的第一停靠站，同时孟买也是印度最大的港口城市。孟买是印度最具活力的金融城市，拥有两个最大的区域性股票交易中心，其中包括标志性的孟买证交所。

然而，孟买最著名的是它的全球电影产业，声名远扬，因其丰富的创造力，美妙的音乐和丰富的产品能满足所有人的品位。众所周知的宝莱坞，带动了许多相关行业如时尚设计、旅游、珠宝、广告和其他富有创造力的行业。此外，孟买的其他行业也广受赞誉，如纺织、汽车、非耐用品消费和其他制造行业，虽然许多生产线都已经搬迁。

孟买的目标是成为一个新基础设施网络系统的核心，可以将孟买与印度整个西部地区以及首都新德里连接起来。德里—孟买专用铁路货运通道是一项铁路项目，跨越印度六个邦和计划新建的工业园与工业镇，将两个大城市连接起来。德里—孟买工业长廊由国家投资与制造区域和城市设施组成，预估的投资额为 900 亿美元。连接孟买和古吉拉特邦的艾哈迈达巴德的两个工业中心的印度首个高速铁路也正处于设计阶段。根据麦肯锡全球研究所的数据，到 2030 年孟买的消费市场将达到 2 450 亿美元之多，远高于如今的马来西亚。

这两大沿海城市和他们周边的其他主要大城市在许多领域正享受着经济得天独厚的优势。特别是，作为国内大企业的总部所在地，它们受益于经济和产业的协同效应，共同开拓全球机遇。

表 1　上海和孟买的经济指标

经 济 指 标	上海（2014 年数据）	孟　买
人口	2 400 万	2 300 万（2011）
国内生产总值	23 568 亿元	1 240 亿美元（2012）
人均国内生产总值	97 370 元	5 900 美元（2012）
国内生产总值组成： 第一 第二 第三	0.5% 34.7% 64.8%	无
旅游者 国内 国外	2.68 亿 791 万	马哈拉施特拉邦 9 410 万（2014） 480 万（2011）
对外直接投资	182 亿	95 亿美元（2015 年 4 月至 2016 年 3 月）
主要行业	汽车制造 电子设备 化工 机械设备 电子机械和设备 旅游和酒店管理 金融服务	消费品 纺织 汽车 电影、娱乐传媒 宝石与珠宝 金融服务 旅游和酒店管理

4. 在经济，工业和基础设施的合作

从城市层面来说，孟买和上海在城市经济管理方面有着强大的合作远景。

上海转型中的城市规划和发展吸引了全球的关注。浦江对岸的浦东地区更是经历了翻天覆地的变化，1990 年后，它从沉睡、低洼的河畔变成了高楼耸立商业荟聚的大都市。它体现了一个城市的奇迹，包括完善的公共基础设施、高效的公共交通道路网络、智能设备，以及令人惊叹的未来城市景观。

战略性的城市规划以迅速和稳健的步伐影响着这种变革，而这也正是孟买所需要的，一座充满着发展空间的城市。这个城市中关键区域的发展潜力还没有完全被挖掘出来，虽然也有一些崭新的区域如班德拉库尔拉中心（BKC）已经发展成世界级水平。孟买必将从上海城市规划的模式中获益良多。

孟买同样可以汲取上海在城市设施建设方面取得的成功经验。孟买正在建造一个现代化的公共交通系统，譬如郊县铁路、地铁系统、单轨轨道公共交通系统也正在筹划中。这个城市将成为印度首个高速铁路所在地，铁路的建成将孟买和

　　提升投资贸易便利化水平，构建开放型经济新体制

艾哈迈达巴德连接起来，未来高铁站的建造规划也在商讨中。

在城市卫生和废弃物管理方面，孟买可以学习上海的经验，因为印度正在进行 Swachh Bharat 运动（即打造清洁的印度）。上海在将城市旧区改造成新的房产开发方面拥有丰富的经验和技术，孟买一定会对此感兴趣。上海的防洪抗旱控制系统，污染管理和城市能源战略，尤其是新能源方面更是值得孟买借鉴。特别是，上海处理紧急状况的指挥控制中心值得孟买多加学习，因为孟买经常发生自然灾害和攻击的情况。

孟买也是信息技术产业中心，可以与上海分享和共同开发管理系统，定位和监测基础设施的运营与维护。孟买的企业非常乐意与上海的企业在医疗保健，生物技术和创新方面共同合作。

作为孟买—上海对话的一部分，印度工业联合会（CII）将组织一次专场交流会，邀请来自不同城市规划和公共基础设施部门的专家参加。两个城市的行业领袖、专家和管理者可以定期会面、洽谈合作、分享信息和探讨实践。我们可以在这两个城市中确定一些具体的项目，建立合资企业，充分利用各自的优势。

潜在合作领域：

• 城市规划

• 公共交通

• 智慧城市，基础设施网络和信息技术

• 能源效率

• 灾难管理规划

• 水务，卫生设施和废物处理

• 医疗保健和生物技术

5. 可持续城市化

上海在可持续城市化方面已经遥遥领先，特别是在浦东新区的规划建设方面。城市当局可以考虑在孟买建立一个可持续城市化中心，将其作为印度的知识中心。

印度政府已经推出了智慧城市项目，98 个印度城市有望通过一系列基础设施和公共设施建设实现现代化和改造的梦想。这个项目已经列出 33 个城市作为第一批改造的对象，这些城市将加强城市化管理，并且一些项目也将进行投标。

孟买是智慧城市项目第三阶段将要被启动的城市之一。孟买的人口超过 1 400 万，110 万新孟买人将被纳入这个项目中。在孟买，一系列的项目都在规划中，包括位于帕雷尔地区的中心商业区、位于西安泰里的信息技术中心、位于马拉德的多生物旅游区，以及位于纳里曼和 Kala Ghoda 的商业旅游区。智慧道路交通管理系统正在规划四条重要公路的建设。孟买也正计划在跨城市的 800 个点建立移动、便利的信息亭。

新孟买的理念是鼓励紧凑睦邻、宜居的城市住房，以此带动整个城市发展的凝聚力。地面电网将被完全摒弃，从而降低电力故障发生的危险性。人们可以亲近红树林，森林和湿地等大片城市自然绿化。

此外，印度计划在未来二十年改造 500 个现代化城市，至 2050 年，印度的城市人口有望增长到 4 亿，印度计划为他们提供宜居的、实惠的、干净整洁的居住环境。这些城市需要基本的水电供应基础设施、卫生设施和固体废物处理，高效的城市交通和公共交通设施、经适房、信息技术的连接和保健教育设施。智慧和可持续城市化包括水务管理、能源管理、可再生能源，以及绿色建筑。

上海智慧城市知识中心能够帮助孟买规划这些项目，甚至其他的一些项目。在孟买建立这样一个资源中心，也将帮助印度其他城市在不久的将来共同迈入智慧城市项目。

6. 教育文化关系合作

上海和孟买蕴含丰富的教育和文化资源，学术和创造性思维独占鳌头。大学可以在两个世界级的城市中扮演重要的角色，就两国丰富的古代历史和现代经济文化层面，帮助青年人建立联系，合作与理解。由上海和孟买两个充满活力的文化中心组织频繁的学术和文化方面的会议，有利于加深两国相互了解，为未来两国的交流起到领头羊的作用。

上海的六所教育机构跻身 2015—2016 年 QS 世界大学排名，包括复旦大学排名第 51 位，上海交通大学排名第 70 位。上海的一些教育机构已将印度研究作为部分选修课，学生们对印度的杰出人物圣雄甘地和泰戈尔非常感兴趣。

孟买许多教育机构如印度理工学院、塔塔社会科学研究院和孟买大学是印度学生学成后继续深造的首选。这些学院为印度当下发展的不同层面扮演着重要的角色，为创新、企业家精神、创造力和思想领导力起着铺垫的作用。从这些机构毕业的青年男女决定了印度这个国家的发展趋势和思想高度。

两个姊妹城市充满活力的历史和现代文化背景为它们的合作提供了一个良好的平台。孟买是一些印度出色传统的起源地，如文学、电影艺术和戏剧、舞蹈和音乐、艺术和雕塑，以及其他艺术追求的形式。它的国家现代艺术美术馆，贾汗季美术馆和大量的顶级画家使得孟买成为艺术家的殿堂，吸引着全世界的艺术家。舞蹈和古典音乐节在这个城市相当流行。每年二月举办的 Kala Ghoda 艺术节，以艺术的多种形式捕捉文化的精髓，吸引了来自世界各地的观众。

同样地，上海国际艺术节每年都受到艺术爱好者的高度期待和追捧，他们从世界各地飞来上海，欣赏最新的中国艺术。上海的设计行业已经成为全球时尚的热点，大家对上海时装周充满兴趣，紧跟时尚潮流。来自中国和世界的艺术大师将最好的作品带入上海音乐节。

电影产业是两个城市合作的又一特殊领域。印度电影产业以宝莱坞而闻名，它在印度出品的电影数量最多，越来越多的全球观众被印度电影明星所吸引，宝莱坞正在迅速跻身世界顶级行列。它出品了大量的艺术电影，获得了全球电影艺术节的好评。上海同样是一个传媒中心，中国的第一部电影在上海出品，它已经成为中国的电影之都，拥有顶级的电影工作室。许多上海出生的明星已经走向国际舞台，参与了好莱坞和香港的流行和艺术电影。中印已就电影合作方面签订了协议，并且已经合作出品了几部电影。两个姐妹城市可以通过共同出品电影，繁荣两国的电影产业。

两个姐妹城市拥有丰富的文化遗产和前沿的产物，孟买和上海可以设计出一个充满活力的文化交流形式，融合各行各业的人。两大城市可以就以下方面考虑共同建立项目：

- 孟买—上海时尚周
- 孟买—上海国际设计节
- 孟买—上海电影合作和共同制片

7. 旅游和运动的合作

上海与孟买是各自国家的知名旅游景点。国外旅游者来中国都会想去上海看看，去印度也会将孟买纳入行程中。在这两个熙熙攘攘的城市中逗留，被视作是在富有异国情调的亚洲地区寻找刺激的终极体验。

与此同时，随着可支配收入的不断增长，远赴海外旅游来度过休闲时光的中国及印度公民越来越多。中国出境旅行的人数排世界首位，超过 1 亿的中国人选择乘坐飞机出国旅游。印度出境游旅客数量在全球发展速度排名第二，在未来的五年，出境游客的数量预测将达到 5 000 万。购物、观光和学习是旅游的主要动力，中国和印度的旅行者已经为他们自己贴上了高价值游客的标签。

除了观光旅游，两座城市可以考虑一些创意来吸引对方国家的游客来本国旅游。上海的中国时尚产业和孟买多彩的纺织品织物，都让购物成为一种巨大的吸引力。上海的南京路和孟买的 Linking 路相似。中国游客也可能对宝莱坞电影公司感兴趣。两国的文化表演可以融入对方国家的特色，吸引更多的游客。

两座城市将受益于高水平的旅游交流，有助于扩大人与人之间的联系。促销和品牌活动可以在双方城市开展。

孟买—上海对话的进程将包含这些推动措施和会议交流活动，以姊妹城市作为门户，打开两国的旅游通道，促进两国旅游业的繁荣发展。

体育互动成为合作的新领域。上海的专家可以与孟买的管理者合作，为体育促进建立适宜友好的运动氛围，包括在公园、体育馆、公共健身中心等场地的普通民众。两座城市顶级的运动员可以互相交流，丰富孟买—上海对话的内容。印度的国球板球也可以成为中国人民创新运动的项目。

8. 结论

显而易见，两国的领导人以缔结姊妹城市关系的方式将上海与孟买紧密联系起来。这两个城市拥有许多共同点，注定将中国和印度塑造成两大新兴的亚洲巨头。现在，我们可以定义这种合作伙伴关系的轮廓，发展具体的行动方向和项目，使这两大亚洲城市不断靠拢融合。

印度工业联合会将是上海与孟买和谐关系进程中的伙伴，积极促进两座姊妹城市之间的紧密联系。

推动全球治理与贸易便利化

陈子雷

上海对外经贸大学教授

在经济全球化背景下，贸易便利化开始取代贸易自由化为各国所瞩目。尽管各国通过多边及双边自由贸易的制度安排，有效地提高了贸易规模，推动了区域经济一体化的进程，但是通关手续作为一种新的隐性壁垒却制约着各国贸易的发展。近年来，各国开始认识到简化贸易程序，提高贸易效率的重要性。如何实现贸易便利化，规范和合理安排各种贸易管理程序，建立一个高效合理、协调的贸易体系，已成为各国学者普遍关注的问题。

1. 贸易便利化

目前世界贸易在便利化方面主要存在三个障碍：一是海关信息不公开，缺乏透明度与可预见性；二是海关程序繁琐，通关效率低下，甚至存在乱收费的现象，使通关成本提高；三是各国海关间缺乏应有的合作，对信息交换、延迟或拒绝、互惠、行政负担等问题未进行统一的规范。推动贸易便利化有利于简化包括国际货物贸易流动所需要的收集、提供、沟通及处理数据的活动、做法和手续在内的贸易程序，加强管理协调。实现贸易便利化有利于解决贸易自由化过于强调推动各国制度改革、政策调整和关税和配额减少等有形的限制措施，转而从技术、程序和管理层面强调为贸易畅通提供一个更加便捷的环境。可以说，贸易便利化有利于在国际公认的规范和惯例基础上，为国际贸易创造一个连续的、透明的和可预见性的环境，从而简化和协调与贸易有关的程序和行政障碍，降低成本，推动货物和服务更好地流通。因此，贸易便利化的关键不但在于消除政府的在贸易管制、通关、出入境检验检疫等领域中的壁垒，还要求企业和社会众多行为体积极参与，以构建一个货畅其流的贸易治理体系。简言之，贸易便利化的核心是推动治理革新，简化程序，为贸易畅通营造一个便捷通畅的营商环节。

2.《贸易便利化协定》的意义

2015 年 9 月 4 日，中国正式接受 WTO《贸易便利化协定》议定书，成为第 16 个接受《协定》的成员。按照规定，《协定》将在 WTO 2/3 以上成员接受后正式生效。《协定》实施后，无疑将大大降低企业的交易成本，提高交易效率。据测算，《协定》实施将带动全球 GDP 增长 9 600 亿美元，增加 2 100 万个就业岗位。其中，贸易伙伴 GDP 每提升 1 个单位，中国贸易总额和出口额分别增长 0.587 和 1.378 个单位；中国自身贸易便利化水平每提升 1 个单位，能带动中国贸易总额提升 4.602 个单位，进口 4.977 个单位，出口 3.069 个单位；如果中国和贸易伙伴从 2016 年开始执行《协定》的话，2020 年中国出口将因此额外增加 30.79%。除了直接带来贸易额和 GDP 增长外，贸易便利化对于规范各成员政府行为，促进各成员认真贯彻 WTO 的透明度原则也有着不容忽视的制度改进作用。从国内层面来看，《协定》的实施还将有助于中国更好地参与国际分工，在全球价值链布局中谋求有利的地位，有利于推动中国产业结构升级，促进经济增长方式转变。同时，贸易便利化将提高我国企业的货物进出口效率，降低对外进出口贸易成本，提高跨境货物流动效率，推动中国与主要贸易伙伴的经济关系，提升我国口岸基础设施、管理方式和职能部门综合管理和协同能力，形成有效的口岸综合管理体系；在多边层面，有利于促进世界贸易的增长和各国经济的发展。在区域层面，在《协定》范本的基础上，可以根据需要探索更高水平的区域内便利化协定，促进区域生产网络及参与国贸易和经济的进一步发展。简言之，《协定》的达成将极大地提高通关效率，削减贸易成本，在推进 WTO 成员贸易便利化的同时，将大大促进国际贸易的发展。

3. 实现贸易便利化的途径

（1）各国贸易部门的信息网络化和行政一体化。贸易便利化涉及众多部门，包括商务、发改、税务、工商、金融、外管、海关、商检等，每个部门都具有复杂严密的规章制度，极其容易形成管理的"条块化"。因此，在处理贸易问题时，各个部门之间办事效率低下，部门间协调成本极高。根据"帕金森定理"和"尼斯卡南模型"，"本位主义"决定了各部门往往从本部门立场和利益出发，希望在公共事务上获得更大的权力，为此不惜造成复杂繁琐的繁文缛节，最终对贸易和投资形成阻碍

（2）构建各国贸易部门的"互联互通"机制。首先，建立管理部门之间的对口交流机制，致力于消除制约贸易畅通的技术障碍、程序障碍和机制障碍。其次，提高各国执法管理的透明度，实现管理法规透明、行政程序透明、管理机构和人员透明、执法监管透明等，建立和完善新闻发布会、公布年度报告、举办专题听证会等多种制度。再次，推动各国贸易政策的互联互通，进一步制定和完善多边体制下的贸易议题，共同推动多领域的政策协调，建立多边贸易共同管理平台。

（3）共同推动法治化建设。依靠法治化可以发挥市场在资源配置中的决定性作用。其中，各国间签订相关贸易、投资协定、成立国际组织、制定国际组织章程的做法，有利于将经贸往来有效地纳入法治化和制度化轨道。因此，加强规则体系、监管机制和贸易投资争端制度建设的本质就是构建法治化体系：首先，以法律为准绳，有效利用法律手段来解决各种贸易与投资问题，推动各国在降低关税、简化通关手续、制定相互认证的商品检验检疫程序和标准等领域的合作，为贸易畅通提供完善的法律体系。其次，以建立自贸区和自贸协定为抓手，支持相关国家在边境地区建立跨境共同市场，鼓励在一些贸易和投资枢纽成立设立政策灵活的产业园区、经济技术开发区和高新产业开发区等贸易和投资平台，加强在重点贸易领域的合作，从点到线，从块到面，推动区域内商品服务和人员往来的自由化。再次，要着眼于建设一整套贸易和投资争端解决机制，尤其是在劳工标准、环境标准、人权和知识产权保护等领域，要和贸易便利化结合起来一并考虑，在易发贸易摩擦的问题上建立共同接受的争端解决机制。在这一过程中，既要充分考虑与以 WTO 为代表的一系列现有的国际贸易和投资争端解决机制的对接，又要根据各国实际情况，探索创建新的贸易争端解决机制，夯实贸易畅通的制度和机制基础。

上海打造全球电子商务中心城市的思路与对策

芮晔平

华略智库·上海城市创新经济研究中心研究总监

随着电子商务在全球贸易中的地位日益突出,电子商务正在打破区域和国家界限,成为全球化发展的重要推动力量。在这样的背景下,以往野蛮式的发展方式已不符合当前形势的要求,电子商务发展对规则、制度、营商环境等要求越来越高,那些能够为电子商务发展提供更好的创新环境、制度环境以及国际化发展环境的城市必将脱颖而出,成为电子商务全球化发展的枢纽城市。

本文通过分析梳理电子商务发展的重大趋势,研究总结国内外电子商务发展的典型案例,结合上海电子商务发展的现状与基础,提出上海打造全球电子商务中心城市的基本思路,以及相应的实施路径与对策建议。

1. 全球电子商务发展的重大趋势

一是电子商务正加快成为全球经济新的增长点。在世界经济持续低迷、贸易格局深刻调整、投资规则体系加快重构的背景下,以电子商务为代表的信息经济正成为全球经济的新引擎。二是电子商务新技术、新业态、新模式层出不穷。重点表现在电子商务全面进入移动互联网时代,电子商务正迎来影响深远的"场景革命",线上线下融合已成为电商发展的"新常态",区块链技术或将对电子商务产生深远影响,电子商务正加快向民生服务领域渗透等方面。三是我国加速融入全球电子商务产业链和创新链。随着我国电子商务发展日益成熟以及国内竞争日益激烈,很多企业也将目光投向海外市场,通过兼并、整合、合作等方式,加速融入全球电子商务产业链;与此同时,国内电子商务企业不断学习并引入国外电子商务创新理念和经营模式,加快融入全球电子商务创新链体系。四是龙头企业对大电商生态产业链的整合力度不断加强。BAT将投资触角延伸到了我们所能想象到的几乎所有领域,阿里不仅打通了平台、物流、支付等传统电子商务产业链，还整合了包括金融、影视、娱乐、交通、生活服务等众多领域资源。五是电子商务创新资源加速向中心城市集聚。经历电子商务企业爆发式增长，电子商务模式、技术和业态的不断调整，电子商务的区域竞争格局也不断改变。随着电子商务行业的整合兼并力度不断加大，电子商务逐步走向成熟，电子商务创新要素加速向中心城市集聚。六是跨境电子商务在国际贸易的作用日益凸显。在全球贸易持续低迷的态势下，跨境电子商务逆势增长，占贸易额的比重逐年上升。国际贸易正从传统的货期长、数量大、金额大，转变为多次、少量、交易频繁的跨境订单模式。

2. 国内外相关国家和城市促进发展电子商务的经验

总体来看，美欧等发达国家电子商务发展起步较早，发展优势明显，各国电子商务政策和战略方向各有千秋。美国是全球电子商务发展的领先者，在电子商务发展策略与政策上，率先提出立足于全球化，侧重于强调市场化运作原则，以民营企业作为主导，政府只负责必要的法律环境建设；欧盟的政策框架同样着眼于立法建设，旨在消除各国电子商务跨境贸易之间的各类交易壁垒；而亚洲新加坡政府在注重立法环境之外，还侧重于政策扶持和提供必要的资金支持，协助中小企业发展电子商务活动、拓展海外市场。发达国家和地区的电子商务发展案例的共性特点表现为：在贸易前阶段，注重建设法律法规和基础设施环境；在贸易过程中阶段，制定安全、信用和电子支付政策；在贸易后阶段，完善税收制度和物流体系。

我国电子商务走的是"先发展、后规范"道路，政府更多侧重于企业培育和产业发展，但在知识产权、交易与服务、交易保障、监管责任等领域基础较弱，电子商务制度环境建设相对滞后。部分城市提出了电子商务发展战略目标，如北京提出打造全球电子商务核心节点城市，积极创建国家电子商务示范城市；深圳提出形成华南地区乃至全国有重要影响力的商品交易中心和定价中心；广州提出建设成为全国跨境电子商务中心城市和发展高地。

3. 上海打造全球电子商务中心城市的总体思路

建设全球电子商务中心城市是一个系统工程。既要具备国际化的战略视野，全面融入全球电子商务发展环境、消费市场以及创新网络；也要把握我国电子商务发展的进程与趋势，积极促进国际国内资源要素对流，辐射带动国内其他城市发展；更要立足并服务于上海城市发展的核心功能，充分发挥电子商务在促进国际贸易中心、国际金融中心、全球科技创新中心、制造业转型升级等方面的作用，体现上海在开放、创新、法制等营商环境方面的优势。

上海打造全球电子商务中心城市，就是要以提升电子商务资源要素配置能力为主线，以促进电子商务创新发展与开放发展为抓手，以完善电子商务交易保障和监管服务等基础环境为支撑，加快形成开放程度高、创新能力强、应用领域广、营商环境优、具有全球电子商务资源要素配置能力的发展格局。具体来看，上海建设全球电子商务中心城市，需要重点提升六个方面的能力，即要素集聚能力、交易保障能力、创新发展能力、综合应用能力、开放合作能力、监管服务能力。

4. 上海打造全球电子商务中心城市的对策建议

根据深化上海电子商务创新发展的基本思路，提出相应的实施路径与对策建议如下：一是加强要素集聚能力，打造电子商务资源配置中枢。包括引进和培育电子商务龙头企业；打造大宗商品全球交易平台与定价中心；构建电子商务在内外贸市场的互促、互动和互通平台；建立符合一体化要求的电子商务市场规则与税收制度等方面内容。二是加强创新发展能力，着力推动电子商务创新发展。包括打造全球电子商务创新创业高地；推动电子商务产业园和孵化器建设；完善电子商务创新创业支撑环境；培育和引进电子商务创新人才等方面内容。三是加强开放合作能力，提升电子商务对外开放水平。包括参与推动跨境电商贸易规则体系建设；提升跨境电子商务企业发展能级；完善跨境电子商务公共服务体系；建立跨境电商多双边国际合作机制；构建电商企业引进来和走出去通道等方面内容。四是加强综合应用能力，积极培育专业领域垂直电商。包括打造国内领先的制造业电子商务平台；支持医疗医药电子商务平台企业发展；支持教育文化等电子商务平台企业发展；支持旅游电子商务平台企业发展；促进航空、交通、汽车、家居等专业领域的电子商务平台企业发展等方面内容。五是加强交易保障能力，完善电子商务交易支撑体系。包括完善全市信息基础设施建设布局；构建适应电子商务发展的物流体系；创新电子商务金融及支付服务；完善电子商务专业服务支撑体系；建立健全电子商务安全认证体系；建立电子合同、电子发票、电子会计档案等管理制度等方面内容。六是加强监管服务能力，加快政府服务管理模式创新。包括放宽市场准入；加大财税支持力度；完善上海电子商务地方标准；强化电子商务知识产权保护；完善电子商务统计与运行监测；建立电子商务网络化监管与执法平台等方面内容。

跨境并购要补上哪些短板

周师迅

上海市人民政府发展研究中心信息处处长

中国企业国际化和跨境并购潜力巨大，提升跨境并购能力有助于加快推进中国企业"走出去"步伐，服务我国创新驱动转型发展的战略目标。为此，在战略选择上，第一，应以上海自贸区建设为抓手，加快投资贸易便利化体制机制创新；第二，积极参与双边、区域和多边国际投资规则制定，为中国企业跨境并购提供国际规则保障；第三，立足国家战略和企业转型升级战略目标；第四，强化企业跨境并购能力建设。

跨境并购是对外直接投资的重要形式，改革开放以来我国企业跨境并购取得了较快发展。2014 年 11 月，习近平主席在北京 APEC 工商领导人峰会上表示未来十年中国对外投资将达到 1.25 万亿美元，跨境并购将迎来新的发展机遇。鉴此，归纳总结我国跨境并购经验，分析发展趋势与特征，剖析存在的问题，把握未来发展趋势，对于促进跨境并购发展，稳步推进中国企业"走出去"，服务我国新型开放战略具有十分重要的现实意义。

1. 我国跨境并购趋势与特征

（1）中国跨境并购规模稳步增长。在全球化和经济一体化大背景下，企业国际化浪潮席卷全球，中国企业跨境并购持续升温。据 Thomson ONE Banker 数据，2004—2014 年间，中国企业跨境并购市场规模复合增长率高达 35%，交易数量年复合增长率为 9.5%。另据汤姆森研究表明，中国企业已完成的跨境并购金额从 2004 年占全球不到 1% 增长到 2013 年的近 10%，2015 年中国企业已完成并购交易金额达 610 亿美元，较 2014 年增加 16%，达到了创纪录的最高水平。

（2）跨境并购主体日益多元化。总体看，中国 500 强企业在跨境并购中较为活跃。根据 2009 年到 2014 年间的交易金额统计，中国 500 强企业占海外并购交易总额的 65%，占海外并购交易数量的 31%。2004 年以来，在以国企大型基建项目并购为先导，民企制造业项目随后跟进的作用下，跨境并购主体日益多元化，呈现出最初以国企为主，逐渐发展到民企、上市公司和私募基金等多种主体并存的格局。

（3）并购行业附加值逐渐高端化。能源和资源性标的向来是中国企业跨境并购的重要目标，但对其偏好已逐渐下降，2015年仅占全部境外并购支出的16%，远低于2011年83%的峰值。2008年金融危机以来，被并购的行业逐渐向非资源类产业转移，其中以金融业、工业、高科技产业、娱乐业和房地产业为主，并都取得了创纪录的高增长，呈现出附加值产业高端化趋势。

（4）并购目的地逐渐向发达国家集中。对成熟资产的偏好增强以及对新兴经济体政治和商业风险更清晰的认识，加速了中国投资从发展中经济体向发达经济体转移的进程。以欧美发达区域为并购目的地的交易数量显著增加，2014年占中国海外并购数量的六成以上，而针对东南亚等传统区域的并购数量比例下降较快。数据显示，北美的并购数量占比从2004年的11%上升到2014年的23%；欧洲的并购数量占比更是从2004年的13%上升到2014年的37%；东亚的并购数量占比从2004年的53%下降到2014年的15%。欧洲和北美已经超过亚洲成为中国企业最热门的海外并购目的地。

2. 哪些因素驱动跨境并购

中国企业跨国并购取得的成就，主要得益于我国改革开放以来企业经济实力的快速增长。其主要驱动因素主要有：

（1）全球化和经济一体化的驱动。2001年中国加入WTO后，中国融入全球化的障碍大幅度减小，全球化推动的国际产业分工为我国跨境并购提供了良好的国际大环境，信息通信、交通运输技术等成本的下降，极大地提高企业在全球范围配置资源的能力，全球投资贸易便利化规则和治理体系的逐渐完善为跨境并购提供了切实保障。

（2）国家战略和对外投资政策的驱动。自"走出去"国家战略、"一带一路"倡议实施以来，国家陆续出台了系列配套政策，为跨境并购提供了战略和政策支持。对外投资并购政策正在大幅放宽，2010年以来，国务院、发改委、商务部及外汇管理局分别发布《关于进一步优化企业兼并重组市场环境的意见》《境外投资项目核准和备案管理办法》和《跨国公司外汇资金集中运营管理规定（试行）》，简化跨境并购外汇管理，大幅放宽跨境并购的政府核准权限，减少了项目核准程序，简化了核准内容，尤其是2013年上海自贸区挂牌以来，为跨境并购提供了投融资政策支持，有效提升了企业跨境并购能力。

（3）受低估值机会驱动。在跨国并购中，目标企业的估值受宏观经济、产业周期、股市波动、并购双方的谈判能力等因素的影响。2008年国际金融危机、欧洲债务危机以来，受全球经济增速放缓等影响，国外企业股价大幅下跌，很多企业出现财务困境，国外企业低估值机会和将外汇储备投资实体经济等多元化投资需求为中国企业提供了跨境并购的良好机会，驱动了我国跨境并购的增长。

（4）市场需求和企业转型升级驱动。早期跨境并购主要受企业自然资源、矿产资源等生产要素约束，因此，对自然资源的跨境并购能有效解决结构性短缺问题。近年来，国内市场逐渐饱和产能过剩凸显，企业转型压力日趋增大，加之相对宽松的海外并购政策、充裕的现金储备以及中国企业的崛起和日益提升的国际影响力，使不少发达国家企业意识到与中国企业合作的重要性。在此背景下，中国企业借助跨境并购实现企业转型升级的战略意图日趋明显，旨在通过海外并购获取国外先进的技术、品牌和管理经验，力图通过海外并购寻求新的利润增长点、占领新的市场以及成为全球竞争的领导者。对企业的调查分析显示，过去五年中，希望获取能源矿产等战略性资产的海外并购项目数量占比仅为20%，而希望获取技术、知识产权或生产能力、进入当地市场以及收购品牌的海外并购占比却高达75%。

3. 中国企业跨境并购面临的主要挑战

在新的外部形势下，受中国企业国际化程度低等制约，在跨境并购上存在宏观和微观两方面的挑战。

（1）宏观方面。一是政治、外交因素的挑战。跨境并购并非简单的经济活动，往往涉及政治、外交、文化等诸多复杂因素，随着中国崛起，发达国家的"中国威胁论"甚嚣尘上，以及"一带一路"沿线国家存在的地缘政治风险超越经济风险，对我国跨境并购形成了严重挑战。二是国际投资协调机制滞后于跨境并购发展。金融危机以来，国际双边、区域和多边投资协议尚待完善，目前国际投资协定一致性滞后，呈现碎片化，甚至规则之间相互矛盾，造成大量国际投资争端。三是发达国家"国家安全审查制度"形成的挑战。在我国国企主导的跨境并购活动中，由于国企的身份导致发达国家对我国跨境并购持有怀疑和排斥态度，经常诉诸国家安全审查，并赋予并购活动过多的政治色彩，使得我国跨境并购步履维艰。

（2）企业微观方面。企业跨境并购交易环节和整合执行环节面临诸多挑战，尤其体现在并购战略制定、尽职调查和并购后整合三个阶段。这些主要问题表现在以下几个方面：一是企业跨境并购战略不清。清晰的并购战略以及对标的的深入了解和全面评估是中国企业成功实现海外并购不可或缺的因素。不少企业缺乏清晰的并购路线图，并购目的含混不清，对协同效应理解不足或缺乏清晰可操作的海外并购路线图来为其"走出去"战略提供支持。二是缺乏足够的国际资源和专业经验，过分依赖投行等国际中介提供目标企业信息，导致中国企业自搜寻和筛选并购目标时困难重重。三是尽职调查专业能力不足。中国企业跨境并购尽职调查常遇到缺乏国际化经验、对海外商业法律环境和盈利模式理解不深，组织和协调商务、法律、财务、人力资源等内外部资源的能力缺失，对尽职调查风险点评估和决策的能力不足等问题。一方面，一些企业对并购标的所处地区的经济社会环境知之甚少，加上语言、文化和理念的差异，在当地招募的商务、财务和法务顾问的专业指导意见有时不被采信，或不能及时送达关键决策方。另一方面，许多中国企业内部的决策权高度集中在后方，身处一线的尽调团队授权不足，导致内外部资源的协调沟通困难，效率低下。四是并购后整合困难重重。在并购发达国家的先进企业时，一些并购企业对自身的管理制度和人员素质缺乏信心，过分依赖标的企业的原有管理班子，遵循原有管理架构和经营模式，不进行重组改革。另外，有些跨境并购只有粗线条的顶层设计，缺乏细致、可操作的执行层的配套计划，导致实施过程中的盲目性。此外，缺乏清晰的海外公司治理结构、缺乏具有跨境跨文化管理经验和对当地营商环境熟悉的高管，以及文化习惯和管理风格冲突等问题，也严重阻碍了一些中国企业跨境整合目标的实现。

4. 提升跨境并购能力是促进中国企业"走出去"的战略选择

尽管近年来中国企业跨境并购增速较快，但中国企业全球化程度仍然较低，与中国是全球第二大经济体相比，跨境并购总量和规模依然偏小，在经济全球化深入推进和国资国企改革大背景下，中国企业国际化和跨境并购潜力巨大，提升中国企业跨境并购能力有助于加快推进中国企业"走出去"步伐，服务我国创新驱动转型发展的战略目标。为此，提出以下战略选择。

（1）以上海自贸区建设为抓手，加快投资贸易便利化体制机制创新。投资贸易便利化是自贸区建设的一项重要任务，要积极探索国际投资贸易便利化体制机制创新。一是下放跨境并购的审批，简化审批手续，放宽外汇额度的控制，放松企业跨境并购的政策限制，加大跨境并购的事中事后监管，为企业开展跨境并购活动搜寻跨境并购项目、提供海外法律、制度方面的信息服务。二是要制定产业优惠政策，强化国内产业政策对跨境并购的引领和支撑作用，针对不同的跨境并购行业和项目进行分类管理，采取差异化的策略，对于涉及国家战略和战略性资源并购项目，政府应积极支持并承担相应风险。三是以自贸区人民币国际化为重点，加快资本项目开放，为企业跨境并购提供跨境融资等创新金融工具支持。

（2）积极参与双边、区域和多边国际投资规则制定。中国是全球第二大经济体和最大的贸易国，有必要也有能力从经济全球化的被动参与者向全球化推进者转变。新形势下，要加快中美 BIT 和中欧投资规则谈判，推进国际投资贸易规则的制定，为中国企业跨境并购提供国际规则保障。

（3）立足国家战略和企业转型升级战略目标。"一带一路"建设以及与之配套的亚投行、丝路基金和金砖银行为跨境并购提供了良好的战略支撑和政策配套支持。企业跨境并购时要立足于服务我国创新驱动转型发展的战略目标，跨境并购目标选择时重点放在产业纵向关联度高的制造业领域，着力在获取高新科技等产业并购方面有新的突破。并购金融等服务业，应以中国消费市场为依托，把国外资源与我日益增长的需求紧密结合起来，特别是要有利于我国人民币国际化战略的推进。

（4）强化企业跨境并购能力建设。一是厘清跨境并购战略。充分利用"外脑"和内部资源，根据企业战略，结合政策走向、技术发展趋势、消费习惯变化等行业发展趋势，梳理企业海外并购的优先发展领域，制定清晰的海外并购战略。二是有效执行跨境并购举措。管理好尽职调查、谈判和审查流程，鉴别交易风险，有效整合规划和规划执行，实现协同效应。三是培养和提升与跨境并购相关组织管理、风险管控等一系列核心能力，细分行业和交易方式、标的筛选流程及并购频次和时间点的决策等，建立并购知识数据库，储备并留住国际化高端管理人才，优化并购流程管理和绩效考核体系。

投资贸易便利化措施现状及存在问题

周师迅

上海市人民政府发展研究中心信息处处长

王孝钰

上海市人民政府发展研究中心博士后工作站

1. 中国对外投资和贸易发展现状

（1）对外直接投资情况。中国对外直接投资持续扩张。2015 年，中国对外直接投资实现了连续 13 年增长，对外直接投资存量首次超过万亿美元，成为国际投资市场上的重要生力军。从投资区域看，北美洲、欧洲与亚洲成为中国企业海外投资的主要目的地，三者吸纳了同期中国海外兼并收购总投资额的 85.5%、总项目数的 83.5%。此外，中国对"一带一路"沿线国家的投资呈高速增长态势，2015 年，对沿线 49 个国家进行了直接投资，投资额合计 148.2 亿美元，同比增长 18.2%。从投资行业看，中国海外投资行业持续向多元化和高端化发展，服务业"走出去"强劲，主要集中于金融业、租赁和商务服务业和信息技术业。从投资模式看，兼并收购成为中国对外直接投资的重要形式。从投资主体看，民营企业引领海外投资新浪潮，由早期的国企主导模式逐渐演变为国企和民企并驾齐驱。截至 2014 年底，非国有企业对外直接投资存量占中国对外直接投资总存量的 46.4%。

（2）吸收外商直接投资情况。中国吸收外商直接投资呈增长态势，2015 年，全国设立外商投资企业 26 575 家，同比增长 11.8%；实际使用外资金额 7 813.5 亿元人民币（折 1 262.7 亿美元），同比增长 6.4%。其中"一带一路"沿线国家对华投资增速最快，对华投资新设立企业 2 164 家，同比增长 18.3%，实际投入外资金额 84.6 亿美元，同比增长 23.8%。主要国家或地区对华投资总体保持稳定。对华投资前十位国家 / 地区依次为：中国香港、新加坡、中国台湾、韩国、日本、美国、德国、法国、英国和中国澳门。

（3）对外贸易发展情况。中国国际市场份额继续扩大。2015 年，中国货物贸易进出口和出口额稳居世界第一。中国出口占国际市场份额升至 13.8%，比 2014 年提高 1.5 个百分点。商品结构进一步优化。中国出口商品的附加值有所提高，机电产品等高新技术产品出口额逐年提升，纺织品、服装等七大类劳动密集型产品出口呈下降趋势。服务贸易占整体外贸的比重进一步提高。2015 年，中国服务进出口总额 7 130 亿美元，同比增长 14.6%。服务贸易占对外贸易总额的比重达 15.3%，比 2014 年提高 3 个百分点。跨境电子商务、市场采购贸易等新型商业模式成为外贸发展的新热点。2015 年，跨境电子商务增长 30% 以上，市场采购贸易方式出口增长 60% 左右。市场多元化成效显著。欧盟、美国、东盟是中国前三大贸易伙伴，同时，中国对部分新兴经济体出口增长较快，其中对印度、泰国、越南出口分别增长 7.4%、11.6% 和 3.9%。民营企业成为出口的主力军。2015 年，中国民营企业出口 1.03 万亿美元，同比增长 1.8%，占出口总额的比重为 45.2%，占比第一次超过外资企业。

2. 促进投资贸易便利化的相关政策和措施

（1）市场准入方面。第一，外资准入由正面清单模式转向负面清单模式，且负面清单逐步优化。2015 版负面清单内容从 2014 版的 139 条减少为 122 条。在清单结构上，减少制造业在清单中的比例，同时，清单透明度和操作性进一步提升。第二，服务业开放模式多样化。上海、天津和北京服务业开放主要以放宽股权为主，广东和福建则主要以放宽资质为主，集中表现为内地与港澳台从业人员资质的互认。

（2）海关边境管理方面。第一，实施系列通关便利化措施。区内企业海关注册登记纳入企业准入"单一窗口"；先进区，后报关；自主报税、自助通关、自动审放、重点稽查；一次备案、多次使用；海关智能化卡口管理；批次进出，集中申报；货物流转"自行运输"。第二，实施货物分类监管。根据保税货物、非保税货物、口岸货物三类不同货物状态进行分类监管，实行同仓存储，采用"联网监管＋库位管理＋实时核注"监管模式。第三，实施企业分类监管。推行"经认证的经营者（AEO）"互认制度（目前已与新加坡、韩国、中国香港地区、中国台湾地区、欧盟签署 AEO 互认的合作协议）。区内高资信报关企业在全国首次实现"一地注册，全国申报"。第四，区港一体运作。推行区内企业货物流转自行运输、简化统一进出境备案清单等，进一步推进自贸试验区四大区域联动和港区一体。上海自贸试验区洋山保税港区启用"区港直通道"。

（3）进出口检验检疫方面。第一，取消许可证委托加工备案；第二，进口货物预检验制度；第三，自贸试验区全面推广"即查即放"现场查验放行模式。

（4）海事方面。第一，创新国际船舶检查方式，提升海事监管服务效能。通过整合海事执法力量，做到能够不登轮检查的不再登轮检查，必须登轮检查的事项，一次完成海事监管所有执法检查。第二，先许可，后查验。船舶可享受到"船舶出口岸许可"即到即放、多份申请材料开航前一次提交、多艘船舶一次办结的便利服务，实现了船舶出口岸查验业务办结"零等待"。

（5）企业设立准入方面。第一，外资审批制度改革，转变为备案制。第二，商事登记制度改革。一是注册资本由"实缴制"改为"认缴制"；二是企业注册由"先证后照"改为"先照后证"。第三，企业准入的"单一窗口"制度。

（6）税收方面。第一，实行税收优惠政策。一是鼓励投资政策主要涉及非货币性资产对外投资、股权激励等两项。二是促进贸易政策主要涉及融资租赁出口退税、进口环节增值税、选择性征税、部分货物免税、启运港退税等五项。第二，实行"办税一网通"，提高涉税事项办理效率。

（7）金融方面。第一，实施资本账户开放。一是居民自由贸易账户实现分账核算管理；二是居民自由贸易账户与境外账户、境内区外的非居民账户、非居民自由贸易账户以及其他居民自由贸易账户之间的资金可自由划转。第二，投融资汇兑便利。一是促进企业跨境直接投资便利化。试验区跨境直接投资，可直接向银行办理所涉及的跨境收付、兑换业务。二是便利个人跨境投资。在区内就业并符合条件的个人可按规定开展包括证券投资在内的各类境外投资。第三，稳步开放资本市场。区内金融机构和企业可按规定进入上海地区的证券和期货交易场所进行投资和交易。区内企业的境外母公司可按国家有关法规在境内资本市场发行人民币债券。第四，扩大人民币跨境使用。区内企业可根据自身经营需要，开展集团内双向人民币资金池业务，为其境内外关联企业提供经常项下集中收付业务。第五，稳步推进利率市场化。一是全面放开金融机构贷款利率管制；二是放开小额外币存款利率上限的改革试点，由上海自贸区扩大到上海市。第六，深化外汇管理改革。一是简化对外直接投资外汇管理政策。取消直接投资项下外汇登记核准；取消境外再投资外汇备案；取消直接投资外汇年检，改为实行境外直接投资存量权益登记。二是取消金融类租赁公司境外租赁等境外债权业务的逐笔审批，实行登记管理。三是取消区内机构向境外支付担保费的核准。

（8）监管方面。实行企业年度报告公示和企业经营异常名录制度。

（9）争端解决机制方面。第一，仲裁成为上海自贸区争端解决的首选方式。第二，对仲裁规则有较大的突破和创新。一是开放仲裁员名册；二是在审理方式上提出了"合并仲裁"；三是仲裁调解；四是友好仲裁；五是小额案件，或经双方当事人同意可适用简易程序。

（10）促进对外投资方面。第一，建设对外投资合作公共服务体系。主要措施有：一是搭建信息服务平；二是举行投资促进活动，为各方构筑沟通桥梁；三是编写国别与行业投资报告；四是商务部印发《境外经贸合作区服务指南范本》，加强各地商务主管部门、有关中央企业对合作区建区企业的指导；五是制定国际产能和装备制造合作的指导意见，选择钢铁、有色金属等国际竞争优势明显的 12 个重点行业，有针对性地指出了相应行业"用何种方法走出去更好"。第二，扩大融资资金来源。一是支持符合条件的企业和金融机构通过发行股票、债券、资产证券化产品在境内外市场募集资金，用于"走出去"项目；二是实行境外发债备案制，募集低成本外汇资金，更好地支持企业"走出去"资金需求。第三，加大金融支持力度。一是鼓励国内金融机构开展 PPP 项目贷款业务；二是鼓励国内金融机构提高对境外资产或权益的处置能力；三是支持中资金融机构加快境外分支机构和服务网点布局，提高融资服务能力。第四，加强和完善出口信用保险。建立出口信用保险支持大型成套设备的长期制度性安排，对风险可控的项目实现应保尽保。第五，鼓励开展境外股权投资。第六、涉及敏感国家和地区、敏感行业的境外投资项目由国家发改委核准，其他投资项目实行备案管理。

3. 投资贸易便利化存在的主要问题

（1）市场准入方面。第一，当前扩大开放措施的项目落地效果不均衡。开放措施中，"首次开放"较少，"政策放宽"较多，且服务业开放程度较低。第二，开放政策缺乏解释、配套和相关法律支持，导致企业在项目落地方面存在诸多问题。比如，中资非五星船舶沿海捎带业务，交通部已经出到文件予以明确，且中海、中远等企业已经试点操作，但该政策涉及海关、检验检疫、港务集团等多家部门，还需要研究制定配套方案。

（2）边境管理方面。第一，区内政策统一协调性不够。例如，海关监管模式和实际操作流程在自贸试验区四个区域之间仍未统一。第二，企业分类监管制度不够完善。例如，即使已经签署双边互认协议，但单证上还没有 AEO 的标志，企业就无法享受 AEO 的便利化政策。第三，部门政策缺乏协同联动。例如，有些进口商品在一线放开方面相关部门实际操作不统一。

（3）企业设立方面。第一，商事登记制度改革的执行效果差。商事登记制度改革后，部分政府主管部门仍然参照传统审批流程和方法执行。试验区管委会承诺有更大开放，但各政府主管部门审批流程和方法依然如旧，企业来来回回跑，办事人员无权做主。第二,一些企业被卡在员工资格认证环节,无法投入运营。例如,建筑设计企业外籍员工的原籍国不存在建筑业从业人员的资格认证。企业提交的员工在本公司的多年从业经验证明,没有通过行业主管单位批准,理由是企业无法证明自己员工的从业经验,需要有独立第三方证明。但企业外籍员工的原籍国也没有该行业的独立第三方认证机构。企业被卡在员工从业资格认证的环节,无法投入运营。第三,"单一窗口"服务功能有待拓展。虽然国际贸易"单一窗口"管理制度为企业通关提供极大便利,但目前仅限于海关、检验检疫、口岸、海事四部门,税务外管等部门尚未纳入,在一定程度上影响了"单一窗口"的便利。

(4)税收方面。目前,上海自贸试验区在税收方面还未形成一套完善的制度框架,一些高端功能的主体引进和功能拓展仍受到税收政策的制约,不仅表现在税率方面,还有征收机制、征收方式等方面的问题。

(5)金融方面。第一,受资本外流压力影响,外汇管制有逐步收紧的趋势。第二,银行业非居民业务税率高、FTN项下人民币存款利率非市场化、FT账户功能空转。自贸区金融机构开展非居民金融业务(离岸业务),除了5%的营业税,还有25%的所得税,税率较重。与国际对标,相对税负较重,因此金融企业缺乏开展离岸业务的积极性。FTN项下人民币存款利率是参照境内人民银行公布的存款利率执行,而国际上实行利率市场化管理。FT账户缺乏实质性功能,在资金联通境内外进出上没有做到真正自由。外资公司都开设有外资账户,FT账户对于他们的意义不大,甚至有银行为了完成开户指标,极力劝说企业开设FT账户,但开设后并没有真正运转。

(6)监管方面。第一,年报内容及时性不足。年报的内容仅可以在1月1日至6月30日提交期间进行更改,在经营期间企业的通信地址等内容的变化以及歇业、清算等情况得不到及时公示。第二,我国非政府组织如民间协会、行业协会等组织的作用不大,社会监督不力。第三,企业信用信息采集、处理、公开和监管体系不完善。

(7)争端解决机制方面。上海自贸区仲裁规则的创新可能因未能得到立法的支撑而在实际运行中难以取得良好效果。例如,《中国(上海)自由贸易试验区仲裁规则》增加了当事人意思自治的程度和仲裁庭的权限,但过于"国际化"的规则却与我国《民事诉讼法》和《仲裁法》的立法难以衔接。看似创新性的开放仲裁员名册制虽然有利于扩大当事人意思自治程度,但可能会延长仲裁期限、降低仲裁效率。

(8)对外投资方面。第一,国有企业跨境并购容易受到西方国家"歧视"。

"主权基金"受到西方国家的普遍猜忌，西方发达国家对中国国有企业的特殊身份背景非常敏感。国有背景的企业进行跨国并购或投资时容易受到西方国家更严格的安全审查，导致国有企业需要承担更大的信息披露责任或在其他方面进行让步。此外，"竞争中立"原则也更进一步加大了国企"走出去"的难度。第二，我国投资促进服务供给不足并效率低。一是资源配置行政化，容易发生资源错配。二是资源配置倾向国有大型企业，不仅抑制了民营企业"走出去"，也提高了整体的政治风险概率。三是信息支持问题多，如信息服务偏宏观；缺少与企业或项目密切联系，实用信息少；收费项目多；人员和企业培训少；缺少帮助投资者协同合作，制定长远战略和规划等。四是缺乏支持小企业的专门计划。第三，法律制约。我国目前针对企业境外投资行为的法律规定比较薄弱，主要是一些办法和暂行规定，立法的滞后已经严重影响到企业的海外并购活动，既造成政府的相关支持政策效果大打折扣，又使企业在海外并购过程中发生纠纷后缺少法律法规的保护。第四，外汇管理限制。我国尚未完全实现资本项目下的自由兑换，导致企业海外并购活动受外汇额度的制约较大。此外，国家外汇管理局与国家商务部、各地商务部门在外汇风险审查与项目立项两者的关系上及先后顺序上存在不同看法，导致企业常常无所适从，难以办理。这对于需要配套现汇的实物投资项目，以及需要较多外汇汇出我国的非生产性投资（例如售后服务项目、研发项目等），具有十分不利的影响。第五，海外投资保险的作用未得到充分发挥。与快速扩大的海外投资规模相比，我国海外投资保险存在参保费率较高，缺乏专门的海外投资保险制度，承包机构设置不合理，投保人范围界定不合理等问题，使得我国的海外投资保险覆盖面仍然较低。难以达到支持和鼓励本国投资者积极主动地开拓海外市场，促进本国经济发展的目的。第六，中介服务机构不健全，服务水平未达到提供国际并购服务要求。目前，我国虽已形成了包括信托投资公司、证券公司、财务公司在内的投资银行格局，但无论是实力还是经验都明显欠缺，行业协会和专业组织不健全，服务水平远未达到提供国际并购服务的要求，许多中介机构甚至还从未接触过跨国并购业务。这使得中国企业在开展跨国并购时很难得到中介机构的高质量服务，无法获得有用的信息和帮助，从而导致企业在并购中出现问题。第七，企业自身条件的限制。例如，与国外企业在经营文化和管理上的冲突；跨国并购专业人才的缺乏；高估海外资产价值和投资回报等等。

上海自贸区促进投资贸易便利化相关政策措施梳理汇总

王孝钰

上海市人民政府发展研究中心博士后工作站

1. 市场准入

（1）现状。

外资准入由正面清单模式转向负面清单模式。负面清单制度的核心在于建立"法无禁止即可为"的政府管理理念，从根本上和制度上实现简政放权。目前，大部分国家都实行准入前国民待遇和负面清单的外资管理模式，正在进行的中美 BIT 谈判也以准入前国民待遇和负面清单为基础进行实质性磋商。在这种情势下，从"正面清单"到"负面清单"的跨越使得中国与国际接轨。

2013 年 9 月 30 日，上海市人民政府公布了《中国（上海）自由贸易试验区外商投资准入特别管理措施（负面清单）（2013 年）》。这是我国首份负面清单，共有 190 条特别管理措施，占行业比重的 17.8% 左右。由此，自贸试验区对外资的准入管理由原来的"核准制"向"备案制 + 核准制"转变。2014 年 6 月 30 日，上海市人民政府公布了《中国（上海）自由贸易试验区外商投资准入特别管理措施（负面清单）（2014 年修订）》，进一步扩大了开放力度。与 2013 版相比，2014 版负面清单里的特别管理措施从 190 条缩减为 139 条，减幅达 26.8%，并且取消了 14 条管理措施，放宽了 19 条管理措施，进一步开放比例达 17.4%。此外，2014 版负面清单在制造业、建筑业等领域继续扩大开放。此次负面清单关于制造业领域的 14 条措施中，有 5 条注重于产品的研发、设计；在建筑业扩大开放方面，体现了基础设施建设对外资的开放；在采矿业扩大开放方面注重新技术的开放应用。同时，2014 版负面清单也扩大了服务业领域的开放措施。服务业领域扩大开放的 14 条措施，其中航运服务领域 6 条，商贸服务领域 3 条，专业服务领域 4 条，社会服务领域 1 条，进一步扩大开放商贸物流、会计审计、医疗等领域。

2015 年 4 月 8 日国务院办公厅发布《自由贸易试验区外商投资准入特别管理措施（负面清单）》，清单内容从 2014 版的 139 条减少为 122 条。在清单结构上，减少制造业在清单中的比例。2015 版负面清单在制造业方面的条款由 2014 版的近 50 条减少到 17 条。这更符合国际惯例，也标志着我国对于服务业的管理趋向成熟。同时，2015 版负面清单的透明度进一步提升。例如，金融领域负面清单的条款内容由 2014 版的 4 条上升为 14 条，文化、体育、娱乐业的条款内容由 2014 版的 8 条上升为 24 条。增加的内容都是将两大领域对于外商的限制具体化，不但没有削弱开放度，负面清单的透明度和操作性反而更高。

（2）存在的问题及未来发展。

当前扩大开放措施的项目落地效果不均衡，开放措施中，"首次开放"较少，"政策放宽"较多，且服务业开放程度较低。另外，开放政策缺乏解释、配套和相关法律支持。比如，中资非五星船舶沿海捎带业务，交通部已经出到文件予以明确，且中海、中远等企业已经试点操作，但该政策涉及海关、检验检疫、港务集团等多家部门，还需要研究制定配套方案。

自加入 WTO 以来，我国服务贸易进出口已上升至世界第五位，在传统服务行业领域业形成了一定的优势，但我国新兴服务业、高端服务业（高附加值、高人力资本含量）发展仍较为滞后，服务业国际竞争力整体还比较弱。我国在自身发展水平和承受能力的基础上，仍需要通过不断扩大开放，强化市场竞争，进一步提升新兴服务业和高端服务业的竞争力，带动我国服务业发展水平的整体提升。因此，未来我国将进一步推动服务业，尤其是金融、文化、教育、医疗、航运、专业服务等新兴服务业、高端服务业的开放，同时完善和细化法律法规，以支持相应的产业开放。

2. 边境管理

（1）现状。

• 海关

① 通关便利化措施。区内企业海关注册登记纳入企业准入"单一窗口"：企业准入"单一窗口"是投资者通过"中国（上海）自由贸易试验区投资办事直通车"网上平台一次性报送相关注册登记的申请信息，各政府部门（包括工商、税务、质监、商务委、海关等）受理并办理投资者所申请的相关注册登记，办事结果将通过平台统一反馈至投资者的企业注册模式。

"先进区，后报关"："先进区、后报关"是指在试验区境外入区环节，经海关注册登记的试验区内企业（以下简称"区内企业"）可以凭进境货物的舱单等信息先向海关简要申报，并办理口岸提货和货物进区手续，再在规定时限内向海关办理进境货物正式申报手续的作业模式。

"自主报税、自助通关、自动审放、重点稽查"："自主报税、自助通关、自动审放、重点稽核"作业模式是指，企业登录关企共用平台预录入客户端，自主如实申报报关单数据，并主动申报税款，海关信息系统对于企业申报数据进行自动审放一体作业。试点初期，该作业模式仅适用于试验区"分送集报"进口业务。

"一次备案、多次使用"："一次备案、多次使用"是指试验区内企业（以下简称"区内企业"）在账册备案环节通过"中国（上海）自由贸易试验区海关监管信息化系统"（以下简称"信息化系统"）向试验区主管海关一次性备案企业、进出货物等信息，经主管海关核准后，可以在试验区各项海关业务中多次、重复使用的海关监管模式。区内企业经账册备案后，在开展"批次进出、集中申报""保税展示交易""境内外维修""期货保税交割"、"融资租赁"等经海关核准开展的业务中，可以在信息化系统中直接调用已备案的企业和进出口货物等信息，无需再向海关重复备案。

海关智能化卡口管理：试验区智能化卡口验放是指海关依据卡口核放单，运用智能化设备自动读取电子车牌号码、集装箱号、车载重量（电子地磅数据）、安全智能锁等监管数据，进行海关监管信息的自动比对、风险判别，完成车辆GPS运行轨迹自动核销、货物查验或者放行指令处置等卡口智能化管理作业，实现车辆分流、自动验放。

"批次进出，集中申报"："批次进出、集中申报"，是指允许试验区内企业（以下简称区内企业）与境内区外企业（含区外海关特殊监管区域以及保税监管场所内企业）、区内其他企业之间分批次进出货物的，可以先凭卡口核放单（以下简称"核放单"）办理货物的实际进出区手续，再在规定期限内以备案清单或者报关单集中办理海关报关手续，海关依托"中国（上海）自由贸易试验区海关监管信息化系统"（以下简称"信息化系统"）进行监管的一种通关模式。

货物流转"自行运输"："自行运输"是指经海关注册登记的试验区内企业（以下简称"区内企业"），可以使用经海关备案的车辆，在试验区内自行运输货物的作业模式。

② 货物分类监管。根据保税货物、非保税货物、口岸货物三类不同货物状态进行分类监管，实行同仓存储，采用"联网监管＋库位管理＋实时核注"监管模式。

③ 企业分类监管。推行"经认证的经营者（AEO）"互认制度（目前已与新加坡、韩国、中国香港地区、中国台湾地区、欧盟签署 AEO 互认的合作协议），使区内 118 家 AA 类企业同时享受国内及货物出口国海关最高等级通关便利措施。区内高资信报关企业在全国首次实现"一地注册，全国申报"。

④ 区港一体运作。推行区内企业货物流转自行运输、简化统一进出境备案清单（备案格式由原来外高桥保税区和保税物流园区备案清单申报项 36 项、洋山保税港区和浦东机场综保区备案清单申报项 42 项，统一为 30 项）等，进一步推进自贸试验区四大区域联动和港区一体。2014 年 9 月 1 日，上海自贸试验区洋山保税港区正式启用"区港直通道"。"区港直通道"是连接自贸试验区洋山保税港区岛域和陆域的内部通道，启用后，一线进出境车辆通过"区港直通道"直接验放，进一步完善了自贸试验区洋山保税港区交通网络的整体布局，降低了区内企业的物流成本，提高了物流实效。与此同时，"区港直通道"实施 7×24 小时验放模式，对进出境车辆过卡口实行自动比对、自动判别、自动验放等智能化管理，有效提高了企业承运车辆的通行效率，也完善了洋山保税港区的物流监控系。

• 进出口检验检疫

① 取消许可证委托加工备案。上海市质监局自 2014 年 2 月 1 日起在上海自贸试验区开展取消工业产品生产许可证委托加工备案试点，并于 2014 年 4 月 15 日起推广至上海市所有区（县）。

② 进口货物预检验制度。2014 年 5 月 1 日起，上海出入境检验检疫局在上海自贸试验区范围内全面推行进口货物预检验制度，企业可在货物入境进区或在区仓储时申请预检验，对预检验合格的货物实施核销放行，免于检验。通过预检验及核销制度的实施，可以在自贸试验区"二线"严密防范质量安全风险的同时，有效地将刚性的进口现场检验和实验室检测时间前置到货物的在区仓储期间，实现了货物出区时"零等待"和预检验后，货物进境到进口通关的整个流程时间至少缩短 50%。进口工业品从 7 到 8 个工作日缩短至 3 到 4 个工作日，进口化妆品从 12 个工作日缩短到 5 个工作日。

③ 自贸试验区全面推广"即查即放"现场查验放行模式。"即查即放"现场查验放行模式，是利用物联网、云储存等先进技术与口岸查验监管、服务外贸措施相结合的一种查验放行方式，通过手持式移动执法终端，可以实现检验检疫现场查验无纸化以及多系统一键放行（已实现与国家质检总局业务主干系统、上海口岸海港电子闸口系统的联动）。这种模式解决了监管人员和被监管人员在查验现场和办公区域往返奔波、查验过程无法追溯、查验结果重复录入、现场放行等

候排队等问题，在规范执法把关流程的同时又有效加快了查验放行速度。

• 海事

① 创新国际船舶检查方式，提升海事监管服务效能。通过整合海事执法力量，做到能够不登轮检查的不再登轮检查，必须登轮检查的事项，一次完成海事监管所有执法检查，有效降低了海事现场检查对国际航线船舶运营可能产生的影响，大大提高了自贸试验区港口运营效率。

② 先许可，后查验。2013 年 10 月在自贸试验区开始试点国际航行船舶驶离洋山港口岸查验"先许可，后查验"制度。船舶可享受到"船舶出口岸许可"即到即放、多份申请材料开航前一次提交、多艘船舶一次办结的便利服务，实现了船舶出口岸查验业务办结"零等待"。

（2）存在的问题及未来发展

需要完善的地方：区内政策统一协调问题，例如，海关监管模式和实际操作流程在自贸试验区四个区域之间仍未统一；企业分类监管制度完善问题，例如，即使已经签署双边互认协议，但单证上还没有 AEO 的标志，企业就无法享受 AEO 的便利化政策；部门政策协同联动问题，例如，有些进口商品在一线放开方面相关部门实际操作不统一。

未来发展：第一，制定并完善制度实施细则。自贸试验区可以通过制定条例实施细则完善贸易便利化的制度环境，同时进一步通过部门执行使得贸易便利化的规则能够落到实处。第二，建立制度创新协同推进机制。建立跨部门的沟通交流平台，对涉及多部门的改革事项进行联动协调，以加强部门政策创新的联动性、协同性、配套性，特别是对新开放跨界领域探索建立标准统一、流程优化、高校边界的联合监管机制。完善信息共享和服务平台建设，借鉴新加坡公共平台模式，加强信息共享和服务平台的信息整合、服务整合、监管整合功能，整合各部门服务资源和流程，强化"一站式"对外服务和公众参与互动，推动跨部门协同联合监管和服务。第三，完善以信用档案为基础的企业分类监管制度。完善 AEO 互认制度，推动海关与检验检疫等部门统一认证，根据不同授权类型的 AEO 资格实施差别化监管，确保企业享受与其 AEO 资格授权相对应的便利措施。完善企业信用档案建设，推动第三方评估、检验和结果采信制度建设，共享企业诚信信息，真正建立以企业信用档案和信用评级制度为核心的差异化监管制度。第四，完善区域一体监管制度。完善自贸试验区四个海关特殊监管区域的统筹监管机制、监管模式和实际操作流程，建立统一的海关监管机构，整合统一四个海关特殊监管区域的海关代码、优化区内自行运输的运作机制和管理机制，尽快扩大推广，真正实现四个区域间自行运输的无障碍。积极探索与区外海关特殊监管区域的监管联动。

3. 营商环境

（1）现状。

• 企业设立

① 外资审批制度改革，转变为备案制。

借鉴国际通行规则，自贸试验区外资准入备案制，按照负面清单管理管理模式的要求和内外资一致的原则，将外商投资项目有核准制改为备案制（国务院规定对国内投资项目保留核准的除外），将外商投资企业合同章程审批改为备案管理，备案后按国家有关规定办理相关手续。由于外资审批制、核准制需要对主体资格、投资领域行业、投资方式、投资金额、公司合同章程等合法性进行审查认可，负面清单管理模式下的备案制仅需掌握主体资格、投资领域行业等基本信息即可，因此，自贸实验区备案制大大简化了外资进入程序，并降低外资准入门槛和成本，更体现了外资管理体制由注重事前审批向注重事中事后监管的理念转变。

② 商事登记制度改革，注册资本由"实缴制"改为"认缴制"，企业注册由"先证后照"改为"先照后证"。

注册资本认缴登记制是指自贸试验区试行有条件的公司注册资本认缴登记制，除法律、行政规定对公司注册资本实缴登记另有规定的企业外，其余试行认缴制，不再登记实收资本，也不提交验资报告。相对实收资本登记制度而言，在自贸试验区内试行注册资本认缴登记制，由企业股东对认缴出资自行约定，不再受最低注册资本限额、货币出资比例规定以及出资限期等规条约束。这意味着公司设立时不再需要验资，营业执照上不再出现实收资本，无形资产等其他资产也可算作注册资本，从而进一步降低了商事主体进入市场的门槛，消除了商事主体办理实收资本登记的负担，体现了工商登记改革"宽进"的理念。

"先照后证"登记制是指除法律、行政法规、国务院决定规定的企业登记前置许可事项外，自贸试验区企业向工商部门申请营业执照后即可从事一般生产经营活动。对于其他许可项目，应当在领取营业执照及许可证或批准文件后，方可从事经营活动。"先照后证"登记制取消了我国现行商事登记中的前置审批环节，实现商事主体资格和经营许可资格相分离，有利于企业降低市场准入成本，且符合国际惯例做法。

③ 企业准入的"单一窗口"制度。

自贸区建立了企业准入单一窗口工作机制，企业只需按规定提供一个表格，通过一个窗口提交申请材料，实现外商投资项目核准（备案）、企业设立和变更审批（备案）等行政事务的一门式办理。自贸区内工商注册实行"一口受理"政策，即由上海市工商分局、质监局、国税局、公安局等职能部门设立"一口受理"窗口，统一接收申请人向各职能部门提交的营业执照、组织机构代码证、税务登记证及印章等申请材料。也就是说，"多证联办"将直接步入"三证合一"阶段。"一口受理"可三证一块出，办理时间约4天，比原来需要的29天时间大幅减少。

• 税收

上海自贸试验区《总体方案》中提出了一些税收政策，可以概括为"7+2"，即7项明确实行的税收政策和2项探索实行的税收政策。明确的7项税收政策包括鼓励投资的政策和促进贸易的政策，鼓励投资政策主要涉及非货币性资产对外投资、股权激励等2项；促进贸易政策主要涉及融资租赁出口退税、进口环节增值税、选择性征税、部分货物免税、启运港退税等5项政策。主要涉及企业所得税、个人所得税、增值税、关税4个税种。探索的政策即适应境外股权投资和离岸业务发展的2项税收政策。

2014年7月8日，国家税务总局发布《关于支持中国（上海）自由贸易试验区创新税收服务的通知》在征税方式上进行了一定的创新，以提高征税效率。自贸试验区创新税收服务的主题是"税收一网通办、便捷优质高效"（简称"办税一网通"），主要包括：网上自动赋码；网上自主办税；电子发票网上应用；网上区域通办；网上直接认定；非居民税收网上管理；网上按季申报；网上备案；纳税信用网上评价；创新网上服务；网上信息收集，通过税企互动平台、网上在线、网上调查问卷等功能，对纳税人需求进行分类采集；网上信息推送，根据纳税人需求有针对性地提供个性化政策推送、风险提示提醒等主动推送服务；网上信息查询，提供网上涉税事项办理进度等信息查询服务。

• 金融

为进一步促进贸易投资便利化，扩大金融对外开放，"一行三会"先后颁布14项政策法规，着力推进人民币跨境使用、人民币资本项目可兑换、利率市场化和外汇管理等领域改革试点。其中部分措施已经落实，部分措施正在推进阶段。自由贸易账户体系、投融资汇兑便利、人民币跨境使用、利率市场化、外汇管理改革等五个方面，形成了上海自贸区金融创新框架，上海自贸区的金融服务功能不断增强。

① 资本账户开放。

试验区内的居民可通过设立本外币自由贸易账户（以下简称居民自由贸易账户）实现分账核算管理。非居民可在试验区内银行开立本外币非居民自由贸易账户（以下简称非居民自由贸易账户），按准入前国民待遇原则享受相关金融服务。

居民自由贸易账户与境外账户、境内区外的非居民账户、非居民自由贸易账户以及其他居民自由贸易账户之间的资金可自由划转。同一非金融机构主体的居民自由贸易账户与其他银行结算账户之间因经常项下业务、偿还贷款、实业投资以及其他符合规定的跨境交易需要可办理资金划转。居民自由贸易账户与境内区外的银行结算账户之间产生的资金流动视同跨境业务管理。居民自由贸易账户及非居民自由贸易账户可办理跨境融资、担保等业务。建立区内居民自由贸易账户和非居民自由贸易账户人民币汇兑的监测机制。上海地区金融机构可根据人民银行规定，通过设立试验区分账核算单元的方式，为符合条件的区内主体开立自由贸易账户，并提供相关金融服务。

② 投融资汇兑便利。

促进企业跨境直接投资便利化。试验区跨境直接投资，可按上海市有关规定与前置核准脱钩，直接向银行办理所涉及的跨境收付、兑换业务。

便利个人跨境投资。在区内就业并符合条件的个人可按规定开展包括证券投资在内的各类境外投资。个人在区内获得的合法所得可在完税后向外支付。区内个体工商户可根据业务需要向其在境外经营主体提供跨境贷款。在区内就业并符合条件的境外个人可按规定在区内金融机构开立非居民个人境内投资专户，按规定开展包括证券投资在内的各类境内投资。

稳步开放资本市场。区内金融机构和企业可按规定进入上海地区的证券和期货交易场所进行投资和交易。区内企业的境外母公司可按国家有关法规在境内资本市场发行人民币债券。

促进对外融资便利化。根据经营需要，注册在试验区内的中外资企业、非银行金融机构以及其他经济组织（以下简称区内机构）可按规定从境外融入本外币资金，完善全口径外债的宏观审慎管理制度，采取有效措施切实防范外债风险。

提供多样化风险对冲手段。区内机构可按规定基于真实的币种匹配及期限匹配管理需要在区内或境外开展风险对冲管理。允许符合条件的区内企业按规定开展境外证券投资和境外衍生品投资业务。试验区分账核算单元因向区内或境外机构提供本外币自由汇兑产生的敞口头寸，应在区内或境外市场上进行平盘对冲。试验区分账核算单元基于自身风险管理需要，可按规定参与国际金融市场衍生工具交易。经批准，试验区分账核算单元可在一定额度内进入境内银行间市场开展拆借或回购交易。

③扩大人民币跨境使用。

上海地区银行业金融机构可在"了解你的客户""了解你的业务"和"尽职审查"三原则基础上，凭区内机构（出口货物贸易人民币结算企业重点监管名单内的企业除外）和个人提交的收付款指令，直接办理经常项下、直接投资的跨境人民币结算业务。

上海地区银行业金融机构可与区内持有《支付业务许可证》且许可业务范围包括互联网支付的支付机构合作，按照支付机构有关管理政策，为跨境电子商务（货物贸易或服务贸易）提供人民币结算服务。

区内金融机构和企业可从境外借用人民币资金，借用的人民币资金不得用于投资有价证券、衍生产品，不得用于委托贷款。

区内企业可根据自身经营需要，开展集团内双向人民币资金池业务，为其境内外关联企业提供经常项下集中收付业务。

④稳步推进利率市场化。

我国利率市场化正处于加快推进阶段，2013年7月20日央行全面放开金融机构贷款利率管制。2014年3月1日起放开中国（上海）自贸试验区小额外币存款利率上限，在全国率先实现外币存款利率的完全市场化。2014年6月26日，放开小额外币存款利率上限的改革试点，由上海自贸区扩大到上海市。

⑤深化外汇管理改革。

支持试验区发展总部经济和新型贸易。扩大跨国公司总部外汇资金集中运营管理试点企业范围，进一步简化外币资金池管理，深化国际贸易结算中心外汇管理试点，促进贸易投资便利化。

简化直接投资外汇登记手续。将直接投资项下外汇登记及变更登记下放银行办理，加强事后监管。在保证交易真实性和数据采集完整的条件下，允许区内外商直接投资项下的外汇资金意愿结汇。

支持试验区开展境内外租赁服务。取消金融类租赁公司境外租赁等境外债权业务的逐笔审批，实行登记管理。经批准，允许金融租赁公司及中资融资租赁公司境内融资租赁收取外币租金，简化飞机、船舶等大型融资租赁项目预付货款手续。

取消区内机构向境外支付担保费的核准，区内机构直接到银行办理担保费购付汇手续。

支持银行开展面向境内客户的大宗商品衍生品的柜台交易。

• 监管

投资管理由政府单一监管转向政府和社会综合监管，由静态监管转向动态监管。2013年3月，上海市工商行政管理局印发《中国（上海）自由贸易试验区企业年度报告公示办法（试行）》以及《中国（上海）自由贸易试验区企业经营异常名录管理办法（试行）》，开始在自贸试验区内试行企业年度报告公示和企业经营异常名录制度，推进企业信用信息公示，引导政府职能转变，强化社会监督。2014年8月，该制度进一步推广至全国。

- 争端解决机制

《中国（上海）自由贸易试验区总体方案》（以下简称《总体方案》）提到"着力培育国际化和法治化的营商环境"。在培育上海自贸区国际化、法制化的营商环境过程中，要注重建立起一个健全的争端解决机制。从某种程度上说，是否能公正、便捷地进行争端调处，事关上海自贸区的前途和命运。由于商贸与金融服务的溢出效应，相关的争端解决远非上海自贸区法庭可一己承担，自贸区建设所带来的司法创新需求将呈线性增长。仲裁作为在贸易和投资领域中被各国和各国际性经济组织所普遍采用的争端解决方式，其具有自治、灵活、高效等优势，满足了国际化、法治化的自贸区营商环境对于纠纷解决措施便利化的要求，契合了自贸区纠纷的新特点，应当成为上海自贸区争端解决的首选方式。

为了与自贸区相适应，《自贸区仲裁规则》相对中国现有仲裁机构的仲裁规则，有较大的突破和创新。

第一，开放仲裁员名册。《自贸区仲裁规则》规定，仲裁庭的组成可以由当事人在仲裁员名册中选定，也可以自行推荐或共同推荐名册外的人士担任，只要得到仲裁委员会主任的确认。该名册外的人也可以担任首席仲裁员或独任仲裁员。开放仲裁员名册是世界主要国际仲裁机构普遍适用的规则。自贸区仲裁院对开放仲裁员名册的采用，给予当事人更大的自主权，提升仲裁的灵活性和专业性，充分尊重当事人意思自由，标志着自贸区仲裁制度与国际接轨。

第二，在审理方式上提出了"合并仲裁"。针对仲裁案件中第三人，当仲裁标的为同一种类或者有关联的两个或两个以上案件，经一方当事人申请并经所有当事人同意，仲裁庭可以决定合并审理。合并仲裁在国际仲裁机构中亦属前沿，它有效扩大了仲裁庭的案件审理范围（即使被合并的案件当事人并未签订仲裁协定也可以进行合并审理），从而为争端的解决提供更多途径，尤其是纠纷存在多方当事人时。同时它还提高了仲裁的审理效率和专业程度，使当事人可以得到便利，一案审理、一裁终局，有助于纠纷涉及的多方当事人提高对纠纷解决的认同感。

第三，仲裁调解。调解可以在仲裁程序的任何阶段进行。通过调解程序，案件的一部分在仲裁开始之前就得到了解决，从而节省资源，降低当事人的争端解决成本，并缓和当事人之间的关系，利于商业环境和社会环境的稳定；另一方面，仲裁的调解以一方当事人申请、另一方当事人同意为启动条件，充分尊重当事人的意思自由。和解协议达成后（即便该协议是在仲裁委员会之外达成的），裁决书或调解书即具有强制执行的效力，有效解决执行难题，使得争端真正得到解决，结果公平而注重效率。

第四，友好仲裁。即"可仅依据公允善良的原则作出裁决"，而不是依据法律规范。友好仲裁对于中国目前的仲裁制度是极大的突破，它要求仲裁员具备更高的专业素质和仲裁水平，从而可以在法律允许的范围内，作出公正、公平的裁决，真正地解决争端。这对于中国的仲裁制度是挑战，当然也是促进发展的机遇。

第五，《自贸区仲裁规则》还规定了小额案件、或经双方当事人同意可适用简易程序。在证据制度上，从仲裁庭自行调查、专家报告及鉴定意见等方面予以强化。

目前，新加坡国际仲裁中心、香港国际仲裁中心均已在上海自贸试验区设立代表处。

（2）存在的问题及未来发展。

企业设立方面：商事登记制度改革后，部分政府主管部门仍然参照传统审批流程和方法执行。试验区管委会承诺有更大开放，但各政府主管部门审批流程和方法依然如旧，企业来来回回跑，办事人员无权做主。另外，虽然国际贸易"单一窗口"管理制度为企业通关提供极大便利，但目前仅限于海关、检验检疫、口岸、海事四部门，税务外管等部门尚未纳入，在一定程度上影响了"单一窗口"的便利。未来将进一步完善"单一窗口"管理制度，进一步纳入外管、税务等部门业务功能，推进企业运营信息与口岸监管系统全面对接，简化通关要素和流程，实现企业与进口、出口（包括转口）贸易有关的申请、申报、审核、许可、管制等全部手续均通过统一平台进行。企业准入"单一窗口"通过进一步纳入统计、商务、海关、检验检疫等相关准入环节，拓展延伸服务功能，通过对企业需要提交审核的相关材料一口明示，提高服务效率。并且整合各部门服务资源和流程，强化"一站式"对外服务和公众参与互动，推动跨部门协同联合监管和服务，简化审批流程。

税收方面：目前，上海自贸试验区在税收方面还未形成一套完善的制度框架，一些高端功能的主体引进和功能拓展仍受到税收政策的制约，不仅表现在税率方面，还有征收机制、征收方式等方面的问题。未来一定时期，我国仍会合理安排一些税收优惠政策，但将会尽量削减区域优惠，而转向产业优惠为主，通过改进和完善税收政策引导地方政府更多地关注经济发展质量，更加注重经济结构调整和发展方式转变。进一步探索促进离岸业务发展、境外投资发展、总部经济发展、新兴服务业发展的税收制度。

金融方面：将继续参照国际水准，以国际通行制度、规则和惯例为标杆，在人民币国际化和国家金融开放总体战略中，进一步推进资本账户开放、利率市场化改革、外汇管理改革以及离岸金融发展。

监管方面：年报内容及时性不足，年报的内容仅可以在1月1日至6月30日提交期间进行更改，在经营期间企业的通信地址等内容的变化以及歇业、清算等情况得不到及时公示。并且我国非政府组织如民间协会、行业协会等组织的作用不大，社会监督不力。我国社会信用制度特别是企业信用制度极不健全，企业缺乏自律机制，信用意识淡薄。企业信用信息采集、处理、公开和监管体系不完善。未来要进一步协调和组织市场经营主体参与市场监督，做好诚信体系建设，加强自律；推动区内协会、商会、专业服务机构发挥其在制定行业公约、维护竞争秩序、评审评估、认证监管等方面的作用。建立健全由政府主导的全国联网信息库，建立以工商部门经济户籍库为基础的市场主体信用信息公示系统，推动整个社会诚信体系建设。在不侵犯商业秘密的前提下，公开透明披露公司各项信息，包括年检、财务、信用记录、产品质量、社保缴费等信息，尤其是公司资产的变动及结构。

4. 促进对外投资

（1）现状。

• 境外投资促进体系

上海自贸试验区构筑对外投资服务促进体系，充分体现了放松投资管制、加强事后服务、促进境外投资自由化的导向。自贸试验区境外投资促进体系的核心与亮点是试行境外投资备案制，大大减少前置审批的环节和流程，无疑更加契合企业自主投资决策的需求，更符合市场导向和国际投资自由化的发展趋势。

• 境外股权投资

鼓励开展境外股权投资是上海自贸试验区推进我国对外投资发展的重要举措。上海自贸试验区的投资管理制度创新和金融服务创新为国内投资者开展境外股权投资提供了良好的支撑环境。通过鼓励在试验区内设立专业从事境外股权投资的项目公司，支持有条件的投资者设立境外股权投资母基金，有利于拓展我国对外投资模式、降低海外投资风险、实现盈利模式多元化，有利于把握全球行业发展新趋势、进一步推动我国"走出去"战略的实施。

（2）存在的问题及未来发展。

考虑到境外股权投资需要面对来自不同层面的风险，如信息不对称风险、企业运营风险、投资标的行业风险、投资价格风险以及退出风险等，建立健全境外股权投资风险防控体系，也将成为上海自贸试验区构筑对外投资服务促进体系的重要内容。

从相关协议标准看上海自贸试验区贸易便利化存在的问题

张明海　谭　旻

上海市人民政府发展研究中心信息处

1.《贸易便利化协议》是贸易便利化评估的重要标准

根据《上海自贸试验区总体方案》(简称"总体方案"),上海自贸试验区要"全面深化改革和扩大开放探索新途径、积累新经验的国家战略需要","探索构建相对独立的以贸易便利化为主的货物贸易区域和以扩大服务领域开放为主的服务贸易区域。在确保有效监管的前提下,探索建立货物状态分类监管模式"。这个目标要求对上海自贸试验区提升贸易便利化具有重要的指导意义,也是这方面工作评估的主要依据。

同时,目前国际上对贸易便利化标准也有了新的重要进展。2014年11月WTO总理事会特别会议通过的《贸易便利化协议》提出了"通过简化贸易流程、增加规则的透明度和可预见性、消除技术性和机制性障碍,形成和完善贸易的法律基础和配套措施,减少贸易风险、不确定性和交易成本,在整个国际供应链贸易上实现自由与开放,提升资源配置水平和效率"为目标的贸易便利化标准。根据这个协议,贸易便利化内容覆盖了口岸海关管理高效化和国内因素便利化两个领域,包括了贸易流程简化、数据元标准化、信息处理无纸化、程序法治化、监管信息化、成本节约、机构协调、海关合作等多方面事项。《贸易便利化协议》涉及的内容非常丰富,具有较强的国际范围的可比性和实际评估中可操作性,既为上海自贸试验区评估贸易便利化工作提供了重要标准,也为上海借鉴发达国家在提升贸易便利化上的经验提供了视角和框架。

2. 上海自贸试验区在贸易便利化上的成绩和问题

根据"总体方案"的目标要求和《贸易便利化协议》的标准,上海自贸试验区在贸易便利化上成绩评估如下:

（1）对照"总体方案"的目标要求。

总体方案在贸易便利化上提出了4个方面、3个层次和21项要求。截至2014年10月，上海自贸试验区完全达标的有17项，占80%，基本达标的有2项，占10%，不达标的有2项，占10%（见表1）。总的来说，上海自贸试验区在提升贸易便利化水平上取得了稳步而长足的进步。[1]

（2）对照《贸易便利化协议》标准

对照WTO《贸易便利化协议》的标准，上海自贸试验区达到其中贸易流程简化标准的11项，成本节约标准的10项，海关合作标准的4项，监管信息化标准的3项，信息处理无纸化和机构协调标准的分别1项，程序法治化和数据元标准化标准的基本全部没有达到（见表2）。根据上述评估结果，上海自贸试验区在提升贸易便利化上存在四个方面的问题：

一是法律法规建设上，上海自贸试验区虽然制定了一系列有关进出口监管的法规和制度，但这些法规和制度内容不一致，政策经常调整，与国际脱轨，现有的通关等政策与贸易便利化趋势明显不相适应。

二是单一窗口服务上，2014年洋山保税港区在国内首推了国际贸易单一窗口服务，但是单一窗口服务只覆盖海关、商检等少数几个部门和一般贸易进口货物的申报与结果反馈、船舶出口岸联网核放等方面，可实现的功能不多，不能对贸易便利化形成整体性的影响；同时，单一窗口最终是采取单一机构、单一系统还是单一资料自动处理系统的目标模式不明确；有关单一窗口的法律法规建设和数据元标准化工作也没有启动。

三是风险管理意识上，上海自贸试验区风险管理意识总体来说仍然较弱，缺少完整的评估指标和系统。对风险的管控主要依靠人工审单和查验，信息资源分散在各部门，缺少对信息整体监管和信息共享平台；信息的利用仅停留在查询上，分析不深入，不能为整体风控提供支持；缺少风险管理的协作机制。同时，信息技术应用相对滞后，不能适应风险管理智能化的需求。

四是协同监管效率上，上海自贸试验区与有效的监管协作差距尚远。例如，在海关实行无纸通关的情况下，税务部门继续要求提交纸质单据，加上数据格式不统一，与国际不接轨，使通关便利整体上大打折扣，也增加了国际合作的难度。

---

[1] （1）总体方案提出了满足拓展贸易类型、延伸贸易业态、升级贸易功能和创新贸易制度等在4个方面贸易便利化要求。（2）指标结果中的不达标，是指没有执行方案，无出台相关政策，政策没有落实；基本达标是指出台了政策，但没有落地；完全达标是指政策出台并落地。

表 1　上海自贸试验区贸易便利化效果评估（对照总体方案）

总体方案			方案执行		综合评估
			政策出台	政策落地	
拓展贸易类型	1	发展离岸业务	银监发〔2013〕40 号	无落地	基本达标
	2	统筹开展国际国内贸易	上海海关公告 2014 年第 24 号	落地	完全达标
延伸贸易业态	3	设立国际大宗商品交易和资源配置平台	沪商市场〔2014〕595 号	落地	完全达标
	4	扩大完善期货保税交割试点	上海海关公告 2014 年第 11 号	落地	完全达标
	5	加快培育跨境电子商务	上海海关公告 2014 年第 13 号	落地	完全达标
	6	在特定区域设立保税展示交易平台	上海海关公告 2014 年第 9 号	落地	完全达标
升级贸易功能	7	鼓励跨国公司建立亚太地区总部	上海汇发〔2014〕26 号；银总部发〔2014〕22 号	落地	完全达标
	8	拓展国际贸易结算专用账户的服务贸易跨境收付和融资功能	银总部发〔2014〕22 号	无落地	基本达标
	9	支持融资租赁公司设立项目子公司并开展境内外租赁服务	上海汇发〔2014〕26 号；上海海关公告 2014 年第 12 号	落地	完全达标
	10	鼓励设立第三方检验鉴定机构	《关于在中国（上海）自由贸易试验区进口法检商品（重量）鉴定工作中采信第三方检验鉴定结果的通知》	落地	完全达标
	11	试点开展境内外高技术、高附加值的维修业务	上海海关公告 2014 年第 10 号；沪商机电〔2013〕698 号	落地	完全达标
创新贸易制度	12	先入区、后报关		落地	完全达标
	13	实行"进境检疫，适当放宽进出口检验"模式，先许可，后查验	上海海关公告 2014 年第 6 号、7 号、8 号等多个文件；署加发〔2013〕108 号	落地	完全达标
	14	探索建立货物状态分类监管模式		落地	完全达标
	15	优化卡口管理，加强电子信息联网		落地	完全达标
	16	"方便进出，严密防范质量安全风险"检验检疫监管	署加发〔2013〕108 号；国质检通〔2013〕503 号；特级署加函〔2014〕44 号	落地	完全达标
	17	加强电子账册管理，推动货物在各海关特殊监管区域之间和跨关区便捷流转		落地	完全达标
	18	加强海关、质检、工商、税务、外汇等管理部门的协作	上海海关公告 2014 年第 30 号	落地	完全达标
	19	组建统一高效的口岸监管机构	无	无落地	不达标
	20	探索试验区统一电子围网管理	特级署加函〔2014〕44 号	无落地	不达标
	21	促进贸易的税收政策	财关税〔2013〕75 号	落地	完全达标

注：表中为截至 2014 年 10 月总体方案的执行情况。

表 2　上海自贸试验区贸易便利化措施评估（对照贸易便利化评价标准）

序号	措施	贸易便利化标准							
		贸易流程简化	数据元标准化	信息无纸化	程序法制化	成本节约	机构协调	监管信息化	海关合作
1	先进区、后报关	✓				✓			
2	区内自行运输	✓				✓			
3	加工贸易工单式核销							✓	
4	保税展示交易	✓				✓			
5	境内外维修					✓			
6	期货保税交割	✓				✓			
7	融资租赁					✓			
8	批次进出、集中申报	✓				✓			
9	简化通关作业随附单证	✓		✓		✓			
10	统一备案清单						✓		
11	内销选择性征税					✓			
12	集中汇总征税	✓				✓			
13	仓储企业联网监管							✓	
14	智能化卡口验放管理	✓						✓	
15	企业注册登记	✓							
16	海关 AEO 互认								✓
17	企业协调员试点								✓
18	企业信用信息公开								✓
19	企业自律管理								✓
20	跨境电子商务	✓							
21	取消通关单核验	✓							

3. 发达国家在贸易便利化上借鉴的做法

根据《贸易便利化协议》框架和视角，发达国家开展了许多有益的探索，总的来说在贸易便利化处于比较领先的地位，为上海自贸试验区提供了许多可资借鉴的经验（见表 3）。一是信息技术上，如美国普遍应用了电子数据交换（EDI）、自动化贸易环境管理作业系统（ACE）等无纸化通关技术，实现信息处理无纸化、自动化、标准化和高效化。二是单一窗口服务上，有 40 多个国家在资料单

表3 发达国家提升贸易便利化的措施

	具　体　做　法
信息技术先进	• 信息处理无纸化：美国电子数据交换（EDI）无纸化通关技术 • 信息处理自动化：美国自动化贸易环境管理作业系统（ACE），自动边境管理系统 • 信息处理标准化：欧盟统一海关法典，统一报关单，"海关2007"计划
单一窗口成熟	• 单一机构：单一窗口的最高模式，瑞典荷兰 • 单一系统：系统单一，机构分散，美国国际贸易数据系统（ITDS） • 单一资料自动处理系统：系统集成，机构分散，新加坡贸易网络系统（TN）
海关合作广泛	• 与商业企业合作：美国海关与商业企业建立"伙伴关系"，1993年开始实施"海关现代化法案"，引入"知法自律"、"商业守法"概念 • 国际间合作：美国利用WCO平台推行制度，日本开展AEO制度及"贸易程序改革计划"
风险管理完善	• 应用系统风险控制技术：美国海关边防风险管理法，对风险排序，动态管理，对企业评定风险级别 • 风险分析模式成熟完善：荷兰中央计算机系统（TAGITTA）和特色保税仓库系统
海关程序简化	• 事前答复制度：进口前就货物归类、适用税率等想海关书面查询并得到答复，如日本 • 预审查制度：货物抵达前提前进行海关审查已明确是否需要查验，如日本
税收机制灵活	• 动态调整：美国针对关税倒置问题重新设计关税制度 • 优化税制：日本实行延缓纳税（含个别延缓、集中延缓、特例延缓），纳税申报与进口申报分离

证递交和处理上采取了单一机构、单一系统或单一资料自动处理系统模式。[①]三是海关合作上，建立了海关与国内外企业和机构的合作。与企业关系上，新加坡建立了海关与大客户定期对话机制；荷兰建立"海关与企业的守法便利与伙伴合作"关系[②]；澳大利亚在"客户导向"战略下，形成了企业参与海关管理的平台。在国际间合作上，美国在国际海关组织（WCO）框架下，推进了国际贸易安全和便利多边合作机制；日本积极拓展国际认证范围，推进守信企业的国际互认制度安排。四是风险管理上，加强风险分析，加强各监管环节风险控制，保持执法和便利的平衡。五是通关程序上，如日本实行海关事前告知货物报关事项和在货物抵港前对文件预审的制度。六是灵活税收机制，对税收动态调整优化，如美国

[①] "单一机构"是指成立或者授权单一的政府监管机构处理所有的进出口监管业务，瑞典、荷兰是这种模式的典型代表。"单一系统"模式是指建立一个系统统一处理贸易业务，但各监管机构仍相互独立，即"系统单一，机构分散"，美国、日本是这种模式的典型代表。"单一资料自动处理系统模式"模式是指提供一个统一的信息处理门户平台，该平台集成各个政府监管部门的系统，实现不同监管部门在信息流、业务流的共享协作，为贸易商提供单一窗口和一站式服务体验，特点是"系统集成、机构分散"，新加坡系统采用了这种模式。

[②] 在上述模式下，新加坡定期举办了"海关单证课程"和"海关指导计划"等课程；荷兰这个模式形成了"企业申请—海关评估确认—区别管理"工作机制，强调海关全面掌握企业信息、海关与企业共同确定风险指标、实时更新和动态维护风险指标等三个方面。

为解决中间品进口关税率高于最终品的问题，重新设计了关税结构，并对部分中间品采取了免征关税的措施。

4. 政策措施建议

为加快提升上海自贸试验区贸易便利化水平，提出以下建议：

（1）构筑法律基础。

提升有关贸易便利化立法的法律位阶，形成符合国际规则和承诺（包括 WTO 和 WCO 等国际组织）的贸易便利化法律基础。借鉴 WTO《贸易便利化协议》，建立上海自贸试验区的执法和行政行为标准，完善贸易便利化行政执法程序。出台相关的法律法规，对上海自贸试验区管委会的性质、定位、功能、机构设置、权限、职责等予以明确，形成其管理运行的依据和保障。

（2）实行快捷通关。

在保证贸易安全的条件下，最大限度简化通关程序，实行快捷通关制度。建议探索以下制度：一是预裁定制度。对原产地管理实施预确定，提高企业申报的便利度。二是预审查制度。在"先进区，后报关"的基础上，进一步实施货物达到上海（或相关进口手续完成）前即可在上海自贸试验区海关提交进口申报文件，提前进行海关审查。三是通关后审计制度。在完善风险评估规范运作，提升外部审计的纸质单证和现场审计能力的基础上，实行通关后审计制度。四是提前放行制度。在货物符合要求和企业提供计税所需基本信息的条件下，通关和放行分离，提前放行。

（3）推进单一窗口。

加快推进上海自贸试验区贸易单一窗口服务。一是选择适合的单一窗口模式。为避免监管权限的转移，建议选择"单一系统"或"单一资料自动处理系统"作为单一窗口模式。二是实现数据元与国际标准对接。成立专业机构，推进和协调数据元标准化；借鉴新加坡、瑞典和美国等国经验，采用 WCO DATA Model 数据元参考标准。

（4）强化风险管理。

为实现便利化与有效管理的双重目标，把风险管理作为海关管理的中心环节。形成"一个系统、一套指标、一项机制"的风险管理体系框架：一是依托互联网和计算机等技术，建立统一的风险信息系统；二是建立风险参数维护管理中心，形成和完善风险预警和管理指标体系；三是风险信息和管理要在业务流程、数据格式等方面实现统一和兼容，统一技术标准。在各贸易管理部门职责分工基础上，结合各方资源和优势，明确信息采集、风险评估、风险处置等工作的方法和职责任务，整合管理资源和风控手段，建立和完善风险信息共享和风险管理协调的运作机制，提高海关管理效率。

（5）搭建合作平台。

加强海关企业、国际间及海关政府部门之间的合作，一是树立"亲商"理念，以企业需求为核心，创新合作方式，提升海关服务效能和服务水平，提高企业话语权。探索合作谅解备忘录（MOU）制度，约定海关与企业合作方式；与大客户签订服务协议。二是配合 WCO 推动建设"全球网络化海关"，推进 AEO 贸易文件的国际互认、跨国认证和合作[①]。三是建立海关与政府相关管理部门的合作机制，明确职能分工，形成"一口对外"的工作机制，促进口岸管理一体化；在海关内部形成统一领导和协作配合的工作机制。

（6）加强信息技术。

积极推进海关信息的标准化、无纸化和自动化，应用电子数据标准、WCO 数据模型、信息通信技术安全、数据保密等，实行高效率的实时监管。加大在信息化监管建设和维护上的投入，实现上海自贸试验区监管系统在全部环节和领域的无缝对接，加快在其他地区的复制推广和与国际接轨。

---

① 如原产地证明、检验检疫证书等电子信息或证明文件。

跨国公司对上海发展跨境电商的建议

周师迅　谭　旻　张明海

上海市人民政府发展研究中心信息处

在沪跨国公司普遍关注近年来本市出台的跨境电商发展促进政策，特别关注本市在被列为国家电商试验地（2016 年 1 月）、启动建设跨境电商示范区等方面的最新进展。美中贸易全国委员会上海首席代表欧文认为，2016 年美中贸易全国委员会《关于中美贸易关系中重点问题的声明》，对近年中国电子商务的发展给予了高度关注，美资企业正在积极探索在华和在沪跨境电商投资机会。对 4 月份以来出台的一系列跨境电商"新政"政策，各跨国公司提出了以下建议：

1. 加强税收和监管政策的稳定性

亚马逊等企业提出，政策变化快、执行中的不确定性是影响中国和上海跨境电商发展的主要障碍；建议中国和上海加强跨境电商政策的稳定性，特别要加强"新政""过渡期内"与"过渡期后"监管政策的衔接。一些跨国公司认为，为形成政策稳定性，要对跨境电商贸易和涉及的物品的性质做出准确定位，在明确其一般贸易或服务贸易、有关物品是商品或物品的前提下，形成有关税收和监管政策安排。这将为跨国企业选择跨境电商主流模式提供基本依据。

2. 提高政策制定和更新的公开性

宝洁等公司认为，要提高"正面清单"制定和更新程序（清单产品增补和进入清单的申请方式）和调整频率的透明度。强生公司建议，为适应全球商务创新发展对清单归类不明确的创新和跨界产品要设立咨询平台，帮助跨国企业澄清有关政策界限。

3. 细化用足浦东化妆品进口优惠政策

跨国公司专家极大关注最近出台的浦东新区化妆品进口备案制政策。[①] 强生等公司建议，应根据这个"决定"精神，加快出台"进口非特殊用途化妆品备案"管理细则，推动化妆品市场准入制度改革，实现线上线下同步，为跨境电商和自贸区发展争取新的机遇。同时，要探索推广这个"决定"的可能性；在实施"正面清单"和"通关单"等"新政"政策上，上海要有所创新突破，形成比其他口岸更便利的通关环境。

4. 完善具体运作办法和操作流程

联邦快递等物流企业建议，完善跨境电商公共服务平台建设；探索大类备案的通关方式，适应电商进出口物品"种类多、更新快"的特点，并建议尝试跨境电商海外物品退货中就近（如香港）退回办法，减少向原发货地退回数量，降低物流成本。雅诗兰黛、美赞臣等企业建议探索化妆品、保健品和奶粉等物品进口中，把境外政府和第三方机构的验证充当"通关单"部分功能的可行性。

[①] 2016 年 5 月 5 日《国务院关于在上海市浦东新区暂时调整有关行政法规和国务院文件规定的行政审批等事项的决定》（国发〔2016〕24 号），进口（非特殊）化妆品由审批制改为备案制管理。

对接国际贸易新规则，加快自贸试验区改革实践

周师迅　张明海

上海市人民政府发展研究中心信息处

1. 自贸试验区面临的四大问题

目前，四大自贸试验区改革开放成绩显著，但出现了四个问题。

（1）普遍存在"外冷内热"现象。

自上海自贸试验区设立以来，国内媒体及学术界报道和研究层出不穷，而国外对中国自贸试验区的学术研究极少，仅有的一些论文，作者多为中国学者或在中国任教的外国学者。在具体业务上，商务部数据显示，2015 年 1—9 月，广东、天津、福建自贸试验区新设企业 4.5 万家，其中外资企业 4639 家，仅占约 10%。根据 4 个自贸试验区的公开数据计算，开设较早的上海自贸试验区运行两年来新设外企数量约占新设企业总数的 20%。截至 2015 年 10 月底，天津新设外企数量占比约为 4.4%，广东新设外企数量占比约为 5.0%，福建挂牌 7 个月新设外企数量占比约为 7.1%。同时，在改革措施上，自贸试验区在着眼于对外开放制度创新同时，也承担着转变政府职能等对内改革任务，而现在出台政策更多地在于后者。

（2）缺少直接开展试验的权力。

自贸试验区方案中列出的许多改革试验项目，在实际操作中还必须得到有关部委批复才可落地，自贸试验区自身没有直接试验的权力。例如，在天津自贸试验区，虽然国务院提出了要"积极发展跨境电子商务"，但由于海关系统未能与电商平台对接，仍无法注册开展跨境电商业务；甚至在天津列入进口跨境电商试点城市后，也不能开展这些业务。再如，上海自贸区总体方案提出"研究完善适应境外股权投资和离岸业务发展的税收政策"，上海自贸区管委会已就此和中央财税部门进行了深入研究，但迄今为止尚无方案出台。

（3）改革政策便利程度不高。

由于总体监管体制机制没有优化，一些改革政策便利程度不高。例如，上海

自贸试验区在具体实施启运港退税中，有关部门仍对企业管得过细，对这项业务的铺开形成了一定限制（如试点启运港退税的船舶，在运输途中不能挂靠，目的地只能是上海洋山港，外高桥港区不行），严重影响了这些改革的实际效果。再如天津自贸试验区在保税商品展示交易实践中，现在要求展示过程中企业用现金缴纳100%的税款担保，使得很多商品事实上变成了完税展示，使本来可以减少流通环节的现金流的保税展示交易失去了制度创新的意义。

（4）金融改革具体细则出台缓慢。

四大自贸试验区金融改革是对接高水平国际贸易规则的重要内容，但是"金融改革方案"实施细则没有出台，金融改革的实质性进展很少，很多业务其实没有能正常展开。例如，天津自贸试验区"金改30条"出台后，媒体报道了渤海钢铁集团国际贸易有限公司通过中信银行实现天津自贸试验区内开展首笔跨境直贷业务。而实际上因为细则没有出来，这项业务并未完成。同时，自贸试验区也不能对"金融改革方案"的"进一步提高对外放款比例"等提法决定具体的比例数。福建自贸试验区，在金融和医疗领域开放上试验区总体方案中的14项对台开放措施也未落地。

2. 自贸试验区困境的原因

自贸试验区出现上述四个问题，原因在两个方面：

（1）自贸试验的承担任务过多。

世界上的主权国家境内的自贸区（FTZ）有一套典型的运行规则，比如贸易自由、金融自由等。由此，内企怀着进驻开发区可能享受优惠税收等不切实际的幻想，"一厢情愿"非常热心，而很多外企并不理解中国的自贸试验区究竟想要做什么，加上天津等自贸试验区至今都没有颁布总体方案以及针对外资的负面清单等重要文件的官方统一英文版，致使许多外资持续保持观望态度，形成了"外冷内热"的困局。

（2）国家有关部委的权力下放没有到位。

自贸试验区运行以来，中央高度重视，地方政府也有先行先试的诉求。但中央部委权力下放没有到位，表现如下：一是自贸试验区的许多改革与相关部委原有的许多规定相左；改革涉及权力的减法，也有一定的风险。面对日益严格的干部追责制度，不少部门在批复改革方案时效率低下甚至不予批复。二是不同部委缺少协调，例如在探索启运港退税上，虽然海关表示可以有效监管，但是财税部门认为海关监管不住，存在税收流失风险，缺少有效沟通协调，放缓了向自贸试验区的放权。三是再加上一些重大事故的影响，例如在天津港，"8.12"爆炸事故处理一批干部之后，原来的海关等自贸试验区改革也收紧了改革步伐。所有这些都严重影响了自贸试验区改革开放的有效推进。

3. 对策建议

为完善自贸试验区的改革实践，提出以下四个建议：

（1）坚持尝试国际贸易新规则的基础。

依托自贸试验区推进政府职能转变非常重要，但自贸试验区仍然要聚焦对接国际高标准贸易规则这一目标，要加强自贸试验区的扩大开放，勇于试验国际贸易新规则。自贸试验区要积极引入和提前试验国际贸易新规则。具体地说，自贸试验区目前可以围绕 TPP，探索和尝试国企公平竞争、知识产权保护等国际贸易新环境和新规则。同时加强自贸试验区相关文件政策的标准翻译工作，加强国际宣传，加强自贸区对外资的吸引力制度设计和对外创新政策落地、改变目前自贸试验区"内热外冷"的局面。

（2）建立鼓励改革的风险激励机制。

充分认识到自贸试验区改革对部门权力的影响，认识到改革存在的风险。由此，要建立干部改革激励机制，加强对改革出成果的干部进行奖励，对有突出贡献的部门和干部予以物质奖励，或者在提拔任用时优先考虑。同时，要形成合理的风险保护机制，部委不应动不动就将自贸试验区的创新"一棍子打死"，不要对改革试出风险的干部简单"打板子"，要允许合理试错。自贸试验区的风险不应该被人为夸大，要把关注点放在试验遇到风险后怎样应对上来，探索应对出错的机制。

（3）加强自贸试验区改革的协调。

在国家层面建立统一的领导机构，协调相关部委对四大自贸试验区改革提供支持和服务，形成自贸试验区积极对接高水平国际贸易标准和惯例的基础。同时，要加强对国际贸易新规则的研究和培训，加强国内 FTZ 和国家间自贸区（FTA）对接。

（4）加快落实自贸试验区金融改革。

在自贸试验区发展中，对内不能形成税收的洼地，对外也不能形成税收高地。根据国际惯例，适当放开对外资的税收优惠，出台离岸业务的所得税税率优惠政策，进一步扩大国际航运保险税收优惠范围，探索有吸引力的离岸保险税制。要依托创新和企业"走出去"，进一步优化负面清单，加快金融改革、投资贸易便利化改革政策落地，特别是要加快落实离岸金融改革措施，增强国际竞争力。

以韩国为标杆，促进上海国际贸易单一窗口发展

周师迅　姚　治

上海市人民政府发展研究中心信息处

1. 选择韩国 UNI-PASS 系统作为标杆的理由

经多维度对比韩国和新加坡国际贸易单一窗口建设后发现，韩国更适合成为我国单一窗口对标学习的典范。

（1）韩国通关环境世界第一，单一窗口已在 8 国推广。

韩国通过集成海关电子通关系统 UNI-PASS，向用户提供单一登录窗口，实现一站式通关服务。在单一窗口的推动下，韩国成为世界海关组织（WCO）成员国中通关最快的国家之一，多次荣获世界银行通关环境评价第一名。单一窗口作为韩国电子政务实践最佳案例[①]已在多米尼加、哈萨克斯坦等 8 国推广使用，并有扩大之势。

（2）韩国贸易体量更大，是我国第三大贸易伙伴国。

据 WTO 统计，2014 年韩国贸易约相当于 1.415 个新加坡的贸易规模。韩国是全球三大经济体的重要贸易伙伴，近年来一直是中国第三大贸易伙伴，中国则是韩国最大贸易伙伴。刚生效的中韩自贸协定将进一步促进中韩双边贸易。

（3）韩国对外贸易结构与我国更为相似。

新加坡转口贸易与本国实际对外贸易之比从 1999 年 68.8% 跃升为 2014 年 99.7%，其转口贸易占新加坡对外贸易很大比重。而韩、中均为贸易顺差国家，且出口、进口贸易之比都在 1.06—1.20 区间内波动，韩国的贸易结构比新加坡更接近于我国。

---

① 韩国是全球领先的电子政务发展国家，其电子政务发展指数 EGDI 于 2010、2012、2014 年连续三次排名世界第一。

2. 韩国单一窗口的运行模式

（1）UNI-PASS 建设背景与系统架构。

韩国单一窗口项目起源于贸易量迅速增长对贸易自动化的客观需求。韩国海关于 1992 年推出基于电子数据交换（EDI）通关系统，2005 年正式引入单一窗口 UNI-PASS 系统。此后 UNI-PASS 不断发展完善，增加了空运货管 RFID 技术、一体化风险管理、经认证的经营者（AEO）管理等功能[①]，参与机构数量也不断增长：2005 年至 2011 年从 8 家增加到 33 家。[②]

UNI-PASS 系统采用的是 WCO 数据模型等国际标准，以及开放性技术标准，以便于对接国际单一窗口。该系统主要由互联网通关门户和业务操作系统两部分构成（如图 1）。前者向用户提供一个登录窗口，完成注册申请和认证、上传通报关申请及相关文件，并反馈通关结果信息；后者主要由征税、退税、场地监控等业务流程组件构成，是自动化海关监管的最基本模块。业务服务控制（BCS）、一体化人力资源管理（i-HRM）、客户知识管理（CKM）、客户关系管理（CRM）、海关数据仓库（CDW）和企业架构（EA）六大系统对 UNI-PASS 形成了有效支撑。

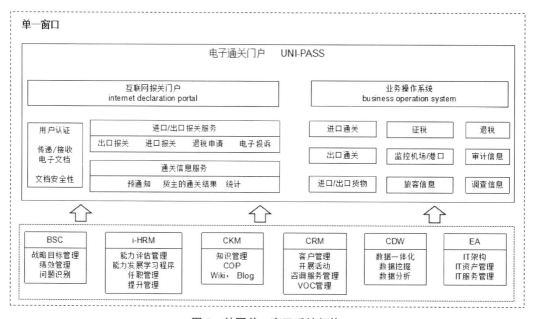

图 1　韩国单一窗口系统架构

---

① 参见 Korea Customs e-Clearance System（2014）。
② 参见 Republic of Korea Single Window Case（2010）。

（2）基本服务功能。

除提供一站式无纸化服务外，UNI-PASS 有两项基本服务功能：一是实时货物跟踪服务，通过使用电子舱单和仓库库存管理、运输管理与跟踪、实时货物处理状态报告等手段，实现对货物全程供应链管理。二是"提前乘客信息系统"（APIS），通过提供所有乘客和机组人员的预到达信息、出发舱单数据，让海关能在飞机到达前结合移民局和其他政府部门的数据库对入境人员进行风险分析，有效控制高风险乘客，保卫国家安全，同时给予低风险乘客快速通过。

（3）运行模式。

UNI-PASS 系统的开发、运行、维护由非营利组织——海关单一窗口国际服务机构（CUPIA）负责。经过 10 年发展，CUPIA 已成长为国内、国际电子通关方面的专业机构，能够向国外海关提供包括单一窗口、海关数据仓库和风险管理在内的个性化解决方案。

韩国 UNI-PASS 系统建设获得了政府预算支持，由韩国海关拨款资助，用户免费使用。

3. 韩国单一窗口对上海的经验借鉴

上海以电子口岸平台为依托，2014 年首先在洋山保税港区试点单一窗口，2015 年 6 月正式上线单一窗口 1.0 版，试点范围扩展到整个上海港区，2015 年底又推出单一窗口 2.0 版。单一窗口实施一年来，在优化监管作业流程、提高口岸通行效率、降低企业经营成本方面取得了明显效果。对标韩国，上海单一窗口可从以下方面完善提高。

（1）扩增单一窗口参与机构类型，提高口岸服务效率。

韩国政府不断推动、吸引更多机构加入单一窗口，既有口岸管理相关的政府机构，又有承担需求验证任务的非政府机构。2009 年，韩国政府要求食品和药品管理局、国家渔产品质量检查服务局等 4 家政府机构加入，还推动制药贸易商协会、医学设备行业协会、动物健康产品协会等 13 家私有化机构加入。相比于上海单一窗口 17 家参与机构中 15 家政府机构、2 家大型国企的构成，韩国单一窗口更能充分发挥非政府组织的作用，提高口岸服务效率。建议上海扩增单一窗口参与机构类型，加强不同行业对单一窗口的支持，更大范围地加强互联互通，提高口岸效率。

（2）注入进出口舱单传输功能，加强供应链全程管理，提高口岸安全性。

进出口舱单是记录进出口货物流动的基础数据，是海关实施监管的有效依据。韩国单一窗口通过电子舱单有效实现了对货物全程供应链管理。目前，中国电子口岸已建立了海运、空运运输方式下的舱单数据传输体系，但上海单一窗口目前尚不具备进出口舱单传输功能。建议在上海单一窗口中增加电子舱单传输，让用户可以了解到完整的物流与通关信息，实现货物实时追溯和物流透明化管理，加强供应链上各环节的有效监管，降低贸易风险和执法风险，提高口岸管理的安全性。

（3）着力推进旅客申报功能，实现客运单一窗口服务。

旅客申报是上海单一窗口 2.0 版提出的拓展应用领域之一，但至今仍未实现。在上海邮轮母港经济快速发展和迪士尼乐园对外开放的推动下，上海出入境旅客数量将会大幅增长。完善旅客申报服务不仅是落实 2.0 版的规划方案，更是在客流量大幅增加的同时加快旅客进出境速度的客观需求。可考虑借鉴韩国单一窗口的旅客申报功能，在单一窗口中集成一个乘客信息预报系统，通过与民航系统、邮轮公司的乘客数据共享或调用，让海关能够提前获取出入境乘客的个人信息并进行风险分析，提前做好高、低风险乘客的甄别，快速放行低风险乘客，有效控制高风险乘客。

（4）加强后端执法部门的互联互通，推进"三互"人通关的落实。

上海单一窗口为企业提供了良好的前端平台，企业可以通过单一入口提交标准化的信息和单证，减少重复输入的无效劳动，降低运作成本。然而，由于单一窗口推出时间不长，在数据转入到各执法部门的业务平台后，由于不同部门之间缺少有效的互联互通机制，使一些环节不能有效实现共同执法，难以更进一步地便利企业。以海关、检验检疫"一次申报、一次查验、一次放行"为例，现有系统不能有效建立起口岸执法部门之间的联合执法机制，仍旧存在多次查验、多次放行的情况。建议在单一窗口中建立执法部门之间的信息互换机制，如预约查验场地、查验时间，便于执法部门的联合执法，切实便利企业，促进货物快速通关。

（5）采用统一的数据标准，进一步简化申报数据。

与韩国一样，上海也非常注重数据的国际标准化问题，采用了 WCO 数据模型。上海作为国内单一窗口建设的领航者，还可以向韩国学习简化单一窗口申报数据，形成统一的单一窗口数据标准，并复制推广到其他省、市，以便与有关省市单一窗口对接，进一步实现全国单一窗口。

提升自贸区贸易监管水平

周师迅　谭　旻

上海市人民政府发展研究中心信息处

1. 自贸区存在虚假贸易情况

上海市浦东新区人民检察院发布的 2014 和 2015 年度《自贸试验区刑事检察白皮书》显示，自贸区犯罪具有"自贸"特质，一些不法分子为牟取非法利益，假借转口贸易等跨境贸易活动的环节复杂、真假难辨、境外取证难及境内外经贸制度的差异等因素，故意虚构跨境贸易项目，实施逃汇、信用证诈骗、骗取出口退税等犯罪行为。根据两年的数据来看，上海自贸区内犯罪数量及罪名分布情况与自贸区成立之前相比，并没有发生实质性变化。但随着自贸区内各项措施纷纷落地，区内企业对政策越来越了解的情况下，风险系数将逐步提升，监管要求只升不降。

当前，上海自贸区虚假贸易主要采取两种形式。一是企业利用保税区、出口加工区等境内关外的贸易便利，通过所谓的"保税区一日游"[①]，实现境内购汇、境外结汇套利，例如，上海外高桥保税区就存在此类行为；二是企业利用假单据套利[②]，通过银行或其他渠道实现跨境套利。、

2. 自贸区存在虚假贸易的原因分析

（1）自贸区高度开放为虚假贸易提供了更便捷的条件。

为加快推进自贸区建设，尤其是促进跨境贸易发展，上海自贸区制定并实行了有关外汇汇率、外贸税率等一系列优惠政策，使跨境贸易成本降低、便捷高效；尤其以资本项目可兑换和金融服务业开放为目标的金融创新制度的确立，更加便利了与自贸区有关的融资租赁业务的发展，为虚假贸易提供了可乘之机。例

---

① 境内企业与境外关联企业构造两笔金额相同、方向相反的国际贸易，构成转口贸易。

② 境内外双方签订虚假购销合同，制造虚假发票、货运单据等。

如，自贸区金融操作细则落地以来，银行境外借款业务发展迅猛，一方面境外融资利率较低，另一方面与常规的"内保外贷"相比，境外融资取消了对境内企业的身份限制。相比于保税区和其他自贸区，上海自贸区高标准的建设和改革为虚假贸易提供了更开放、更便利的条件，同时对金融系统的风险管理带来更多挑战，提出更高要求。

（2）在岸市场和离岸市场汇差的出现为虚假贸易提供了新的平台。

自贸区的人民币离岸市场使境内形成汇率双轨制[1]，人民币内外价格差异驱使一些企业借道自贸区进行虚假贸易。

2015年以来，离岸和在岸市场人民币汇差不断扩大，以套利为目的的虚假贸易量明显增加。根据海关总署资料，我国2015年12月出口同比下降1.4%，优于预期及11月表现。其中，内地对香港出口同比上涨10.8%，总值高达460亿美元；内地从香港进口飙升65%，总值达21.6亿美元。在海关出口先导指数、波罗的海指数均显示出外贸疲软的情况下，外贸数据改善可能部分来源于虚假贸易。

3. 提升自贸区贸易监管水平的对策建议

（1）细化分账核算管理方法，推进监管制度保障。

自贸区实施分账核算系统，是防范热钱借自贸区流入境内的有效监管措施，也是虚假贸易没有在自贸区集中爆发的原因所在，但在标准完善、系统测试、数据监测、风险控制等方面仍需不断细化落实，应加快出台相关细则，以更好地防范虚假贸易、热钱套利等金融风险，为自贸区监管提供制度保障。

（2）落实国家外管局政策，打通各环节监管链条。

虚假贸易帮助企业"空手套白狼"，给商业银行带来巨额利润，给当地政府增加名义GDP，各方诉求不同却形成了链条。上海自贸区在建设过程中应加强对链条上三个环节的有效监管，遏制虚假贸易。一是加强企业分类管理。加大对贸易收支异常企业，特别是远期贸易融资规模异常增长且具有典型套利交易特征企业的监测核查力度，按货物贸易外汇管理规定进行分类管理，对列为B类或C类企业予以重点监管。二是继续督促银行完善贸易融资真实性、合规性审核。积

---

[1] 香港离岸市场和大陆在岸市场广度和深度完全不同，离岸人民币资金池相较于在岸市场规模更小，流动性严重不足，加之国际金融市场的影响，使离岸市场的汇率浮动较大。相反，在岸汇率受到中间价上下2%范围的限制，投资者身份不同使其对于风险偏好、同样的经济状况及政策的解读和反应，都有所差异，因此形成了在岸市场和离岸市场不同的汇率价格。

极支持实体经济真实贸易融资需求，防止企业虚构贸易背景套取银行融资。鼓励银行加强内控督导，及时报告可疑交易，严禁变通执行或协助规避外汇管理规定。三是剥离外贸增长硬性考核指标，完善政府监管职能。虚假贸易存在着制度性根源，考核各级政府政绩的硬性指标应从预先设定外贸增长目标切实转为完善政府事中事后监管职能。但随着自贸区改革创新中新措施不断落地，给予企业方便的同时要充分考虑潜在风险，防范于未然。①

（3）利用信息技术平台，实现海关精准监管。

海关总署 2016 年 3 月起在全国海关开展打击走私"国门利剑 2016"联合专项行动，打击虚假贸易违法行为被列为重点之一。针对上海自贸区虚假贸易的风险态势及监管现状，上海海关可依托自贸区信息共享平台，通过大数据分析提高监管精准度，探索对低资信企业实行系统性的风险管控措施。同时，在管理方式上可依托自由贸易账户管理系统，采用风险转换因子等现代管理手段，对风险进行 24 小时逐笔实时监测，确保金融安全。

（4）采取系统集成方式，全方位提升监管实效。

改变过去各部门碎片化管理方式，推进上海海关、航运、金融等部门展开协作，在政策、数据及信息共享等方面加强沟通，进行系统集成监管，建立多形式、多层次、多渠道的协调机制、联络机制和会议制度，定期开展信息、数据交换，加强物流与资金流的匹配程度，提高贸易信贷调查数据质量和调查效率，联合打击虚假贸易，共同维护自贸区经贸秩序和金融安全，全方位提升监管实效。

---

① 例如，从虚假贸易爆发的时间节点上看，2015 年"8·11"汇改后，境内外汇差较大，以套利为目的的虚假贸易上升。

Shanghai Outbound Investment—Review and Outlook (2015—2016)

Shanghai Municipal Commission of Commerce
Ernst & Young (China) Advisory Limited

Summary

With accelerating paces of the "go-out" strategy, China's outbound direct investment (ODI) has experienced rapid growth in recent years, and the investment subjects and paths are increasingly diversified. According to the statistics from the Ministry of Commerce, China's non-financial ODI recorded a historical high of 118.02 billion US dollars[①] in 2015, a 14.7% growth over the previous year. It is the 13th consecutive year that witnesses an ODI growth of the country. The large-scale entry of Chinese capital in international arena has also become an impressive phenomenon in global investment markets.

With the promotion of the "The Belt and Road" (the Silk Road Economic Belt and the 21st Century Maritime Silk Road) strategy and the policy of international cooperation in production capacity as well as advancement and implementation of "Made in China 2025" and other national strategies, investment cooperation along the Belt and Road focused on infrastructure construction and production capacity optimization is on the rise. New historical opportunities are approaching for extending the international influence of "Made in China".

As one of the global leaders of professional services, EY is honored to prepare the Shanghai Outbound Investment Annual Report under the patronage of Shanghai Municipal Commission of Commerce for 2015 and 2016. In the preparation of

---

[①] Unless indicated otherwise, all opinions and statistics in this article come from the *Report on Development of Outbound Investment and Economic Cooperation of Enterprises in Shanghai (2015)* and the *Report on Development of Outbound Investment and Economic Cooperation of Enterprises in Shanghai (2016)* by Shanghai Municipal Commission of Commerce.

the reports, we have gained deep understanding of the status quo of the outbound investment of China, particularly of Shanghai, in recent years and gained insights into the commonly adopted models and the potential risks enterprises may encounter in their efforts to explore the international market. On the basis of our researches, analyses, interviews and surveys over the past two years, this article will summarize and discuss the outbound investment of China and Shanghai in recent years from the following aspects to serve as an additional resource for investors' reference and a better support for the outbound investment initiatives by Shanghai investors:

(1) Current situation and future trends of outbound investment and economic cooperation of China and Shanghai: portrays the trends of outbound investment of China and Shanghai in recent years via the big data.

(2) Policies of China and Shanghai on outbound investment: provides an overview of the policies of China and Shanghai on outbound investment and economic cooperation and their public service systems.

(3) Analysis of the questionnaire survey results of outbound investment and economic cooperation of Shanghai's enterprises: reveals key information on investment subjects, investment areas, investment risks through research and analysis.

(4) Shanghai corporate investors' approaches to "going out" and case studies: summarizes the *modus oprandi* of "going out" of Shanghai's enterprises and presents different case studies based on the variances in the driving factors of economic cooperation and strategic positioning for outbound investment, with a particular focus on the analysis of the equity fund investment approach.

(5) Assessment of risks in outbound investment and economic cooperation and countermeasure suggestions: summarizes six major risks in outbound investment and economic cooperation confronting outbound investors based on the findings in questionnaires and interviews, and proposes suggestions to deal with different risks in terms of corporate risk prevention and countermeasure preparation.

(6) Effective post-investment integration as a plus to Chinese enterprises' success in overseas M&A: probes into the common challenges confronting enterprises in the process of post-deal integration and shares the best practice through survey of Shanghai's enterprises performing M&A overseas.

1. Current situation and future trends of outbound investment and economic cooperation of China and Shanghai

Driven by the demands of domestic industrial transformation and the "One Belt One Road" policy, an increasing number of Chinese enterprises are witnessing their role transition from global manufacturers to global investors. In 2014, China's actual total outbound investment exceeded its total use of foreign fund for the first time in history, which immediately caught the attention of the global investment market. According to the *Report on Development of Outbound Investment and Economic Cooperation of Enterprises in Shanghai*'s analysis for recent two consecutive years, the footprint of Chinese investors has covered 156 countries and regions around the world. With the transformation and upgrade of the Chinese economy and the growth and expansion of Chinese enterprises, the target of investment has gradually evolved from an early stage featured by obtaining production factors such as resources to obtaining advanced technology and brands as a means to strengthening the competitiveness of enterprises in an international environment and satisfying the growing customer demands at home. Driven by this motive, the destinations of outbound investment are becoming increasingly diversified, and the footprint of Chinese enterprises have spread from resource-based countries and regions in Asia, Africa and Latin America to developed countries in Europe, North America and other areas. In addition to traditional businesses, real estate industry and manufacturing industry, the proportion and growth rate of investments in telecommunication, media and entertainment, automotive and transportation and financial service industries also embodies the diversity and high-end orientation of China's outbound investment.

As a window of opening up to the outside world for China, Shanghai has become a major destination for China's inward foreign investment as well as a cradle for the country's outbound investment thanks to its advantageous geological position and its strategic positioning as "four centers" (namely, international economic center, international financial center, international shipping center, and international trade center). Shanghai's actual outbound investment volume has maintained continuous growth in the past two years. In 2015, the volume reached 16.636 billion US dollars, a growth of 382% over the previous year, and accounted for more than 14% of national outbound investment over the same period, making Shanghai rank the

| 提升投资贸易便利化水平，构建开放型经济新体制

first in the country. In terms of total investment, the investment made by private enterprises as a percentage of overall investment has maintained an upward trend and become the absolute main force of outbound investment. Private equity funds have been providing guidance and capital support for Shanghai's enterprises in their outbound investments, while the Free Trade Zone has become the preferred platform for enterprises in Shanghai and other provinces and municipalities to go out. As to investment destinations and key industries, the regional layout of outbound investment by Shanghai's enterprises is more diversified, with their investment footprint covering developed countries and regions in North America, the Oceania, Europe and other developed countries and regions. Thanks to the national leadership to build "One Belt One Road", Singapore, Indonesia, Kazakhstan, Thailand and other countries and regions along "One Belt One Road" have also become hot spots favored by Chinese investors. According to the *Report on Development of Outbound Investment and Economic Cooperation of Enterprises in Shanghai*'s analysis, main industries of outbound investment by Shanghai's enterprises include leasing and business services, real estate, wholesale and retail, information transmission, software and IT services.

2. China and Shanghai's outbound investment policies

To promote the implementation of the "go out" strategy, the Chinese government has been streamlining administration and delegating power to the lower levels to stimulate outbound investment. The government is also improving the support system for outbound investment in multiple aspects. China's policies on outbound investment cooperation include promoting the construction of "The Belt and Road", development of resources, industrial and financial cooperation, stimulating domestic capital export, streamlining administration and delegating power to the lower levels, simplifying approval procedures, expanding financing channels, improving the service system, encouraging enterprises to go out, stimulating advancement of the manufacturing industry and the financial industry toward medium and high levels, and improving the service system supporting the outbound investment, including protection of rights and interests, promotion of investment, and risks precaution.

Table1 below lists some important policies in relation to outbound investment introduced by the Chinese government since April 2015.

Table 1

Date of issuance	Policy content	Significance
April 2015	The State Administration of Taxation issued the ten measures for serving "One Belt One Road" development strategy	The measures would give full play of the role of tax treaties as the legal basis of international tax relationship and tax cooperation, in order to enhance tax certainty, avoid double taxation, and defend the legal rights and interests of taxpayers
May 2015	The State Council issued "Made in China 2025" strategy	This is the first ten-year action plan for implementing the strategy of strengthening the country by developing the manufacturing industry, deploying a comprehensive promotion and implementation of the strategy
May 2015	The State Council issued the Guiding Opinions on Promoting Cooperation of International Production Capacity and Equipment Manufacturing	As a key guiding document for promoting cooperation of international production capacity and equipment manufacturing at present and for a fairly long time to come, the opinions put forward the guiding concept and basic principle, targets and tasks, policies and measures of promoting cooperation of international production capacity and equipment manufacturing
June 2015	The State Administration of Taxation issued Announcement No. 47 [2015] on Relevant Matters concerning Withholding of Enterprise Income Tax in the Payment of Interest by a Domestic Institution to an Overseas Branch of a Chinese Bank	The announcement reduced the tax burden on banks making outbound investments
August 2015	The Ministry of Commerce issued the Model Service Guidelines for Overseas Economic and Trade Cooperation Zones	The model guidelines would contribute to the construction of overseas economic and trade cooperation zones, stimulate expansion and development of the cooperation zones, and exert agglomeration effects of overseas industries and platform effects
October 2015	The National Development and Reform Commission (NDRC) issued the Action Plan on "One Belt One Road" Standardization and Communication (2015—2017)	To proactively adapt to the new normal of economic development, actively cultivate new advantages for international competition, adhere to the general requirements of "policy coordination, facilities connectivity, unimpeded trade, financial integration and people-to-people bonds", continuously strengthen multilateral cooperation on standardization and interconnectivity with countries along the Belt and Road, vigorously promote international recognition of Chinese standards, accelerate the globalization of standards, in order to serve the needs of "One Belt and One Road" in all aspects
April 2016	NDRC made Decision on Amending the Measures for the Administration of the Confirmation and Reporting of Overseas Investment Projects	• Cancelled the NDRC requirement of confirmation for projects with Chinese investment no less than 1 billion US dollars • Cancelled the requirement of NDRC confirmation comments for the review of the State Council for outbound investment projects with Chinese investment no less than 2 billion US dollars and involving sensitive countries and regions and industries • Streamlined government review and approval procedures and liberalized government restrictions

Source: government gazettes, compiled by EY.

At the same time, all levels of government in Shanghai are also effectively supporting enterprises to "go out" from various aspects, such as formulating the plans and concepts, creating favorable policies and environments, supporting market participants, and establishing service systems. In September 2015, an outbound investment service alliance was launched at Shanghai Free Trade Zone; in February 2016, the plan for the 13th Five-Year Period issued by the Development and Reform Commission of Shanghai Municipal Government specified that Shanghai would explore new space for "going out" and play an indispensable role in the national strategy of "One Belt One Road" during the 13th Five-Year Period; Shanghai Municipal Commission of Commerce will pivot on the "going out" strategy to construct a comprehensive service system covering information service, investment promotion, talent training and risk control to provide a solid backing for enterprises to "go out".

3. Analysis of the questionnaire survey results of outbound investment and economic cooperation of Shanghai's enterprises

EY and Shanghai Municipal Commission of Commerce have carried out a questionnaire survey according to the *Report on Development of Outbound Investment and Economic Cooperation of Enterprises in Shanghai*'s analysis, targeting Shanghai's enterprises with ongoing outbound investment and economic cooperation activities or with the intent to carry out such activities and made a statistical analysis of the actual situation and the trend of development of major "going-out" enterprises in Shanghai.

According to the feedbacks of the questionnaire survey, private companies are taking a more active part in outbound investment and economic cooperation activities. According to the *Report on Development of Outbound Investment and Economic Cooperation of Enterprises in Shanghai*'s analysis, quite a number of investment companies in the city are actively participating in outbound investment activities. Apart from traditional industries such as manufacturing, commerce, construction and real estate, fields related to science and technology such as information transmission, software and IT services, scientific research and technical services are expected to play a more active role in the future. Most enterprises are cautiously optimistic about outbound investment and economic cooperation activities, and outbound M&A activities are expected to see a further growth in the future.

Main driving factors for outbound investment and economic cooperation include development of overseas markets, enhancement of brand influences, increase of competitiveness in domestic market, and development of both upstream and downstream along the value chain. The degree of globalization of Shanghai's enterprises needs to be improved, particularly in terms of international integration, international marketing capability, brand reputation and market share. It is a common view of Shanghai's enterprises that accurate globalization strategy and business judgment as well as an efficient team overseas are the keys to successful outbound investment and cooperation. According to the survey results, respondent enterprises hold the view that there are three major risks in outbound investment and economic cooperation activities, namely political, economic and legal risks overseas. Outbound investors typically lack knowledge of overseas markets and are normally unfamiliar with the local legal and tax environments. In addition, the investors are also confronted with barriers in post-deal corporate culture integration.

4. Shanghai corporate investors' approaches to "going out" and case studies

In this section we have prepared some case studies based on public information and interviews with the management of enterprises and summarized the four main approaches of "going out" adopted by Shanghai's enterprises:

(1) The outbound investment approach of driving industrial upgrading and transformation through integration of the upper- and down-stream of the industrial chain and supply chain.

Enterprises are actively seeking world-class advanced technologies, striving to obtain proprietary intellectual properties (IPs) and acquire quality resources and brands from abroad, vigorously developing the upper- and down-stream of the industrial chain, working towards industrial upgrading and transformation, further enhancing their competitiveness in domestic and overseas markets, and addressing the demands in domestic and overseas markets.

Take the Bright Food Group as an example. At the early stage, the group was not fully aware of the investment environment overseas. However, as it learned to adopt discreet manners, handle publicity affairs with goodwill, objectively price the deal, seek government support and form alliances with M&A partners, the group has been making continuous progress in its overseas investments. In May 2012, the group announced a £1.2 billion purchase deal of 60% of shares of Vitamax Food, a UK company, which marks the largest overseas acquisition by the Chinese food industry.[①]

(2) The outbound investment approach of optimizing production layout, exploring overseas markets and transferring capacity surplus.

Under this approach, Shanghai's corporate investors are not only vigorously exploring overseas markets and transfering capacity surplus in the form of single proprietorship enterprise, joint venture or cooperative, but they are also actively optimizing their production layout overseas in concert with the international strategic planning to realize global sales and optimization of resource allocation via the acquisition of foreign technology, brands and channels.

The Shanghai Automotive Industry Corporation (SAIC) has taken full advantage of its overall competitive edge in the industrial chain and its leading position in domestic market to make further innovations and application to the domestic market via its independent research and development institutions on the basis of acquiring world-class technologies and core proprietary IPs. In addition, SAIC is actively exploring overseas sales channels for domestically established brands.[②]

(3) The approach of investment in overseas resources and infrastructure construction by utilizing advanced industry experience and project operation capabilities at home.

Under this approach, the outbound investor makes use of their mature industry experience and advanced management expertise to pursue investment and economic cooperation opportunities around the globe, pull the trigger for business and revenue growth, and explore overseas markets or resources while elevating their own brand influences.

Take Shanghai Construction Group (SCG) as an example. The group has successfully completed a number of landmark construction projects at home and abroad and established the "SCG brand" via undertaking building projects of local landmarks. The group now has obtained adequate knowledge of potential risks of overseas projects from abundant overseas projects experience and is capable of containing the risks through reasonable and effective risk management.[③]

① Source: "Top ten Chinese enterprises going out in 2015", ForbesChina, http://www.forbeschina.com/news/news.php?id=40149, 15 Jan 2015.

② Source: "SAIC Indonesia plant officially in operation", AutoChina, http://auto.china.com.cn/news/corp/20150202/648116.shtml.

③ Source: SCG overseas official site information, compiled by EY, http://www.cscgoversea.com/.

(4) The outbound investment approach of interactive industry development led by equity investment funds.

In recent years, most cross-border M&As of Chinese industry investors took domestic synergy as the departure point and aimed to bring home advanced technology and well-known brands from developed countries or to explore the upper- or down-stream industrial chain via M&A to increase their shares in their niche market at home. Departing from the needs of the domestic market, the number of cross-border M&A transactions with similar strategic intentions under the direction or with the participation of equity investment funds also displayed an upward trend over the past years. Equity investment funds, which have abundant investment and trading experience as well as technology and financial resources, are actively looking for overseas assets with "Chinese perspectives" that can bring about win-win outcomes with Chinese enterprises.

The *modus operandis* for equity investment funds to participate in overseas investment mainly include: Equity investment funds complete the acquisition independently or play a dominant role in the acquisition; Equity investment funds complete the acquisition in association with industry investors; Equity investment funds complete the acquisition with financial support from financial investment funds; Other special investment approaches. The second approach includes: equity investment funds team with Chinese enterprises to complete overseas M&A, and equity investment funds together with Chinese enterprises set up an acquisition fund for cross-border M&A purposes.

Chinese cross-border equity investment funds usually have the following characteristics:

• Efficient financing capability: equity investment funds raise capital from certain investment institutions or individuals privately, and are able to raise adequate funds for M&A transactions more effectively thanks to the resources of fund managers and flexible arrangement of financing structures.

• Considerable investment operation and management experience: in general, equity investment funds have considerable experience in industry analysis and valuation of targets as well as flexible negotiation skills, and play an active role in selecting appropriate targets and facilitating the transaction.

• Sensitivity in commercial, cultural and political matters: equity investment funds serve as professional investment agencies and directly contact investment targets during M&A transactions. They are able to largely reduce the concerns from various aspects by virtue of an active attitude and a professional position, and obtain approval of local governments and support from the shareholders and management of M&A targets.

Since 2014, domestic equity investment funds have presented more clearly defined strategic goals and more independent operation models. It is not unusual for equity investment funds to complete overseas M&A transactions independently, or play a dominant role in such transactions, or team with other Chinese enterprises in such transactions. Equity investment funds used to play a single role of financial investors in earlier years, however, the strategic intents of Chinese funded cross-border M&A equity funds are becoming increasingly prominent. For instance, in July 2014, Hony Capital purchased UK leisure food and beverage company Pizza Express[1], and CITIC Capital acquired US dental instrument and service company DDS Lab.[2] In July 2015, Bohai Harvest and AVIC Automobile jointly acquired US company Henniges Automotive,[3] China Minsheng Investment Group acquired Sirius International Insurance Group,[4] and Uphill Investment acquired ISSI.[5]

As the national financial center, Shanghai is home to numerous professional service organizations and international talents. The city offers an institutional innovation platform via the Free Trade Zone as well high administrative efficiency. Thanks to Shanghai, Chinese equity investment funds and Chinese companies have made remarkable achievements in cross-border M&A. Technology/media/telecommunication (TMT), auto manufacturing, real estate, wholesale and retail, biological medicine industries are becoming popular industries for outbound investment by equity investment funds.

5. Assessment of risks in outbound investment and economic cooperation and countermeasure suggestions

As mentioned in the analysis of questionnaire survey results, enterprises "going

---

[1] Source: "Nearly 10 billion acquisition of British pizza company made by Hony Capital", Sina Finance, http://finance.sina.com.cn/chanjing/gsnews/20140714/015919690126.shtml.

[2] Source: "CITIC Capital announced the completion of the acquisition of US dental equipment company DDS Lab", Ceweekly, http://www.ceweekly.cn/2014/0702/86040.shtml.

[3] Source: "Li Xiangsheng reveals the secret of the acquisition of Henniges Automotive", Morningwhistle, http://www.morningwhistle.com/website/news/5/46923.html?bsh_bid=955468482.

[4] Source: "CMIG invested RMB 14 billion in the acquisition of US reinsurance group Sirius", Guancha Syndicate, http://www.guancha.cn/economy/2015_08_17_330910.shtml.

[5] Source: "Uphill Investment beated Cypress, the successful acquisition of ISSI", Laoyaoba, http://toutiao.com/a4639287601/.

out" are faced with many risks in practice. We have summarized the six major risks in outbound investment as follows, and made suggestions on dealing with such risks from the perspectives of risk prevention and counter-measure preparation by such enterprises.

(1) Political risks of host countries: establish a risk prevention and emergency response mechanism, take corporate social responsibilities, balance the interest of all parties, and utilize insurance tools for overseas assets.

(2) Lack of clear strategic positioning: conduct robust market survey of the industry, strengthen technology and brand development, build on synergy effects, and look for strategic cooperation alliances.

(3) Lack of awareness and capability for risk prevention: improve management system for internal control, emphasize pre-investment due diligence, make use of commercial insurance as appropriate, and actively manage exchange risks.

(4) Lack of ability and credibility for cross-cultural integration: formulate detailed integration plans, respect local culture and custom, enhance transparency of corporate information, and strengthen effective communication and publicity.

(5) Lack of international talents: respect local labor environment, establish good employer brands, adjust global talent allocation, and optimize the incentive mechanism for talents.

(6) Legal risks, tax risks and other institutional risks: observe the laws and regulations of host countries, play by international rules, strengthen communication with government agencies, and improve tax planning for financing activities.

6. Effective post-investment integration as a plus to Chinese enterprises' success in overseas M&A

Post-M&A integration is a key factor for successful cross-border M&As. Successful integration will enable full utilization of resources of both the buyers and the acquired companies, realize synergy of businesses and improved operations of both parties, and maximize both enterprise value and shareholder value. Similarly, we have probed into post-investment integration based on the questionnaire survey results and summarized a series of targeted countermeasures:

(1) Establish effective corporate governance structure to prevent and control risks: delineate of the power of stakeholders of acquired companies and clearly define the power operation mechanism as an important prerequisite to integration of the

organization and management of acquired companies.

(2) Incentivize core teams to ensure business stability and personnel consistency: for buyers, understanding the risks of losing core members and key terms for them to stay are fundamental to retaining and motivating them.

(3) Clearly define financial management requirements, and obtain relevant information in a timely manner: enterprises with successful integration experience would normally evaluate and analyze the financial management systems of both parties to set specific financial management requirements for the acquired companies, and to align the financial management system of acquired companies with the buyers' strategic targets and management requirements.

(4) Emphasize communication and cultural integration, and gradually realize team integration: Chinese enterprises with successful overseas M&A experience would establish an effective mechanism for internal and external communication, carefully balance the relationship among stakeholders with different cultural backgrounds, and gradually realize team integration.

(5) Prudently promote business coordination to gradually obtain synergy effects: form synergy in post-M&A integration through integration of brand marketing, client resources, sales channels and network, purchase models, R&D systems etc. to enhance the core competitive advantages of both parties.

(6) Accelerate cultivation of Chinese international talents and expand the expatriate talent pool: international talents are a crucial guarantee to support cross-border operations of enterprises. Successful enterprises would place great emphasis on cultivation of international talents from within, expansion of the expatriate talent pool, and more effective management of expatriate staff.

Conclusion

Against the tide of globalization 4.0,Chinese enterprises adhering to the development principle of optimizing industry layout and economic transformation and upgrading will definitely play a more active role in overseas investment and economic cooperation activities. Looking to the future, outbound investment of enterprises in China and Shanghai will maintain a strong upward momentum. Further transformation of the Chinese economy include efforts to build Shanghai into a global scientific innovation center, which will encourage more Shanghai's enterprises to make investment in high technology, high-end manufacturing, high-end services and other upper-stream areas of the industrial chain. At the same time, the consumer demand-oriented global industry integration on the basis of domestic market demands will become an important direction for future investment and economic cooperation of Shanghai's enterprises. Following the guidance of the strategic policy of "One Belt One Road", outbound investments in areas such as infrastructure construction and high-end manufacturing can expect good opportunities to transfer excess capacities to countries along the Belt and Road. For such an international financial center as Shanghai, it will remain an essential approach for its investors to promote diversified investment with the help of financial capital, which will facilitate the Shanghai capital to go global and reshape the world economy landscape.

It can be foreseen that the road for Shanghai's enterprises to "go out" will become smoother with continuous introduction and improvement of supporting policies and services of the government for outbound investors, with the experience and guidance of professional service organizations on the market in the field outbound investment and economic cooperation, as well as with their own experience of overseas investment. At the same time, we are delighted to see during the preparation of the reports that most "going-out" enterprises are able to proactively and sufficiently assess the potential issues and risks they might encounter in the course of overseas investment and economic cooperation, and collaborate with the government and service organizations on the market to actively seek solutions.

The ever-changing international market is full of opportunities and risks. According to the *Report on Development of Outbound Investment and Economic Cooperation of Enterprises in Shanghai*'s analysis, it is now been aware that an absolute majority of Chinese enterprises are in a primitive stage of globalization, with many enterprises still lacking in long-term strategic planning and risk awareness. Furthermore, they lack adequate understanding of the investment and cultural environment of the host country, and also overseas investment management experience and international talents. We sincerely hope more and more enterprises would "go out" successfully with strategic planning and appropriate risk control in the process of acquiring advanced technologies to promote the upgrading of industrial chain, and contribute to China's great economic transformation.

Mumbai-Shanghai Dialogue: Vision for Multi-modal Sister City Partnership

Madhav Sharma

Head-Greater China and Chief Representative，Confederation of Indian Industry (Shanghai Representative Office)

1. Introduction

China and India are two Asian giants and close neighbors as well as the fastest-growing large economies of the world. The forthcoming Asian century is founded upon the success of the two countries in their common endeavor to address developmental challenges. With the personal attention of President Xi Jinping and Prime Minister Narendra Modi to enhancing and deepening the bilateral engagement, new dimensions of cooperation and convergence are rapidly emerging.

A key component of the bilateral engagement outlined during President Xi's landmark visit to India in September 2014 was creation of sister-city relationships between like cities of the two countries. The sister-city relationships inked during the visit were Mumbai-Shanghai and Ahmedabad-Guangzhou, as well as the sister state/province relationship between Gujarat and Guangdong. Prime Minister Modi's visit to China in May 2015 further cemented this engagement by establishing the state/provincial leaders' forum to intensify relations at the sub-regional level. Bilateral visits of state/provincial leaders to each other's countries have become more frequent as opportunities are explored.

Within this overall framework, the sister-city relationship of Mumbai and Shanghai is of special significance and can emerge as a key growth driver of the overall bilateral engagement.

Mumbai and Shanghai are the vibrant nerve-centers of two of the largest global economies. Both enjoy rich commercial histories, progressive perspectives, wide spectrum of industries, and robust infrastructure, and both are the primary financial hubs of their nations. Combining financial leadership with strong external orientation, the two massive urban centers are home to the largest ports in their countries with extensive hinterland connectivity. They have assumed the key role in driving exports, attracting foreign investments and engaging with the world. With large and diverse populations, the two mega-cities represent key fonts for new thoughts and ideas, cultural leadership, creativity, and innovation, and serve as thriving global centers for the entertainment and media industries.

Mumbai has had a small but special role to play in China's history. Merchants from the city were among the first to venture into Chinese markets in the 18th and 19th centuries with shipping and cotton trade, among others. Many Mumbaikars, or people from Mumbai, were instrumental in building infrastructure and institutions in Chinese cities of Guangzhou, Hong Kong SAR and even Shanghai. A large Indian community with strong linkages in Mumbai resides in Hong Kong, acting as a strong link between the city and the mainland. Mumbai residents David Sassoon and later Victor Sassoon built some of the landmark buildings of both Mumbai and Shanghai.

Mumbai and Shanghai embody the dreams of their aspirational nations, positioned as growth centers and leaders of their respective countries in many diverse fields of human endeavor, including economic, cultural, political, sports, and technology. As sister-cities, the two metropolises can be the chief connectors for the new Asian century, bringing together the large urban populations of two dynamic emerging economies in a partnership of mutual understanding, friendship and cooperation.

2. Mumbai-Shanghai Dialogue

The establishment of sister-city relations between Mumbai and Shanghai was taken forward after President Xi Jinping's visit to India in September 2014 to further enhance people-to-people exchanges and foster understanding. The Confederation of Indian Industry (CII), India's apex industry body, aims to facilitate this partnership to build closer relations among the residents of the two mega-cities. Thus, we propose to commence the Mumbai-Shanghai Dialogue, a forum that will bring together key stakeholders from diverse fields of business and industry, arts and culture, and others to drive the agenda for cooperation.

By adding the economic component of industry, the Mumbai-Shanghai Dialogue will ensure that a broad-based multi-modal exchange program is implemented, encompassing diverse dimensions of daily life and interests of the people.

The four key planks of the Mumbai-Shanghai Dialogue to enhance sister-city relationship as envisioned by CII include:

- Economy, industry and infrastructure
- Sustainable urbanization
- Education and cultural relations
- Tourism and sports

CII through its Head Quarters in New Delhi and its offices in Shanghai and Mumbai would drive forward the sister-city engagement with the guidance, encouragement and support of the leaders and administrations of the two metropolises. A range of interactions on a regular basis covering the above areas are planned for the present as well as for the medium and long-term to build an enduring partnership. CII is excited about the potential of this partnership to segue into a closer friendship of the two neighboring nations.

3. Mumbai and Shanghai Economic Snapshot

Shanghai is China's main financial center and largest port, located at the mouth of the Yangtze River. It covers a total area of 6340 square kilometers, extending to 18 districts and a county. One of the 4 autonomous municipalities of China, Shanghai was home to a population of 24.25 million people in 2014.

Shanghai's per capita income in 2014 stood at RMB 97370 or about $15 000. A key industry hub of China, Shanghai's largest manufacturing sectors are automotive, computers, communications and other electronic equipment, chemical materials and products and machinery and equipment.

Shanghai attracts major multi-national companies across all sectors. It is home to 320 investment companies, 402 R&D centers, and 558 MNC regional headquarters. The financial sector of Shanghai is well-developed and it aims to emerge as a global financial center. The Shanghai Free Trade Zone, set up in 2013, is an impressive and innovative center for free trade on the lines of the Hong Kong model with relaxed rules for foreign investment and proposed full convertibility of RMB.

Mumbai, covering 4 350 square kilometers for the larger metropolitan area, is positioned as India's most open city, as reiterated by the famed architectural landmark of Gateway of India. Major Indian corporates have located their headquarters in the city, and it attracts a significant proportion of India's foreign investments and joint ventures. The Mumbai airport is the first port of call for most foreign tourists to India and the city is home to the largest port of the country. With two of the largest regional stock exchanges including the iconic Bombay Stock Exchange, Mumbai is India's most vibrant financial city.

However, the city is most famous for its global film industry, reaching out to wow populations across the world with its creativity, music, and rich offerings to suit all tastes. Bollywood, as it is universally known, has spawned multiple related industries such as fashion design, tourism, gems and jewelry, advertising and other creative industries. In addition, Mumbai was also acclaimed for its textile, automotive, consumer non-durables, and other manufacturing industries, but many production facilities have since relocated.

Mumbai aims to emerge as the locus of a new infrastructure network system that will connect it across India's western region right up to the national capital of New Delhi. The Delhi-Mumbai Dedicated Rail Freight Corridor is a railway project, linking the proposed new industrial parks and industrial townships across 6 states of India between the two large cities. The Delhi-Mumbai Industrial Corridor will consist of National Investment and Manufacturing Zones and urban facilities in this region with an estimated investment of $90 billion. A high-speed rail link—India's first - between the two industrial hubs of Mumbai and Ahmedabad in Gujarat is also on the drawing board. According to McKinsey Global Institute, Mumbai's consumer market in 2030 will be as much as $245 billion, more than that of Malaysia today.

The two coastal cities and leading megacities of their respective regions enjoy economic convergence across many fields. In particular, as the headquarters of major domestic firms, they benefit from economic and industry synergies and together can unlock global opportunities.

Table 1   Economic indicators of Shanghai and Mumbai

Economic Indicator	Shanghai (Data for 2014)	Greater Mumbai
Population	24 million	23 million (2011)
Gross Domestic Product	2 356.8 billion RMB	$124 billion (2012)
GDP per capita	97 370 RMB	$5 900 (2012)
GDP composition: Primary Secondary Tertiary	 0.5% 34.7% 64.8%	 n.a.
Tourists: Domestic Foreign	 268 million 7.91 million	(Maharashtra state) 94.1 million(2014) 4.8 million(2011)
FDI	$18.2 billion	$9.5 billion(April 2015 to March 2016)
Key industries	Automotive manufacturing Electronic equipment Chemicals Machinery and equipment Electrical machinery and equipment Tourism and hospitality Financial services	Consumer goods Textiles Automotives Films, entertainment and media Gems and jewelry Financial services Tourism and hospitality

4. Cooperation in Economy, Industry and Infrastructure

At a city-to-city level, Mumbai and Shanghai can envision a strong cooperation in urban economic management.

Shanghai's transformational urban planning and development has attracted global attention. The Pudong area across the Huangpu River underwent dramatic change from a sleepy, low-lying riverside into a megalopolis with soaring skyscrapers and a spectacular business hub after 1990. It represents an urban miracle, including outstanding public infrastructure, efficient public transport connectivity and roads, smart facilities, and a futuristic cityscape designed for breathtaking views.

Strategic urban planning effected this transformation at a rapid and sustained pace. Such coordination and vision is required for Mumbai, a city in which spaces are developing at different speeds. Key areas of the city are not developed to their potential, while newer areas such as the Bandra Kurla Complex have progressed to world-class standards. Mumbai would greatly benefit from insights regarding the Shanghai urban planning model.

Mumbai can also imbibe many teachings from Shanghai's success in urban facilities. The city is setting up a modern public transport system as the suburban rail, subway system and mono-rail along with the bus system are underway. The city will also be home to India's first high-speed railway line, linking it to the city of Ahmedabad, with plans for a futuristic railway station being deliberated.

In urban sanitation and waste management, Mumbai can learn from the experiences of Shanghai as it proceeds in the Swachh Bharat, or Clean India, campaign. Shanghai has also displayed exemplary expertise in revitalizing urban slums into new real estate developments, which would be of interest to Mumbai. Shanghai's flood and drought control systems, pollution management, and urban energy strategy, particularly for renewable energy, could be replicated in Mumbai. In particular, Shanghai's Command and Control Center for handling emergency situations would bear many lessons for Mumbai which has often been subject to natural disasters and attack situations.

Mumbai, which is also a hub for IT industries, can share and develop management systems with Shanghai for mapping and monitoring infrastructure facilities, operations and maintenance. Mumbai companies would also like to work with Shanghai in the sectors of healthcare, biotechnology, and innovation.

As part of the Mumbai-Shanghai Dialogue, CII would coordinate a structured interaction of experts from different urban planning and public infrastructure departments. Industry players, experts and administrations of the two cities could meet on a regular basis for highlighting areas of cooperation as well as for sharing materials and best practices. Specific projects could be identified in each city where joint ventures could be established, leveraging the respective strengths of the two cities.

Potential areas of cooperation:

- Urban planning

- Public transport

- Smart city infrastructure networks and IT

- Energy efficiency

- Disaster management planning

- Water, sanitation and waste management

• Healthcare and biotechnology

5. Sustainable Urbanization

Shanghai has taken great strides in sustainable urbanization, especially in the newly constructed areas of Pudong. The city administration could consider establishing a center for sustainable urbanization as a knowledge hub for India in Mumbai.

The Indian government has launched the Smart City program under which 98 Indian cities are expected to be modernized and renovated through a range of infrastructure construction facilities as well as public utilities. The program has shortlisted 33 cities in the first phase where urban governance will be strengthened and projects will be identified for bidding.

Mumbai is one of the cities where the Smart City project will be initiated in the third phase. The areas of Greater Mumbai with a population of over 14 million and Navi Mumbai (New Mumbai) with a population of 1.1 million will be included in the program. In Greater Mumbai, a range of projects are planned, including central business district in Lower Parel, IT hub in Andheri West, biodiversity tourism in Malad and commerce and tourism in Nariman Point and Kala Ghoda. Four key roads are proposed to be placed under smart road traffic management. The city also plans to establish mobility, utility, and information kiosks at 800 locations across the city.

In Navi Mumbai, the idea is to encourage livable urban housing in compact neighborhoods to bring cohesion to the city's growth. Over-ground electrical networks will be completely eliminated, leading to lower risk of power failure. Large swathes of the city's natural greener such as mangroves, forests and marshes will be made accessible.

In addition, India plans to modernize 500 cities over the next two decades to provide livable, affordable, clean spaces for the rising urban population for the expected urban population increase of 400 million by 2050. Basic infrastructure of water and electricity supply, sanitation and solid waste management, efficient urban mobility and public transport, affordable housing, IT connectivity and health and education facilities are required to be actioned across cities in India. Smart and sustainable urbanization will include water management, energy management, renewable energy and green buildings.

A Shanghai knowledge center for Smart Cities could help in planning for these and other projects in Mumbai. Such a center could also emerge as a resource for other Indian cities coming up in the Smart City program over the next few years.

6. Cooperation in Education and Cultural Relations

Shanghai and Mumbai are imbued with rich educational and cultural resources, standing out as vanguards of intellectual and creative thought. Universities can assume a strong role in the partnership of the two world-class cities, helping to build connectivity, cooperation and understanding among the youth regarding the rich ancient histories as well as the modern economic and cultural interface of India and China. Such a common understanding within an academic and cultural framework with frequent meetings sets the pace for the future interaction of the two countries, led by the vibrant cultural hubs of Shanghai and Mumbai.

Six of Shanghai's educational institutions are ranked among the top QS World University Rankings 2015—16, including Fudan University at 51st and Shanghai Jiao Tong University at 70th rank. Indian studies are part of the course options at a few of Shanghai's learning places already, and there is interest in Indian luminaries such as Mahatma Gandhi and Rabindranath Tagore.

In Mumbai, many educational institutions such as IIT Bombay, Tata Institute of Social Sciences, and Mumbai University, are among India's most sought after study options. These institutions play a leading role in diverse facets of India's contemporary preoccupations, setting the trends for innovation, entrepreneurship, creativity and thought leadership. The young men and women coming out from the portals of these institutions often go on to define trends and thoughts in the country.

The dynamic historical and modern cultural contexts of the two sister cities also provide an excellent platform of cooperation. Mumbai is home to the some of the finest Indian traditions of literature, cinema and theater, dance and music, arts and sculpture, and other cultural pursuits. Its National Gallery of Modern Art, Jehangir Art Gallery, and large number of top painters make it a vibrant city of artists, attracting world players in the art market. The dance and classical music festivals are extremely popular events in the city. Kala Ghoda Arts Festival, held in February each year, captures the essence of culture across many art forms and attracts a high audience from across the

　　　提升投资贸易便利化水平，构建开放型经济新体制

world.

Similarly, the Shanghai International Arts Festival is keenly anticipated each year by art aficionados who flock in from all over the world to imbibe the latest in Chinese art. The design industry in Shanghai has emerged as one of the world's hotspots for fashion with the Shanghai Fashion Week drawing high interest and setting the trend for everyone to follow. The Shanghai music festivals bring in the best of offerings from artistes around China and the world.

The film industries of the two cities are a special area of cooperation. Mumbai's film industry, known as Bollywood, produces the highest number of films in the country, and is rapidly emerging as a global player as more and more audiences across the world are enamored by Indian film stars. It also produces a large number of art films that earn accolades at global film festivals. Shanghai too is a media hub, having made the first Chinese movie and emerging as the movie capital of the country with top studios. Many Shanghai-born stars have gone on to win international acclaim and have acted in popular and art films in Hollywood and Hong Kong SAR. India and China have also signed an agreement for co-production of films and a couple of movies have already been produced. This could be taken forward by the two sister-cities through more co-production ventures.

With their rich cultural heritage and avant garde cutting-edge interests, the two sister cities can devise a vibrant cultural interaction that will embrace people from all walks of life. Some of the joint programs that the two megapolises can consider include:

- Mumbai-Shanghai Fashion Week
- Mumbai-Shanghai International Design Festival
- Mumbai-Shanghai Film Cooperation and co-production

7. Cooperation in Tourism and Sports

Shanghai and Mumbai are the top destinations of their countries for tourism purposes. International travelers make it a point to include Shanghai if they are visiting China, and Mumbai while visiting India, in their itineraries. A sojourn in these two bustling and thrumming cities is considered as an ultimate experience for those seeking thrills in exotic Asian locations.

At the same time, with growing disposable incomes, citizens of both China and

India are increasingly venturing overseas for their leisure time. China's outbound tourism numbers are the highest in the world with over 100 million Chinese people emplaning for global cities. India is the second fastest growing source for outbound tourists and is forecast to send 50 million overseas travelers in the next five years. Shopping, sight-seeing, and learning about the world are the chief travel impulses, and Chinese and Indian tourists have made a name for themselves as high-value tourists.

Apart from sight-seeing, the two cities can think of innovative ideas to entice visitors from the sister city. Shopping can be a huge attraction with Shanghai's Chinese fashion industry and Mumbai's colorful fabrics and textiles. Nanjing Street in Shanghai is matched by Linking Road in Mumbai. Bollywood studios could be interesting for Chinese tourists to visit. Cultural performances can also be tailored for respective audiences.

The two cities would benefit from a high level of tourist exchanges which would serve to expand people-to-people links. Promotional and branding activities could be undertaken in both cities.

The Mumbai-Shanghai Dialogue process would include such promotional measures as well as conferences to look at ways to promote tourism between the two countries with the two sister-cities as gateways.

Sports interaction emerges as a new area of collaboration. Experts in Shanghai could work with Mumbai administrators to build a congenial and welcoming climate for sports promotion including for ordinary people in public parks, stadia, public fitness centers and so on. An exchange of top sportspersons from both cities could serve to enrich the Mumbai-Shanghai Dialogue. The inclusion of cricket, the flagbearer of the Mumbai sporting culture, could emerge as an innovative sport for Chinese people.

8. Conclusion

It is evident that our leaders have rightly sought to link Shanghai and Mumbai with the strong bonds of sister-city relations. The two cities converge on many common points and are perfectly destined to shape the two emerging Asian giants of China and India. Now, we can define the contours of this partnership and evolve specific action points and programs that will bring the two megapolises of Asia together.

CII will be a partner on this journey of harmonious relations and facilitate a closer connectivity of the two sisters of Shanghai and Mumbai.

Promote Global Governance and Trade Facilitation

Chen Zilei

Professor of Shanghai University of International Business
and Economics

In the context of economic globalization, all the countries are shifting their focus from trade liberalization to trade facilitation. With the help of multilateral and bilateral free trade institutions, all of us have successfully expanded trade scale, and promoted regional economic integration. Therefore, how to realize trade facilitation, how to design and well implement trade management programs, and how to set up an efficient, rational and balanced trading system have been the wide concerns of academics around the world.

1. Trade Facilitation

Three main challenges are facing global trade facilitation. First, due to customs information is not adequately disclosed, there is the lack of transparency and predictability. Second, customs procedures are so tedious that customs clearance is rather low efficient. What are worse, arbitrary charges make customs clearance more expensive. Third, there is the absence of necessary cooperation between customs authorities around the world. They have not unified rules to deal with problems concerning information exchange, delay or rejection, reciprocity, and administrative burdens, etc. Promoting trade facilitation can help to simplify trade procedures including handling formalities of information gathering and providing, communication and data processing, all of which are required in international trade in goods. And it also helps regulation and coordination. With trade facilitation realized, tangible restrictions will be reduced, such as overemphasis on promoting institutional reforms and policy shifts in each country, and cutting down tariffs and quotas for trade liberalization. Attention thus will be shifted to creating a more business-friendly environment by improving technologies, procedures and management. On the basis of universally recognized standards and practices, trade facilitation offers international trade a consistent, transparent and predictable environment where trade-related procedures are streamlined, administrative barriers are eradicated, and costs are reduced to promote the flow of goods and services. Therefore, to achieve trade facilitation, what matters is not only governments' efforts to lift restrictions in areas like trade, customs clearance, and entry-exit inspection and quarantine, but also the active role that enterprises and other market players are expected to play, so that a trade management system which ensures smooth flow of goods can be established. In brief, the key to realizing trade facilitation is pressing ahead with management reforms and simplifying procedures to create a business-friendly environment for international trade.

2. The Significance of *Trade Facilitation Agreement*

On September 4th, 2015, China became the 16th WTO member to formally accept the WTO's Trade Facilitation Agreement (TFA). It will only enter into force when two-thirds of WTO members ratify the Agreement, whose implementation will surely reduce transaction cost and increase trade efficiency for enterprises. It is estimated that the Agreement can realize a world GDP increase of \$960 billion and create 21 million new jobs. If our trading partners' GDP increases 1 unit, we will see our trade value and export go up by 0.587 units and 1.378 units respectively. One unit improvement in our country's trade facilitation will lead to the increase of 4.602 units in our trade value, 4.977 units in import and 3.069 in export. If China and its trading partners would begin to implement the TFA since 2016, we would see an extra increase of 30.79% in our export in 2020. Apart from the direct increase in trade value and GDP, trade facilitation that drives forward institutional reform plays an undeniably important role in regulating WTO's member states' practices and encouraging them to carefully follow the organization's transparency principle. Domestically, the implementation of TFA will help China to play a better role in global division of labor, gain a beneficial position in global value chain, upgrade its industrial structure and transform its economic growth model. Besides, trade facilitation can make it more efficient for Chinese enterprises to export and import goods, reduce cost in international trade, make cross-border flow of goods more efficient, and improve our economic ties with major trading partners. It can also improve China's port infrastructures, port management mode, and the integrated administration and collaboration capability of functional departments. Multilaterally, it can boost the growth of global trade and economic development of each country. Regionally, higher-level regional trade facilitation agreement may be explored on the basis of TFA, so as to further the development of regional production network as well as the trade and economy of each state player. In a word, TFA can promote trade facilitation in WTO's members and stimulate international trade development by impressively increasing customs clearance efficiency and reducing trade costs.

3. Methods to Realize Trade Facilitation

(1) Create an information network and integrated administration among each country's trade department. Trade facilitation covers multiple departments including the departments of commerce, development and reform, taxation, business, finance, foreign exchange regulation, customs and goods inspection etc. As all of them have their own complicated and sophisticated rules, fragmented regulation are always found. When they are dealing with trade issues, interdepartmental management is low-efficient, and the cost for interdepartmental coordination is rather high. According to Parkinson's Law and Niskanen Model, departmentalism leads all departments to try to maximize their own power in public affairs out of the concern for their own position and interests. Therefore, they will try all means to create red tapes, impeding the development of trade and investment.

(2) Establish a connectivity mechanism between each country's trade departments. First, an interdepartmental communication mechanism should be set up to eradicate technical, procedure and institutional barriers that are in the way of trade flows. Second, each TFA member should increase their transparency in law-enforcement management. Laws and regulations, administrative procedures, the composition of authorities and personnel, and regulations on law-enforcement should be disclosed to the public. The government should establish and improve the systems of press conference, annual report publication and public hearings on specific issues. Third, all the members should cooperate more closely with each other in trade policies to optimize trade topics under multilateral mechanism, to jointly strengthen policy coordination in various sectors, and

to establish a common management platform for multilateral trade.

(3) Propel the legal system construction through jointed efforts. With the help of legal system, the market is able to play an essential role in resource allocation. With member states concluding trade and investment agreements, and establishing international organizations and rules, business and trade will be covered by rule of law and other institutions. Therefore, to improve the legal system of rules, regulation mechanism, and trade and investment dispute resolution mechanism is to develop the rule of law. First, with laws as the criteria, trade and investment issues should be handled through legal means. All countries should enhance cooperation on cutting down tariffs, streamlining customs clearance and establishing mutually recognized procedures and standards for goods inspection and quarantine, so that a well-established legal system can be created to ensure smooth flow of trade. Second, with focus on the establishment of free trade zone and free trade agreement, some member states should be encouraged to set up a common market for cross-border business in order areas, to establish industrial parks provided with flexible policies in trade and investment hubs, to strengthen cooperation in trade sectors, and realize regional free movement of goods, services and labor force step by step. Third, member countries should take trade facilitation into consideration and set of a series of mechanism centered around trade and investment dispute settlement, particularly on labor standards, environmental standards, and human rights and intellectual property protection. Universally accepted dispute settlement mechanism should be created for areas where trade frictions easily emerge. In this process, they are expected to follow the existing international trade and investment dispute settlement mechanisms like that of the WTO. Meanwhile, they should improve their systems and consolidate institutional foundations to ensure smooth flow of trade.

Insights and Measures on Developing Shanghai into a Global E-commerce Center

Rui Yeping

Chief Research Officer at Urban Innovation Think-tank

With its increasing importance in global trade, e-commerce is breaking the boundaries between regions and countries, and is driving globalization forward. Against the backdrop, the aggressive development mode adopted in the past can no longer fit into the current situation, as the development of e-commerce requires more in improving rules, systems and business environment. If a city can offer the e-commerce industry a better climate for innovation and going global, and improve its institutions, it will surely stand out and become a global center for the globalization of e-commerce.

This paper combs through the major development trend of e-commerce, looks into typical cases both at home and abroad, and finally put forward insights and suggest measures on developing Shanghai into a global hub of e-commerce on the basis of the current situation of the city's e-commerce development.

1. The Major Development Trend of E-commerce in the World

First, e-commerce is turning into a dynamo for global economic growth at a faster pace. When the world is undergoing weak economic growth, dramatic change in trade patterns, and faster restructuring of the system of investment rules, information economy with e-commerce as a representative is serving as a new engine for global economy. Second, new technologies, business forms, and modes continue to emerge. Particularly, the whole industry of e-commerce is entering into the age of mobile internet, and is faced with a far-reaching situated revolution. The integration of online and offline businesses has become a "new normal" in the development of e-commerce. Blockchain is likely to have a profound effect on the industry. And it is permeating into areas like public services at a faster speed. Third, China is speeding up in integrating itself into the global value chain and innovation chain of e-commerce. As our e-commerce is growing mature and domestic competition increasingly intense, a number of domestic enterprises have shifted their attention to the overseas market. They try to accelerate their pace of integrating into the global industrial chain of e-commerce through merge & acquisition, consolidation and cooperation. Meanwhile, they keep learning from their foreign counterparts and introducing innovative philosophies and operation modes from abroad to join the global innovation chain of e-commerce more quickly. Fourth, leading companies are stepping up their efforts in the consolidation of eco-industrial chain of e-commerce. BAT (Baidu, Alibaba, and Tencent) are expanding their investment into almost all areas. Alibaba has not only connected the traditional industrial chains of e-commerce, such as platform, logistics and payment, but also consolidated various areas including finance, film and TV, recreation, transport and daily services. Fifth, innovation resources for e-commerce are concentrating at big cities at a faster pace. With the explosive growth of e-commerce companies and the constant development of e-commerce mode, technologies and business forms, the regional landscape of competition in the e-commerce industry keeps changing. Because the consolidation and M&A of the industry is growing, e-commerce is becoming more mature, and factors for innovation are concentrating at big cities at a faster speed. Sixth, cross-border e-commerce is playing an increasingly significant role in international trade. In the continued slowdown of global trade, cross-border e-commerce is against the trend, whose contributions to the trade are increasing year by year. Global trade is shifting from the traditional mode featuring in long delivery time, large volume, and huge value to the new mode of cross-border orders that are made more frequently with a smaller value.

2. Experience on Boosting the Development of E-commerce from Other Countries and Cities both at Home and Abroad

Generally, the developed world including the US and European countries are among the first to develop their e-commerce industry and has outstanding advantages. Countries vary from each other in terms of e-commerce policies and strategies. As a pioneer in the development of global e-commerce, the US first declared that it would adopt globalized strategies and polices for e-commerce development. It relies on the principle of market-oriented operation with private companies playing a leading role, and the government is only responsible for developing the required legal environment. Similarly, the EU centers its policy framework on legislation to eliminate all sorts of trade barriers of e-commerce between different countries. But in Singapore, the government not only focuses on legal environment, but also emphasizes a lot over policy support and necessary capital support to assist small and medium enterprises to develop their e-commerce activities and expand business into the global market. According to some cases, wealthy countries and regions share some commonalities in the development of e-commerce. At the pre-trade stage, they focus on the establishment of law, regulations and infrastructures. At the trade stage, setting up security, credit and electronic payment polices is the priority. At the post-trade stage, improving the taxation and logistics systems are on the top of the agenda.

China's e-commerce industry goes on the path of "development first and rule-making next". The government pays more attention to the development of enterprises and the industry. Thus, we only have relatively weak foundation in the area of IP protection, trade and services, transaction security, and regulation and accountability. We also lag behind in the development of institutional environment for e-commerce. Several cities have set up strategic goals of e-commerce development. For instance, Beijing has decided to develop itself into a global nodal city of e-commerce. Shenzhen has put forward the idea to become a significant goods trading center and pricing center in south China and even around the country. Guangzhou has made up the decision to construct itself into a national hub and breeding ground for e-commerce.

3. General Strategy on Building Shanghai into a Global E-commerce Center

In this systemic project, the government should adopt a global strategy and vision, and should be fully involved in the development of global e-commerce, in the consumer market and in the innovation network. It should understand the developing trend of China's e-commerce, actively promote the exchange of resources and factors within China and with foreign countries, and prompt the development of other domestic cities. More importantly, it should focus on the main effects of urban development in Shanghai, and take full advantage of e-commerce to promote the development of international trade center, international finance center, and global technology and innovation center, as well as the transformation and upgrading of manufacturing, so as to manifest the city's advantages in business environment, like openness, innovation and rule of law.

To develop Shanghai into a global e-commerce center, the government is supposed to focus on enhancing the capability to allocate e-commerce resources by promoting the innovation and opening of the industry. To support the project, the government should improve the infrastructures for e-commerce transaction such as the security system and regulations. The government should accelerate the pace of creating a development landscape in which opening up is at high level, innovation capability is impressive, application can be widely used, business environment is friendly, and the capability to allocate global e-commerce resources makes its contribution. To be exact, six types of capabilities need to be enhanced: the capability to concentrate resources, the capability to secure transactions, the capability of innovative development, the capability of comprehensive application, the capability of opening and cooperation, and the regulatory capability.

4. Suggestions on Building Shanghai into a Global E-commerce Center

In accordance with the general strategy to deepening the innovative development of the city's e-commerce industry, corresponding measures are put forward as follows. First, the government should enhance the capability to concentrate resources to develop a resource-allocation hub for e-commerce. Concrete measures include introducing and developing e-commerce giants, setting up a global commodity trading platform and pricing center, establishing a platform for the mutual furtherance, interaction and connection between e-commerce activities both at domestic and overseas markets, and creating market rules and taxation system for e-commerce in accordance with integration principles. Second, the government should strengthen the capability of innovative development and press ahead with the innovative development of e-commerce. Specific measures include developing a global breeding ground of innovation and entrepreneurship for e-commerce, promoting the construction of e-commerce industrial park and incubator, improving the environment to support the innovation and startup in the e-commerce industry, and cultivating and attracting innovative talents in this field. Third, the government should enhance the capability of opening and cooperation to further open the e-commerce industry to the outside world. Concrete measures are as follows: taking part in promoting the construction of rule systems for cross-border e-commerce, enhancing the growth capacity of cross-border e-commerce enterprises, improving the public service system for cross-border e-commerce, establishing multilateral, bilateral and international cooperation mechanism on cross-border e-commerce, and building up channels to attract e-commerce enterprises and for them to go global. Fourth, the government should sharpen the capability of comprehensive application and actively develop vertical e-commerce in certain areas. Specific steps are as follows: building up a national leading e-commerce platform in manufacturing; supporting the growth of companies that provide e-commerce platforms for medical care, medicine, education, culture, and tourism; and boosting the development of e-commerce platforms in the areas of aviation, transport, automobile and home ware. Fifth, the government should improve the capability to secure transactions and optimize the supporting system for e-commerce transaction. Concrete steps are as follows: improving the planning of information infrastructure construction around the city, creating a logistics system that fits into e-commerce development, innovating financial and payment services for e-commerce, improving the supporting system for e-commerce services, establishing and strengthening the security authentication system for e-commerce, and setting up the management systems that cover electronic contracts, invoices, and accounting archives. Sixth, the government should enhance the regulatory capability and pick up the pace of innovation the management mode on government services. Specific measures are as follows: expanding market access, improving the city's own standards on e-commerce, enhancing IP protection in the e-commerce industry, improving the monitoring on e-commerce statistics, and setting up a networked regulation and law-enforcement platform for e-commerce.

The Weak Links to be Improved for Cross-border M&A

Zhou Shixun

Director of Information Department of the SDRC

Chinese enterprises have huge potential in internationalization and cross-border merger and acquisition. Improving their competence in cross-border M&A benefits them in going global and serves our country's transformation strategy of innovation-driven development. So firstly and strategically, the government is supposed to promote the innovation of trade facilitation mechanism by starting from developing China (Shanghai) Pilot Free Trade Zone. Secondly, it should take an active part in drawing bilateral, regional, multilateral and international investment rules so that Chinese companies can get protected in cross-border M&A. Thirdly, it should focus on the national strategy and the strategic goal of business transformation and upgrading. Fourthly, the government should step up efforts to enhance companies' competence in cross-border M&A.

Cross-border M&A is a significant part of foreign direct investment. Chinese companies have made fast progress in this field since the reform and opening-up. In the 2014 APEC CEO Summit held in Beijing in November, 2014, President Xi Jinping stated that China's FDI would reach $1.25 trillion, offering new opportunities in cross-border transactions. Therefore, the government needs to learn lessons from the past, explore the development trend, break down existing problems, and follow the future trend. These are of vital significance for promoting cross-border M&A, pressing ahead with the internationalization of Chinese companies, and realizing the new national strategy of opening-up.

1. The Features and Development Trend of China's Cross-border M&A Activity

(1) China's cross-border M&A market is growing in a steady way.

In the context of globalization and economic integration, the tide of enterprise internationalization is sweeping across the world, and Chinese companies are increasingly interested in cross-border M&A. According to statistics from Thomson ONE Banker, during the decade from 2004 to 2014, China's outbound M&A market has flourished, growing at a CAGR of up to 35% by size and 9.5% by number of deals. Thomson's research also suggests that the completed deals amounted to less than 1% in 2004, but nearly 10% in 2013. The deal value in 2015 totaled a record-high of $61 billion, up by 16% compared with 2014.

(2) Entities joining in the cross-border M&A market are more and more diverse.

Generally, China's Top 500 Companies have been substantial players in cross-border M&A deal making. As the statistics on the transaction volume between 2009 and 2014 suggest, they accounted for 65% of outbound deal value and 31% by the deals completed. In 2004, Chinese state-owned enterprises took the lead by striking outbound M&A deal on larger-scale infrastructures, followed by private sector that pursed transactions on manufacturing projects. Since then, groups joining in the outbound M&A activity have been more diversified with SOEs as the leading force, private groups, listed companies and private equities playing their due role in the market.

(3) M&A industries tend to be high value added.

Chinese companies always had the goal of acquiring energy and resources in outbound investment. But with their focus and intent shifting, their foreign investment on energy and resources were only responsible for 16% of the total, far lower than the peak volume of 83% in 2011. After the recession in 2008, M&A industries have gradually become non-resource industries, mainly financial sector, industrial sector, high-tech sector, media and entertainment sector and real estate industry. All of them have achieved record-high growth and tend to be high value added.

(4) M&A targets are concentrated in developed countries.

Stronger preference for mature assets and better understanding on the political and business risks in emerging economies enable Chinese investors to pick up pace in moving from developing countries to developed countries. The number of transactions with Europe and the US as the M&A destination had hiked to roughly 60% of outbound M&A deals by Chinese companies in 2014. By contrast, the number of deals targeting traditional destinations, such as Southeast Asia has plummeted. More precisely, the number of deals targeting North America rose from 11% in 2004 to 23% in 2014; deals with Europe as the destination accounted for 37% in 2014, but only 13% in 2004; while East Asia had witnessed the deal drop from 53% in 2004 to 15% in 2014. So Europe and North America have surpassed Asia as the China's most sought-after targets for outbound M&A.

2. Factors Driving China's Cross-border M&A

Thanks to their fast economic growth after the reform and opening-up policy implemented, Chinese companies have made success in cross-border M&A, which is also driven by:

(1) Globalization and Economic Integration.

After the entry into WTO in 2001, China has found much fewer barriers in its way to integrate into the global market. The international division of labor, driven by globalization, has created a favorable environment for China's cross-border M&A activity. Telecommunication and transportation becoming less expensive have greatly strengthened Chinese companies' capability to allocate resources worldwide. The improved global investment and trade facilitation rules and management system are the guarantees for outbound transactions.

(2) National Strategy and OFDI Policies.

After the implementation of "Go Global" national strategy and "Belt and Road" initiative, the state government has introduced a set of accompanying polices as strategy and policy support for cross-border M&A. The authority has also lowered threshold on outbound deal making. Since 2010, the State Council, the National Development and Reform Commission, and the State Administration of Foreign Exchange released *Opinions on Further Promoting Enterprise Merger and Restructuring, Measures for the Administration of Confirmation and Recordation of Overseas Investment Projects, Provisions on the Centralized Operation and Management of Foreign Exchange Funds of Multinational Companies (For Trial Implementation)* respectively.

All of these policies and procedures are issued to simplify the foreign-exchange management scheme for outbound M&A, substantially relax restrictions on the power to authorize outbound M&A projects, reduce project approval procedures and streamline confirmation process. In particular, the establishment of China (Shanghai) Pilot Free Trade Zone in 2013 has offered investment and financing policy support for cross-border M&A, and effectively improved companies' ability for outbound M&A.

(3) Undervalued Opportunities.

In cross-border M&A, the contributing factors to the valuation of target enterprise include macro economy, industrial cycle, fluctuation in the stock market and the negotiation ability of stakeholders, etc. Since the 2008 financial crisis and the euro zone crisis, global economic growth has slowed down, leading to the tumbling of the stock price of many foreign enterprises who have found themselves in financial dire. Thus these companies are undervalued and aspire to invest their foreign exchange reserves into real economy. Their diversified investment needs create great opportunities for Chinese companies, driving China's cross-border M&A.

(4) Market Demand and the Transformation and Upgrading of Enterprises.

The early-stage outbound M&A activity was limited by the structural shortage of essential productive factors like natural and mineral resources. So acquiring natural resources overseas could help to meet companies' need. But in recent years, due to the emergence of overcapacity in domestic market, Chinese companies are under mounting pressure of transformation. Besides, more relaxing overseas M&A polices, large cash reserve, the rise of Chinese enterprises and the improvement of national image have enlightened a number of companies in wealthy countries the importance of cooperating with Chinese counterparts. Therefore, it's more evident that Chinese deal-makers are looking to realize transformation and upgrading through outbound M&A. Acquirers also view outbound M&A as a way to obtain cutting-edge technology as well as brand and management experience in overseas market. They are engaging in outbound M&A to access new profit pools, capture new markets and tap the skills of globally competitive leaders. Our research reveals that only 20% of outbound M&A deals made during the past five years had the goal of acquiring strategic resources, while roughly 75% were aimed at accessing technology, intellectual property, production capacity, brands, and market share.

3. Challenges Facing Chinese Acquirers in Cross-border M&A

In a new global landscape, challenges facing Chinese buyers arise from both macro and micro environment because of their low-level internationalization.

(1) Macro Environment.

Firstly, political and diplomatic challenges are exerting their influence. Cross-border M&A is not a simple economic activity, but is entwined with politics, diplomacy and culture. With the rise of China, western countries are more prone to regard China as their threat. Geopolitical risks in countries along the "Belt and Road" outweigh their economic risks. These are challenges facing us in making outbound deals. Secondly, the international investment coordination mechanism lags behind the development of cross-border M&A. In the wake of recession, international bilateral, regional and multilateral investment agreements are all broken yet to be improved. They are so fragmented and even contradictory to each other that a large number of international investment disputes have been caused. Thirdly, the national security review systems in developed countries have been imposing challenges to China. In outbound M&A activities led by Chinese state owned enterprises, our buyers are always suspected and rejected by wealthy countries just for being as a SOE. The target country often resorts to their national security review system and taking political factors into consideration, making our acquirers struggle in outbound M&A activities.

(2) Micro Environment in Companies.

Chinese companies have encountered continuing challenges in the international deal-making marketplace. These challenges center on M&A strategy, due diligence and post-merger integration (PMI) and are as follows. Firstly, M&A strategy is often unclear. A clear strategy, deep understanding of the target and comprehensive evaluation are all indispensible for Chinese companies to succeed in outbound deals. But many of them lack a clear M&A roadmap, have only a vague idea of the purpose of any given deal, and know little about the value of possible synergies or how to capture them. And the absence of any discernible M&A strategy has hampered their globalization drive. Secondly, due to an insufficiency of international resources and required expertise, Chinese companies over-rely on foreign agents such as the investment bank for information about target enterprises, which makes it harder for Chinese players to seek and select targets. Thirdly, Investigation with due diligence is often incomplete. Chinese companies' due-diligence investigation teams face challenges, such as a lack of experience with internationalization; insufficient knowledge of overseas commercial and legal environments or profitability models; a limited ability to organize and coordinate commercial, legal, financial, and HR due diligence; and incapability to assess, identify, and evaluate risk points in the due diligence process. Compounding the problem, different languages, cultures and ideologies make leadership turn a deaf ear to the company's local commercial, financial and legal advisors, and inhibit local teams from speaking up at crucial moments. Problems may also arise when decision-making power is highly concentrated at headquarters. In that case, the due-diligence team in the field may be left without sufficient power, rendering it all but impossible for the would-be acquirers to effectively coordinate internal and external resources, and respond efficiently. Fourthly, PMI proves to be difficult to master. After merging and acquiring pioneer enterprises from the developed world, some acquirers, who do not have faith in their own management system and personnel, over-depend on the executives of the acquired company and follow the management and operation modes without any modification. What's worse, some acquirers have only a rough top-down design for outbound M&A and lack a detailed and feasible operation plan, thus running the combined entity in a blind way. Compounding the problem, the absence of a clear management structure for the foreign target, the lack of cross-border and cross-cultural management experience, the absence of executives familiar with local business environment and disparities in culture and management mode impede their cross-border M&A efforts.

4. Enhancing Capabilities for Cross-border M&A is Strategically Important for Chinese Companies' Globalization Drive

In recent years, Chinese companies have been experiencing a surge in outbound M&A, but remain at a low level of globalization. But as the second largest economy in the world, China has only a relatively small number and size of cross-border deals. As economic globalization is still developing and reforms on the state asset management and state owned enterprises are ongoing, Chinese companies have huge potential in globalization and cross-border M&A, enhancing their competence in making outbound

M&A benefits their "Go Global" drive, and serve the national strategy of innovation-driven transformation and development. So, suggestions are as follows.

(1) Promote the Innovation on Investment and Trade Facilitation Mechanism by Focusing on the Construction of China (Shanghai) Pilot Free Trade Zone.

Facilitating investment and trade is an essential part of FTZ construction, so the government needs to proactively promote the innovation of international investment and trade facilitation mechanism. To do so, firstly, it should delegate the power for review on cross-border M&A, simplify approval procedures, relax controls on foreign exchange quota, ease restriction policies on companies' outbound M&A, strengthen operational and post-operational regulations, inform would-be acquirers of potential projects, and offer them advice on foreign legal system and institution. Secondly, the government is supposed to introduce preferential industrial policies to provide more support for Chinese companies' outbound M&A. It should carry out separate management modes and methods for different industries and projects. It should be supportive and ready to take risks when the overseas deal has something to do with national strategies or targets strategic resources. Thirdly, with focus on RMB internationalization drive of China (Shanghai) Pilot Free Trade Zone, the government should pick up the pace of opening capital account to support companies in cross-border M&A with innovative financial tools like cross-border financing.

(2) Take an Active Part in Drawing Bilateral, Regional, Multilateral and International Investment Rules.

As the second largest economy and the largest trader in the world, it should and can change its role from a passive participator to a pioneer in economic globalization. In the era, the government should accelerate negotiations on US-China BIT and EU-China Investment Agreement, and promote the establishment of international investment and trade rules, so as to protect Chinese companies in cross-border M&A.

(3) Focus on the National Strategy and the Strategic Goal of Business Transformation and Upgrading.

The development of the "Belt and Road" together with accompanying projects including Asian Infrastructure Investment Bank, Silk Road Fund and The New Development Bank can effectively support outbound M&A activities. In cross-border M&A, Chinese companies are expected to help to realize the national strategic goal of innovation-driven transformation and development, focus on manufacturing which is vertically highly correlated with other industries when selecting targets, and try to make new breakthroughs in advanced and emerging high-tech industry M&A. Financial sector and other service sectors M&A should be domestic consumption market oriented, so that increasing domestic needs can be satisfied with foreign resources and the national strategy of RMB internationalization can be promoted.

(4) Step up Efforts to Enhance the Companies' Competence in Cross-border M&A.

Firstly, the government should clarify outbound M&A strategy. It can take advantage over foreign talents and domestic resources. It is suggested to study enterprise strategies, policy change, technology development, and shifts in consumers' habits to figure out sectors that should be priorities in cross-border M&A and then make a clear strategy. Secondly, it should effectively implement measures on cross-border M&A. It is supposed to well manage due diligence, negotiation and approval procedures, identify deal risks, and integrate planning and execution to derive genuine synergies. Thirdly, the government should foster its outbound-M&A-related core abilities to manage systems and risk. It should make a detailed division of industry and the way of deal-making, should clarify selection procedures, and companies' M&A frequency and timing, so as to set up an outbound M&A information database, create a talent pool of excellent executives with an international view, and optimize the management and assessment systems.

The Status Quo and Existing Problems of Investment and Trade Facilitation Measures

Zhou Shixun

Director of Information Department of the SDRC

Wang Xiaoyu

Postdoctor of the SDRC

1. The Status Quo of China's Foreign Investment and Trade

(1) Outbound Foreign Direct Investment: China's Outward Foreign Direct Investment (OFDI) continues to increase. In 2015, China's OFDI had been growing for 13 consecutive years, and exceeded trillions of US dollars for the first time, making China the powerhouse in international investment market. In respect of investment destination, North America, Europe and Asia, as the sought-after destinations, attracted 85.5% of China's outbound M&A investment, accounting for 83.5% of total deals. Besides, China's investment in countries along the "Belt and Road" has been rising at a quick pace. In 2015, we directly invested in 49 out of them with the amount totaling $14.82 billion, up by 18.2% over the previous year. In terms of the investment industry, the industries for China's OFDI have been more diversified and moved up the value chain. The service sector is growing at a strong momentum of going global, mainly the financial industry, leasing industry, commercial services industry and IT industry. M&A has become the major way of China's OFDI. Private sectors are taking the lead in overseas investment. At the early stage, it was the state owned enterprises that played a dominant role, but now both SOEs and private companies are equally important in overseas investment. Non-SOEs had contributed 46.4% to our country's OFDI as of the end of 2014.

(2) The Inflow of Foreign Direct Investment: The inflow of FDI into China remains to go up. In 2015, 26,575 foreign invested enterprises were set up in China, representing an increase of 11.8% over the previous year. Foreign capitals used amounted to 781.35

billion RMB (about $126.27 billion), 6.4% more compared with last year. Among the foreign countries, countries along the "Belt and Road" expand their investment in China at the fastest speed. They set up 2,164 foreign-funded enterprises in China, up by 6.4% compared with the last year; and invested $8.46 billion in real terms with an increase of 23.8% over the previous year. Investment from the major countries and regions remain stable. The top investor was Hong Kong of China, followed by Singapore, Taiwan of China, South Korea, Japan, the US, Germany, France, the UK and Macao.

(3) The Development of Foreign Trade: China is taking up more shares in the international market. In 2015, China ranked first in terms of international trade in goods and the value of export. China's export as a proportion of the international market rose to 13.8%, up by 1.5 percentage points compared with 2014. The composition of exports has been furthered improved. China's exports have more value added. High-tech products such as mechanical and electrical products account for more proportion in exports year by year, while the proportions of seven types of labor-intensive products like textiles and clothing are decreasing in exports. The proportion of trade in services continued to increase. In 2015, China's international trade in services reached $713 billion, representing a year-on-year increase of 14.6%; and accounted for $713 billion of the total, up by 3 percentage points compared with 2014. New business mode like cross-border e-commerce and market procurement trade has become new hotspots for developing international trade. In 2015, cross-border e-commerce grew by at least 30%, and market procurement trade increased by nearly 60% in export. Market diversification has brought about impressive effects. The EU, the US and ASEAN are now China's three largest trading partners. China's export in some emerging countries is expanding fast. For example, our export to India, Thailand and Vietnam rose by 7.4%, 11.6% and 3.9% respectively. The private sector has become the engine power in export. In 2015, the export of private enterprises amounted to $1.03 trillion, up by 1.8% over the previous year. Their proportion of total export reached 45.2%, making private sector surpass foreign-funded enterprise for the first time.

2. Policies and Measure for Promoting Investment and Trade Facilitation

(1) Market Entry: Firstly, The management mode of the admission of foreign

investment has changed from the positive list to the negative list, and the negative list mode is being improved. The 2015 Negative List details 122 prohibited or restricted areas, reduced from 139 in the 2014 Negative List. The updated list has smaller proportion of restrictions on manufacturing, and greater transparency and feasibility. Secondly, the mode to open up service sector is diversified. Shanghai, Tianjin and Beijing try to open up their service sectors by relaxing equity rules. Guangdong and Fujian do so by easing qualification rules with the mutual recognition on the qualification of employees from mainland China, Hong Kong, Macao and Taiwan as the main method.

(2) Customs and Border Control: Firstly, a series of measures to facilitate customs clearance have been implemented, including incorporating the customs registration of enterprises in the China (Shanghai) Pilot Free Trade Zone in the "Single Window" administration system for enterprise access; first entering and then declaring to the customs; independent tax declaration, self-service customs clearance, automated review and release, and priority review; one-off archival filing for repeated uses; intelligent inspection and release at customs pass; centralized declaration for import/export in batches; and goods flow by "transportation under self-control". Secondly, the goods status classification supervision system has been enforced. Goods status covers bonded goods, non-bonded goods, and port goods. By means of "network supervision + storage location administration + real-time verification and endorsement" (as a mode for customs supervision), real-time control and dynamic verification of goods can be achieved as storage in the same house. Thirdly, enterprise status classification supervision system has been launched. With the implementation of Mutual Recognition of AEO programs, a cooperation agreement that has been concluded with Singapore, South Korea, Hong Kong, Taiwan, and the EU for the mutual recognition of AEOs, highly credited enterprises in the Zone for the first time have the access to declaration services nationwide wherever they are registered. Fourthly, zone-port integrated operation has been achieved. The operation mode of goods flow by "transportation under self-control", the measure to simplify and unify filing list for goods entry into and exit from the zone (refers to the simplification and unification of 36 declaration items in filing form format in Waigaoqiao Bonded Zone and Waigaoqiao Bonded Logistics zone, as well as 42 items in Pudong Airport Free Trade Zone and Yangshan Free Trade Port Area into 30 declaration items), and many other measures have been implemented

to further promote the interaction between the four zones and zone—port integration. A direct channel between bonded zones and ports has been opened in Yangshan Free Trade Port Area.

(3) Entry-exit Inspection and Quarantine: Firstly, industrial products production license manufacturing consignment has been cancelled. Secondly, entry-exit pre-inspection system has been enforced. Thirdly, the onsite inspection and release mode of "inspection and release upon cargo arrival" has been widely implemented across the Free Trade Zone.

(4) Maritime Affairs: Firstly, inspections on offshore vessels have been innovated to upgrade the performance of maritime regulation. With the interaction between maritime law enforcement authorities, unnecessary boarding for vessel inspections can be avoided and necessary on-board inspection is completed once for all. Secondly, in the "approval first and then verification" pilot system, vessels are provided with convenient services including release upon arrival, one-off submission of multiple application documents and one-off verification and endorsement for multiple vessels, thus enjoying zero waiting time in inspection for port departure.

(5) Establishment and Access of Enterprises: Firstly, in the Reform of FDI review system, the filing system is adopted. Secondly, in reforming the commercial registration system, the registered capital registration system has been changed from "capital paid-in system" to "capital subscription system", and the enterprise registration system has been transformed from the system of "business certificate with precedence over license" to the system of "license with precedence over business certificate". Thirdly, the "single window" system for enterprise access has been enforced.

(6) Taxation: Firstly, the implemented favorable tax policies refer to two policies covering external investment of non-monetary assets and equity incentives installments; and other five policies including export tax rebate for finance leasing, import VAT policy, selective tax collection (levying Customs duties on goods for domestic sale according to the imported materials or parts or according to the actual inspection declaration status), tax exemption for necessary goods, and tax rebate at the port of departure. Secondly, the efficient and accessible One-Stop Tax Service Online system has been enforced to improve the efficiency of handling tax-related matters.

(7) Finance: ① Capital account liberalization: Resident Free Trade Account is accounted for and managed separately. Free fund flow is allowed between a Resident

Free Trade Account and an overseas account, a domestic nonresident account but opened outside the Pilot Zone, a Nonresident Free Trade Account or another Resident Free Trade Account. ② The convertibility administration system to facilitate financing and investment: (a) Promote institutional cross-border direct investments: For the purpose of cross-border direct investments made by Pilot Zone investors, relevant parties may directly arrange the receipt or payment of the funds, currency conversion with banks without obtaining pre-approvals pursuant to relevant regulations in Shanghai. (b) Facilitate individual cross-border investments: Qualified individuals who are working in the Pilot Zone may make various outbound investments including investments in securities pursuant to relevant regulations. ③ Steadily open up the capital market: Financial institutions and enterprises in the Pilot Zone may conduct investments and trading in securities and futures exchanges in Shanghai pursuant to relevant regulations. Foreign parent companies of Pilot Zone enterprises may issue RMB bonds in domestic capital market according to relevant laws and regulations. ④ Enhancement of cross-border use of RMB: According to business needs, enterprises in the Pilot Zone may launch a two-way RMB cash pooling within the group to carry out a centralized payment and receipt under current account for their domestic and overseas related parties. ⑤ Steady progression of interest rate liberalization: Lending rate control on financial institutions has been removed. The ceiling of interest rate for small-denomination deposits in foreign currencies was first lifted in the Pilot Zone, and then the pilot program was expanded to other areas in Shanghai. ⑥ Deepening reform in foreign exchange administration: (a) Streamline Forex procedures for foreign direct investment: The foreign exchange registration and approval requirement under direct investments has been abolished. The record filing of foreign exchange for overseas reinvestment has been cancelled. The annual inspection of direct investment-related foreign exchange has been cancelled and replaced with registration of stock rights and interests. (b) The foreign credits approval requirement on transaction basis for finance leasing companies engaged in foreign leasing has been replaced by a registration management system. (c) The pre-approval for payment of guarantee fees to overseas parties by Pilot Zone institutions has been removed.

(8) Supervision and Regulation: The programs of the publication of annual reports by enterprises in China (Shanghai) Pilot Free Trade Zone and administration on directory of enterprises with abnormal operation in China (Shanghai) Pilot Free Trade

Zone have been implemented.

(9) Dispute Resolution Mechanism: Firstly, arbitration has become the preferred way to resolve disputes in the Free Trade Zone. Secondly, great breakthroughs and innovations have been made for arbitration rules, including opening up of the panel of Arbitrators, consolidation of arbitration cases, mediation in arbitration proceeding, amicable arbitration procedure, the use of simple procedures for small claims with consent from both parties.

(10) Overseas Investment Promotion: ① To establish a public service system for overseas investment cooperation, several measures have been implemented. Information service platform has been set up. Investment promotion activities are held to bridge different parties for communication. Report on investment in different countries and industries are written. The Ministry of Commerce has issued the "Model Service Guidelines for Overseas Economic and Trade Cooperation Zones" to help local administration of commerce and central enterprises to improve their guidelines for the establishment of enterprises in cooperation zones. In the "Guiding Opinions on Promoting International Cooperation in Industrial Capacity and Equipment Manufacturing", with twelve sectors where China obviously has an advantage over other countries, such as iron and steel, as well as nonferrous metals picked out as the priority sector, methods are tailored for corresponding sectors to go global. ② Expand sources of financing: Qualified enterprises and financial institutions are supported to raise funds in both domestic and overseas markets through issuing shares, bonds and asset-backed securitization products for "going global" projects. The filing system for issuance of foreign debts by enterprises has been implemented to help raise foreign exchange funds at low cost, which better meets enterprises' capital needs in internationalization. ③ Enhance financial support: Domestic financial institutions are encouraged to provide loans for PPP (public-private partnership) projects, and are driven to enhance the ability to deal with assets (or equities) abroad. Chinese-funded financial institutions are supported to set up offshore subsidiaries and service outlets to strengthen financing service. ④ Optimize export credit insurance: Export credit insurance has been established to support long-term institutional arrangement for complete sets of large equipment. Universal coverage for eligible projects whose risks are controllable has been realized. ⑤ Promote outbound equity investment. ⑥ Investment projects are managed by the filing system, except the overseas

investment projects that have something to do sensitive countries, regions and sectors and should go through verification by the National Development and Reform Commission.

3. Major Problems of Investment and Trade Facilitation

(1) Market Entry: Firstly, the implementation of projects on further opening-up has only brought about unbalanced results, as there are two few projects for opening up certain sectors for the first time, while too many for relaxing policies. And the service sector is at a low level of opening. Secondly, there is the lack of interpretations, accompanying policies or legal support for opening-up policies. For instance, the Ministry of Transport has specified on the policy on coastal carriage. International vessels not flying a five-star flag which are owned or controlled by Chinese-funded shipping companies shall be allowed to engage in the coastal carriage of foreign trade import and export containers. Companies such as China Ocean Shipping (Group) Company and China Shipping (Group) Company have been implementing the policy on a trial basis. But the implementation is involved with departments like the Customs, the Administration of Inspection and Quarantine, and Shanghai International Port (Group) CO., LTD, so accompanying policies are to be designed and enforced.

(2) Border Control: Firstly, there are inconsistencies in China (Shanghai) Pilot Free Trade Zone policies. For example, customs regulatory mode and the practice in every one of the four zones of the China (Shanghai) Pilot Free Trade Zone are inconsistent with each other. Secondly, enterprise classification supervision system is not well-established. For example, the bilateral recognition system has been concluded, but enterprises can't have access to the benefits provided by the AEO due to the lack of AEO label on bills. Thirdly, there is the lack of interaction and consistency between policies issued by different departments. For example, departments differ from each other in terms of the opening-up of the front-line (which refers to the national border) for imports.

(3) Establishment of Enterprises: Firstly, reform on enterprise registration system is not well-implemented. Some departments keep their practice of traditional review and approval procedures and measures. China (Shanghai) Pilot Free Trade Zone Administration has pledged further opening-up, but some authorities haven't

changed their review and approval procedures and measures, leading to the repeated visits of enterprises and the lack of rights for office staff to make decisions. Secondly, some enterprises are faced with insurmountable difficulties in employee qualification authentication and thus are not allowed to run their business. For example, in the home country of foreign employees who are working in architectural design companies, there is no qualification authentication for people working in construction industry. So the documents to prove the multi-year working experience of employees submitted by the company fail to get approval from competent authorities, as when the company has no legal certificate to prove employees' working experience, they need proof from independent third parties. However, in the home country of foreign employees, there is no independent third-party authentication institution for the construction industry. Thirdly, the service of single window system should be extended. Though the Single Window management system for international trade has greatly facilitated enterprise customs clearance, the system only covers four departments, namely the Customs, the Administration of Inspection and Quarantine, Entry-exit Port Bureau, Maritime Safety Administration, but not Administration of Taxation or Administration of Foreign Exchange. This partly impairs the efficiency of the system.

(4) Taxation: Up to now, China (Shanghai) Pilot Free Trade Zone has not set up a well-established framework for tax system. Tax policies are constraining the introducing of entities with high-end functions and function enhancement, which can be found in tax rate system, as well as tax collection mechanism and methods.

(5) Finance: Firstly, due to capital outflow, foreign exchange control is going to be tightened. Secondly, ① non-resident banking business is facing high tax rate. Financial institutions in the Free Trade Zone are exposed to relatively high tax rates compared with foreign countries. They have to pay 5% of business tax and 25% of income tax when running non-resident financial business (offshore business), thus not active in running offshore business; ② RMB deposit rate has not been liberalized for FTN. The RMB deposit rate for FTN is benchmarked against the onshore deposit rate unveiled by the central bank, but internationally, interest rate is decided by the market; ③ FT account does not have substantive functions. The connectivity of onshore and offshore funds is not provided with real freedom. Foreign-funded enterprises all have their foreign currency accounts, so FT account does not make any difference to them. What's worse, a few banks try very hard to persuade enterprises to open a FT account only to

finish their target. Therefore, these accounts are not used in real terms.

(6) Supervision and Regulation: Firstly, Annual reports by enterprises are not timely, as they can only be revised during the submission period from January 1st to June 30th. So the enterprise cannot disclose information about disclosure and settlement, or any modification like the change of address. Secondly, Chinese NGOs, such as folk association and trade association are not playing a major role, and is under weak supervision of the public. Thirdly, a robust system of enterprise credit information gathering, handling, disclosing and regulation is in absence.

(7) Dispute Resolution Mechanism: Innovations in arbitration rules for China (Shanghai) Pilot Free Trade Zone may not achieve good results due to the lack of legislation support. For example, the "China (Shanghai) Pilot Free Trade Zone Arbitration Rules" gives more autonomy to the parties, better respects their wishes and expands rights for arbitration tribunals. However, too internationalized rules may sometimes work in contradiction with provisions in Law of Civil Procedure and Arbitration Law. The innovative rule of opening the panel of Arbitrators though gives more autonomy to the parties and better respects their wishes, it is likely to prolong the arbitration and reduce efficiency.

(8) Overseas Investment: ① Western countries are prone to have prejudice against Chinese state-owned enterprises, do not have faith in China's sovereignty fund and are sensitive about the identity of being Chinese SOEs. So Chinese SOEs are likely to undergo stricter security review by wealthy countries when conducting overseas M&A or investment. This puts greater responsibility of information protection on SOEs and forces them to make concessions in other aspects. Moreover, the principle of competitive neutrality makes it harder for SOEs to go global. ② Investment promotion services are insufficient and inefficient. The administration of resource allocation can easily lead to misallocation. As the allocation measures are more favorable to large-scale SOEs, private enterprises are contained in internationalization and political risks are more likely to emerge. There are plenty of problems related to information support, such as information services being too macro, the lack of close connection with enterprises and projects; too little useful information; too many charging items; too few trainings for employees; and the lack of coordination and cooperation with investors in designing long-term strategies and plans. Plans tailored to support small enterprises are insufficient. ③ Legal restrictions: There are only a few laws helping enterprises in overseas

investment. Most of the support comes from measures and provisional regulations. Lagging behind in legislation has gravely weakened enterprises in cross-border M&A activities, made supporting policies made by the government much less effective, and deprived enterprises of legal protection when disputes appear during outbound M&A. ④ Restrictions from Foreign Exchange Management: As our government has not realized full convertibility on capital account, Chinese enterprises are faced with many restrictions in overseas M&A. Besides, the State Administration of Foreign Exchange, Ministry of Commerce and local administrations of commerce have different ideas on the relationship between the review on foreign exchange risk and project approval, and on which of the two should be the priority. So enterprises usually feel puzzled and find it hard to handle formalities. It also exerts negative impacts on direct investments that need spot exchange and non-productive investments in which a large amount of foreign currency needs to be remitted out of China (like after-sale service and R&D). ⑤ Overseas investment insurance has not fully played its due role. Our country's overseas investment is growing rapidly. But there are many problems related to overseas investment insurance, such as high insurance rate, the lack of a professional overseas investment insurance system, the inappropriate structuring in insurers, and the unreasonable insurance coverage for the insured. So our country's overseas investment insurance is not widely applied, fails to drive Chinese investors to actively expand their business to overseas market for China's economic growth. ⑥ Intermediaries are not well developed and not able to provide services for outbound M&A. Though we have our investment banking comprised of trust and investment companies, security companies and finance companies, we are not very capable and experienced in this area. Trade associations and professional organizations are not well established, and far from being able to provide services for outbound M&A. What's worse, many intermediaries have never participated in outbound M&A. So Chinese investors hardly get quality intermediary services, useful information or help, which only leads to the emergence of problems in outbound M&A. ⑦ Restrains from enterprises within: For example, the operation and management philosophies of Chinese enterprise are in conflict with that of foreign companies. Talents for cross-border M&A activities are insufficient. Overseas assets and investment returns are overvalued.

Policies and Measures for Promoting Investment and Trade Facilitation in China (Shanghai) Pilot Free Trade Zone

Wang Xiaoyu

Postdoctor of the SDRC

1. Market Entry

(1) Status Quo.

The management mode of the admission of foreign investment has changed from the positive list to the negative list. The essence of the negative list mode is embodied by the law-based governance principle, which is to basically and systematically streamline administration and delegate powers. Pre-establishment national treatment and negative list are the most universally exercised management mode in the world. And based on the mode, the US-China BIT negotiation is under the way. In this sense, the shift from positive list to negative list makes China be in line with international norms.

On September 30th, 2013, Shanghai Municipal People's Government issued "The Special Administrative Measures (Negative List) on Foreign Investment Access to the China (Shanghai) Pilot Free Trade Zone (2013)". As the first of this kind in China, the list has 190 special administrative measures, covering 17.8% of all industries. It means the management mode on the entry of foreign investment in the pilot free trade zone has changed from approval system to filing plus approval system. On June 30th, 2014, the Municipality released the "Special Administrative Measures (Negative List) on Foreign Investment Access to the China (Shanghai) Pilot Free Trade Zone (2014 Amended Version)" to further open up the free trade zone. Compared with the 2013 version, the 2014 updated one has reduced the number of special administrative measures on the list from 190 to 139, down by 26.8%. The 2014 Negative list lifts 14 administrative measures and relaxed other 19 measures, making it 17.4% less restrictive than the previous one.

In addition, the 2014 list further opens up manufacturing and construction industries. 5 out of the 14 measures on manufacturing are focused on product R&D and design. Less restrictive measures on the construction industry opens up access for foreign investment in infrastructures. Further opening up the mining industry is for the application of new technologies. The 2014 list also eases measures on the service sector. Among the concerning 14 measures, 6 are about shipping service, 3 commercial service, 4 professional service and 1 about social service. What's more, the revised version creates a wider access into business logistics, accounting and auditing, and medical care sectors.

On April 8th, 2015, the State Council issued the "Special Administrative Measures (Negative List) for Foreign Investment Access to Pilot Free Trade Zones". The 2015 Negative List details 122 prohibited or restricted areas, reduced from 139 in the 2014 Negative List. Under the 2015 list, less proportion of measures are focused on manufacturing, which means the number of prohibited items is shrunk from 50 stipulated in the 2014 list to 17, making the revised version more in consistence with international practice and representing the maturity of China's management methods on the service sector. Moreover, the 2015 negative list is more transparent. For example, the number of prohibited items in the list related to the financial sector increases from 4 in the previous version to 14, and that of items concerning culture, sports and entertainment industry rises from 8 to 24. The increase is only to materialize restrictions on the entry of foreign capitals into the two sectors. So the updated list is not more restrictive, but more transparent and more feasible.

(2) Existing Problems and Future Development.

The implementation of projects on further opening-up has only brought about unbalanced results, as there are too few projects for opening up certain sectors for the first time, while too many for relaxing policies. And the service sector is at low level of opening-up. Besides, there is the lack of interpretations, accompanying policies or legal support for opening-up policies. For instance, the Ministry of Transport has specified on the policy on coastal carriage. International vessels not flying a five-star flag which are owned or controlled by Chinese-funded shipping companies shall be allowed to engage in the coastal carriage of foreign trade import and export containers. Companies such as China Ocean Shipping (Group) Company and China Shipping (Group) Company have been implementing the policy on a trial basis. But the implementation is involved with departments like the Customs, the Administration of Inspection and Quarantine, and Shanghai International Port (Group) CO., LTD, so accompanying policies are to be designed and enforced.

After the entry into WTO, China has ranked 5th in the world in terms of international trade on services. It indicates that we have had some advantages in traditional service sector. However, we are lagging behind in emerging service industry and high-end service industry, an industry that is high value-added and rich in human capitals, showing that we remain to be relatively weak in the service sector globally. According to our current stage of development and affordability, we need to continue to expand the opening-up to improve competitiveness in the global market, further enhance competitiveness in emerging and high-end service industries and promote the development of China's service sector as a whole. So, the government is supposed to expand the opening-up of the service industry, especially the emerging and high-end service industries of finance, culture, education, medical care, shipping and professional services. Meanwhile, it should improve and refine concerning laws and rules to support the opening-up of relating industries.

2. Border Control

(1) Status Quo.

• The Customs

(a) Measures for Facilitating Customs Clearance.

Including the customs registration of enterprises in the China (Shanghai) Pilot Free Trade Zone in the "Single Window" administration system for enterprise access: Enterprise may, through the single window which is set up in the FTZ to form a comprehensive management service platform, make one-time submission of standardized electronic information as required by different administrations such as the Administration for Industry and Commerce, the Administration of Taxation, the Administration of Quality Supervision, Inspection and Quarantine, the Commission of Commerce and the Customs. And the feedback of handling outcome shall be given through the single window.

"First entering and then declaring to the customs" (hereinafter referred to as "first entering and then declaring"): "First entering and then declaring" means the operation mode in the Pilot Zone entering from abroad link, where enterprises registered with the customs in the Pilot Zone (hereinafter referred to as the "enterprise in the Zone") may, by presenting the manifest of entering goods and such other information, make brief declaration to the customs first and handle formalities for picking up goods at port and goods entering the zone, and, in the prescribed time limit, handle formal declaration formalities for entering goods with the customs.

"Independent tax declaration, self-service customs clearance, automated review and release, and priority review": It is an operation mode where enterprises log onto the pre-entry client side of the customs-enterprise sharing platform to report data on the Customs Declaration Form and declare taxes. The Customs Information System will conduct the integrated operation of automated review and release. At the early stage of the pilot program, the operation mode only applies to the centralized declaration for import/export in batches.

"One-off archival filing for repeated uses": It refers to a customs supervision mode where enterprises in the Zone when filing books should go through one-off recordation of information about the enterprise and entry-exit goods on the China (Shanghai) Pilot Free Trade Zone Customs Supervision Informatization System (hereinafter referred to as the "Informatization System"). With the approval from the competent customs, they can use the recordation repeatedly in various customs-allowed operations like centralized declaration for goods imported or exported in batches, bonded exhibition and trading, domestic and overseas maintenance, futures bonded delivery business and financing lease business without handling filing formalities with competent customs again.

Intelligent inspection and release at customs pass: Intelligent clearance at checkpoint is an intelligent management mode whereby intelligent facilities are used to read data including electronic license plate number, container number, vehicle weight provided by electronic weighbridge and data on the intelligent security lock, and compare them with information on the examination and review form to identify risks. The intelligent facilities are also used to verify and cancel GPS vehicle tracking data, examine goods and emit release instruction. This mode helps to ease traffic flow and realize automatic examination and release.

"Centralized declaration for import/export in batches": It is a customs clearance mode whereby enterprises in the Zone may finish formalities for goods entering or leaving the Pilot Zone with checkpoint examination and release form (hereinafter referred to as the examination and release form), and then submit Archival Filing Form and Customs Declaration Form to handle customs declaration formalities within prescribed time limit, if goods are to be transported in batches between such enterprises and domestic enterprises outside the Zone (including enterprises at special customs supervision areas and enterprises at bonded supervision premises), or to be traded in batches between enterprises in the Zone. The mode is supervised and regulated by the Customs on the basis of "Informatization System".

Goods flow by "transportation under self-control": Transportation under self-control is an operation mode whereby enterprises in the Zone may use vehicles registered with the customs to conduct the operation mode of goods transportation under self-control.

(b) Goods Status Classification Supervision.

Goods status covers bonded goods, non-bonded goods, and port goods. By means of "network supervision + storage location administration + real-time verification and endorsement" (as a mode for customs supervision), real-time control and dynamic verification of goods can be achieved as storage in the same house.

(c) Enterprise Status Classification Supervision.

With the implementation of Mutual Recognition of AEO programs, a cooperation agreement that has been concluded with Singapore, South Korea, Hong Kong, Taiwan, and the EU for the mutual recognition of AEOs, 118 AA-level enterprises are subject to the greatest clearance facilitation granted by customs administrations in China and export countries. Highly credited enterprises in the Zone for the first time have the access to declaration services nationwide wherever they are registered.

(d) Zone-port Integrated Operation.

The operation mode of goods flow by "transportation under self-control", the measure to simplify and unify entry and exit filing list for goods from the zone (refers to the simplification and unification of 36 declaration items in filing form format in Waigaoqiao Bonded Zone and Waigaoqiao Bonded Logistics Zone, as well as 42 items in Pudong Airport Free Trade Zone and Yangshan Free Trade Port Area into 30 declaration items), and many other measures have been implemented to further promote the interaction between the four zones and zone—port integration. On September 1st, 2014, a direct channel between bonded zones and ports was opened in Yangshan Free Trade Port Area to connect islands and land areas in Yangshan. After crossing the "front line" (refers to the national borderline), vehicles can travel through the direct channel and be released without any further inspection. This project improves the transport system of the Area, reduces enterprise logistics cost and enhances transportation efficiency. What's more, in its 24-7 operation, intelligent management including automatic comparison, automatic judgment, automatic inspection and release, is applied when vehicles are going through the checkpoint. The management mode improves traffic efficiency for companies' transport vehicles and the logistics monitoring system in Yangshan Free Trade Port Area.

• Entry-exit Inspection and Quarantine

(a) Cancel Filing for Industrial Products Production License Manufacturing Consignment.

On February 1st, 2014, Shanghai Municipal Bureau of Quality and Technical Supervision started the pilot project to cancel industrial products production license manufacturing consignment in China (Shanghai) Pilot Free Trade Zone, and began to promote it around Shanghai on April 15th, 2014.

(b) Entry-exit Pre-inspection System.

On May 1st, 2014, Shanghai Entry-Exit Inspection and Quarantine Bureau carried out imports and exports pre-inspection program in China (Shanghai) Pilot Free Trade Zone. Since then, enterprises have been allowed to apply for pre-inspection for imported cargos at the free trade zone and goods at storage in zone. If goods are pre-inspected to be qualified, they will be will released and exempt from inspection. This program not only helps to ward off quality risks at "the second line" (which refers to the line dividing China (Shanghai) Pilot Free Trade Zone from the domestic market), but also advance the on-site and laboratory inspections on imports to the storage period, which reduces the waiting time to zero when goods are to leave the zone and halve the flow time from crossing the border to going through the customs pass. The flow time for importing industrial products has gone down form 7-8 working days to 3-4 working days, and that for importing cosmetics down from 12 working days to 5 working days.

(c) The Full Implementation of the Onsite Inspection and Release Mode of

"Inspection and Release upon Cargo Arrival".

The mode of "inspection and release upon cargo arrival" uses cutting-edge technologies such as the Internet of Things and cloud storage in customs inspection regulation and foreign trade facilitation. The use of handheld mobile terminals for law enforcement realizes paperless clearance in inspection and quarantine as well as one-touch release granted by multiple administrative systems, as the terminal is connected with the major service system of AQSIQ and the Shanghai Port Electronic Out-Gate System. This mode eliminates the need to make repeated visits to inspection site and office buildings, make it possible to trace the origin of goods, avoid duplication of data entry, and prevent waiting in lines for onsite inspection and release etc., thus not only ensuring law enforcement, but also speed up the whole process.

• Maritime Affairs

(a) Innovate Inspections on Offshore Vessels to Upgrade the Performance of Maritime Regulation.

With the interaction between maritime law enforcement authorities, unnecessary boarding for vessel inspections can be avoided and necessary on-board inspection is completed once for all. It effectively reduces the impact of the onsite inspection by maritime officers on the operation of vessels sailing in international routes and remarkably enhances the port efficiency of China (Shanghai) Pilot Free Trade Zone.

(b) Approval First and Verification Later.

The "approval first and verification later" pilot system was first implemented in the free trade zone in October, 2013 for offshore vessels to be leaving the Yangshan port. In the system, these vessels are provided with convenient services including release upon arrival, one-off submission of multiple application documents and one-off verification and endorsement for multiple vessels, thus enjoying zero waiting time in inspection for port departure.

(2) Existing Problems and Future Development.

Problems to be solved:

Inconsistencies in China (Shanghai) Pilot Free Trade Zone policies: For example, customs regulatory mode and the practice in every one of the four zones of the China (Shanghai) Pilot Free Trade Zone are inconsistent with one another.

Problems in the enterprise classified supervision system: For example, the bilateral recognition system has been concluded, but enterprises can't have access to the benefits provided by the AEO due to the lack of AEO label on bills.

The lack of interaction and consistency between policies issued by different departments: For example, departments differ from each other in terms of the opening-up of the front-line (which refers to the national border) for imports.

Future Development:

Make and improve detailed rules for implementing systems: The government can make detailed rules for implementing regulations and laws to improve the institutional environment for trade facilitation. And through department practices, trade facilitation rules can be implemented.

Set up a co-promotion mechanism for system innovation: The government should establish a cross-department communication platform and coordinate reforms in various departments to enhance interaction and consistency in innovating department polices which are supposed to be matched up with supporting measures. Particularly, a standardized, effective and procedure-optimized joint regulation mechanism should be set up for newly opened crossover sectors. The government is also expected to promote the development of information sharing and service platforms by drawing experience from Singapore's public platform mode so as to strengthen information, service and regulation integrations of information sharing and service platform. It should integrate service resources and procedures of each department, improve one-stop service and encourage public participation and interaction, and promote cross-department joint and coordinated regulation as well as public serving.

Improve the enterprise classified supervision which is based on credit record: The government is suggested to optimize the AEO mutual-recognition system, realize unified certification among authorities like the customs, and the administration of inspection and quarantine, and implement differentiated regulations in accordance with enterprises' AEO certifications so that they can enjoy their due benefits. It should promote the development of enterprise credit record and of the system of third-party evaluation, test and acceptance of results. It should share information about whether enterprises have faith and comply with laws. All these are done to establish a differentiated regulation mechanism with enterprise credit record and credit rating system as the essence.

Optimize regional-integration-based regulation system: The government should optimize the coordinated regulation mechanism, mode and procedures for the four special customs supervision areas inChina (Shanghai) Pilot Free Trade Zone, establish a unified customs regulatory authority, unify the HS code of the four special customs supervision areas, and improve the operation and management mechanisms of self-transportation in the Zone. It should accelerate the spreading of these measures to eradicate the barriers in the way of practicing self-transportation in the four special customs supervision areas. It should actively explore how to achieve the interaction between the special customs supervision areas in and outside China (Shanghai) Pilot Free Trade Zone.

3. Business Environment

(1) Status Quo.

• Establishment of Enterprise

(a) Reform on FDI Review System and the Adoption of the Filing System.

To follow the international practices, the filing regulatory system for foreign direct investment entry into China (Shanghai) Pilot Free Trade Zone has been launched. Upon the establishment of administration via a negative list, it is necessary to follow the principle of the same treatment for domestic investment and foreign investment, including changing from the approval system to the filing system for foreign investment projects (unless the decisions the State Council provide otherwise), and shifting from review and approval for articles of association of foreign-invested enterprises to a filing administration whereby enterprises need to handle statutory formalities after filing. Under the review and approval system, it is required to examine the qualification of the enterprise and the legitimacy of the industries they are going to invest in, their investment mode, investment amount, and articles. But under filing system which is part of the management mode of negative list, it is only necessary to gather some basic information such as the qualification of the enterprise and the legitimacy of the industries they are to invest in. So the filing system has greatly simplified the FDI entry procedures, and lowered the threshold and cost for foreign enterprises. More importantly, it is an embodiment of the shift in ideology from prior approval to in-process and ex post administration in terms of administration for foreign-funded enterprises.

(b) In reforming the commercial registration system, the registered capital registration system has been changed from "capital paid-in system" to "capital subscription system", and the enterprise registration system has been transformed from the system of "business certificate with precedence over license" to the system of "license with precedence over business certificate".

In the registered capital subscription system, except for enterprises that are otherwise provided by laws and administrative regulations in terms of paid-in registered capital of a company, other companies in the FTZ are subject to the capital subscription system, and are no longer required to register the paid-in capital amount or hand in capital-contribution verification report. In contrast to the capital paid-in system, the capital subscription system allows shareholders to decide the capital contribution by themselves. And they are exempt from the restrictions of minimum registered capital, capital contribution and contribution schedule. Accordingly, companies don't have to verify capital contribution, the amount of paid-in capitals are not written on the business license, other assets like intangible assets can be used as registered capitals. This further lowers the threshold for businesses to enter the market, releases the burden imposed by capital paid-in system and reflects the idea of access-widening in commercial registration reform.

In the registration system of "license with precedence over business certificate", except for the pre-licensing items of enterprise registration provided by the laws, administrative regulations and decisions of the State Council, enterprises in the FTZ may engage in general production and operation activities after applying for registration in the registration authority and obtaining a business license. Operation projects that involve pre-approval items of enterprise registration shall apply for a business license in the registration authority after obtaining the permit or approval documents. This registration system eliminates preset review and approval items and separates business qualification from operation certification, thus not only helping to cut down market entry cost for enterprises, but also in line with international practices.

(c) The "Single Window" System for Enterprise Access.

China (Shanghai) Pilot Free Trade Zone has launched a "single window" working mechanism for enterprise access. Enterprises are only required to submit a format and application documents to one centralized system and finish administrative matters such as the approval (filing) of FDI projects and the review (filing) of the establishment and modification of enterprises at one location. With the implementation of "one-window handling" policy for enterprise registration, various departments like the branch office of Shanghai Administration for Industry & Commerce; Shanghai Municipal Bureau of Quality and Technical Supervision; Shanghai Municipal Office, SAT and Shanghai Municipal Public Security Bureau have realized concentrated handling through one window and one-off acceptance of application materials including business license, organization code certificate, tax registration certificate and official stamp. It means the mechanism of joint handling of the application for licenses and certificates has been improved to be the one whereby enterprises only have to apply for business license, organization code certificate, tax registration certificate through one window at one time. They can expect to receive the relevant licenses and certificates simultaneously within four working days, which is significantly cut from the original 29 working days.

- Taxation

The tax policies stated in the Framework Plan for the China (Shanghai) Pilot Free Trade Zone can be concluded into "7+2", which refers to seven formal tax policies and two pilot policies. The seven formal policies consist of two policies encouraging investment and five policies promoting trade. The former covers external investment of non-monetary assets and equity incentives installments; and the latter include export tax rebate for finance leasing, import VAT policy, selective tax collection (levying Customs duties on goods for domestic sale according to the imported materials or parts or according to the actual inspection declaration status), tax exemption for necessary goods, and tax rebate at the port of departure. The seven policies cover four types of taxes, namely corporate tax, individual income tax, VAT, and Customs duty. The two pilot tax policies are adapted to boost the development of overseas equity investment and offshore business.

As required by the State Administration of Taxation in the "Notice on Supporting Tax Service Innovation in China (Shanghai) Pilot Free Trade Zone" which was released on July 8th, 2014, China (Shanghai) Pilot Free Trade Zone has innovated tax collection measures to improve levying efficiency. The tax service innovation, namely efficient and accessible One-Stop Tax Service Online, include ten measures, i.e. automatic online code assignment, independent tax service online, the use of online invoices, regional one-stop tax service online, online qualification determination, online tax administration of non-resident enterprises, quarterly tax declaration, online approval recording, online tax credit assessment, and innovative online tax service. What's more, authorities can achieve separate collection of information concerning taxpayers' needs by using Shanghai Municipal office, SAT-enterprise interaction platform, online questionnaire and website survey. They can feed taxpayers with personalized policy information and risk warning according to their needs. They can inform taxpayers of the progress of handling tax-related matters online.

• Finance

To further promote trade and investment facilitation and expand financial opening, People's Bank of China, China Banking Regulatory Commission, China Securities Regulatory Commission, and China Insurance Regulatory Commission have issued 14 polices and regulations to press ahead with pilot programs such as the cross-border use of RMB, the convertibility of RMB capital accounts, interest rates liberalization and foreign exchange management. Some of the programs have been fully implemented, while some others haven't. The free trade account system; the convertibility administration system to facilitate financing and investment; the cross-border use of RMB; interest rates liberalization; and reform on foreign exchange management, all of which are part of the framework for financial innovation in China (Shanghai) Pilot Free Trade Zone, have increasingly improved the financial services provided by the Free Trade Zone.

(a) Capital Account Liberalization.

Residents in the Pilot Zone may open a domestic/foreign currency free trade account (hereinafter as the "Resident Free Trade Account"), which will be accounted for and managed separately. Nonresidents may open a domestic/foreign currency free trade account (hereinafter as the "Nonresident Free Trade Account") with banks in the Pilot Zone and is granted to the relevant financial services pursuant to the national treatment principle.

Free fund flow is allowed between a Resident Free Trade Account and an overseas account, a domestic nonresident account but opened outside the Pilot Zone, a Nonresident Free Trade Account or another Resident Free Trade Account. Fund flow between Resident Free Trade Accounts and settlement accounts in other banks of the same non-financial entity is allowed if the fund flow is for the purposes of current account transaction, loan repayment, industrial investment and other qualified cross-border trading activities. Fund flow between a Resident Free Trade Account and an onshore bank settlement account but opened outside the Pilot Zone is deemed as cross-border fund flow for management purposes. Cross-border financing and guarantee businesses may be carried out through Resident and Nonresident Free Trade Accounts. Domestic and foreign currencies in such accounts will be freely convertible when conditions permit. A system will be established to monitor the status of RMB conversion in Resident and Nonresident Free Trade Accounts. Pursuant to regulations of the People's Bank of China (hereinafter as the "PBOC"), financial institutions in Shanghai may, by establishing a separate unit to account for the Free Trade Accounts (hereinafter as the "Pilot Zone Unit"), help qualified Pilot Zone entities open Free Trade Accounts and provide relevant financial services.

(b) The Convertibility Administration System to Facilitate Financing and Investment.

Promote institutional cross-border direct investments: For the purpose of cross-border direct investments made by Pilot Zone investors, relevant parties may directly arrange the receipt or payment of the funds, currency conversion with banks without obtaining pre-approvals pursuant to relevant regulations in Shanghai.

Facilitate individual cross-border investments: Qualified individuals who are working in the Pilot Zone may make various outbound investments including investments in securities pursuant to relevant regulations. Legal income derived by individuals from the Pilot Zone may be remitted to overseas after tax clearance. Individual industrial and commercial households within the Pilot Zone may extend loans to their overseas business entities according to the business needs. Qualified foreign individuals who are working in the Pilot Zone may open nonresident individual accounts with Pilot Zone financial institutions to make various domestic investments including investments in securities pursuant to relevant regulations.

Steadily open up the capital market: Financial institutions and enterprises in the Pilot Zone may conduct investments and trading in securities and futures exchanges in Shanghai pursuant to relevant regulations. Foreign parent companies of Pilot Zone enterprises may issue RMB bonds in domestic capital market according to relevant laws and regulations.

Facilitate financing from overseas: According to business needs, Pilot Zone institutions (including Chinese or foreign-funded enterprises, non-banking financial institutions and other economic organizations registered in the Pilot Zone) may borrow funds from overseas in domestic or foreign currencies pursuant to relevant regulations.

The macro-prudential management system on the overall status of foreign debts will be improved with effective measures introduced to control the foreign debt risk.

Offer diversified risk-hedging tools: Based on real management needs in respect of matched-currency or maturity, Pilot Zone institutions may conduct risk hedging within the Pilot Zone or in overseas pursuant to relevant regulations. Qualified Pilot Zone enterprises may be allowed to make foreign securities and foreign derivative investments pursuant to relevant regulations. A Pilot Zone Unit's open positions arising from free currency conversion with institutions in the Pilot Zone and overseas should be closed or hedged in the Pilot Zone market or in overseas. A Pilot Zone Unit may participate in derivative trading in international financial markets to control its own risk. Subject to approvals, a Pilot Zone Unit may conduct inter-banking lending or repos in the domestic inter-bank market within approved amounts.

(c) Enhancement of Cross-border Use of RMB.

Based on the three principles (i.e. "Know your client", "Know your business" and "Due diligence"), for items under current accounts or direct investments, banking institutions in Shanghai may directly arrange cross-border RMB settlements for Pilot Zone institutions and individuals (except for those entities on a monitoring list for cross-border RMB settlement purpose) according to their fund receiving or payment instructions.

Banking institutions in Shanghai may cooperate with Pilot Zone payment service institutions which hold "Payment Business Permit" and whose business scope includes online payment service, and provide RMB settlement service to cross-border e-Business (goods or service) pursuant to relevant payment service policies.

Financial institutions and enterprises in the Pilot Zone may borrow RMB funds from overseas. Such RMB funds cannot be used to invest in securities, derivatives, or used for entrust loan purpose.

Financial institutions and enterprises in the Pilot Zone may borrow RMB funds from overseas. Such RMB funds cannot be used to invest in securities, derivatives, or used for entrust loan purpose.

(d) Steady Progression of Interest Rate Liberalization.

China's interest rate liberalization is at an accelerating stage. On July 20th, 2013, the central bank announced removal of lending rate control on financial institutions. On March 1st, 2014, it lifted the ceiling of interest rate for small-denomination deposits in foreign currencies in the Pilot Zone and began to expand the pilot program from the Zone to other areas in Shanghai.

(e) Deepening Reform in Foreign Exchange Administration.

Support development of headquarter economy and new trade forms: The pilot scope of multinational headquarters which are allowed to manage their foreign exchange on a centralized basis will be expanded. The administration of foreign exchange cash pooling will be further simplified. The pilot of foreign exchange administration for international trading and settlement centre will be enhanced to facilitate the trading and investment.

Simplify the foreign exchange registration formalities for direct investments: The foreign exchange registration under direct investments and relevant changes will be delegated to banks, with subsequent supervision being strengthened. Based on the conditions that the authenticity of relevant transactions are ensured and complete information has been collected, foreign exchange funds under foreign direct investment may be converted to RMB according to the enterprise's wishes.

Support domestic and overseas leasing service in the Pilot Zone: The foreign credits approval requirement on transaction basis for finance leasing companies engaged in foreign leasing will be replaced by a registration management system. Subject to approvals, finance leasing companies in financial system (which are under administration of the Chinese Banking Regulatory Commission) and Chinese-funded finance leasing companies may be allowed to receive rental payments in foreign currencies for domestic finance leasing business. The procedures for pre-payments in large finance leasing projects (i.e. aircrafts, ships) will be simplified.

The pre-approval for payment of guarantee fees to overseas parties by Pilot Zone institutions will be removed; Pilot Zone institutions may directly purchase the foreign exchange and make the payment with the bank.

Banks are supported to carry out over-the-counter transactions of commodity derivatives for domestic clients.

• Supervision and Regulation

The investment management used to be static and solely rely on a single party, but now it is dynamic and depends on the joint efforts of the government and the public. In March, 2013, Shanghai Administration for Industry & Commerce promulgated the *"Procedures for Publication of Annual Reports by Enterprises in China (Shanghai)*

Pilot Free Trade Zone (For Trial Implementation)" and "*Procedures for Administration on Directory of Enterprises with Abnormal Operation in China (Shanghai) Pilot Free Trade Zone (For Trial Implementation)*". Since then, the two programs have been carried out in the Free Trade Zone to promote publication of enterprises' credit information, transform government functions, and strengthen social supervision. The two programs began to be implemented nationwide in August, 2014.

- Dispute Resolution Mechanism

According to the "*Framework Plan*", an internationalized and regulated business environment should be cultivated. In this process, a robust dispute resolution mechanism is expected to be established, as whether a dispute can be settled in a fair and convenient way partly determines the future of China (Shanghai) Pilot Free Trade Zone. But because of the spillover effect of commerce and financial services, dispute resolution is far beyond the sole capacity of China (Shanghai) Pilot Free Trade Zone Court and the need for judicial innovation emerging in the construction of the Free Trade Zone will undergo linear growth. Commonly used by other countries and international economic organizations, arbitration featuring in independence, flexibility and high-efficiency, well satisfies the need to settle disputes in a convenient way in an internationalized and regulated business environment in the FTZ. Also it matches up with the new features of the disputes in the Free Trade Zone, so it is the preferred way to resolve disputes in the Zone.

To meet the need of the Free Trade Zone, there are more breakthroughs and innovations in "*China (Shanghai) Pilot Free Trade Zone Arbitration Rules*" (hereinafter as *Arbitration Rules*) than in the rules of other Chinese arbitral authorities.

(a) Opening up of the panel of Arbitrators: According to the "*Arbitration Rules*", any party may recommend person(s) from outside the Panel of Arbitrators as an arbitrator and parties may also reach an agreement with the director of the arbitration commission on jointly recommending a person from outside the Panel of Arbitrators as the presiding / sole arbitrator. Opening up of the panel of Arbitrators is a commonly-used way by most international arbitration organizations. This measure conforms to the international practice, as it provide more autonomy for parties, makes arbitration more flexible and professional, and respect parties' wishes.

(b) Consolidation of arbitration cases: The FTZ Arbitration Rules states that the tribunal may, on the application of any party and with the consent of all other parties concerned, order the consolidation of related arbitrations or arbitrations involving the same or similar subject matter. As a pioneer rule in the world's arbitration field, the consolidation effectively expands the scope of proceeding for tribunals (Even in the absence of agreement from the party concerned in cases to be consolidated, the power of consolidating cases for trial can also be exercised.). Therefore, more methods are created to resolve disputes, particularly the ones with multiple parties. As this rule makes arbitration more efficient and professional by allowing the consolidation of multiple cases into one for one-off arbitration, parties will be benefited and agree more on the result of dispute resolution.

(c) Mediation in arbitration proceeding: Mediation may be utilized at any stage of arbitration proceedings. If mediation is launched before the composition of the arbitral tribunal to partly settle the dispute, resources will be saved, settlement cost be cut down, relationship between different parties be improved, and business environment and the whole society will be benefited in terms of stability. But mediation procedure can only be started on the application of any party and consent from all other parties concerned. This is to show respect to their wishes. If the settlement agreement is concluded, even though it is concluded without the involvement of arbitration commission, the award must be enforced. This requirement effectively avoids the problem of enforcement, realizes efficient dispute resolution and ensures fair results.

(d) Amicable arbitration procedure: The tribunal may render the award on the principle of "ex ae quo et bono" instead of based on laws and regulations. Amicable arbitration is a great breakthrough for China's arbitration system, but it requires more on the expertise and arbitration ability of arbitrators, so that they can issue fair and just verdicts under the scope of the laws and settle disputes. This measure poses challenges to China's arbitration system, but also creates an opportunity to develop the system.

(e) The FTZ *Arbitration Rules* is introducing simple procedures for small claims. If the amount is small, the parties shall be able to apply for this procedure. The rules of evidence like the independent investigation by arbitration tribunals, expert evidence, and examination of evidence should be improved.

To date, Singapore International Arbitration Center and Hong Kong International Arbitration Center have set up their offices in China (Shanghai) Pilot Free Trade Zone.

(2) Existing Problems and Future Development.

Establishment of enterprise: Though the enterprise registration system has been reformed, some departments keep their practice of traditional review and approval procedures and measures. China (Shanghai) Pilot Free Trade Zone Administration has pledged further opening-up, but some authorities haven't changed their review and approval procedures and measures, leading to the repeated visits of enterprises and the lack of rights for office staff to make decisions. Besides, though the single window management system for international trade has greatly facilitated enterprise customs clearance, the system only covers four departments, namely the Customs, the Administration of Inspection and Quarantine, Entry-exit Port Bureau, Maritime Safety Administration, but not Administration of Taxation or Administration of Foreign Exchange. This partly impairs the efficiency of the system. So to improve the single window management system, departments like the administrations of taxation and foreign exchange will be included in the its scope, the connectivity of enterprise operation information and port regulation system be promoted, customs clearance requirements and procedures be simplified, and enterprises will handle all formalities for the application, declaration, review, approval and regulation, etc. related to export and import (including entrepot trade) through a unified platform. In the single window system for enterprise access, more departments like the Bureau of Statistics, Commission of Commerce, the Customs, and the administration will be covered to expand the their services and functions. Enterprises will be informed of all the documents need for review at one time to enhance efficiency. The service resources and procedures of each department will be integrated to improve one-stop service, encourage public participation and interaction, promote interdepartmental coordinated regulation and public-serving, and streamline review and approval procedures.

Taxation: Up to now,China (Shanghai) Pilot Free Trade Zone has not set up a well-established framework for tax system. Tax policies are containing the introducing of entities with high-end functions and function enhancement, which can be found in tax rate system, as well as tax collection mechanism and methods. In the future, the state government will continue to implement favorable tax policies, but less for certain regions while more for certain industries. It will optimize tax policies to lead local governments to focus more on the quality of economic growth, economic restructuring and the transformation of development pattern. The central government will continue to explore the tax system which can promote the development of offshore business, overseas investment, headquarters economy and emerging service industry.

Finance: In reference to international standards and with prevailing international system, rules and practices as the example, the government will continue to promote the capital account liberalization, interest rate liberalization reform, foreign exchange administration reform and the development of offshore finance.

Supervision and regulation: Annual reports by enterprises are not timely, as they can only be revised during the submission period from January 1st to June 30th. So the enterprise cannot disclose information about disclosure and settlement, or any modification like the change of address. What's more, Chinese NGOs, such as folk association and trade association are not playing a major role, and is under weak supervision of the public. Our country's social-credit system, especially the enterprise credit system is far from being well-established. Many enterprises are in lack of self-discipline mechanism, and good understanding about credit. A robust system of enterprise credit information gathering, handling, disclosing and regulation is in absence. In the future, the government will have to coordinate and organize market players to participate in market supervision, develop their credibility system, and strengthen self-discipline mechanism. It will encourage associations, chamber of commerce and professional service institutions to make a difference in drawing up conventions for industries, safeguard competition order, and play a role in review, verification and regulation. It will set up and improve the government-led national internet-connected database, establish a market player credit information publication system which is based on the enterprise and individual business registration database of administration for industry & commerce. On the condition that business secrets will not be disclosed, the government will unveil information about enterprises, including annual inspection results, finance, credit record, product quality, social security contributions and the change in and the structure of their assets.

4. Promote Overseas Investment

(1) Status Quo.

• Overseas Investment Promotion System

The establishment of overseas investment promotion system in the Free Trade

Zone reflects the idea to relax investment control, enhance ex post services and promote the liberalization of overseas investment. The essence and highlight of the system is the pilot program of the filing of overseas investment, which remarkably streamlines the pre-approval procedure, undoubtedly better satisfies enterprises' need to make decisions on investment by themselves, and conforms to market development and the trend of international investment liberalization.

• Outbound Equity Investment

Encouraging outbound equity investment is an important measure by China (Shanghai) Pilot Free Trade Zone to promote the development of overseas investment. The Free Trade Zone's innovations on investment management system and financial services have created a good environment to support domestic investors in outbound equity investment. Promoting the establishment of enterprises specialized in outbound equity investment in FTZ and helping capable investors to set up outbound equity investment fund are beneficial to expand our foreign investment mode, reduce risks in overseas investment, diversify profit model, follow the global trend of industries and drive forward the national strategy of going global.

(2) Existing Problems and Future Development.

Given risks facing outbound equity investment come from various aspects, like information asymmetry, business operation, investment target industry, investment amount and exit strategy, setting up and improving outbound equity investment risk prevention system will be the key in the construction of overseas investment promotion system in China (Shanghai) Pilot Free Trade Zone.

Existing Problems in SFTZ's Trade Facilitation from the Perspective of Relevant Protocol Standards

Zhang Minghai   Tan Min

Information Department of the SDRC

1. *The Trade Facilitation Agreement* is an Important Standard in the Assessment of Trade Facilitation

As required by *Framework Plan for the China (Shanghai) Pilot Free Trade Zone* (hereinafter referred to as *Framework Plan*), China (Shanghai) Pilot Free Trade Zone (SFTZ for short), against the background of the "national strategy" to "explore new channels and accumulate new experience for the deepening of reform and expansion of opening-up on a full scale", shall explore the establishment of a relatively independent area for trade in goods focusing on trade facilitation and an area for trade in services focusing on the expansion of opening-up of the service field. Conditioned upon ensuring effective regulation, the SFTZ shall explore the establishment of a model of categorized regulation according to the status of goods." This is an important guideline for the SFTZ to boost trade facilitation; it is also the main standard for assessing the progress made in this aspect.

At the same time, the international community has also achieved important milestones in trade facilitation standards. In November, 2014, at a special session of the General Council of the WTO, *The Trade Facilitation Agreement* (*TFA*) was adopted in which trade facilitation standards are proposed with the aim to "streamline trade flow, enhance the transparency and predictability of the standards, remove technical and institutional obstacles, develop and improve the legal basis and supporting measures for trade, reduce trade risks, uncertainties and transaction costs, achieve freedom and open-up in international supply-chain trade and optimize resource allocation and efficiency." According to *TFA*, trade facilitation includes efficient management of the customs and favorable domestic situations, covering many aspects such as streamlining trade flows, establishing standards for data elements, paperless-oriented information processing, legalizing procedures, information-based regulation, cost savings, coordination among departments and cooperation among customers. *TFA* covers many aspects. It can be compared with other international standards and carried out with great practicability in assessment. It provides important standards for the assessment of the SFTZ's trade facilitation progress; it is also another perspective and framework for Shanghai to learn from the experience of foreign countries in trade facilitation.

2. Achievements and Problems of the SFTZ in Trade Facilitation

According to the general requirements and the standards stipulated in *Framework Plan* and *TFA*, the achievement assessment of the SFTZ in trade facilitation is as follows:

(1) Compared with the requirements of *Framework Plan*.

Framework Plan has put forward 21 requirements of 3 levels in 4 aspects. As of October, 2014, the SFTZ has met 17 requirements (accounting for 80%), reached the basic standards of 2 requirements (accounting for 10%) and failed to reach the rest 2 requirements (accounting for 10%). For details, see Table 1. In general, the SFTZ has made steady and significant progress in improving trade facilitation.[①]

(2) Compared with *TFA*.

According to *TFA*, the SFTZ has met the standards of 11 items in the streamlining of trade flows, 10 items in cost savings, 4 items in customs cooperation, 3 items in information-based regulation, 1 item in paperless-oriented information processing, and 1 item in coordination among departments. But the SFTZ failed to pass the basic standards of procedure legalization and establishing standards for data elements (For details, see

---

① (1) *Framework Plan* has put forward requirements in 4 aspects for trade facilitation: expand trade types, extend trade activities, upgrade trade functions and innovate trade policies. (2) "Failing to reach the requirements" means no implementation plans and relevant policies have been made, nor have the policies been implemented; "reaching the basic standards" means policies have been made, but they have not been implemented yet; "meeting the requirements" means policies have been made and implemented.

Table 1　The result assessment of the trade facilitation of the SFTZ
(compared with Framework Plan)

		Framework Plan	Plan execution Policy development	Implementation	Comprehensive assessment
Extend trade types	1	Develop offshore businesses	Yin Jian Fa (2013) No. 40	Not implemented	Reach the basic standards
	2	Carry out domestic and international trade in an integrated way	Shanghai Customs Notice, 2014 No. 24	Implemented	Meet the requirements
	3	Set up international bulk commodity trading and resource allocation platform	Hu Shang Shi Chang (2014) No. 595	Implemented	Meet the requirements
Extend trade activities	4	Improve the pilot work of futures' bonded physical delivery	Shanghai Customs Notice, 2014 No. 11	Implemented	Meet the requirements
	5	Accelerate the nurturing of cross-border e-commerce	Shanghai Customs Notice, 2014 No. 13	Implemented	Meet the requirements
	6	Set up bonded product exhibition and trading platforms in designated areas	Shanghai Customs Notice, 2014 No. 9	Implemented	Meet the requirements
	7	Encourage multinational companies to establish headquarters in the Asia-Pacific region	Shang Hai Hui Fa (2014) No. 26 Yin Zong Bu Fa (2014) No. 22	Implemented	Meet the requirements
	8	Upgrade the cross-border receipt and payment and financing functions of the designated account for international trade settlement	Yin Zong Bu Fa (2014) No. 22	Not implemented	Reach the basic standards
Upgrade trade functions	9	Support financial leading companies to set up project subsidiaries and carry out domestic and foreign leasing services	Shang Hai Hui Fa (2014) No. 26 Shanghai Customs Notice, 2014 No. 12	Implemented	Meet the requirements
	10	Encourage to set up third-party inspection bodies	Notice on the Adoption of the Results of Third-party Inspection Bodies on the Inspection of Imported Commodities (Weights) in China (Shanghai) Pilot Free Trade Zone	Implemented	Meet the requirements
	11	Carry out domestic and foreign high technology and high value-added maintenance service on pilot basis	Shanghai Customs Notice, 2014 No. 10; Hu Shang Ji Dian (2013) No. 698	Implemented	Meet the requirements

		Framework Plan	Plan execution Policy development	Implementation	Comprehensive assessment
Innovate trade policies	12	First entering and then declaring		Implemented	Meet the requirements
	13	Use the model of "entry quarantine, and appropriate import and export inspection relaxation" and "first approving and then checking"	Shanghai Customs Notice, 2014 No. 6, 7 and 8; Shu Jia Fa (2013) No. 108	Implemented	Meet the requirements
	14	Explore the establishment of a model of categorized regulation according to the status of goods		Implemented	Meet the requirements
	15	Improve bayonet management and strengthen electric information networking		Implemented	Meet the requirements
	16	Inspection and quarantine supervision featuring "entry/exit convenience and prevention of quality safety risks	Shu Jia Fa (2013) No. 108; Guo Zhi Jian Tong (2013) No. 503; Te Ji Shu Jia Han (2014) No. 44	Implemented	Meet the requirements
	17	Strengthen electric account management, facilitate the circulation of goods in different customs' special supervision areas and among different customs		Implemented	Meet the requirements
	18	Strengthen the coordination among different administrative departments such as customs, quality inspection, industry and commerce, taxation and foreign currency	Shanghai Customs Notice, 2014 No. 30	Implemented	Meet the requirements
	19	Form unified and efficient customs regulation bodies	N/A	Not implemented	Fail to reach the requirements
	20	Explore unified electric fencing management in the SFTZ	Te Ji Shu Jia Han (2014) No. 44	Not implemented	Fail to reach the requirements
	21	Accelerate trade taxation policies	Cai Guan Shui (2013) No. 75	Implemented	Meet the requirements

Note: as of October, 2014.

Table 2). Based on the above-mentioned assessment results, the SFTZ has four problems in improving trade facilitation:

First, the development of laws and regulations. Despite the fact that the SFTZ has enacted a series of rules and regulations about import and export regulation, they are different in contents and relevant policies are often adjusted and derailed from international standards. Current policies such as customs clearance are increasingly not compatible with the trend of trade facilitation.

Second, one-stop service (single window). In 2014, Yangshan Bonded Port

Table 2　Assessment of the trade facilitation measures in the SFTZ (compared with FTA)

No.	Measures	Trade facilitation standards							
		Streamlining of trade flow	Standardiz-ation of data elements	Information paperless-ness	Procedure legaliza-tion	Cost savings	Coordin-ation among institutions	Information-based regulation	Customs cooper-ation
1	First entering and then declaring	✓				✓			
2	Self-transport Policy within the SFTZ	✓				✓			
3	Processing trade work Order type verification							✓	
4	Bonded exhibition	✓				✓			
5	Domestic and foreign maintenance					✓			
6	Futures' bonded physical delivery	✓				✓			
7	Financial lending					✓			
8	"Import/export goods in batches" and "centralized declaration" policy	✓				✓			

No.	Measures	Trade facilitation standards							
		Streamlining of trade flow	Standardization of data elements	Information paperless-ness	Procedure legalization	Cost savings	Coordination among institutions	Information-based regulation	Customs cooperation
9	Simplification of customs clearance attachment documents	✓		✓		✓			
10	Unified customs record list						✓		
11	Domestic selective taxation					✓			
12	Centralized consolidated tax payment	✓				✓			
13	Bonded logistics network supervision							✓	
14	Intelligent bayonet clearance management	✓						✓	
15	Enterprise registration	✓							
16	Customs' AEO mutual recognition								✓
17	Enterprise coordinator on pilot basis								✓
18	Enterprise credit information disclosure								✓
19	Enterprise self-discipline management								✓
20	Cross-border e-commerce	✓							
21	Cancelling of clearance receipt review	✓							

Area—for the first time in China—rolled out one-stop service for international trade. However, the scope of the service only covers several departments such as customs and commodity inspection; it only has functions such as declaration for ordinary imported goods and result feedback and the networking and release approval for outbound vessels. In a word, the one-stop service does not have many functions, which cannot have a general impact on trade facilitation. Meanwhile, it is still not clear that which model (one institution, one system or one automatic material processing system) will be adopted as the goal for the service. Laws and regulations on one-stop service have not been developed yet, nor has the standardization for data elements.

Third, the awareness of risk management. Generally speaking, the SFTZ does not have the full awareness of risk management, lacking complete assessment metrics and systems. Risks are mainly managed by people who carry out paperwork examination and inspection. Information resources are scattered among different departments; information is only used for inquiry purpose without being analyzed thoroughly. It cannot help with risk control in general and lacks coordination mechanism for risk management. At the same time, the application of information technology relatively lags behind and cannot adapt to the needs of intelligent risk management.

Fourth, the SFTZ still lacks efficient coordinated regulation. For example, though paperless clearance is being carried out, taxation departments still require that written documents be handed out. Besides, no standard has been established for data format and as international standards have not been used instead, the convenience for customs clearance has been greatly reduced; moreover, it makes harder for international cooperation.

3. The Practices of Developed Countries in Trade Facilitation

Based on the framework and from the perspective of *TFA*, developed countries have conducted many valuable explorations. Generally speaking, they are the leader in trade facilitation and can offer many valuable experiences for the SFTZ to learn (For details, see Table 3). First, in terms of information technology, the US has a wide application of paperless clearance technologies such as Electronic Data Interchange (EDI) and Automated Commercial Environment System (ACE), making information processing paperless, automated, standardized and efficient. Second, regarding one-stop service, more than 40 countries have adopted one institution, one system or one automatic material processing system.[①] Third, in terms of customs cooperation, cooperation has been established between customs and foreign and domestic enterprises and institutions. As to the relations with enterprises, Singapore has set up a regular dialogue mechanism between customs and major clients; the Netherlands has built "Compliance and Facilitation and Partnership between Customs and Businesses"[②]; Australia has formed the platform where enterprises can participate in the management of customs under the "client-oriented" strategy. With regard to international cooperation, under the framework of World Customs Organization (WCO), the US has furthered the multilateral cooperation network trade security and facilitation in the international community; Japan is actively extending the scope for international certification and advancing the international mutual recognition system for honest enterprises. Fourth, in terms of risk management, risk analysis and risk control for all regulation work should be strengthened and balance should be stricken between law enforcement and facilitation. Fifth, regarding clearance procedures, Japan has introduced the system of ex-ante notification for clearance of goods and the system of preliminary document review before the arrival of goods at port. Sixth, with flexible taxation mechanism, adjust and optimize the status of taxation. For example, in order to solve the problem that the tariff rate for imported intermediate goods is higher than that of final goods, the US has redesigned tariff structure and taken the measure that part of intermediate goods will be exempted from tariffs.

---

① "One institution" refers to the establishment or the authorization of one government regulation body to handle all import and export regulation work. Countries adopting this model include Sweden and the Netherlands. "One system" refers to the establishment of a system to handle trade businesses together with all regulation bodies being independent from each other. In other words, this model features "one system and several institutions". Typical examples include the US and Japan. "One automatic material processing system" refers to the providing of one information processing portal where all systems of the government regulation bodies have been integrated, making information and business sharing and coordination a reality among all regulation bodies. By providing "single window" and one-stop service, this model features "one integrated system and independent institutions". Singapore is a typical country that adopts this model.

② With the above-mentioned models, Singapore has regularly opened courses such as "Customs Documents" and "Customs Guidance Program"; the Netherlands has formed "enterprise application—customs assessment and approval—differentiated management" mechanism and put the focus on the full understanding of customs of enterprise information, risk metrics determined both by enterprises and customs", real-time update and dynamic maintenance of risk metrics.

4. Policy Suggestions

To further enhance the level of trade facilitation of the SFTZ, the following suggestions are proposed:

(1) Establish law basis.

Upgrade the legal hierarchy of trade facilitation legislation and form the law basis for trade facilitation that is in line with international rules and commitments (including those of international organizations such as WTO and WCO). *TFA* of the WTO can be used for reference to establish the standards for law enforcement and administration and improve the law enforcement procedures for trade facilitation. Relevant laws and regulations should be made to make clear the nature, positioning, functions, institution

Table 3　Measures of developed countries in improving trade facilitation

	Measures
Advanced information technology	• Paperless-oriented information processing: the US (EDI) • Automated information processing: the US (ACE), automated border management system • Standard information processing: Europe, unified customs code, unified declaration forms, "Customs 2007" Program
Mature one-stop service	• One institution: the best model in one-stop service, Sweden and the Netherlands • One system: one system and several institutions, the US's International Trade Data System (ITDS) • One automatic material processing system: one integrated system and independent institutions". Singapore's TradeNet (TN) System
Extensive cooperation among customs	• Cooperation with commercial companies: the customs of the US has established "partnership" with commercial companies, *Customs Modernization Act 1993* has introduced concepts such as "informed compliance" and "law-abiding commercially" • International cooperation: the US has made use of WCO platform to advance the implementation of its policies; Japan has implemented AEO policy and "Trade Procedure Reform Plan"
Complete risk management	• Systematic risk control technologies: according to the US's customs risk control administrative laws, risks are ranked and managed dynamically and risk levels of enterprises are assessed • Mature and complete risk analysis model: the Netherlands' TAGITTA and special bonded warehouse system
Simplified customs procedures	• Ex-ante reply system: goods are classified before import and written inquiries are submitted to the customs on subjects such as applied tax rates and then replies are given. Japan is an example. • Preliminary inspection system: goods are inspected before the arrival at customs to make sure whether there is need to do inspection. Japan is an example.
Flexible taxation mechanism	• Dynamic adjustment: the US has resigned its tariff system because of tariff inversion. • Optimized taxation: Japan has carried out delayed taxpaying system (including individual delay, collective delay and special delay) and tax declaration and import declaration are separated.

settings, limits of authority and responsibilities of the management committee of the SFTZ, thus providing the law basis for its running and operation.

(2) Roll out fast clearance system.

Under the condition of trade security, clearance procedures should be simplified to the most degree and fast clearance system should be rolled out. The following systems are suggested to be explored: firstly, preliminary determination system. Pre-determine the management of the place of origin in advance to facilitate clearance. Secondly, preliminary review system. On the basis "first entering and then declaring" policy, further carry out the preliminary review system, that is to say, submit declaration documents for import to the SFTZ customs before the arrival of goods (or before the completion of relevant import procedures) and customs can conduct inspection in advance. Thirdly, auditing system after clearance. Under the condition that the risk assessment standards are improved and the capabilities of paper documents of outside auditing and on-site auditing are enhanced, the auditing system after clearance can be carried out. Fourth, release in advance system. When goods are met relevant requirements and the enterprise has provided needed basic information for taxpaying, clearance and release should be separated and the release in advance system should be carried out.

(3) Further one-stop service.

Accelerate the one-stop service of the SFTZ. First, suitable one-stop service model should be adopted. To avoid the shifting of regulation authority, "one system" or "one automatic material processing system" is suggested to be adopted as the suitable one-stop service model. Second, data elements should be compatible with international standards. Professional institutions should be set up to facilitate the standardization for data elements; learn from the experiences of Singapore, Sweden and the US and adopt the WCO DATA Model as the data element standard.

(4) Strengthen risk management.

In order to achieve dual goals of trade facilitation and efficient management, risk management should be taken as the focus of customs management. A framework of risk management featuring "one system, one set of metrics and one mechanism" should be established: first, relying on technologies such as the Internet and computer technology, a unified risk information system should be set up; second, build a risk parameter maintenance management center to form and improve risk pre-warning and management metrics system; third, risk information and management should be unified and be compatible in terms of business flows and data formats and technical standard should also be the same. Based on clear division of work for all trade management departments and by making full use of all resources and advantages, clarify the method and responsibilities for information collection, risk assessment and risk disposition. Develop and improve risk information sharing and risk management coordination mechanism to improve the efficiency of customs management.

(5) Set up cooperation platform.

Strengthen cooperation among customs, enterprises and government departments around the globe. First, set up the "commerce-friendly" concept, that is to say, focus should be on the needs of businesses. Innovate the ways of cooperation, improve the efficiency and level of customs service and let enterprises have more voice. Explore the mechanism of memorandum of understanding (MOU) on cooperation, reach agreements on the cooperation methods between customs and businesses; sign service agreement with major clients. Second, to cooperate with WCO to further the construction of the "global network of customs", and accelerate international mutual recognition, cross-border recognition and cooperation for AEO trade documents[1]. Third, set up cooperation mechanism for customs and relevant government administration departments and clarify their division of work to form "single window" mechanisms and facilitate the integration of customs management; for the customs itself, unified leadership and cooperation and coordination mechanism should be formed.

(6) Strengthen information technology.

Actively advance the standardization of customs information, paperlessness and automation. Apply electronic data standards, WCO data model, information and communication technology security and data privacy. Carry out efficient real-time supervision. Invest more in the construction of information-based supervision and maintenance to achieve seamless joint in all links of the supervision system of the SFTZ and accelerate the rolling out in other areas and be compatible with international standards.

---

[1] For example, electric information or certificates such as certificate of the place of origin as well as inspection and quarantine certificate.

Suggestions from Multinationals for Shanghai to Develop its Cross-border E-commerce

Zhou Shixun Tan Min Zhang Minghai

Information Department of the SDRC

Multinationals in Shanghai are concerned about the policies introduced by the municipality in recent years to facilitate the development of cross-border e-commerce. In particular, they pay close attention to the up-to-date policies designated for China (Hangzhou) Cross-Border E-Commerce Comprehensive Pilot Zone established in January 2016, and to the policies for the construction of cross-border e-commerce demonstration area. Owen, the Chief Representative from the Shanghai Office of the US-China Business Council (USCBC) stated that in the USCBC 2016 Board Priorities Statement, great importance was attached to China's e-commerce development. He said America-based companies are vigorously seeking opportunities in China to invest into Shanghai's cross-border e-commerce industry. Based on latest policies introduced for cross-border e-commerce since April, multinationals offered their suggestions as follows.

1. Enhance the Stability of Taxation and Regulations

Amazon and other companies believed fast changes in policies and uncertainties emerging in implementation are the major challenges in the way of the development of cross-border e-commerce in Shanghai and China as a whole. So they suggested that the central government and the municipal government should enhance the stability of policies, and especially the consistency in regulatory policies at the initial stage, and during and after the transition period. Some of them stated that precise classification of cross-border e-commerce trade and that of traded items are necessary for the stability of policies. Not until government has made it clear whether the trade is general trade or service trade, and whether the traded item is goods or service, can it effectively introduce corresponding taxation and regulatory policies, thus creating a basic foundation with reference to which multinationals can pick up a cross-border e-commerce model among the mainstream.

2. Improve the Transparency of Policy Drafting and Upgrading

P&G and other companies pointed out that the government should make the process of drafting and upgrading the positive list (adding new items into the list and the application for the access of new products) more transparent. The government should reveal to the public how frequently it would upgrade the list. Johnson & Johnson proposed that to adapt to global business innovation and development, the government is expected to establish a consultancy platform for the innovations and crossover products that are not clearly categorized in the positive list, so that multinationals will be able to fully acquire the boundaries stated in the policy.

3. Refine and Make the Most of the Favorable Policies for the Imported Cosmetics in Pudong New Area

Experts focused on multinationals are greatly concerned about the recently launched filing system for the imported cosmetics in Pudong New Area.[1] Enterprises including Johnson & Johnson suggested that on the basis of the circular, the municipal government should pick up the pace of introducing management rules for the filing system of imported non-special use cosmetics, promote the reform on the access into the cosmetics market, and realize online and offline synchronization, so as to create new opportunities for the development of cross-border e-commerce and the Free Trade Zone. Meanwhile, the government is expected to explore the possibility of enacting the decision throughout the city. When implementing the new policy of positive list

---

[1]　The State Council decided to make temporary changes to 11 administrative regulations and some administrative approval items stated in the cabinet's documents in Shanghai's Pudong New Area, according to a circular issued on May 5, 2016. It means the regulatory regime of the imported non-special use cosmetics in Shanghai Pudong New Area will change to record-keeping from current registration.

and customs clearance, it is advised to make innovative breakthroughs to build a more favorable environment for customs clearance than any other ports.

4. Improve Operations and Procedures

FedEx and other logistics companies advised that the government should improve the development of public service platform for cross-border e-commerce. The method of category filing should be explored for customs clearance to serve e-commerce industry where imports and exports are various in kinds and new products can quickly replace the less needed one. The government is also suggested to pilot the method of allowing goods purchased abroad to be returned to the nearest market such as Hong Kong, so as to reduce the number of goods returned to the place of departure and cut down logistics cost. Other companies like Estee Lauder and Mead Johnson proposed that the government should explore the feasibility of using verification by overseas governments and third-party organizations in the customs clearance of imported cosmetics, health products and milk powder.

Conforming to Amended International Trade Rules and Quickening the Pace of Reform in China(Shanghai) Pilot Free Trade Zone

Zhou Shixun   Zhang Minghai

Information Department of the SDRC

1. Four Main Issues Confronting the Reforming of Free Trade Zones

Despite the notable achievements in the reform and opening-up of the four Free Trade Zones, four main issues stand out to be resolved.

(1) Enthusiasm from home and cold response from abroad.

Since its setup, China (Shanghai) Pilot Free Trade Zone (SFTZ for short) has attracted consistent coverage of domestic press and study of domestic academic institutions. Contrarily, foreign academic world has attributed only a scanty number of research papers, the majority of which come from Chinese scholars or foreign ones teaching in China. Specifically speaking, according to the statistics published by the Ministry of Commerce, during January to September in 2015, 45,000 new enterprises were set up in Free Trade Zones from Guangdong, Tianjin and Fujian, among which only 10 per cent were foreign-funded. According to the published data from the four Free Trade Zones, the new foreign-funded enterprises set up since the start of the SFTZ two years ago accounted for 20 per cent of the total number of newly established ones. By the end of October 2015, among all the new foreign-funded enterprises, the ones in Tianjin FTZ took up 4.4%, and the ones in Guangdong FTZ took up 5.0% and the ones in Fujian FTZ took up 7.1% since its setup seven months ago. Meanwhile, regarding specific reform practices, apart from institutional innovation, the transformation of government functions is emerging as the focus in the Free Trade Zones, on which currently issued policy is also centered.

提升投资贸易便利化水平，构建开放型经济新体制

(2) Lack of power to directly carry out experiments.

Free Trade Zone administration has no right to carry out experiments directly as examination and approval is required from concerned ministries in practices for many pilot projects listed in the Free Trade Zone program. Take Tianjin Free Trade Zone for instance, despite the advocate of "proactive development of cross-border e-commerce" from the State Council, the failed docking between customs system and e-commerce platform strangled its registration and development, even after Tianjin had entered the list of pilot cities for import cross-border e-commerce. Take the SFTZ for a further example. It's advised in the SFTZ Framework Plan to "deepen tax policy for overseas equity investment and offshore business", despite the comprehensive discussion between the SFTZ administration committee and the central financial and taxation departments, no result is published until now.

(3) The inconvenience of reform policy.

Due to the lack of optimization of overall oversight mechanism, some policies failed to facilitate reform practices. For example, regarding the tax refund in port of departure, the regulation on business are over-tight (e.g. ships refunding at pilot port of departure shall not anchor underway until they reach at Shanghai Yangshan Port instead of any port in Waigaoqiao Port Area), impeding the development of this business and crippling the effects of reform in the SFTZ. Take the exhibition and exchange of bonded goods in Tianjin Free Trade Zone for another example. Enterprises are required to pay full duty guarantee in cash for its exhibition, in which sense, the original significance of reducing cash flow in the exhibition and exchange of bonded goods vanishes with its institutional innovation.

(4) Slow publication of Regulations of financial reform.

The financial reform in the four Free Trade Zones is aimed at accommodating high-level international trade rules, yet it turns out to witness no publication of implementing regulations, scarce substantial progress in financial reform and no smooth development of relevant businesses. For example, after the publication of Thirty Regulation Rules of Financial Reform in Tianjin Free Trade Zone, reports from the press showed that Bohai Steel Group International Trading C.o. had made the first cross-border direct loan via CITIC Bank, while in fact due to the absence of detailed rules and regulations, this transaction didn't take place. Besides, to which extent the foreign loan proportion should be raised in the Plan for Financial Reform is out of reach of Free Trade Zone administration. In Fujian Free Trade Zone, the fourteen measures for opening-up to Taiwan in the fields of finance and medical care are also yet to be implemented.

2. Causes for the FTZ dilemma

The above-listed four issues confronting the Free Trade Zones result from the following two reasons.

(1) Overload of tasks for FTZs.

As a common practice, there is a set of typical operational procedures, e.g. freedom to trade or financial freedom for Free Trade Zones (FTZs) in the sovereign states of this world. Therefore, domestic enterprises harbor impractical expectation that moving into the Development Zone will bring tax cuts to their business. Contrary to their one-sided enthusiasm, the foreign companies have no idea of what the Free Trade Zones in China is planning and hence remain their cautious observing position in reaction to the continuous absence of unified English version of essential documents including the Framework Plan and the negative list for foreign investment in Tianjin and other FTZs.

(2) Failure of power delegation from the state ministry to the lower levels.

The setup of Free Trade Zone has attracted high attention of central government as well as the appeal of local government to carry out pilot programs. However, there is failed delegation of power to the lower levels. First of all, many FTZ related reforms contradict against previous regulations published by concerning ministries, hence the risk of undermining the power of the higher levels. Faced with the increasingly rigorous officials-accountability system, many ministries or administrations give slow or even no examination and approval to reform programs. Second, the lack of trans-ministry coordination slows down the delegation of power to FTZ administration. For example, regarding the tax refund of port of departure, the customs shows its ability to regulate but the finance and taxation department thinks otherwise and shows its concern over potential tax evasion. Third, major accidents like the 8.12 explosion in Tianjin harbor have led to the dismissal of some government officials and slowed down the reform of FTZ including the customs part, All above-listed reasons can be attributed to the stagnancy of reform and opening-up in the FTZs.

3. Suggestions

Four suggestions are presented here to improve the reform in the Free Trade Zones.

(1) Stick to the basis of new international trade rules.

Though it is very important to advance the transformation of government function by developing the Free Trade Zone, the priority of FTZ should be accommodating high-standard international trade rules. Courage is needed to introduce and apply new international trade rules in order to deepen opening-up in the FTZs.

Specifically, centered on TPP, encouraging practices should be introduced to boost fair competition between domestic and overseas enterprises and intellectual property protection. Moreover, to fill in the attention gap between the domestic and overseas enterprises, we should work on the standard translation of documents on policy, on the image promotion of the FTZ, on the framework plan and policy innovation aiming at attracting foreign investment.

(2) Establish incentive mechanism against risks.

It should be fully acknowledged that the reform of FTZ will have an influence on the power shift among different administrations. Therefore, an incentive mechanism for government officials should be established to reward officials or departments who have made achievements or contributions to the reform, and to prioritize them on the promotion list. Meanwhile, ministries should not knock down innovative practices at one stroke as officials who dare to take risks in reform should be allowed with their try and error method. The focus should be put on working out solutions and a coping mechanism against risks rather than on exaggerating the possible risks.

(3) Enhance the coordination of reform in the Free Trade Zones.

A unified leadership should be established on the national level to coordinate the work among ministries to provide support and service for the FTZ reform and thus to lay the foundation stone for accommodating high-level international trade standards and conventions. Besides, research and training should be enhanced to facilitate the docking of domestic FTZs and trans-national FTAs.

(4) Fasten the pace of financial reform in the Free Trade Zones.

During the development of Free Trade Zones, tax revenue should be allocated in a reasonable proportion. It should be neither too high for foreign enterprises nor too low for domestic ones. According to international practices, we should broaden the tax preference to foreign fund, publish the preferential policy to adjust income tax rate for offshore business, enlarge tax preference range for international shipping insurance and develop an attractive offshore insurance tax system. Besides, we should promote innovation and out-going strategy, optimize negative list, fasten financial reform and facilitation of trade and investment, especially implementing the reform in offshore finance and thus strengthening Chinese international competitiveness.

Promote the Development of Shanghai's Single Window System for International Trade by Learning from South Korea

Zhou Shixun   Yao Zhi

Information Department of the SDRC

1. Reasons to Learn From South Korea's UNI-PASS System

With the comprehensive comparison between South Korea's single window system and that of Singapore, it is found that South Korea is more suitable for us to learn from.

(1) South Korea has the most favorable environment for customs clearance in the world, and its single window system has been learned from in other 8 countries.

With the help of UNI-PASS, an electronic customs clearance system, South Korean government provides one-stop clearance service for clients by enabling clearance processes to be executed through a single window. Thanks to the system, the country has shorter clearance procedure time than other WCO member states, and it has been repeatedly crowned as the best by the World Bank in terms of clearance environment. As the best practice[1] of the country's E-government, the single window system has been practiced in 8 countries including the Dominican Republic and Kazakhstan, and is likely to be implemented in more countries.

(2) South Korea has larger trade volume than Singapore, and is China's third largest trading partner.

According to WTO's statistics, South Korea's trade volume was 1.415 times

---

[1] Taking the lead in the development of e-government in the world, South Korea ranked the first for three consecutive years (2010, 2012, 2014) in terms of EGDI.

that of Singapore in 2014. It is the crucial trading partner of the world's three large economies, and has been China's third largest trading partner in recent years, while China is its largest trading partner. China–South Korea Free Trade Agreement which began to be enacted recently will further enhance the bilateral trade between the two countries.

(3) South Korea's structure of foreign trade is more similar to ours.

Singapore's entrepot trade as a large proportion of its foreign trade rose from 68.8% in 1999 to 99.7% in 2014. While South Korea and China are both countries with trade surplus, and their export-to-import ratio moves within the range of 1.06 and 1.20. Therefore, our country's structure of foreign trade is more similar to South Korea's than to Singapore's.

2. The Operation Mode of South Korea's Single Window System

(1) The Background and Structure of UNI-PASS.

South Korea's Single Window project is launched to meet the objective demand on trade automation resulting from the rapid increase in trade volume. Since 1992, the Korea Customs Service (KSC) has been implementing Electronic Data Interchange (EDI) system for customs clearance. Since the UNI-PASS was first introduced by KCS in 2005, the system has continued to grow with RFID used in the air cargo management, and expand by developing Integrated Risk Management System and AEO management system[1]. The number of agencies participating in it has continued to increase, rising from 8 in 2005 to 33 in 2011.[2]

For the interconnectivity with foreign countries in achieving Global Single Window, the UNI-PASS applies international standards such as WCO DM 3.0, and open technology standards. The system is composed of Internet clearance portal and the business operation system (shown in the Figure 1). The portal allows traders to lodge application and authentication, and submit documents for customs clearance and declaration with a single entry point where they can also receive feedback. The business operation system consists of Procedural business modules (ie. Duty collection,

---

[1] See Korea Customs e-Clearance System (2014).

[2] See Republic of Korea Single Window Case (2010).

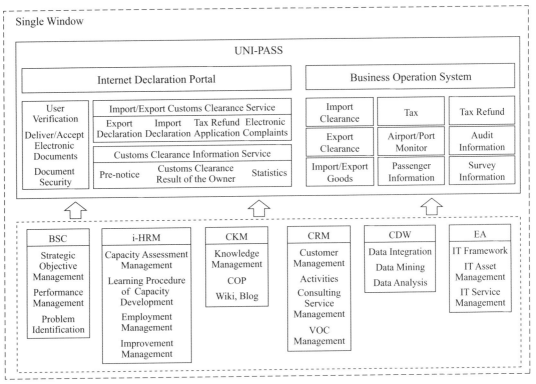

Figure 1   The Structure of South Korean Single Window System

tax rebate, surveillance etc.), and these form the most basic customs modules for the automation of the customs administration. And the UNI-PASS is also supported by six systems: Business Service Control (BSC), integrated Human Resource Management (i-HRM), Customer Knowledge Management (CKM), Customer Relationship Management (CRM), Customs Data Warehouse (CDW), and Enterprise Architecture (EA).

(2) Basic Services.

Apart from one-stop paperless service, the UNI-PASS has other two basic services, one of which is real-time cargo tracking. It manages cargo throughout the supply chain with the help of e-manifest, warehouse inventory management, transport control and tracking, and cargo processing status (real-time). The other service is based on (Advanced Papyrological Information System) APIS. By providing passenger and crew information, and manifest data, it enables customs to analyze the risk of passengers to control high-risk passengers, ensure national security and allow low-risk passengers to pass through a swift clearance prior to the arrival of airplanes. In this process, information from immigration and other Ministries are also taken into consideration.

(3) Operation Model.

The UNI-PASS is developed, operated and maintained by Korea Customs UNI-PASS Information Association (CUPIA), a non-profit organization. Over the past decade, CUPIA has grown into a professional in e-clearance both at home and abroad, who can offer individual solutions including single window system, CDW, risk management, etc. for customs in foreign countries.

The development of UNI-PASS is covered by the government budget, and is funded by KCS. The system is free for clients to use.

3. Experience Gained from South Korea's Single Window System for Shanghai

On the basis of e-port platform, the Shanghai government first piloted the single window system in Yangshan Bonded Port in 2014. With the 1.0 version of the single window system introduced in June, 2015, the pilot program was expanded to ports in Shanghai. At the end of the same year, the 2.0 version was launched. Over the past year, the system has successfully improved regulatory activities, enhanced customs clearance efficiency, and cut down the operation cost for enterprises. To further improve the single window system, Shanghai can learn from South Korea in the following aspects.

(1) Expand the types of agencies participating in the Single Window system to improve the efficiency of port services.

The South Korean government keeps connecting more agencies to its single window system, including port administrations as well as non-governmental organizations responsible for verification. In 2009, the government connected 4 public agencies (i.e. Korea Food and Drug Administration, National Fisheries Products Quality Inspection Service, etc.), and 13 private organizations (like Korea Pharmaceutical Traders Association, Association for Medical Devices Industry and Korea Animal Health Products Association). In contrast, 17 agencies involved in Shanghai's single window system is only composed of 15 government agencies and 2 large state owned enterprises. So South Korean Single Window system can better take advantage of NGOs to make port services more efficient. Shanghai government is suggested to expand the types of agencies participating in the Single Window system to win support from more industries for the system. The government should strengthen

提升投资贸易便利化水平，构建开放型经济新体制

interconnectivity with more industries to improve the efficiency of port services.

(2) Include the function of manifest transmission to strengthen the management through supply chain and to enhance port security.

The manifest records basic data on the flow of imports and exports, based on which the customs execute regulation. With the use of e-manifest, South Korean Single Window System effectively manages cargo through the supply chain. At present, China's e-port has established manifest transmission system for vessels and aircraft, but Shanghai's Single Widow system lacks the function of manifest transmission. So it is suggested that this function be included in Shanghai's single window system to provide users with the full information about logistics and clearance, and to realize real-time cargo tracking and the transparency of logistics administration. It can also make the regulation in each stage of the supply chain more effective, reduce risks in trade and law enforcement, and increase the security during port administration.

(3) promote traveler declaration and carry out passenger service in the Single Window system.

Traveler declaration is one of the extensions of the 2.0 version of Shanghai's single window system, but has not been realized yet. Because of the rapid economic growth at Shanghai Cruise Port and the popularity of Shanghai Disneyland, the number of overseas arrivals and departures will rocket. So improving the service of traveler declaration is not only to implement the 2.0 version, but also to meet the objective need to provide swifter clearance for travelers whose number is increasing dramatically. To do so, Shanghai is advised to look to South Korean Single Window System and include passenger information pre-reporting system to its single window. By sharing or exchanging passenger data with airlines and cruises, the pre-reporting system enables the customs to collect passenger information in advance to analyze risks, and categorize passengers into various levels of risk. low-risk passengers will pass through a swift clearance while high-risk passengers will be subject to stricter control.

(4) Strengthen the connectivity with law enforcers and promote the Implementation of Integrated Faster Clearance.

Shanghai's single window system offers enterprises a user-friendly front-end platform on which they can standardized information and documents with a single entry point. The system helps enterprises to reduce the duplication of futile effort, and cut down costs. However, due to the system at its infancy, when data is transmitted to the operation system of law enforcers, these authorities still fail to cooperate on law enforcement at some stages because of the absence of effective connectivity mechanism. It means they cannot further provide convenience for enterprises. Take the "one-time declaration, one-time inspection, one-time release" service by the customs and the department of inspection and quarantine as an example. In the existing system, due to the lack of joint law enforcement between different port law enforcers, traders have to undergo repeated inspection and release. So it is proposed that information exchange mechanism among law enforcers should be established in the single window system, such as the arrangement of inspection site and time in advance, so as to realize joint law enforcement between multiple departments, create convenience for companies and accelerate cargo clearance.

(5) Adopt unified data standard and further simplify declaration data.

The same as South Korea, Shanghai has applied WCO data model as it emphasizes the international standardization of data. As a domestic pioneer in the development of Single Window system, Shanghai is supposed to learn from South Korea to simplify declaration data and establish unified data standard for the single window system. Ultimately, the standard can be replicated by other places throughout China to connect regional single window systems and realize a national system.

Strengthen Trade Regulations in China (Shanghai) Pilot Free Trade Zone

Zhou Shixun   Tan Min

Information Department of the SDRC

1. False Trading in China (Shanghai) Pilot Free Trade Zone

According to the "*White Paper on the Investigation into Crimes in China (Shanghai) Pilot Free Trade Zone: 2014—2015*" released by the People's Procuratorate of Pudong New Area of Shanghai, crimes in Shanghai Free Trade Zone are generally related to false trading. Law-breakers strike transactions without substances, evade foreign exchange controls, commit letter of credit fraud, and defraud the State of the refunded tax on exports. In order to gain illegal benefits, the offenders commit these crimes by taking advantage over some factors including the complexity of cross-border trade, the problem of distinguishing false trading from real ones, the difficulty to obtain evidence overseas, and the difference on the trading systems at home and abroad. As statistics of the past two years reveal, the quantity and the type of crimes in China (Shanghai) Pilot Free Trade Zone remain almost the same as what they were before the free trade zone was established. However, risk factors are continuing to emerge as enterprises in the zone have a far better understanding of implemented polices. Thus, regulations should be strengthened.

The false trading appears in two forms. One form is through cross-border trade facilitation solutions in the bonded area and export processing zone[1], where enterprises are allowed to purchase foreign exchange at home and sell it in the foreign market for interest arbitrage. This can be found, for example, in Waigaoqiao Free Trade Zone. In the other form, Enterprises realize cross-border arbitrage by submitting fake documents to banks and other institutions.[2]

---

[1] If a company in China and its trading partner abroad export to each other the products of the same price, it can be regarded as an extrepot trade.

[2] The two trading partners at home and abroad forge purchase and sale agreement, invoices and shipping documents.

2. Reasons on the Emergence of False Trading in China (Shanghai) Pilot Free Trade Zone

(1) FTZ Pioneers a High Degree of Openness which yet Makes it More Convenient for False Trading.

To promote the development of the free trade zone, especially the cross-border trade,China (Shanghai) Pilot Free Trade Zone has implemented a series of preferential policies concerning foreign exchange rate and tax on international trade. These policies have reduced the cost and made it more convenient for cross-border trade. Of particular note, the financial innovation mechanism established for capital account convertibility and the opening up of the financial service sector has further facilitated financing and leasing, thus creating exploitable opportunities for false trading. For instance, with the enforcement of "*Operational Guidelines on Financial Innovation in China (Shanghai) Pilot Free Trade Zone*", domestic banks have been witnessing their offshore lending increase dramatically, partly because of the relatively low interest rate overseas. What's more, Chinese companies normally could only be offered overseas loans under domestic guarantees, which made it rather difficult for them to get offshore loans. But now they are no longer restricted in overseas financing for being a domestic company. China (Shanghai) Pilot Free Trade Zone is being constructed and reformed based on higher standards than other bonded areas and free trade zones. This creates a more open and more favorable environment for false trading, and brings about more challenges and greater requirements for risk management in the financial system.

(2) The Exchange Rate Difference between Onshore and Offshore Markets Creates a New Platform for False Trading.

As in the FTZ there is an offshore RMB market, the domestic market has a dual exchange rate system.[1] The exchange rate difference lures some enterprises to carry

---

[1] The offshore RMB market in Hong Kong differs from the onshore market in mainland China in terms of the size and depth. The offshore RMB pool is smaller than the onshore market and lacks liquidity. On top of that, influenced by the global financial market, the offshore exchange rate appears larger fluctuation. On the contrary, the onshore rate is only allowed to fluctuate within a range of 2% above and below the middle rate. With different investors have different risk appetite, different insights into an economic situation, different interpretations of a policy and different reactions; RMB has different prices in the offshore and onshore markets.

out false trading in FTZ.

Due to RMB exchange rate difference having been widening since 2015, the number of false trading driven by interest arbitrage has been growing significantly. According to statistics from the General Administration of Customs, our country's export fell by 1.4% in December on a year-over-year basis, better than expected and outperforming that in November. But in the same period exports from Chinese Mainland to Hong Kong stood as high as $46 billion, up by 10.8% from a year ago; while imports from Hong Kong to Chinese Mainland reached $2.16 billion, rocketing by 65%. The improvement in international trade statistics partly resulted from false trading, as China's Export Leading Indicator released by the Customs and the Baltic Dry Index suggested China's foreign trade had slumped.

3. Suggestions for Enhancing Trade Regulations of China (Shanghai) Pilot Free Trade Zone

(1) Promote the Regulatory Regime by Refining the Measures to Account for and Manage Trade Account Separately.

In the FTZ, trade account is accounted for and managed separately. This has been effective in stopping hot money from flowing into China through the FTZ, and preventing the explosive growth of false trading. But more efforts are needed to refine and implement detailed rules about system improvement, system testing, data monitoring and risk management so as to support the regulation of FTZ and further ward off false trading, hot money flows, arbitrage-seeking activities and other financial risks.

(2) Enforce the Policies Issued by the State Administration of Foreign Exchange and Ensure Separate Regulations on Each Party.

False trading helps companies to gain high incomes without paying anything, brings commercial banks enormous profits and increase nominal GDP for local governments. Different parts are linked together, though have different interests. During the construction of China (Shanghai) Pilot Free Trade Zone, effective regulations should be enforced on the three parties to fend off false trading. First, the government needs to strengthen separate regulations on companies. We need to strengthen supervision on companies with unusual expenditures and incomes in trade, particularly companies undergoing abnormal increase in long-term trade finance and showing the signs of arbitrage. We should carry out separate regulations on companies based on "*Provisions of Trade in Goods and Foreign Exchange Management*", and should focus on the supervision on companies that have a bad record. Second, the government should continue to urge banks to improve their examination on the authenticity and legitimacy of companies' trade finance. It needs to play an active role in meeting the need of real economies in trade finance and prevent companies from illegally obtaining loans from banks in the way of false trading. The government should encourage banks to enhance internal management and supervision, report suspicious trade deals to authorities immediately, and ban on helping companies circumvent foreign exchange management rules. Third, the government is supposed to stop solely emphasizing international trade growth and should improve its regulation. False trading has something to do with the regulatory system. So the government should transfer its focus from international trade growth target to the improvement on operational and post-operational regulation when accessing the performance of lower-levels of government. While a mounting number of policies on FTZ reform and innovation are being introduced for the convenience of companics, the government should take full into consideration potential risks and take precautions measures.[1]

(3) Take Advantage of Information Technology to Realize Customs Precise Regulation.

Since this March, the General Administration of Customs has been launching a nationwide smuggling crackdown movement with fighting against false trading as its priority. To deal with the risks related to false trading in China (Shanghai) Pilot Free Trade Zone and improve the regulation, Shanghai Customs can make its regulation more precise and explore into systemic risk management measures on poor-credit companies by big data analysis on the platform provided by information technology. Meanwhile in management methods, the Customs can rely on the free trade account system and modern methods like the use of risk conversion factor to 24-hour monitor the risks in each deal and ensure financial security.

(4) Improve Regulatory Efficacy in all Aspects through an Integrated Approach.

---

[1] Take the timing of the dramatic increase in false trading as an example. Since the RMB exchange rate reform on August 11th, 2015, the exchange rate difference between the onshore and offshore markets have been widening and the number of false trading for arbitrage has been going up.

The government should change its fragmented management mode in which every department is isolated from each other. It should promote the cooperation between different departments such as the Customs, the shipping department and financial institutions, and strengthen communications on policies, data and information sharing among them, so as to achieve a systemic and integrated regulation. The government is suggested to establish a multi-form, multi-level and multi-channel coordination, communication and meeting mechanisms for regular data and information exchange. It should enhance the interaction between logistics and capital flow, better the quality of data from trade credit investigation and improve the efficacy of investigation. It should work together with different parties to crack down false trading, safeguard economic order and financial security in FTZ, and improve regulatory efficacy in all aspects.

APPENDIX

附　录

2016 年上海国际智库峰会
办会、参会方简介

1. 主办方

上海市人民政府发展研究中心

上海市人民政府发展研究中心（前身是上海经济研究中心）于 1980 年 12 月 26 日正式成立，于 1995 年 12 月 22 日根据市政府决定，更名为上海市人民政府发展研究中心。上海市人民政府发展研究中心是为市政府决策服务，承担上海市决策咨询的研究、组织、协调、管理、服务的市政府决策咨询研究机构。

主要职责：

（1）研究上海市经济、社会发展和改革开放中具有全局性、综合性、战略性的问题。

（2）了解动态、分析矛盾、研究对策、预测前景，及时向上海市委、市政府提出决策建议和咨询意见。

（3）负责上海市两年一度的市决策咨询研究成果奖的评奖工作。

（4）组织、协调市政府系统的决策咨询研究工作。

（5）负责上海市决策咨询系统建议库信息管理和维护工作。

（6）受市政府委托，管理有关组织和事业机构。

（7）编辑出版《上海经济年鉴》和《科学发展》杂志。

（8）承办上海市领导交办的其他事项。

2. 承办方

普华永道中国

普华永道 1849 年创立于英国伦敦，经过百年发展，已经成为一家全球性运营的专业服务机构，通过在 157 个国家和地区中超过 22.3 万名的专业人才，致力于向客户提供基于行业的咨询、审计和税务服务，协助解决复杂的业务难题，提高客户运营效率、风险控制水平及提升自身价值。全球财富 500 强企业中超过 84% 的企业是普华永道的服务客户。

普华永道在中国共拥有员工约 18 000 人，其中包括约 700 名合伙人。普华永道是在中国最具规模的专业服务机构，北京、上海、香港是我们在中国最大的三个办事处。

秉承"解决重要问题，营造社会诚信"的企业使命，普华永道致力于吸引优秀的人才来创建多元包容的团队，持续提升专业服务质量，勇于创新并积极参与社会重大活动，为客户和社会解决各类重要问题。

在品牌价值及战略咨询公司 Brand Finance 最新公布的"2016 全球品牌价值 500 强榜单"上，普华永道名列"全球最强十大品牌"之一，在金融行业企业中名列榜首。2015 年在雇主品牌咨询机构优信（Universum）全球最具吸引力雇主排名中，普华永道被评为"对商学院毕业生最具吸引力雇主"第二位。普华永道中天会计师事务所在 2003 年开始的中国注册会计师协会下属会计师事务所百强评选中，连续十四年名列第一。

上海发展研究基金会

上海发展研究基金会成立于 1993 年，是利用自然人、法人或者其他组织捐赠的财产，以从事公益事业为目的，按照国家有关规定的公募基金会、非营利性法人。

上海发展研究基金会以促进对发展问题的研究、推进决策咨询事业为宗旨；以募集、运作资金，研究、交流、资助、奖励经济、社会、城市发展决策咨询项目为业务范围。

二十多年来，基金会大力支持上海市决策咨询研究工作，资助了许多研究项目，并资助开展了上海市决策咨询研究成果奖评奖工作。同时，基金会也组织研究团队，完成了自行设立的或从其他单位承接的一系列研究项目。

近年来，基金会为实现其宗旨而积极探索。基金会每月举办一次"上海发展沙龙"，邀请国内外知名专家、学者就当前的热点或敏感问题作演讲，并与参会者进形互动讨论；每年举办两到三次高层次的研讨会，邀请多位海内外专家与政、商、学界人士共聚一堂，就全球经济和中国经济的形势进行讨论和交流；举办"中国经济未来"系列座谈会，针对中国经济发展中一些深层次问题，进行深入的讨论。基金会还通过资助的方式，与大学和研究机构合作举办了各种形式的研讨活动。基金会把各种研讨活动中的精彩内容，不定期地编撰出版内部资料《研讨实录》和《研究简报》，在更大的范围内推广对发展问题的研究和讨论成果。

上海国际智库交流中心

上海国际智库交流中心是上海市人民政府发展研究中心搭建的开放式决策咨询研究公共平台之一。2010 年，市政府发展研究中心按照时任市长韩正的指示要求，为进一步拓展上海市决策咨询研究工作，汇集国内外专家学者智慧服务市委、市政府的科学决策、民主决策，不断扩大市政府发展研究中心的国际影响力，由市政府发展研究中心牵头，联合埃森哲、凯捷、博斯、德勤、IBM 等 13 家在沪的国际知名智库于 2011 年 1 月成立并举办了主题为："创新、转型、发展"首届上海智慧论坛。时任市长韩正同志发来贺电，时任市政府秘书长姜平同志出席会议并致词。

上海国际智库交流中心的主要职责是：

(1) 开展政府决策咨询研究。

(2) 服务企业发展开展应用研究、企业规划、管理咨询。

(3) 开展双边和多边国际合作研讨。

(4) 承担国际合作课题研究。

(5) 提供专业人才培养、培训与信息服务。

六年来，上海国际智库交流中心发挥独特的人才、资源和信息优势，对接中心的特聘专家、工作室、社会调查、课题研究、高校论坛等决策咨询研究公共平台，围绕上海的经济社会发展开展了大量国际合作研究，举办了 16 次双边论坛，4 次"上海智慧论坛"，三次上海国际智库峰会，有效地提升了市政府发展研究中心整合国家智库的功能和作用，为市委、市政府科学决策、民主决策提供了大量来自国外知名智库的意见和建议。

3. 参会智库

埃森哲

埃森哲公司注册成立于爱尔兰，是一家全球领先的专业服务公司，为客户提供战略、咨询、数字、技术和运营服务及解决方案。埃森哲立足商业与技术的前沿，业务涵盖 40 多个行业，以及企业日常运营部门的各个职能。凭借独特的业内经验与专业技能，以及翘楚全球的交付网络，埃森哲帮助客户提升绩效，并为利益相关方持续创造价值。埃森哲是《财富》全球 500 强企业之一，目前拥有约 38.4 万名员工，服务于 120 多个国家的客户。埃森哲致力于驱动创新，从而改善人们工作和生活的方式。

埃森哲在大中华区开展业务已 30 年，拥有一支逾 1.3 万人的员工队伍，分布于北京、上海、大连、成都、广州、深圳、香港和台北。作为绩效提升专家，埃森哲将世界领先的商业技术实践于中国市场，帮助中国企业和政府制定战略、优化流程、集成系统、促进创新、提升运营效率、形成整体竞争优势，从而实现基业常青。

麦肯锡

麦肯锡公司是一家全球领先的管理咨询公司，1926 年创立于美国，致力于为企业和公共机构提供有关战略、组织、运营和技术方面的咨询。麦肯锡在全球范围内咨询业务的客户包括了最知名的企业及机构，占据《财富》杂志全球 500 强公司排行榜的 80%。在大中华区，麦肯锡的客户遍及 15 个行业，还包括国家级、地区级及省市级的政府及机构。麦肯锡进入大中华区三十余年来，一直致力于帮助本土领先企业改善管理技能和提升全球竞争力，并为寻求在本地区扩大业务的跨国企业提供咨询，同时也积极参与中国公共政策咨询和公共事业建设。目前麦肯锡在大中华地区开设了北京、上海、深圳、香港及台北五家分公司，共有50 多位合伙人，300 多位咨询师，还有 100 多位研究员及 200 多位专业人员。

波士顿咨询公司

波士顿咨询公司（BCG）是一家全球性管理咨询公司，是世界领先的商业战略咨询机构，客户遍及所有行业和地区。BCG 与客户密切合作，帮助他们辨别最具价值的发展机会，应对至关重要的挑战并协助他们进行行业业务转型。在为客户度身订制的解决方案中，BCG 融入对公司和市场态势的深刻洞察，并与客户组织的各个层面紧密协作。从而确保客户能够获得可持续的竞争优势，成长为更具能力的组织并保证成果持续有效。波士顿咨询公司成立于 1963 年，目前在全球48 个国家设有 85 家办公室。

BCG 在大中华区已运营了 30 多年，并分别设立了北京、香港、上海和台北四个办公室。BCG 的客户是来自各个行业领域的跨国公司或本土企业。BCG 利用国际最佳实践和本土经验及实战技术，帮助他们制定业务战略。

凯捷咨询

凯捷在全世界 40 多个国家拥有超过 18 万名员工，是全球领先的咨询、信息技术和外包服务提供商之一。2015 年，凯捷全球营业额达 119 亿欧元。凯捷通过其独有的"协同业务体验 Collaborative Business Experience™"方式，利用其全球交付模式"Rightshore®"，有效平衡世界各地的最佳资源，帮助客户创建并提供适应其业务需求的最优化解决方案。

1997 年凯捷登陆中国，随着在 2000 年全球性地并购了五大会计师事务所之一安永的咨询业务，凯捷进一步扩大了其在中国的业务。目前，凯捷中国已经成为集团重要的战略新兴市场之一，凯捷的大中华区总部设在上海，并在北京、广州、香港、台北、昆山、佛山、杭州和沈阳等地设有分公司或运营中心。拥有超过 2 500 名专业管理顾问和技术专家团队，业务覆盖管理咨询、信息技术、服务外包、全球研发及本地化解决方案的实施等。凯捷中国有效地将本土团队与全球业务网络和资源高度融合，形成相互支持的网络化服务能力，是数字化转型的最佳合作伙伴。

德勤

德勤凭借遍布逾 150 个国家的全球网络和近 24 万人才的专业智慧，为 80% 的全球 500 强企业提供服务。2016 财年全球营收 368 亿美元，为全球最大的综合咨询服务提供商（按营收计）。德勤自 1917 年进入中国，已经为大中华区客户服务 99 年，亦是德勤全球网络中发展最快的成员所。德勤一向看重本地市场的实际需求，24 个城市近 13 500 名员工，按照当地适用法规以协作方式提供综合服务；帮助更多优秀的中国企业、本地企业做大做强；也通过自身全球网络的优势，将更多的外资企业引进来以及为中国企业走出去提供支持，全面协助中国企业实现优质增长并提升国际地位。1/3 香港联交所上市的企业选择德勤的服务，为 800 多家跨国公司及其在中国的关联公司提供专业服务。除向企业提供服务之外，我们也向中央及各级政府、机构提供专业建议，推动国资发展，帮助"引进来，走出去"。自 1993 年以来，德勤一直作为中国政府财政部在国际会计准则和税务系统建设方面的专业顾问。德勤向国务院国资委、地方国资委提供包括国有企业产权代表、董事长绩效考核等多领域的专业管理咨询服务，协助一些省市国资委成功建设并推广了风险预警机制。此外，德勤为多个省市政府提供产业规划、招商策略、政府创新转型、电子政务等服务，有很多成功经验。

安永

安永凭借在全球和当地的专业知识，协助客户保持投资者对客户的信心、管理企业风险、强化控制措施、抓住机遇和发挥企业的潜能。我们向许多大型和快速增长的中国企业，以及在区内经营业务的跨国公司提供审计、税务、财务交易和咨询服务。中国海外投资业务部（China Overseas Investment Network 简称"COIN"）将安永全球的专业人员连接在一起，促进相互协作，为中国企业的国际化发展提供全球一致的高质量服务。安永在美洲、EMEIA、亚太和日本各大区设置了专业的中国商业顾问团队，服务网络覆盖全球约 65 个国家和地区。

安永是大中华区规模最大的专业服务机构之一，在区内提供专业服务已有45 年。这段期间，安永取得多项具里程碑意义的发展：安永的前身雅特杨会计师事务所（Arthur Young）于 1968 年在香港成立首个办事处；1981 年安永成为首批获准在中国内地开展业务的国际专业服务机构之一。

安永在大中华区设立了共 24 家办事处的网络，分别位于北京、香港、上海、广州、深圳、成都、大连、杭州、澳门、青岛、苏州、天津、武汉、厦门、南京、沈阳、长沙、西安、台北、台中、台南、中坜、新竹和高雄。

高风咨询

高风咨询公司是一家顶尖的战略和管理咨询公司，植根于中国，同时拥有全球视野、能力、以及广泛的资源网络。高风咨询公司为客户解决他们最棘手的问题——在当前快速变化、复杂且不确定性的经营环境之中所出现的问题。高风咨询公司不仅为客户"构建"问题解决方案，同时亦是协助方案的执行与落地，与客户携手合作。高风咨询公司的价值观引领着其工作行为——公司致力于将客户的利益放在最根本和最重要的位置；高风咨询公司是客观的，致力于与客户建立长期的合作关系，而不是单独的项目；高风咨询公司将人才视为战略资产，而非纯粹的"人头"；高风咨询公司，从最基层到最高级的顾问，都以帮助客户解决难题和并肩合作提升价值为信条。

IBM

IBM，即国际商业机器公司，创立于 1911 年，是一家全球整合的信息技术、咨询服务和业务解决方案公司。IBM 公司业务遍及 170 多个国家，运用最先进的信息科技，助力各行各业的客户创造商业价值。同时，IBM 吸引并拥有全球最优秀的人才，助力对客户及整个社会至关重要的事业，致力于让世界更美好。

IBM 的业务涵盖技术与商业领域。IBM 始终寻求高价值创新，推动持续改造与转型自身的业务。通过从行业领先的大数据、云、社交移动与认知计算技术、企业级系统和软件、咨询和 IT 服务中形成的产品与整合业务解决方案，为客户创造价值。同时，所有这些方案都汲取着全球最领先的 IBM 研究机构的创新支持。

目前，IBM 致力于推进三大战略——利用大数据推动行业转型、打造竞争优势；利用云计算，重塑企业 IT 架构，推动业务模式变革；以及利用移动和社交技术、并依托安全能力构建企业互动参与体系。IBM 正在为现代 IT 骨干创建一个专注于开放创新的全新系统基础架构，以满足新计算时代前所未有、日新月异的需求。IBM 员工与客户通力合作，利用公司的业务咨询、技术和研发能力构建稳健的系统，以创造动态高效的组织、更便捷的交通、更安全的空气、食品、更清洁的水源和更健康的生活。

上海美国商会

上海美国商会成立于 1915 年，是美国本土外成立的第三家美国商会。成立之初，商会仅有 45 名男性美国籍会员，彼时商会以促进美国对华贸易出口为宗旨。经过一个世纪的发展，商会已经成为亚太地区规模最大且最具影响力的美国商会之一，会员结构及宗旨也发生了很大变化。如今商会拥有来自 1 650 多家企业的 3 700 余名会员，其中包括众多知名全球五百强企业，也包括很多中小企业。商会除了致力于推动美中双边贸易以外，也帮助中国投资者赴美投资以及促进美中宏观经济合作。商会的服务覆盖整个中国，并在苏州和南京设立了分支机构。

作为一家非营利性、中立的商业组织，上海美国商会崇尚贸易自由、市场开放、私有企业自由发展和信息自由流通的原则，致力于在中国营造健康良好的商业环境，增进美中商务交往。

中国欧盟商会

中国欧盟商会由 51 家会员企业于 2000 年成立，其目的是代表不同行业和在华欧盟企业的共同声音。中国欧盟商会是一个在会员指导下开展工作的、独立的非营利性机构，其核心结构是代表欧盟在华企业的 25 个工作组和论坛。

欧盟商会目前已拥有约 1 600 家会员公司，并在九个城市设有七个分会，分别是：北京、南京、上海、沈阳、中国华南（广州和深圳）、中国西南（成都与重庆）及天津，每个分会都由当地董事会管理，并且直接向执行委员会汇报。

中国欧盟商会上海分会成立于 2002 年 4 月，如今已拥有近 600 家会员企业，是中国欧盟商会最大的分会。其会员企业构成了 25 个活跃的工作组和论坛，广泛覆盖了各行业和跨行业议题。每年，上海分会和北京及其他分会一起，共同起草年度《欧盟企业在中国建议书》和《商业信心调查》，为会员企业创造更好的在华营商环境提供参考意见。

美中贸易全国委员会

美中贸易全国委员会（USCBC）是非政府、无党派的，非营利的机构，拥有大约220家在华经营的美国会员公司。自1973年成立以来的四十多年中，美中贸易全国委员会为会员公司提供了大量的信息以及咨询、倡导等服务，并举办了多项活动。通过设在华盛顿的总部以及北京和上海的办事处，美中贸易全国委员会以其独特的定位优势在美、中两地为会员提供服务。

美中贸易全国委员会的使命是扩大美中商务联系，使全体会员从中受益，进而在更广阔的层面上使美国经济获益。美中贸易全国委员会提倡与中国进行建设性的商务联系——共同致力于消除贸易投资壁垒，并为双方营造一个规范、可预测的、透明的商务环境。在美中贸易全国委员会的会员公司中，既有诸多知名的大型企业，也有相当比例的小型企业和服务业公司。

日本贸易振兴机构

日本贸易振兴机构（JETRO）是促进日本与海外国家和地区间贸易·投资的政府机构。前身"日本贸易振兴会"成立于1958年，当时以"振兴出口"为工作重心。进入21世纪，工作重心已转向吸引海外国家对日本直接投资以及支持中小企业最大限度地开拓全球市场。2003年由日本经济产业省的下属特殊法人变更成了独立行政法人日本贸易振兴机构。现在，拥有东京·大阪总部，亚洲经济研究所和43个国内事务所，在海外55个国家和地区拥有74个事务所。在中国的上海、北京、广州、成都、武汉、大连、青岛、香港分别设有代表处。

JETRO特别支援日本的中坚和中小企业开拓海外市场。根据企业的不同需求，向企业提供从出口到向海外投资的"全程支援"的同时，为协助海外企业快速解决所面临的问题，在海外具有现地律师、会计等专家提供咨询服务的体制。此外，还与当地政府协同合作保护知识产权及活用知识产权的商业服务。JETRO作为国外企业投资日本的最初窗口，也致力于研发及雇用能力充足的行业对日本的投资。针对已进入日本市场的外资企业，也向它们提供扩大地区投资的服务。

印度工业联合会

印度工业联合会 (CII) 致力于通过咨询和顾问服务，联合政府部门和工业界的共同力量，创建和维持一个利于印度工业发展的理想环境。

印度工业联合会是一个非政府、非营利性的行业领导机构，由印度工业界自主领导和管理，对于印度经济的繁荣和发展起到了积极的推进作用。印度工业联合会成立于 1895 年，是目前印度最重要的行业协会。它拥有超过 8 000 家的直属成员机构，涵盖国有及私有性质的各大中小型企业和跨国公司。此外，通过 240 个国家和地区部门性协会，联合会更是与 200 000 多家间接会员保持着紧密联系。

印度工业联合会拥有 9 家海外办事处，分别位于澳大利亚、巴林、中国、埃及、法国、德国、新加坡、英国和美国，以及遍布 106 个国家的 320 家合作机构。今天，它已成为印度工业产业界和国际商业界之间重要的枢纽机构。

北京大学

北京大学创办于 1898 年，初名京师大学堂，是中国第一所国立综合性大学，也是当时中国最高教育行政机关。辛亥革命后，于 1912 年改为现名。

作为新文化运动的中心和"五四"运动的策源地，作为中国最早传播马克思主义和民主科学思想的发祥地，作为中国共产党最早的活动基地，北京大学为民族的振兴和解放、国家的建设和发展、社会的文明和进步做出了不可替代的贡献，在中国走向现代化的进程中起到了重要的先锋作用。爱国、进步、民主、科学的传统精神和勤奋、严谨、求实、创新的学风在这里生生不息、代代相传。

近年来，在"211 工程"和"985 工程"的支持下，北京大学进入了一个新的历史发展阶段，在学科建设、人才培养、师资队伍建设、教学科研等各方面都取得了显著成绩，为将北大建设成为世界一流大学奠定了坚实的基础。今天的北京大学已经成为国家培养高素质、创造性人才的摇篮、科学研究的前沿和知识创新的重要基地和国际交流的重要桥梁和窗口。

BitSE

BitSE 是一家位于上海的区块链科技初创公司，创始人来自 IBM、Louis Vuitton、阿里巴巴及普华永道的高管。

来自全世界 9 个国家的核心研发团队，拥有丰富的技术，产品及市场经验。目前累计已为区块链开发了超过 50000 行代码，并领先全球率先提出了区块链即服务（Blockchain as a Service）的设想和理念。

上海 WTO 事务咨询中心

上海 WTO 事务咨询中心是上海市人民政府主办的非营利性的 WTO 事务专业咨询服务机构，建于中国加入世界贸易组织前夕的 2000 年 10 月。中心成立以来，始终致力于为中国中央政府和地方政府处理与 WTO 有关的事务，以及参与多边、双边、区域性特惠或非特惠性贸易、投资安排谈判，提供短期数据库应用支撑和中长期决策咨询服务。经过多年的积累，目前上海 WTO 事务咨询中心已建成名为"全球贸易与投资运行监控预警系统"业务工作平台，该平台能按细分行业对全球贸易和投资规则体系变化、流量波动和产业产出量之间相互作用进行监控和预警。2012 年，上海市人民政府分别与国家商务部及工业和信息化部签订协议，决定以上海 WTO 事务咨询中心为载体，在已建成的"全球贸易与投资运行监控预警系统"的基础上，共建"全球贸易投资研究咨询中心"和"世界产业运行研究咨询中心"。上述两个"中心"的建设，标志着上海 WTO 事务咨询中心迈上了建设国家级对外经济政策研究咨询平台的新台阶。

上港集团

上海国际港务（集团）股份有限公司（简称：上港集团）目前是我国最大的港口股份制企业，是目前货物吞吐量、集装箱吞吐量均居世界首位的综合性港口。

上港集团已开辟遍布全球国际直达的美洲、欧洲、澳洲、非洲以及东北亚、东南亚等地的班轮航线 300 多条，集装箱月航班密度达到 2 700 多班，其中，国际航班达到 1 300 班，是中国内地集装箱航线最多、航班密度最高、覆盖面最广的港口。全球最大的 20 家中外船公司已全部进驻上海，在上海设立子公司或办事处的外国航运公司已逾 80 多家。

上港集团主业领域包括港口集装箱、大宗散货和杂货的装卸生产，以及与港口生产有关的引航、船舶拖带、理货、驳运、仓储、船货代理、集卡运输、国际邮轮服务等港口服务以及港口物流业务。

上海电气集团

上海电气集团股份有限公司是中国装备制造业最大的企业集团之一，具有设备总成套、工程总承包和提供现代装备综合服务的优势。自 20 世纪 90 年代以来，销售收入一直居于机械行业前三位。

集团主导产品主要有 1 000MW 级超超临界火力发电机组、1 000MW 级核电机组，重型装备、输配电、电梯、印刷机械、机床等。高效清洁能源、新能源装备是上海电气集团的核心业务，能源装备占销售收入 70% 左右。

"上海电气"是中国装备制造业领袖品牌。在"亚洲品牌 500 强"评选中，上海电气为亚洲机械类品牌排名第五名，中国机械类品牌第一名。上海电气正在成为一个主业突出、优势明显，可持续发展的现代化、国际化大型装备集团。

中伦律师事务所

中伦律师事务所创立于 1993 年，是中国司法部最早批准设立的合伙制律师事务所之一。经过数年快速、稳健的发展壮大，中伦已成为中国规模最大的综合性律师事务所之一。如今，中伦拥有 240 多名合伙人以及超过 1 200 名专业人士，办公室分布在北京、上海、深圳、广州、武汉、成都、重庆、青岛、东京、香港、伦敦、纽约、洛杉矶及旧金山 14 个城市，为全球 20 多个国家和地区提供市场领先和高质量法律服务。

毕马威

毕马威在中国 16 个城市设有办事机构，合伙人及员工约 10 000 名，分布在北京、北京中关村、成都、重庆、佛山、福州、广州、杭州、南京、青岛、上海、沈阳、深圳、天津、厦门、香港特别行政区和澳门特别行政区。毕马威以统一的经营方式来管理中国的业务，以确保我们能够高效和迅速地调动各方面的资源，为客户提供高质量的服务。

毕马威是一个由专业服务成员所组成的全球网络。成员所遍布全球 155 个国家和地区，拥有专业人员 174 000 名，提供审计、税务和咨询等专业服务。

1992 年，毕马威在中国内地成为首家获准合资开业的国际会计师事务所。2012 年 8 月 1 日，毕马威成为四大会计师事务所之中，首家从中外合作制转为特殊普通合伙的事务所。

德意志银行

德意志银行于 1870 年在德国柏林成立，是德国的行业领袖，在整个欧洲也享有领先地位，同时在北美洲和亚洲展现强大竞争实力。德意志银行为企业、政府、机构投资者、中小企业及个人提供包括商业银行、投资银行、零售银行、交易银行和资产与财富管理领域的产品及服务。

德意志银行最早于 1872 年在上海设立首间办事处，并于 2008 年 1 月 1 日在北京正式注册成立法人银行——德意志银行（中国）有限公司，把原德意志银行北京分行和广州分行改制为德银中国北京分行和广州分行，并新设上海分行。2010 年 3 月，天津分行正式开业；2011 年 4 月，重庆分行正式开业；2013 年 9 月，青岛分行正式开业；2014 年 5 月，上海自贸试验区支行正式开业。德银中国在中国法律法规和监管部门允许的范围内开展企业银行业务、私人银行业务和其他类型的业务。德意志银行还在北京和上海设有证券业务代表处。德银中国现有业务部门包括企业及投资银行部、环球市场部以及财富管理部。

雅培

雅培是全球首屈一指专注于服务消费者的医药公司，拥有约 69 000 名员工，业务遍布 150 多个国家。1888 年，华莱士·C. 雅培博士开设了属于自己的药店，并开始精心配制生产药物，旨在为病人和医生提供更有效的治疗方法。在雅培博士的经营下，公司迅速跻身制药业的创始企业之一。通过业务拓展，利用公司在全新医疗研究领域的领先地位满足日益增长的全球医疗需求。在不断涉足医疗行业新领域，开阔新市场的同时，雅培逐步树立了公司百年来的传统——帮助全球更多的人过得更健康。雅培与中国拥有着深厚渊源。早在 1937 年，雅培就在中国创立了第一家分公司。雅培致力于为中国消费者开发并生产营养品、药品、医疗器械和诊断产品，不断改善人类健康，激发潜能。

泰科电子

泰科电子（TE Connectivity）是全球技术领军企业，泰科电子是 TE 在中国的成员企业，TE 年销售额达 120 亿美元。在连接日益紧密的当今世界，TE Connectivity 的连接和传感解决方案发挥着核心作用。TE 与工程师协作，帮助他们将概念转变为现实——通过经受严苛环境验证的智能化、高效、高性能 TE 产品和解决方案，实现各种可能。TE 在全球拥有 72 000 名员工，其中 7 000 名为设计工程师，合作的客户遍及全球 150 多个国家和众多领域。

Introduction to Organizers and Think Tanks of 2016 Shanghai International Think Tanks Summit

1. Host

The Development Research Centre of Shanghai Municipal People's Government

The Development Research Centre of Shanghai Municipal People's Government (SDRC) was formerly known as Shanghai Center for Economic Research (SCER) which was founded on Dec. 26th, 1980, and was renamed by SDRC on Dec. 22nd, 1995. SDRC is a decision-making research institution led by Shanghai Municipal People's Government, providing comprehensive consulting services with the functions of organizing, coordinating and managing the government research projects.

Main functions:

(1) Study on the overall and strategic issues concerning Shanghai economy, social development, reform and opening-up.

(2) Trace the dynamic trends, analyze the inconsistency, study the countermeasures and forecast the prospects, submit decision-making proposals and consulting advices to the CPC Shanghai Committee and the Shanghai Municipal People Government in due course.

(3) Organize the assessment of the decision-making and consulting research results as well as the appraisal of the distinguished research achievements once every two years.

(4) Organize and coordinate the decision-making and consulting research work within the government system.

(5) Conduct the information maintenance work of the Shanghai Decision-making and Consulting Proposals System.

(6) Administrate the related organizations and institutions entrusted by the Shanghai Municipal People's Government.

(7) Compile and publish *Shanghai Economy Almanac* and *Journal of Scientific Development*.

(8) Undertake other missions assigned by the leaders of the Shanghai Municipality.

2. Organizers

PwC China

PwC firms help organizations and individuals create the value they're looking for. PwC is a network of firms in 157 countries with more than 223 000 people who are committed to delivering quality in assurance, tax and advisory services. PwC has around 700 partners and a strength of around 18 000 people in China.

Providing organizations with the advice they need, wherever they may be located, PwC's highly qualified, experienced professionals listen to different points of view to help organizations solve their business issues and identify and maximize the opportunities they seek. PwC's industry specialization allows PwC to help co-create solutions with clients for their sector of interest.

PwC firms have provided industry-focused Assurance, Consulting & Deals and Tax services for more than 84% companies in the Fortune Global 500. PwC's many smaller listed, private and government clients benefit from the same depth of industry and technical expertise.

PwC named strongest B2B brand & one of the world's 10 most powerful brands by Brand Finance 2016, and named the second most attractive employer for business students in 2015. The Chinese Institute of Certified Public Accountants published its Top 100 Accounting Firms in China in 2016. PwC China ranked first in the list. This is the 14th consecutive year that PwC won this award.

Shanghai Development Research Foundation

Shanghai Development Research Foundation (SDRF) was established in 1993. As a public-foundation and a non-profit legal person established in accordance with the relevant governmental regulations, SDRF is devoted to the public welfare undertakings by utilizing donations from individuals, legal persons and other organizations.

SDRF aims at actively promoting the research on the development issues and the development of decision-making consultation. Its business scope includes capital raising and operation, and researching, communicating, sponsoring and awarding the consultation projects concerning economic, social and urban development strategy.

Since established, SDRF has been strongly supporting the research work on decision-making consultation in Shanghai, with a lot of projects being sponsored and numbers of awards for great research achievements being held. Meanwhile, we have accomplished many research projects set up by ourselves or other organizations.

For the last several years, SDRF has been continuously endeavoring to fulfill its missions. We hold "Shanghai Development Salon" monthly, inviting distinguished experts and scholars home and abroad to make speeches on hot topics and sensitive questions, and make interactive discussion with the attendees. The high-level symposiums are held twice or thrice annually, gathering numbers of domestic and overseas experts, and the noble guests from political, business and academic circles together to discuss the important issues in the development of global economy and Chinese economy. In addition, SDRF holds a series of mini-seminars themed "The Future of Chinese Economy" for a thorough discussion on the depth-rooted problems in the development of Chinese economy. SDRF has also sponsored and jointly held many academic conferences with Fudan University, Shanghai Jiaotong University (SJTU) and Shanghai University of Finance and Economy (SHUFE). Taking the advantage of the fruitful contents of these conferences, SDRF has compiled its booklets *Discussion Record* and *Research Review* so as to further spread the achievements of research and discussion on the development issues.

Shanghai International Think Tank Exchange Center

Shanghai International Think Tank Exchange Center is one of the open and public decision-making and consulting research platforms, set up by the Development Research Center of Shanghai Municipal People's Government.(SDRC). In 2010, SDRC, as required by the then Mayor Han Zheng proactively made contact with thirteen world-renowned think tanks in Shanghai like Accenture, Capgemini, Deloitte and IBM, aiming to further Shanghai's decision making and consulting research by drawing on the wisdom of experts and scholars form home and abroad to enable the CPC Shanghai Committee and Shanghai municipal government to do decision-making in a more democratic and scientific way and constantly expand the influence of SDRC in the world. In January, 2011, the center was established and the first "Smart Shanghai Forum" with the theme "Innovation, Transformation and Development" was also held.

The main responsibilities for the Shanghai International Think Tank Exchanges Center are as follows:

(1) To conduct decision-making research for the government.

(2) To provide application research, business planning, managerial consulting services for enterprises.

(3) To organize international bilateral and multilateral corporation seminar.

(4) To study international cooperation and exchanges subjects.

(5) To provide development, training and information services for professionals.

For the past six years, the Shanghai International Think Tank Exchanges Center has conducted plenty of international cooperation researches with focus on the economic and social development of Shanghai by taking advantage in talents, resources and information, jointly with the public decision-making consulting research platforms of experts, workshops, social surveys, research projects and college forums. Until now, the Shanghai International Think Tank Exchanges Center has held bilateral forums for 18 times, "Shanghai Intelligent Forum" for 5 times and "Shanghai International Think Tank Summit" for 3 times, which effectively improves the function and role of the Development Research Center of Shanghai Municipal People's Government in integrating the think tank resources at the national level, and provides lots of advices and suggestions to the CPC Shanghai Committee and the Shanghai Municipal People's Government from leading think tanks at home and abroad.

3. Think Tanks

Accenture

Accenture is a leading global professional services company, providing a broad range of services and solutions in strategy, consulting, digital, technology and operations. Combining unmatched experience and specialized skills across more than 40 industries and all business functions—underpinned by the world's largest delivery network—Accenture works at the intersection of business and technology to help clients improve their performance and create sustainable value for their stakeholders. With approximately 384 000 people serving clients in more than 120 countries,

Accenture drives innovation to improve the way the world works and lives.

Accenture has been operating in Greater China for 30 years. Today, the Greater China practice has more than 13 000 people serving clients across the region and has offices in Beijing, Shanghai, Dalian, Chengdu, Guangzhou, Shenzhen, Hong Kong and Taipei.

McKinsey & Company

McKinsey & Company is the leading global management consulting firm and by far the largest global management consulting firm in Greater China. Globally, McKinsey & Company is the trusted advisor and counselor to many of the most influential businesses and institutions in the world. McKinsey & Company serves more than 80 percent of Fortune magazine's list of the Most Admired Companies. In Greater China, McKinsey & Company advises clients in over 15 different industry sectors, and work with dozens of government agencies and institutions at the national, regional and municipal levels. McKinsey & Company's primary mission is to help its clients achieve substantial and enduring impact by tackling their biggest issues concerning strategy, operations, organization, technology and finance. Today McKinsey & Company has more than 350 consultants and over 50 Partners located across four locations in Greater China: Beijing, Shanghai, Hong Kong, and Taipei. They are supported by more than 100 research professionals, and over 200 professional support staff.

The Boston Consulting Group

The Boston Consulting Group (BCG)is a global management consulting firm and the world's leading advisor on business strategy. BCG partner with clients in all sectors and regions to identify their highest-value opportunities, address their most critical challenges, and transform their businesses. BCG's customized approach combines deep insight into the dynamics of companies and markets with close collaboration at all levels of the client organization. This ensures that our clients achieve sustainable competitive advantage, build more capable organizations, and secure lasting results. Founded in 1963, BCG is a private company with 85 offices in 48 countries.

BCG has been in Greater China for more than 30 years. BCG's offices are located in Beijing, Hong Kong, Shanghai and Taipei. BCG's clients are multinational corporations or local enterprises from a multitude of industry sectors. BCG help them design business strategies by leveraging BCG's international best practices and on-the-ground experience and know how.

Capgemini

With more than 180 000 people in over 40 countries, Capgemini is a global leader in consulting, technology and outsourcing services. The Group reported 2015 global revenues of EUR 11.9 billion. Together with its clients, Capgemini creates and delivers business, technology and digital solutions that fit their needs, enabling them to achieve innovation and competitiveness. A deeply multicultural organization, Capgemini has developed its own way of working, the Collaborative Business Experience™, and draws on Rightshore®, its worldwide delivery model.

In 1997, Capgemini began operations in China. In 2000, with the global acquisition of leading accounting firm Ernst & Young, Capgemini expanded its business in China. Capgemini China has today become one of the Group's most important and strategic markets. Capgemini China headquarters in Shanghai provides support to its branch offices and operations centers located in Beijing, Guangzhou, Hong Kong, Taipei, Kunshan, Foshan, Hangzhou, Shenyang. With more than 2 500 professional consultants and technical experts, Capgemini China's business covers consulting, information technology, outsourcing services, and implementation of localized solutions. Capgemini China effectively integrates local teams with global business networks and resources to leverage network service capabilities that are mutually supportive, is the best partner of digital transformation.

Deloitte

With over 240 000 people in more than 150 countries, Deloitte serves more than 80 percent of the world's largest 500 companies. One-third of all companies listed on the Stock Exchange of Hong Kong choose Deloitte's service. Based on the reported global revenue of US $36.8 billion for the fiscal year of 2016, Deloitte again takes the lead among the Big Four and is the world's largest professional services provider. Deloitte set up its first rep office in Shanghai, China in 1917 and just celebrated our 99th-year anniversary. Deloitte China is the fastest-growing member firm of Deloitte global network, drawing increasing attention from the management of DTTL. Deloitte Greater China now has near 13 500 people in 24 cities in Greater China. Deloitte China focuses on the real needs of local markets. It adheres to the localization strategy and is transforming to a full-range professional services firm. Deloitte China serves one-third of all companies listed on the Stock Exchange of Hong Kong and more than 800 MNCs and their affiliated companies on the Chinese Mainland. Apart from providing services to enterprises, we also serve the government at all levels. Deloitte constantly supports the central and local governments. Deloitte hopes to leverage its global network to bring more foreign companies into China and bring more local companies abroad, helping promote "a two-way flow of inbound and outbound business activity". Deloitte has been a firm supporter of Chinese government in developing the accounting profession in China. We have proactively participated in the consultation of proposed rules and regulations relating to accounting and tax systems. We'll continue to bring international accounting practices to China and promote the development of local accounting profession.

EY

At EY, we draw upon our global and local knowledge to help you retain the confidence of investors, manage your risk, strengthen your controls, grasp opportunities and achieve your potential. We offer assurance, tax, transaction and advisory services to many large and fast-growth Chinese companies, and multinationals operating in the region. EY's China Overseas Investment Network (COIN) links EY professionals around the globe, facilitates collaboration, and provides consistent and coordinated services to Chinese clients making outbound investments. Building on the existing China Business Group in the Americas, EMEIA, Asia-Pacific and Japan areas, COIN has expanded our network into 65 countries and territories around the world.

EY is one of the largest professional services organizations in Greater China, having enjoyed a presence in the region for 45 years. We have reached many milestones, including opening our first Hong Kong office in 1968 as Arthur Young and being one of the first international organizations to establish operations in mainland China in 1981.

EY has a network of 24 offices in Greater China, which located in Beijing, Chengdu, Dalian, Guangzhou, Hangzhou, Hong Kong, Macau, Nanjing, Qingdao, Shanghai, Shenyang, Shenzhen, Suzhou, Tianjin, Wuhan, Xiamen, Changsha, Xi'an, Chungli, Hsinchu, Kaohsiung, Taichung, Tainan and Taipei.

Gao Feng Advisory Company is a pre-eminent strategy and management consulting firm with roots in China coupled with global vision, capabilities, and a broad resources network. Gao Feng help clients address and solve their toughest business and management issues—issues that arise in the current fast-changing, complicated and ambiguous operating environment. Gao Feng commit to putting our clients' interest first and foremost. Gao Feng is objective and views client engagements as long-term relationships rather than one-off projects. Gao Feng not only help clients "formulate" the solutions but also assist in implementation, often hand-in-hand. Gao Feng believe in teaming and working together to add value and contribute to problem solving for clients, from the most junior to the most senior.

IBM

IBM is a globally integrated technology and consulting company headquartered in Armonk, New York. With operations in more than 170 countries, IBM attracts and retains some of the world's most talented people to help solve problems and provide an edge for businesses, governments and non-profits.

Innovation is at the core of IBM's strategy. The company develops and sells software and systems hardware and a broad range of infrastructure, cloud and consulting services.

Today, IBM is focused on four growth initiatives-business analytics, cloud computing, growth markets and Smarter Planet. IBMers are working with customers around the world to apply the company's business consulting, technology and R&D expertise to build systems that enable dynamic and efficient organizations, better transportation, safer food, cleaner water and healthier populations.

AmCham Shanghai

The American Chamber of Commerce in Shanghai, known as the "Voice of American Business" in China, is one of the largest American Chambers in the Asia Pacific region. As a non-profit, non-partisan business organization, AmCham Shanghai is committed to the principles of free trade, open markets, private enterprise and the unrestricted flow of information. Founded in 1915, AmCham Shanghai was the third American Chamber established outside the United States.

European Chamber, Shanghai Chapter

The European Union Chamber of Commerce in China (European Chamber) The European Union Chamber of Commerce in China (European Chamber) was founded in 2000 by 51 member companies that shared a goal of establishing a common voice for the various business sectors of the European Union and European businesses operating in China. It is a member-driven, non-profit, fee-based organization with a core structure of 25 working groups and for a representing European business in China.

The European Chamber has nearly 1 600 members in seven chapters operating in nine cities: Beijing, Nanjing, Shanghai, Shenyang, South China (Guangzhou and Shenzhen), Southwest China (Chengdu and Chongqing) and Tianjin. Each chapter is managed at the local level by local boards reporting directly to the Executive Committee.

The Shanghai Chapter was established in April 2002 and currently has over 600 member companies, the largest of all Chamber chapters. It has grown substantially in terms of membership, the number of working groups and fora, as well as its events and lobby activities. The Shanghai Chapter currently has 26 active working groups, desks and fora covering a diverse range of industries and services. Shanghai-based working groups cooperate closely with working groups in Beijing and other chapters to provide input into the annual *European Business in China Position Paper, Business Confidence Survey* and other advocacy initiatives in order to give recommendations to improve business environment in China.

The US-China Business Council

The US-China Business Council, Inc. (USCBC) is a private, nonpartisan, nonprofit organization of roughly 220 American companies that do business with China. Founded in 1973, USCBC has provided unmatched information, advisory, advocacy, and program services to its membership for four decades. Through its offices in Washington, DC; Beijing; and Shanghai, USCBC is uniquely positioned to serve its members' interests in the United States and China.

USCBC's mission is to expand the US-China commercial relationship to the benefit of its membership and, more broadly, the US economy. It favors constructive engagement with China to eliminate trade and investment barriers and develop a rules-based commercial environment that is predictable and transparent to all parties. Among

USCBC's members are many large and well-known US corporations, but smaller companies and service firms make up a substantial portion of the overall membership.

Japan External Trade Organization

The Japan External Trade Organization (JETRO) is a government-related organization that works to promote mutual trade and investment between Japan and the rest of the world. Originally established in 1958 to promote Japanese exports abroad, JETRO's core focus in the 21st century has shifted toward promoting foreign direct investment into Japan and helping small to medium size Japanese firms maximize their global export potential. JETRO has 74 overseas offices in 55 countries worldwide, as well as 8 offices in China, including Shanghai, Beijing, Guangzhou, Chengdu, Wuhan, Dalian, Qingdao and Hong Kong, 46 offices in Japan, including Tokyo and Osaka headquarters.

The Confederation of Indian Industry

The Confederation of Indian Industry (CII) works to create and sustain an environment conducive to the development of India, partnering industry, Government, and civil society, through advisory and consultative processes.

CII is a non-government, not-for-profit, industry-led and industry-managed organization, playing a proactive role in India's development process. Founded in 1895, India's premier business association has over 8000 members, from the private as well as public sectors, including SMEs and MNCs, and an indirect membership of over 200 000 enterprises from around 240 national and regional sectoral industry bodies.

With 9 overseas offices in Australia, Bahrain, China, Egypt, France, Germany, Singapore, UK, and USA, as well as institutional partnerships with 320 counterpart organizations in 106 countries, CII serves as a reference point for Indian industry and the international business community.

Peking University

Peking University is a comprehensive and national key university. The campus, known as "Yan Yuan" (the garden of Yan), is situated at Haidian District in the western suburb of Beijing.

The university has effectively combined research on important scientific subjects with the training of personnel with a high level of specialized knowledge and professional skill as demanded by the country's socialist modernization. It strives not only for improvements in teaching and research work, but also for the promotion of interaction and mutual promotion among various disciplines.

Thus Peking University has become a center for teaching and research and a university of a new type, embracing diverse branches of learning such as basic and applied sciences, social sciences and the humanities, and sciences of medicine, management, and education. Its aim is to rank among the world's best universities in the future.

BitSE

BitSE is a Shanghai-based start up that founded by ex-IBM, Louis Vuitton, and Alibaba employees and is billed as one of the leaders in the blockchain as a service (BaaS) model.

BitSE established in 2013, focusing on the blockchain field and devoting to the blockchain technology to make innovations in industries. Three founders are from IBM, Alibaba and Louis Vuitton, with products and market experiences. BitSE core R&D team are from nine different countries, and have been developed more than 50 000 rows of codes accumulatively. BitSE is a world leader who firstly brought the concept and philosophy of BaaS (Blockchain-As-A-Service).

Shanghai WTO Affairs Consultation Center

Shanghai WTO Affairs Consultation Center, supported by Shanghai Municipal People's Government, is a non-profit professional service center dealing exclusively with WTO affairs consultation. Since establishment, our center has been dedicated to handling WTO related affairs for Chinese central government and local government, and participating in multilateral, bilateral and regional preferential or non preferential trade and investment negotiations, providing short-term database support and mid-and-long term decision consultation services. After years of accumulation, Shanghai WTO Affaires Consultation Center built a business platform, namely the "Monitoring and Early Warning System of Global Trade and Investment", which can monitor and make early warning of dynamics in the interaction between global trade and investment regulations, flow fluctuation, and industrial output, classified by industries.

In 2012, Shanghai Municipal People's Government signed agreements with Ministry of Commerce of People's Republic of China and Ministry of Industry and Information Technology of People's Republic of China respectively, and decided to use Shanghai WTO Affairs Consultation Center as a carrier, to build " Global Trade and Investment Research Consultation Center" and "Global Industry Operation Research Consultation Center", on the basis of "Monitoring and Early Warning System of Global Trade and Investment". The establishment of the above two centers is a sign of Shanghai WTO Affairs Consultation Center reaching a new stage of building national consulting platform of foreign economic policy research.

Shanghai International Port (Group) Co., Ltd.

Shanghai International Port (Group) Co., Ltd. ("SIPG" or "the group")is majority-owned by the Shanghai SASAC with state-owned China Merchants Group as its second largest shareholder. SIPG is the largest joint-stock port operator in China by equity throughput.

As China's main gateway port to the global market, SIPG, an easy access to the vast hinterland, serves 281 container shipping routes covering major ports globally and accommodates over 2 700 monthly calls, which makes it the port with the highest density of container routes, the most frequent shifts and the most extensive coverage in the mainland of China. The world's top 20 shipping companies have deployed their shipping service routes in port of Shanghai; over 80 overseas shipping lines now have offices in Shanghai. SIPG has recorded the container throughput of 35.285mTEU, ranking No.1 for the fifth consecutive year in terms of container volume in the year of 2014.

Shanghai Electric Group Co., Ltd (Shanghai Electric)

Shanghai Electric is one of the largest equipment manufacturing conglomerates in China.

High efficiency and clean energy as well as new energy equipment represent its core business segments, which account for 70% of segmental revenues. Leading products include 1 000MW supercritical thermal power units, 1 000MW nuclear power generation units, heavy-duty equipment, power transmission and distribution equipment, elevators, printing machinery and machine tools.

Shanghai Electric is currently the leader in China's equipment manufacturing sector. According to an assessment for the "Top 500 Asian Brands," Shanghai Electric was ranked the 5th in Asia and the 1st in China in machinery industry. Shanghai Electric is developing itself into a sustainable, modern, and international enterprise group with clearly-defined principal businesses and distinctive advantages within the large-scale equipment sector.

Zhong Lun Law Firm

Founded in 1993, Zhong Lun Law Firm was one of the first private law partnerships to receive approval from the Ministry of Justice. After years of rapid development and steady growth, today Zhong Lun is one of the largest full service law firms in China. With over 240 partners and over 1 200 professionals working in fourteen offices in Beijing, Shanghai, Shenzhen, Guangzhou, Wuhan, Chengdu, Chongqing, Qingdao, Tokyo, Hong Kong, London, New York, Los Angeles and San Francisco, Zhong Lun is capable of providing clients with high-quality legal services in more than 20 countries across a wide range of industries and sectors through its specialized expertise and close teamwork.

KPMG

KPMG China operates in 16 cities across China, with around 10 000 partners and staff in Beijing, Beijing Zhongguancun, Chengdu, Chongqing, Foshan, Fuzhou, Guangzhou, Hangzhou, Nanjing, Qingdao, Shanghai, Shenyang, Shenzhen, Tianjin, Xiamen, Hong Kong SAR and Macau SAR. With a single management structure across all these offices, KPMG China can deploy experienced professionals efficiently, wherever our client is located.

KPMG is a global network of professional services firms providing Audit, Tax and Advisory services. We operate in 155 countries and regions, and have 174 000 people working in member firms around the world.

In 1992, KPMG became the first international accounting network to be granted a joint venture licence in mainland China. KPMG China was also the first among the Big Four in mainland China to convert from a joint venture to a special general partnership, as of 1 August 2012.

Deutsche Bank

Deutsche Bank is Germany's leading bank, founded in Berlin, Germany in 1870, with a strong position in Europe and a significant presence in the Americas and Asia Pacific. Deutsche Bank provides commercial and investment banking, retail banking, transaction banking and asset and wealth management products and services to corporations, governments, institutional investors, small and medium-sized businesses, and private individuals.

Deutsche Bank opened its first office in Shanghai early in 1872, and formally registered as locally incorporated bank—Deutsche Bank (China) Co., Ltd. on 1 Jan 2008, transformed Beijing and Guangzhou branch of DB AG to Beijing and Guangzhou branch of DB China, newly set up Shanghai branch. In Mar 2010, Tianjin branch officially opened; In Apr 2011, Chongqing branch opened; In Sep 2013, Qingdao branch opened; In May 2014, Shanghai FTZ sub-branch opened. Within the scope as permitted by laws and regulations and regulatory authorities in China, DB China conducts corporate banking, private banking and other types of businesses. Deutsche Bank also maintains securities representative offices in Beijing and Shanghai. DB China operates the following business divisions: Corporate & Investment Banking, Global Markets, and Wealth Management.

Abbott

Abbott, as a more global, consumer-focused company than ever before, has approximately 69 000 staff and business over more than 150 countries. In 1888, physician and drug store proprietor Dr. Wallace C. Abbott began producing accurate, scientifically formulated medications with the goal of providing more effective therapies to patients and the physicians providing their care. Under the pioneering leadership of Dr. Abbott, the company was among the founders of the scientific practice of pharmacy, expanding its business to meet rising global health needs by championing new areas of medical research. By continually entering new areas—both scientific and geographic—the company established a now long-standing tradition of helping people live healthier lives around the world. Abbot has a long history with China. As early as 1937, Abbot established its first branch in China. Abbott is dedicated to develop nutrients, medicines, medical instruments, and diagnostic products for Chinese consumers, and wish to continuously make contributions to human health and potential

提升投资贸易便利化水平，构建开放型经济新体制

exploration.

TE Connectivity

TE Connectivity is a global technology leader. TE connectivity and sensor solutions are essential in today's increasingly connected world. TE collaborate with engineers to transform their concepts into creations—redefining what's possible using intelligent, efficient and high-performing TE products and solutions proven in harsh environments. TE's 72 000 people, including over 7 000 engineers, partner with customers in close to 150 countries across a wide range of industries.

POSTSCRIPT

后 记

　　为进一步推进"一带一路"倡议的实施，提升上海投资贸易便利水平，更好地服务上海自贸区和开放型经济建设，并充分发挥上海各类国际智库云集的优势，凝聚更多国际智库参与上海的决策咨询研究工作，上海市人民政府发展研究中心于 2016 年 12 月 9 日牵头召开第三届上海国际智库峰会。峰会以"提升上海投资贸易化水平"为主题，借助上海国际智库交流中心这一开放式、互动式的国际交流平台，深入探讨了上海投资贸易便利化面临的问题和解决思路，为上海未来提升投资贸易便利化水平提供了来自不同国家的专家、学者的卓越见解。为扩大这些宝贵的观点和研究成果的影响，我们将其原汁原味地汇编成书，以飨读者。同时，书中还收录了国际智库成员单位围绕此次峰会主题开展的前期研究成果报告，一并汇集成册。

　　本书的出版得到了各位与会国际智库和专家学者以及上海世纪出版集团格致出版社的大力支持，上海市人民政府发展研究中心国合办承担了大量译校和主要编辑工作，信息处和科研处的同仁也给予了积极协助，在此一并表示感谢！

To further promote the implementation of the Belt and Road initiative, enhance the level of investment and trade in Shanghai to better serve the construction of China (Shanghai) Free Trade Zone and open economy, and organize more international think thanks to pool the wisdom of domestic and foreign experts in Shanghai's decision-making and consulting work, the Development Research Center of Shanghai Municipal People's Government (SDRC) hold the 3rd Shanghai International Think Tank Summit on December 9, 2016 with the theme of "Promote the Investment and Trade Facilitation in Shanghai". Through the open and interactive platform of Shanghai International Think Tank Exchange Center, attendees have an in-depth exchange on the problems and solutions of Shanghai's investment and trade facilitation and offered many remarkable insights. In order to make the most out of these valuable ideas and research achievements, we are compiling them into a book for your reading. Several members from Shanghai International Think Tank Exchange Center did some preliminary study on this topic, and those research papers are also included in the book.

The publication of the book is not possible without the strong support of International Think Tank and experts and scholars as well as Shanghai Century Publishing Group Truth & Wisdom Press. International Cooperation & Exchange Office of the Development Research Center of Shanghai Municipal People's Government undertakes the majority of translation and editorial work, with support from colleagues of Information Division and Scientific Research Management Division of the SDRC. We are truly grateful to all of them for their generous help.

图书在版编目(CIP)数据

提升投资贸易便利化水平,构建开放型经济新体制:
2016 上海国际智库咨询研究报告/上海市人民政府发展
研究中心编.—上海:格致出版社:上海人民出版社,
2017.10
(上海市人民政府发展研究中心系列报告. 国际智库
咨询系列报告)
ISBN 978 - 7 - 5432 - 2787 - 3

Ⅰ. ①提… Ⅱ. ①上… Ⅲ. ①投资环境-研究报告-
上海②国际贸易-经济发展-研究报告-上海 Ⅳ.
①F127.51②F752.851

中国版本图书馆 CIP 数据核字(2017)第 203641 号

责任编辑 忻雁翔
装帧设计 人马艺术设计·储平

提升投资贸易便利化水平,构建开放型经济新体制

——2016 上海国际智库咨询研究报告

上海市人民政府发展研究中心 编

出 版	世纪出版股份有限公司 格致出版社 世纪出版集团 上海人民出版社 (200001 上海福建中路 193 号 www.ewen.co)	印 刷	上海商务联西印刷有限公司
		开 本	787×1092 1/16
		印 张	26.75
	编辑部热线 021-63914988 市场部热线 021-63914081 www.hibooks.cn	插 页	13
		字 数	493,000
		版 次	2017 年 10 月第 1 版
发 行	上海世纪出版股份有限公司发行中心	印 次	2017 年 10 月第 1 次印刷

ISBN 978 - 7 - 5432 - 2787 - 3/F·1055   定价:128.00 元